THE IMAGE OF CHRIST IN RUSSIAN LITERATURE

THE IMAGE OF CHRIST
IN RUSSIAN LITERATURE

DOSTOEVSKY, TOLSTOY, BULGAKOV, PASTERNAK

JOHN GIVENS

NIU PRESS / DEKALB, IL

Northern Illinois University Press, DeKalb 60115
© 2018 by Northern Illinois University Press

27 26 25 24 23 22 21 20 19 18   2 3 4 5
978-0-87580-779-9 (case)
978-1-60909-238-2 (e-book)
Book and cover design by Yuni Dorr

Library of Congress Cataloging-in-Publication Data
is available online at http://catalog.loc.gov

For Anna and Will

IN MEMORIAM MARIAN AND CALVIN SCHWENK

CONTENTS

Acknowledgments

The impetus behind this project emerged from conversations I had with a former Catholic priest about the relationship between the quest for the historical Jesus and the Christ of faith in Mikhail Bulgakov's novel, *The Master and Margarita*, which I was teaching for the first time in my Soviet literature class. Though the historical critical method of biblical scholarship and aspects of Western and Eastern Christology occupied many of our conversations, our dialogue began with one of the first questions Woland asks his two atheist interlocutors on that park bench at Patriarch's Ponds: the question about the five proofs of God. Curiously, neither of the two most recent and well-regarded translations of the novel had any annotations explaining what these proofs were, though presumably many readers might not know who authored them or be able to recall them. My interlocutor could, and without any prompting elaborated on them at length. That priest was my stepfather, and in listening to him recount Thomas Aquinas's Five Ways and in talking with him about what Bulgakov was up to having the devil not only insist on God's existence but that of Jesus as well, I realized I had found an endlessly fascinating subject. Calvin Schwenk, a priest forever in the line of Melchizedek, is thus this study's most important inspiration and guiding light, though he did not live to see its completion. I offer this book in his memory and that of my mother.

I have many other debts to acknowledge, large and small. My colleague, Anna Maslennikova, formerly of Saint Petersburg State University, carefully read every page of my manuscript and offered innumerable insights and suggestions as well as constant support throughout the writing process. Her comments and those of my anonymous readers were crucial in honing my arguments and saving me from missteps and I thank them all for their valuable critical interventions. Other important readers of this manuscript include Gary Saul Morson and Kathleen Parthé, who provided many helpful and insightful comments at different stages of writing and revision. My book is better for the contributions of all of these thoughtful commentators, though any mistakes that persist are strictly my own responsibility.

All of the case studies in my book were presented in one form or another at annual meetings of the Midwest Slavic Conference or the Association for Slavic, East European, and Eurasian Studies, and I thank those organizations for providing such stimulating environments for the airing of scholarly ideas. I thank as well everyone at these conferences who engaged with my ideas and helped me develop them. An early and fruitful forum for my work in this area was a one-day symposium at the Memorial Art Gallery at the University of Rochester on the authority of the image in Russian and Soviet culture in November 2008. I thank Marlene Hamann-Whitmore, McPherson Director of Academic Programs, and Nancy Norwood, curator of European art, for inviting me to participate. My former PhD student and present colleague in the field, Elena Rakhimova-Sommers of the Rochester Institute of Technology, also organized a one-day symposium on Russian culture where I presented on portions of my book in April 2013 in the most supportive and convivial of academic settings, and I thank her as well.

My thanks also to Peter Lennie, dean of faculty at the University of Rochester, who supported a leave request in the spring of 2009 that got the book off to a good start, and to my research assistant, Katharina Schander, for her thorough and professional help in my final year of work on the manuscript. My literature students at UR, especially those in my image of Christ class, were generous interlocutors on many of the questions I treat in this book and I am grateful for their enthusiasm and interest. One of these students in particular, Meaghan DeWaters, deserves special mention. Meaghan wrote an impressive 187-page honors thesis in 2011 on "the pathological believer" in Dostoevsky's fiction. Her interest in the relationship between illness and apophaticism in the writer's metaphysical inquiries was the basis for a fruitful dialogue between us on the riches of the apophatic approach to spirituality, a key element in my own approach to my subject. Ryan Prendergast in my home department at the University of Rochester and Michael Ruhling at the Rochester Institute of Technology provided both support and intellectual dialogue throughout the writing process and I thank them for their insights, collegiality and friendship.

At Northern Illinois University Press I am grateful to acquisitions editor Amy Farranto and Orthodox Studies Series editor Roy Robson for their generous support and help throughout the review process. My sincere thanks as well to my manuscript's superb copyeditor, whose keen editorial eye and pitch-perfect ear for language improved my book in its final revision, and to managing editor Nathan Holmes, who shepherded me through the copy-editing phase and oversaw all apects of production. My manuscript improved immeasurably under their collective guidance and I could not have asked for a more professional and nurturing publishing process.

My twin brother Jim has always been a pillar of support—my stave and my staff, as Turgenev might have put it. His interest in my work and encouragement have been a sustaining presence over the years. Though she did not sew me a cap with the letter "M" on it like Margarita did for her favorite author, my wife Laura was this manuscript's most jealous defender and zealous supporter. She made our basement office—like the Master's basement apartment—a refuge of creative work and like Margarita is far more important to the plot than the author. I dedicate this book to our children, Anna and Will, who grew up watching their father at his computer, writing and rewriting. They kept me grounded in the real world and constantly reminded me that there were other joys to my life besides books.

Parts of this book have appeared elsewhere in altered form. Portions of chapters 2 and 5 appeared as "Tolstoy's Jesus versus Dostoevsky's Christ: A Tale of Two Christologies," in *From Russia, with Love Symposium Proceedings* (Rochester: Rochester Institute of Technology, 2014), 13–26. Chapters 3 and 4 appeared in different versions as, respectively, "A Narrow Escape into Faith? Dostoevsky's *Idiot* and the Christology of Comedy," *Russian Review* 70, no. 1 (January 2011): 95–117, and "Divine Love in *War and Peace* and *Anna Karenina*," *Zapiski russkoi akademicheskoi gruppy v S.Sh.A/Transactions of the Association of Russian American Scholars in the USA* 34 (2010): 165–90. They are reprinted here with the kind permission of these journals.

THE IMAGE OF CHRIST IN RUSSIAN LITERATURE

THE IMAGE OF CHRIST AND RUSSIAN LITERATURE

> Let us preserve the image of Christ, that it may shine forth like a precious diamond to the whole world ... So be it, so be it!
>
> Fyodor Dostoevsky, *Brothers Karamazov*
> (Pevear and Volokhonsky translation)

If you were to read only the works of Fyodor Dostoevsky after his Siberian exile or Leo Tolstoy in his final thirty years, you might easily believe that Jesus Christ and Russian literature are two subjects that cannot be separated from each other, so central does Christ or his teachings seem to be in their lives and creativity. The reality, of course, is quite different. Russian literature of the past two hundred plus years is as secular as any of the literatures of its European neighbors. And yet, at the same time, like European literature, Russian literature was nurtured and developed in a culture whose art, spirituality, and thought were dominated for centuries by the image of Jesus and the beliefs and practices of the Christian faith. Indeed, as far as Russian literature is concerned, we may even argue that in its earliest forms—numerous sermons and saints' lives—there was no literature without Jesus, for these works dealt with little else than living in accordance with the words and deeds of Christ.

Certainly, we can say that Russia has a Christian literature in the same way that we can say England does, whose novels assume a single national faith, shared values, and common religious heritage reflected in the daily lives and assumptions of its heroes and heroines. This shared spiritual heritage and national religion, and the mores they gave rise to, however, figure chiefly as a common cultural background in novels whose concerns are largely elsewhere. One thinks of the novels of Jane Austen, George Eliot, the Brontë sisters, and most of Charles Dickens in nineteenth-century British fiction, for instance, in which England's Anglican faith is but part of the wallpaper of the world inhabited by the characters these authors created. The same is true in Russian literature, as we shall see in chapter 1. That being said, classics of a more overt Christian literature also occupy a significant place in both cultures. In Britain, works like John Milton's *Paradise Lost* (1667), John Bunyan's *The Pilgrim's Progress* (1678), Charles Dickens's *A Christmas Carol* (1843), or C. S. Lewis's *Screwtape Letters* (1942) come to mind. In Russia, *The Life of the Archpriest Avvakum, Written by Himself* (written 1672–1675, first published in Russia in 1861), Nikolai Gogol's *Selected Passages from Correspondence with Friends* (1847), Nikolai Leskov's *The Cathedral Clergy* (1872), or Dostoevsky's *Brothers Karamazov* (1880) are prominent examples. My concern in this book, however, is not Russia's Christian literature but rather its anxiety over its Christian heritage, specifically, its anxiety over the meaning and significance of Jesus Christ.

Beginning in the nineteenth century and corresponding with the rise of the historical school of biblical criticism in Europe, Russian intellectuals became increasingly skeptical of the traditional claims made by the Orthodox Church about the order of the cosmos and Christ's role therein. Partly a consequence of the Russian response to the Enlightenment in the eighteenth century, partly a reaction to the religious revival of Alexander I's reign in the beginning of the nineteenth century, a rising secularism dominated Russian intellectual life throughout the 1800s, gaining momentum just as realism replaced Romanticism in Russian letters and David Friedrich Strauss published his *Life of Jesus Critically Examined* (1835), the first of two immensely influential works in Russia that redefined the meaning of Christ in a non-mystical light. The other work, Ernest Renan's *Life of Jesus*, appeared in 1863 and was translated into Russian a year later, precisely when radical materialism was gaining inroads among Russian intellectuals. Thus, the question of faith, the role of the Church in Russian society, and the identity of Jesus Christ and his significance in history became part of the war waged between progressives, who put their faith in reason, science, and governmental reform, and their opponents, who largely maintained traditional religious values and views.

For his part, Dostoevsky opposed the secularists not only for reasons of faith but also because he could not agree with them that a perfect society could be built on the basis of reason, science, and egalitarian thought. The idea that merely by feeding mankind, providing for its physical comforts, and educating it about its best interests one could bring about the New Jerusalem was ridiculous to Dostoevsky. "Oh, tell me who was the first to declare, to proclaim that man does vile things only because he does not realize his true interests," his unnamed narrator in *Notes from Underground* exclaims, "that if he were enlightened, if his eyes were opened to his true, normal interests, he would immediately cease committing abominations but would immediately become good and noble, because, being enlightened and understanding his true advantage, he would inevitably see that only goodness is to his advantage, and everybody knows that no man will knowingly act against his own interests. [. . .] Oh, child! Oh, pure, innocent babe!"[1]

But even Dostoevsky, in *Notes from Underground* and later, in his mature novels, hesitated to oppose materialist visions of a brave new world with a straightforward case for Christ, as we shall see in chapters 2 and 3. In later republications of *Notes*, for instance, he never attempted to restore chapter 10 of part 1, where in passages paradoxically forbidden by the censor he makes a case for the necessity of faith in Christ. It is as if Dostoevsky feared that an earnest, ardent defense of Christ was no longer possible in the age of skepticism, that a vindication of Christ could only succeed if it were somehow concealed, introduced obliquely, or disguised as something else, such as a revolt against God or a profession of atheism.

At the same time, Dostoevsky could not avoid being affected by the atheism that he spoke out against, admitting in a famous letter that he was "a child of doubt and disbelief" and would ever remain so.[2] Nor was he alone in this regard. Doubt permeates the Christological imagings of all of the writers of this study, each of whom acknowledges both the contestability of faith and the inability of fundamentalist professions of belief or unbelief to persuade. They instead occupy a middle theological position somewhere between faith and skepticism, inhabiting what Charles Taylor calls the space of cultural "cross pressures," where positions of faith are made fragile by the challenges of science, reason, and progressive social attitudes on the one hand but are simultaneously bolstered by the sense of the inadequacy of these "narratives of closed immanence" on the other.[3]

Tolstoy, every bit as opposed to the radical materialists of his day as Dostoevsky, suffers from the same sense of cultural cross pressures in his own approach to belief. He complains in the second epilogue to *War and Peace* about how confidently the materialists had done away with the idea of the human soul: "In our time the majority of so-called advanced people, that is, a crowd of ignoramuses, have taken the works of the naturalists, who study one side of the question, for the solution of the whole question." He goes on to liken "the naturalists and their admirers" to "plasterers assigned to plaster one side of a church wall, who, taking advantage of the foreman's absence, in a fit of zeal smear their plaster all over the windows, the icons, the scaffolding, and the as yet unreinforced walls, and rejoice at how, from their plastering point of view, everything comes out flat and smooth."[4] Like Dostoevsky's defense of belief, however, Tolstoy's comes with a secular caveat, one that acknowledges that the Christian faith narrative needs correcting. In his case, Tolstoy defends Christianity by reinventing it and in so doing, attempts to save it from itself. Sharing the secularists' view that Jesus was no more than a mortal man, Tolstoy nevertheless scolds the radicals of his day for not seeing that what Jesus taught was already a more revolutionary blueprint for establishing true justice on earth than any the materialists were promoting. Thus Tolstoy's intervention was not for Jesus's sake but for that of his message. The former was not divine but the latter was. Tolstoy thus negated Jesus to save his message.

Here is where I begin my inquiry—with the paradoxical nature of these two writers' engagement with the image of Christ in Russia and what it reveals about the anxiety in Russian literature that speaking about Jesus provokes. The need to speak about Christ in an age of unbelief but, at the same time, to affirm him or his teachings through indirect, even negative, means struck me as an intriguing and important commonality between the two writers. As I moved into the twentieth century, I noticed that this anxiety persisted, but in a different way, in the two great Easter novels of the Soviet period: Mikhail Bulgakov's *Master and Margarita* and Boris Pasternak's *Doctor Zhivago*. Writing in a new age of belief in the quasi-religion of the Soviet state, Bulgakov and Pasternak also describe a negative path toward Christ, in part because positive depictions of Jesus were hardly going to be published in the Soviet Union but also because both writers were intent on rescuing the image of Christ from both the caricatures of propaganda and the certainties of religious dogma. Like Dostoevsky and Tolstoy before them, Bulgakov and Pasternak tell us much about what Jesus is not, the better to reveal what the true Jesus must be and, at the same time, avoid making statements about him that diminish, compartmentalize, or otherwise define the Godhead. As the poet Gavriil Derzhavin in his 1814 poem

"Christ" proclaims, Jesus is someone whom "neither pen, / nor mortal vision nor hearing / nor language can describe,"[5] hence the need for an apophatic approach to the Godhead.

A prominent part of Eastern Orthodoxy, apophatic theology emphasizes the ineffability of the Godhead and proposes that, since God cannot be understood through positive assertions, we must approach God through negative means, by emptying ourselves of all conceptual language, since God is beyond all human intellectual comprehension. As the fifth-century Christian theologian Pseudo-Dionysius the Areopagite writes,

> The supreme Cause of every conceptual thing is not itself conceptual. It cannot be grasped by understanding since it is neither knowledge nor truth. It is not kingship. It is not wisdom. It is neither one nor oneness, divinity nor goodness. Nor is it a spirit, in the sense in which we understand that term. It is not sonship or fatherhood and it is nothing known to us or to any other being. [...] There is no speaking of it, nor name nor knowledge of it. Darkness and light, error and truth—it is none of these. It is beyond assertion and denial.[6]

In his *Theological Outlines* (now lost) and treatise *Divine Names*, Pseudo-Dionysius interrogates the way we understand God by first asserting what God is and then, in his *Mystical Theology*, negating those same assertions by saying all that God is not. He thus explores the tension between cataphatic theology (expressing what God is by making affirmative assertions) and apophatic theology (which eschews such concept formation). In Eastern Christianity, apophatic theology is often acknowledged as the superior of the two ways of knowing God. As Vladimir Lossky explains:

> God is beyond all that exists. In order to approach Him it is necessary to deny all that is inferior to Him, that is to say, all that which is. If in seeing God one can know what one sees, then one has not seen God in Himself but something intelligible, something which is inferior to Him. It is by *unknowing* that one may know Him who is above every possible object of knowledge. Proceeding by negations one ascends from the inferior degrees of being to the highest, by progressively setting aside all that can be known, in order to draw near to the unknown in the darkness of absolute ignorance. For even as light, and especially abundance of light, renders darkness invisible; even so the knowledge of created things, and especially excess of knowledge, destroys the ignorance which is the only way by which one can attain God in Himself.[7]

The goal of apophaticism is to draw nearer to the Godhead, to achieve ecstatic union with God through the attainment of a "perfect ignorance" that vacates from one's understanding and senses all concepts and preconceptions of "Him who transcends all being and all knowledge." It is only then, Lossky writes, "that one may penetrate to the darkness wherein He who is beyond all created things makes his dwelling."[8]

The literary apophaticism that I argue is at work in all four of my case studies describes a similar apprehension about imaging God, in this case, God incarnate as Jesus Christ. Affirm Christ too directly and you paradoxically risk diminishing him, either by deploying faith explanations that no longer persuade in an age of skepticism or by reducing Christ to a mere argument in an ideological dispute. These writers understood that to reimage, rescue, or rehabilitate Christ for their age, they had to make him known through indirect, even negative ways, lest what they said about him be mistaken for cliché, doctrine, fashionable interpretation, or naïve apologetics. Their Christology is thus polemical, oppositional, and self-conscious. Their approach to Christ is apophatic because they avoid descriptions or depictions of him that are declarative and definitive. In other words, they avoid a cataphatic approach to describing the Godhead.

Apophaticism as a theological approach, but also adopted and modified as a tool of literary analysis in my book, is thus the golden thread that runs through the Christological inquiries of this investigation. The Jesus of these four writers is affirmed negatively, not as a theological exercise but a literary one, and always in the cause of truer discernment. He is a hidden Christ, sometimes unrecognizable or seemingly absent, like the resurrected Jesus on the road to Emmaus, who is identified by his disciple traveling companions only after he departs from them.[9] The writers in my study image this mysterious Jesus in various ways, revealing him either through problematic and unlikely Christ figures or by means of contradiction, refutation, or radical theological reconfiguration. He is disguised, absent, hidden, even distorted. When he is affirmed, he is most often affirmed through negative means, in seeming repudiation, but always in the service of revealing the real Jesus, as each writer understood him. In this way, these writers can be said to be traveling a *via negativa* or negative way toward Christ, one negotiated primarily through their fiction. While the goal of literary and theological apophaticism is the same—truer discernment of the Godhead—my adaptation of apophaticism as a literary approach needs to be understood in the broader terms that I have been using here to mean not only the deployment of negative statements about God, but also the use of a discursive approach that deflects, contradicts, complicates, and renders mysterious what we know about Christ in order to reveal Christ anew to a society for whom he had become invisible.

For Dostoevsky, this "apophatic" Jesus is the Christ revealed by atheists or concealed behind the ridiculous façade of a unique comic Christology: the Christ of faith, but estranged so that we might see him as if for the very first time. It is a Christ discovered by negative means, a Christ revealed through misdirection and allusion because to affirm him directly risks uttering falsehoods about him. He is thus an ambiguous or paradoxical Christ. Tolstoy's literary apophaticism, by contrast, is as exacting in its negative Christology as the apophaticism of mystical theology. Where Tolstoy's apophatic Christology leads him, however, is quite startling if not sacrilegious, at least from the perspective of the church. The Christ of faith and object of worship is a distraction that gets in the way of our doing the will of God that Jesus revealed to us. We must therefore negate that Christ in order to find the Godhead in Jesus's teachings alone. Only by acting on these teachings can we do the bidding of the God we cannot know.

Both Dostoevsky's and Tolstoy's apophatic Christologies are expressions of faith in the century of unbelief even as each leads us in different directions: Dostoevsky toward the affirmation of the beauty and perfection of Christ as the necessary agent of humanity's salvation; Tolstoy away from Jesus altogether, as a corrective measure necessary in order to recover what is truly important: Jesus's teachings. Both Tolstoy and Dostoevsky lay the critical Christological groundwork for Bulgakov's and Pasternak's famous Easter novels, each of which practices its own literary apophaticism. Together, these four authors express images of Christ that are the most enduring and most important in Russian literature of the last two centuries. Their unique images of Christ are emblematic of their times and universally appealing. They also represent intriguing Christological formulations in their own right.

My reading of all four of these writers will be guided by their shared literary apophaticism, as I follow where their negative Christology leads them. I will also comment, however, on two other common Christological concerns in their works, both of which originate in the Gospels and Orthodox theology, namely the tension between the two dominant kinds of love—eros (physical love) and agape (spiritual love);[10] and the theme of personhood conspicuous in each writer's work—the idea that the human being created in the image of God possesses an inviolate dignity, value, and uniqueness that Christ's incarnation has confirmed for all time.

As with the concept of personhood, the tension between physical and spiritual love—a common enough theme in literature—plays a heightened role in the Christological novels I will be treating. Konstantin Dmitrievich Levin himself announces this theme in *Anna Karenina* when he tells Stiva (Stepan Arkadievich) Oblonsky that the two loves that Plato defines in his *Symposium*—earthly, carnal love versus heavenly, spiritual love—"serve as a touchstone for people."[11] While Levin's comment is obviously important for understanding the novel, it is but the early articulation of a cardinal distinction between the spirit and the body that would dominate Tolstoy's thought over the next quarter century, culminating in its rearticulation in *Resurrection*, a clear measure of its importance for Tolstoy.

This same opposition between kinds of love (eros and agape) confounds Prince Lev Nikolaevich Myshkin in *The Idiot*, who wants to be allowed to love both ways, that is, to love both Aglaya Yepanchina and Nastasia Filippovna, the first through eros, the second through agape. His rival for Aglaya's hand, Evgeny Radomsky, ridicules him for this strange desire. Dostoevsky views the seeming incompatibility of these two kinds of love as the chief impediment to our capacity to understand Christ and to love as he loves. Indeed, the contemplation of these two kinds of love is the subject of an important April 1864 diary entry Dostoevsky composed while awaiting the burial of his first wife, Masha. Family love and the love between husband and wife interfere with agape as Christ himself preached.[12] "The family—that's the law of nature," Dostoevsky writes, "but it is nevertheless an abnormal, egoistic (in every sense of the word) condition of man. [...] But at the same time man must, by the same law of nature, in the name of the ultimate ideal of his goal [i.e., Christ-like love], constantly deny it."[13] *The Idiot*, whose composition Dostoevsky undertook three years later, represents one attempt on the writer's part to work through this paradox.

While apophaticism, personalism, and the contrast between eros and agape inform all four of my case studies, I also address other questions as they are relevant, such as the meaning of divine love in these writers' Christological formulations—a question linked to the eros/agape question—and the problems and nature of belief in their life and times. At the center of my inquiry is the intriguing phenomenon of two centuries of Russian writers' preoccupation with the concept of Christ and the interweaving of religious and moral themes in their works that resulted from that preoccupation.

I should also say a few words about the title of my book. In the epigraph to this preface, the elder Zosima from *Brothers Karamazov* exhorts us to "preserve the image of Christ [*obraz Khristov*]."[14] *Obraz*/image here is understood as likeness, representation, idea, or concept. In Russian, *obraz* can also be used in the same sense as "icon"—*ikona*, from the Greek εἰκών (eikōn), which itself means "image." Thus, to speak of the image/*obraz* of Christ in Russian is already to evoke depictions of Jesus in Russian Orthodox icons, with all of their attendant cultural and theological associations. For the purposes of my study, the idea of the image of Christ will largely be understood as a given interpretation, imitation, or concept of Christ, not necessarily his visual depiction in icons or paintings. Although I do discuss the meaning of Russian icons with regard to the Orthodox understanding of Jesus and personhood, I leave how Jesus has been portrayed in the visual arts in Russia—an intriguing and important subject in its own right—to other researchers, both past and future.[15] Throughout my book, I am concerned primarily with literary images of Christ, which I further restrict to those mainly found in prose works.

The use of the word "Christ" in my title and elsewhere in the book also requires commentary. Christ (Χριστός in Greek, "Christos") is a translation of the Hebrew מָשִׁיחַ, *Mashiach*, or "Messiah"—literally, "the anointed." To be anointed meant to have oil poured over your head as a sign of divine approbation for a given task. While priests and sometimes prophets were anointed, it is an act (anointing) and a term ("the anointed") that refers primarily to kings. Jesus Christ is thus Jesus the Messiah or Jesus the King. The use of "Christ" to refer to Jesus may thus be interpreted as underscoring his messianic qualities. Indeed, with the advent of the historical-critical school of biblical scholarship, some began to make a distinction between the "Jesus of history" and the "Christ of faith" in order to preserve a certain clarity about what person they were talking about: the human first-century Jewish teacher or the Son of God. However, such a distinction is not as neat as it may seem, for Jesus is also a highly symbolic name. Jesus derives from the Greek Iesous (Ἰησοῦς), which is a rendition of the Hebrew Yeshua (also Joshua, Jeshua, and Jehoshuah), which means "Yahweh saves." Thus, whether you refer to him as Jesus, Christ or Jesus Christ, it is impossible to avoid altogether certain theological or Christological associations. For the purposes of my study, I use both terms interchangeably when referencing Jesus in the works of the Russian authors I am analyzing. I do this in part because neither name can be truly divorced from its theological resonances and also in recognition of the fact that over the centuries the term "Christ" has become something of a second proper noun for Jesus in common parlance. I should also mention that Christology as a term is used in two senses in my work: as a word designating the study of Christ; and in the meaning of a theological interpretation of the person and work of Christ.

A final methodological note. Though my study refers to Christ figures, its use of that term is very specific.[16] Christ figures serve an apophatic function in my analysis. A Christ figure, by definition, is not Christ. Not being Christ, however, they nevertheless point to him, though in my study they do so from a distinctly negative vantage point. Like the absurd Myshkin in Dostoevsky's *The Idiot* or the philandering Yuri Zhivago in Pasternak's eponymous novel, the Christ figures that I address are flawed in a way that problematizes their status as markers of Christ or that impedes the otherwise positive associations that have accrued to Jesus. At the same time, however, they embody recognizable features or attitudes of Christ. To invoke the concept of biblical typology, we could say that these characters are types of Christ in that their behavior corresponds in some way to Jesus's character or actions in the New Testament. The purpose of my investigation, however, is not to identify Christ figures in Russian literature or to account for every mention or fictional treatment of Jesus.[17] Rather, it is to understand why the most important Russian authors who attempted to image Christ over the past two hundred plus years chose to affirm him through strategies of negation or through weak or failed Christ figures.

The structure of the book is straightforward. I focus on each of these four writers' image of Christ, supplementing these case studies with chapters that provide the necessary context—cultural, social, political, and theological—to understand the evolution and shape of Russia's literary engagement with Christ. Chapter 1 contrasts the Jesus of history with the Christ of faith and charts the growing secularism of Russian culture and society in the nineteenth century, what I call the "century of unbelief." I track the rise of secularism in the lives and works of the major writers of the day, in the increasing prominence and influence of the works of the historical school of biblical criticism, and in the advent of a radical materialism. In the face of this secularism, I argue that writers like Dostoevsky and Tolstoy adopted a quasi-apophatic approach to the question of belief as a discursive strategy that allowed them to advocate for their faith positions along a *via negativa*, a method in tune with what Dostoevsky called "our negative age."[18] This approach is explicated at length in the case studies that follow.

Because their engagement with Jesus Christ spans several decades and multiple works, I devote two chapters each to my discussions of Dostoevsky and Tolstoy. Chapters 2 and 3 offer extended analyses of Dostoevsky's apophatic

Christology, whose origins can be found in the writer's paradoxical credo from an 1854 letter in which he pledges an allegiance to Christ, even if Christ is discovered to be "outside of the truth," a negative faith assertion that reappears in his novel, *Demons*. In the first Dostoevsky chapter, I compare *Demons* and *Brothers Karamazov* as apophatic discourses that underscore the difficulty of belief, even among those who profess faith. Both of these novels demonstrate how the apophatic exercise can lead as easily to unbelief as to belief. By contrast, in chapter 3 I argue that one of Dostoevsky's bleakest faith narratives, *The Idiot*, deploys comedy as an apophatic device that reveals in the actions of its comic Christ figure, Prince Myshkin, the possibility of faith even in the face of the death and tragedy that close the novel. Dostoevsky's exploration of the "ridiculous man" Myshkin is an exercise in negative Christology par excellence, where our comic Christ figure articulates that which Christ is not and, in so doing, affirms what Christ must be. Comedy—always a fixture of the writer's works—becomes in *The Idiot* the unexpected vehicle for a quite serious exploration of the nature and challenges of belief.

Like Dostoevsky's, Tolstoy's unique Christology also has a negative formulation as its basis, namely, the negation of Christ's divine attributes, but also the concept of divine love, understood in *War and Peace* and *Anna Karenina* as the ability to love those who hate you. This definition of divine love, first articulated in Christ's commandment from the Sermon on the Mount, foregrounds hatred as a paradoxical negative means by which to measure our ability to love like God. It is both a heretofore-underappreciated theme at the heart of each novel's religious and philosophical inquiries and a concept critical to the writer's own radical imaging of Christ. Chapter 4 argues that Tolstoy's exploration of divine love as love of enemies in these novels is a critical first step toward his own idiosyncratic understanding of Christ.

The next chapter examines Tolstoy's ultimate apophatic exercise: his negating of Jesus's divine qualities altogether, the outcome of a desire, first articulated in an 1855 diary entry, to create a "religion of Christ, but purged of beliefs and mysticism." This undertaking is the subject of a series of works in which Tolstoy's assertion of Christ's non-divinity and his emphasis on reason (*razum*) are worked out as a new form of Christian spirituality. Tolstoy's only sustained attempt in fiction at dramatizing the principles of this new vision and its negative Christology is his final novel, *Resurrection*, the basis of this chapter's case study. At the center of Tolstoy's social and Christological critique in the novel is his preoccupation with the body. As the body is to blame for much of the evil in the world, an embodied God in the form of Jesus Christ cannot be tolerated. But there are unintended consequences both to this critique of the body and its Christological application that threaten to undo Tolstoy's radical Christ project, an outcome I explore in my analysis of the novel.

Chapter 6 provides the context for my two twentieth-century case studies. In this chapter, I view the Soviet century, ironically and in contrast to its predecessor, as a century of belief, an outcome of the movement from realism toward symbolism in literature and from the materialist outlook of the secular age to a renewed interest in spirituality at the fin-de-siècle. I address in particular two symbolist poems—Andrei Bely's "Christ Is Risen" and Alexander Blok's "The Twelve"—that situate Jesus provocatively in the context of the Bolshevik Revolution and that confirm two important truths: that Russian radicals had long invoked Jesus as a kind of forefather of the socialist cause, and that there had always been a quasi-religious character to the revolutionary movement. Indeed, in one sense there were no greater true believers than the architects of the new Soviet order, whose revolution raised the lives, ideas, and historical significance of Lenin and Stalin to a quasi-divine status. These aspects of Soviet society thus prepared the ground for a century in which belief as such was very much in the air, even as religion was suppressed. I address provocative imagings of Christ by early Soviet writers and conclude by situating Bulgakov and Pasternak in the context of the Soviet century of belief, where atheism actually provided the negative space for renewed faith.

In the next chapter, I analyze the first example of a novel of belief born in the negative space of state-sponsored atheism: Mikhail Bulgakov's *Master and Margarita*, whose radically estranged depiction of Jesus is the most dramatic example of negative Christology in Soviet literature. In particular, I attempt to show how Bulgakov reveals Christ anew by creating a tension between the adamantly non-divine Yeshua of the inserted text of the Master's novel and the apparently supernatural Yeshua who appears in Stalin's atheist Russia to grant the Master and Margarita peace and to forgive Pontius Pilate. In the dialectic between the quasi-divine and non-divine Yeshua, Bulgakov offers us a *via negativa* toward discerning Christ and the Godhead, a journey complicated by the indeterminacy of the novel's text itself—whose aporias and disjunctions frustrate attempts at forming definitive conclusions—and illuminated by the fairy-tale love story of the novel's titular heroes, which promises to show us what "real, true, everlasting love" looks like and, indeed, does so, but with a twist.

Like Bulgakov, Boris Pasternak also reveals Christ through a text within a text: the poems of his hero, Yuri Zhivago, which appear as the final chapter of the book and which help to affirm Zhivago's status as an unlikely Christ figure. Like his poems, which juxtapose and blend erotological, meteorological, and Christological themes, Yuri embodies a striking contradiction: he is a Christ figure who sleeps with three women and sires five children. This chapter seeks an explanation for this contradiction in Yuri's consistent personalist philosophy (his seeming inability not to love whomever he is with) and how this personalism informs the novel's pronounced eros/agape opposition (represented by the three love affairs of Zhivago), both simultaneously negating a reading of Yuri as a Christ figure and revealing it: an apophatic operation that ultimately reinscribes the biblical Christ into the Soviet century of belief.

I conclude with observations about the image of Christ in works published after Stalin's death and after the demise of the Soviet Union. The Passion narrative in particular—so prominent in Bulgakov's and Pasternak's novels—continued to resonate, reappearing in works such as Venedikt Erofeev's *Moscow to the End of the Line* (1969, arguably a Christ novel in and of itself), Yury Dombrovsky's *The Faculty of Useless Knowledge* (1978), and Chingiz Aitmatov's *The Place of the Skull* (1987). I briefly analyze these works in the context of my four case studies, survey the current literary interest in Christ and Christian themes, and offer a few concluding remarks on the meaning of Christ in Russian literature.

The image of Christ in Russian literature is a rich and as yet still insufficiently studied topic of broad interest and importance.[19] It is my hope that in putting these authors' images of Christ into dialogic contact with each other and identifying what is common and what is distinct about their quests for the Jesus of history or the Christ of faith, we may better understand the changing face in Russian literature of him who "is the same yesterday and today and for ever" (Hebrews 13:8). When Jesus asked his followers, "Who do people say I am?" his question provoked a variety of answers: "Some say John the Baptist; others say Elijah; and still others, one of the prophets." But when he asked them, "And who do you say that I am," Peter gave the answer of faith: "You are the Messiah" (Mark 8:27–29). The writers studied in this book also took up this question. The answer they gave is the subject of the inquiry that follows.

CHAPTER ONE

THE CENTURY OF UNBELIEF
Christ in Nineteenth-Century Russian Literature

Believe me, your Christ, were he born in our time, would be the most undistinguished and ordinary of men; he would be utterly eclipsed by today's science and by those forces that now advance humanity.

Vissarion Belinsky, quoted by Fyodor Dostoevsky,
"Old People," *Diary of a Writer*

BELIEF AND UNBELIEF IN RUSSIAN SOCIETY

In calling the nineteenth century in Russia "the century of unbelief," I do not wish to argue that a great secularism descended upon the country between 1800 and 1900 due to which no one believed in God any longer. On the contrary, Orthodoxy was alive and well in Russia, which, by 1914, boasted some 55,173 churches and 29,593 chapels,[1] along with hundreds of monasteries and tens of thousands of priests and monks. Russia was truly a Christian nation, united by a single faith whose calendar of feast days and fasts regulated the daily lives of millions of peasants, merchants, and members of the nobility. Icons occupied places of honor in the corners of rooms in peasant huts and estate houses alike and Orthodox practices and beliefs made up a common cultural fabric that bound all levels of Russian society together. At the same time, however, there was also a growing conviction, mainly among the educated strata of Russian society, that religious belief was something of a cultural atavism whose place in human society had long been superseded by the sciences and the ascendancy of rationalism as a guiding principle—the culmination, to be sure, of the secular impulse in the seventeenth and eighteenth centuries that accompanied Peter the Great's Westernization of Russia and Catherine's championing of Enlightenment ideas, marking these centuries as the beginning of unbelief in Russia, at least as far as Russian intellectual life is concerned. But it was in the nineteenth century in particular that various strains of materialism made significant inroads into Russian culture, giving rise to an aggressive secularism that became the very hallmark of the progressive intelligentsia and culminating in a revolution that would usher into existence the first officially atheist state in the world. The nineteenth century, then, more fittingly merits the label of the century of unbelief than do its predecessors.

One of the most eloquent champions of the secular mindset in nineteenth-century Russia was Alexander Herzen, an ardent opponent of the Church who believed religion, like the other institutions of tsarist society, threatened the autonomy of the individual. At the same time, Herzen argued that religion had ceased to be important in the lives of the educated class. He declared in his memoirs that "nowhere does religion play so modest a role in education as in Russia."[2] Here, as Joseph Frank reminds us, Herzen was "talking about the education of the children of the landed or service aristocracy, whose parents had been raised for several generations on the culture of the French Enlightenment and for whom Voltaire had been a kind of patron saint."[3] Other Russian intellectuals were much broader in their indictment of Russian religiosity. In his famous 1847 "Letter to N. V. Gogol," Herzen's friend and fellow socialist visionary, Vissarion Belinsky, proclaimed that the peasants, too, were hardly Christian in the true sense of the word. "The Russian *muzhik* utters the name of the Lord while scratching his behind," Belinsky writes. "He says of the icon: *If it isn't good for praying, it's good for covering the chamber pots.* Take a closer look and you will see that it is by nature a profoundly atheistic people. It still retains a good deal of superstition, but not a trace of religiousness."[4]

Belinsky is surely exaggerating for effect in his assertions about the atheism of the common folk, but he is right to insist that Orthodoxy was far from properly understood or correctly practiced across the Russian Empire. The question Belinsky is really asking is to what extent Orthodoxy can be considered primarily a cultural rather than spiritual force in Russian life, that is, a religion whose believers largely go through the motions of their faith—fasting, receiving the sacraments, attending liturgy, and so on—without understanding what they are doing and without feeling particularly religious about it. This kind of Orthodox Christianity is, at best, no more than a set of acknowledged ethical norms and ritualistic gestures. Certainly, this is the impression given in the story "Peasants" ("Muzhiki," 1897) by Anton Chekhov, whose portrait of the ignorance, filth, and drunkenness of the countryside created a sensation when it was published in partially censored form (the Moscow censorship commission found the piece "too gloomy" and too great a potential indictment of the failures of the emancipation[5]). Belinsky would recognize his own comments about peasant religiosity in the following passage from the story:

> Marya and Fyokla crossed themselves, fasted, and took communion every year, but without any understanding of what they were doing. The children were not taught to pray, nothing was told them about God, and no moral precepts were instilled into them; they were simply forbidden to eat certain foods on fast days. In other families it was much the same: there were few who believed, few who understood. At the same time they all loved the Holy Scripture, loved it tenderly, reverently; but they had no books, there was no one to read the Bible and explain it to them, and because Olga sometimes read them the Gospels, they respected her and addressed her and Sasha as their superiors.[6]

Herzen describes a similar situation in his own family in the late 1820s, about the time he turned fifteen. He writes that his father, a wealthy nobleman from an ancient Russian family, "believed to some extent, from habit, from a sense of decency, and just in case," but notes that he "never himself observed any of the rules laid down by the Church," and received the local priest at his house not out of "religious feeling" but rather as "a concession to the ideas of society and the wishes of Government." Herzen was told "it was necessary to submit to such rites as were required by the Church," but that he "must avoid excessive piety, which is suitable for women of advanced age but improper for a man."[7] He was made to observe the Lenten fasting requirements, "dreaded confession," and found Church ceremonies "impressive" and "awful." The Divine Liturgy caused him "real fear" but no "religious feeling." When Easter brought an end to fasting, he ate all the Easter dishes "and thought no more about religion for the rest of the year." But, like the peasants in Chekhov's story, Herzen reserved "a deep and sincere reverence" for the Gospel.

> In my early youth, I was often attracted by the Voltairian point of view—mockery and irony were to my taste; but I don't remember ever taking up the Gospel with

indifference or hostility. This has accompanied me throughout life: at all ages and in all variety of circumstances, I have gone back to the reading of the Gospel, and every time its contents have brought down peace and gentleness into my heart.

For Herzen, the attractiveness of the Gospels had much to do with their theme of social justice, the cause that became for Herzen "a religion of a different kind."[8]

For progressive thinkers like Herzen and Belinsky, there was no other kind of faith. Christ may have been an admirable moral teacher, but the religion founded in his name was already thoroughly discredited among many intellectuals. One only has to listen to the precocious teenager Kolya Krasotkin in *Brothers Karamazov* to understand to what extent it was fashionable in mid- to late nineteenth-century Russia to denounce religion, even while professing begrudging admiration for the figure of Jesus. Kolya tells Alyosha (Aleksei Fyodorovich Karamazov) that he is "not against Christ," who was, after all, "a very humane person," but as an "incorrigible socialist" he believes that "the Christian faith has only served the rich and noble, so as to keep the lower classes in slavery." Kolya goes on to declare (echoing Belinsky[9]) that Christ, were he alive today, "would go straight to join the revolutionaries, and perhaps even play a conspicuous part."[10] A bemused Alyosha can only wonder aloud how the teenager has managed to acquire such a conviction so quickly. In truth, the secularization of the educated classes in Russia proceeded apace, not only among Orthodox Christians, but also in Russia's Jewish population.[11]

As early as 1861, the conservative critic Mikhail Katkov in the periodical *Russkii vestnik* (Russian herald) declared a new "religion" was already on the scene.[12] That religion was materialism, and writers such as Nikolai Chernyshevsky, Nikolai Dobroliubov, Maksim Antonovich, and Dmitrii Pisarev were preaching it in the pages of the leading radical journals of the day, *Sovremennik* (The contemporary) and *Russkoe slovo* (Russian word).[13] Though materialism as the object of passionate debate and partisan devotion peaked in the 1860s, its sustained influence was felt throughout the final decades of the nineteenth century, when Georgii Plekhanov and, after him, Vladimir Lenin championed a Marxist "dialectical materialism" that fueled the revolutionary movements that would topple the tsarist monarchy. Like Kolya Krasotkin's socialist conversion, the growth of the materialist worldview in nineteenth-century Russia was swift, giving rise to the single most important paradigm shift in nineteenth-century Russian culture: away from belief in God and toward belief in humanity instead.

The century of unbelief in Russia, stretching from Herzen's childhood skepticism to Chekhov's quasi-pagan peasants, is not, of course, to be understood in absolute terms. Though church officials fretted over the declining religious habits of nineteenth-century Russians, parishes and religious communities thrived; Orthodoxy was championed by important writers and thinkers associated with the Slavophile movement; Russian children still learned to read from saints' lives; and personal copies of the New Testament (and, after 1876, the entire Bible in Russian translation) were common possessions.[14] Many of the most prominent writers of the century—Nikolai Gogol, Fyodor Dostoevsky, Leo Tolstoy, Nikolai Leskov, and even the future atheists Nikolai Chernyshevsky and Nikolai Dobroliubov (both of whose fathers were priests)—grew up in conventionally pious and religiously observant families. Tolstoy—no friend of Orthodoxy himself—declared in his *Confession* that the lives of the saints were his favorite reading.[15] But, as Tolstoy also reminds us, the religious heritage one grows up with is easily lost "under the influence of knowledge and experience of life which conflict with it." "A man very often lives on," Tolstoy continues, "imagining that he still holds intact the religious doctrine imparted to him in childhood whereas in fact not a trace of it remains."[16]

A similar argument may be made for Russian culture in the nineteenth century, at least as regards Russian literature. Although V. N. Zakharov claims that "up until the twentieth century, [Russia] had not so much literature per se as *Christian* literature,"[17] a glance at the canonical works of the nineteenth century actually suggests that Russian literature was no more religious in theme or content than any of its European neighbors, and perhaps even less so. With the exception of those of Tolstoy and Dostoevsky, the major prose works of the nineteenth century do not focus on questions of Christian metaphysics and refer to aspects of Christianity or Christian culture chiefly in passing, if they do so at all. As for the writers, most were as conflicted about belief as they were in their attitudes toward their native Orthodox Church.

RUSSIAN WRITERS IN THE CENTURY OF UNBELIEF

A case in point is the father of modern Russian literature, Alexander Pushkin. The product of a childhood that was "French, frivolous, and worldly,"[18] Pushkin was initially remote from religion, vacillating between agnosticism and atheism as a young man. Certainly, he was irreverent. One need only look at a few of his early works on religious themes. His 1821 poem "Christ Is Risen" is addressed to a young Jewish woman whom he promises to kiss on Easter "following the law of the Godman," Jesus Christ, only to add, bawdily, that, for another kiss, he is equally ready to adhere "to the faith of Moses" and even put into her hand "that by which one can tell / a true Jewish man from an Orthodox." Pushkin's "Epistle to Davydov," written the same day as "Christ Is Risen," quips that the poet/narrator's "atheistic stomach / will not digest the Eucharist," but might manage "if the blood of Christ / were a good Chateau-Lafitte." That same year Pushkin penned his blasphemous parody of the Annunciation, *The Gabrieliad* (*Gavriliada*), in which Mary is visited by Satan, the Archangel Gabriel, and God all on the same day, each of whom has sexual relations with her.

While these poems do not necessarily constitute a metaphysical revolt on the young poet's part, they do reflect a deep-seated skepticism over the claims of religion. This skepticism, however, did not prevent Pushkin from hailing Christianity in later years as "the greatest spiritual and political upheaval to have transpired on this planet" or from admiring Christianity as an important moral force in the world.[19] Moreover, as Felix Raskolnikov points out in his article on Pushkin and religion, the poet's poems on death from the 1830s increasingly feature religious motifs, leading some critics to make a case for Pushkin as a Christian writer.[20] By the same token, however, the work he spent the better part of a decade writing—his masterpiece, *Eugene Onegin* (1823–1831)—is devoid of any significant reference to Christianity at all. Indeed, Pushkin's heroine, Tatyana, looks more to superstition and folk belief to guide her actions early in the novel than to Christianity, and while she chooses to remain faithful to her older husband and rejects Eugene's declaration of love at the end of the novel, her moral action does not stem from any apparent religious convictions. Indeed, the clearest kind of immortality the book espouses is that earned not by a prayerful life of faith, but by art. One of Pushkin's last poems, however, "Desert Fathers and Virtuous Women" (1836)—a poetic rephrasing of one of the most famous prayers of the Lenten liturgy, the supplication of Ephraim the Syrian—is often cited as evidence of Pushkin's turn to faith at the end of his life.[21]

Pushkin's heir apparent, Mikhail Lermontov, exhibited a similarly vacillating attitude toward faith. His distinct contribution to Russian literature is the famous psychological portrait he drew of the first bona fide materialist of Russian fiction (identified as such midway through the novel): Grigory Pechorin from Lermontov's 1840 novel *A Hero of Our Time*.[22] Handsome, enigmatic, manipulative, and cruel, Pechorin is also a jaded cynic who has replaced belief with skepticism in his life and worldview. He looks at the starry skies and marvels that humanity once thought to look for aid from the heavens, noting how, unlike past generations, this one passes "with indifference from doubt to doubt, just as our ancestors rushed from one delusion to another" (188).

In an age where belief is no longer tenable, Pechorin is one of the first characters in Russian literature to feel the full burden of his existential isolation and the impossibility of any firm answers to life's burning questions. "How can a man know for certain whether or not he is really convinced of anything?" Pechorin asks. "And how often we mistake, for conviction, the deceit of our senses or an error of reasoning?" (193). An amalgam of Romantic clichés and ironic inversions of that same Romanticism, Pechorin emerges as a thoroughly modern figure. He doubts everything, mistrusts both feeling and cold calculation and, as someone who lives his life "having already lived it through in [his] mind" (189), questions what passes for authentic experience and what, on the contrary, is mere simulacrum: a distorted copy of reality derived from the artificial constructs of culture and filtered through our expectations and misperceptions. His appearance on the literary scene set the tone for the questioning heroes who followed two decades later in the works of Dostoevsky and Tolstoy.

The contemporary of both Pushkin and Lermontov—Nikolai Gogol—would seem to present the first exception to our list of authors whose works are marked by religious or ecclesiastical indifference. Gogol, whose career was launched by an anthology of tales describing how good Christian folk battle the devil and his evil forces (*Evenings on a Farm near Dikanka*, 1831–1832) and was concluded by a collection of essays featuring homilies about the Orthodox Church, good Christian behavior, and Christ's resurrection (*Selected Passages from Correspondence with Friends*, 1847), is the most prominent writer on religious themes in the first half of the nineteenth century. Such a characterization comes with a rather large qualification, however. No writer of "idea novels" à la Tolstoy and Dostoevsky, Gogol does not directly tackle eternal metaphysical questions in his works but rather unmasks quotidian petty evil through grotesque depiction. The whole of his masterpiece *Dead Souls* is built on this idea, that trivial banalities—not "some sweeping, grand longing, but a mean, sneaky yen for something insignificant"—make humanity "forget great and sacred obligations and see something great and sacred in insignificant gewgaws."[23] This inversion of scale is a quintessential Gogolian device. Whatever Christian message is inscribed in the novel can be found here, in Gogol's exposition of the soul-deadening properties of a world awash in triviality. While such unmasking had a larger moral aim as its goal, Gogol's desire to expand *Dead Souls* into a larger work of edifying Christian literature—a kind of Russian "Divine Comedy"—was never realized.

When Gogol addressed religion directly, he did so with disastrous results. Ever desirous of serving as a spiritual guide for his readers but always disappointed that this desire never quite realized itself in his fiction, Gogol published his *Selected Passages* near the end of his life as a kind of "religio-ethical treatise."[24] The book's failure with both conservative and liberal readers, however, was due not just to its reactionary content but also to its anachronism. Gogol was out of step with the times. The writer's pious exhortations were better suited to an earlier age and, in any case, were far less interesting than his fiction. As Russian society shifted toward more secular preoccupations in the 1830s and 1840s, religious inquiry gave way to social ethics and political philosophy.[25]

Russian literature reflected this shift in emphasis, relegating Russian Orthodoxy to the role of a purely cultural or background feature in novels. The best example of this phenomenon is Ivan Goncharov's *Oblomov*. The thematic and poetic centerpiece of the novel, "Oblomov's Dream," published a decade ahead of the novel in 1849, establishes the essentially cultural aspect of Orthodoxy in the lives described in the novel. Central to the dream is the mock-epic description of life deep in the Russian provinces on the Oblomov family estate, where time is marked by the passing of Orthodox feast days (St. Ilya's Day, Pentecost, St. Peter's Day, St. Prokhor's Day, and St. Nikanor's Day are all mentioned). Servants and masters live in mutual harmony, no one is in want of anything, and no one is troubled by "any vague intellectual or moral questions," which is "why they always bloomed with health and good cheer and why they lived so long."[26] It is a veritable Garden of Eden, except that there is no talk of God except in the mention of various Church feast days. In truth, the text is not at all concerned with theology but rather comic mythmaking, complete with biblical and classical allusions and the occasional Homeric catalog. Thus the dream does not describe paradise but rather comically distorts it, in the manner of Gogol.

"Oblomov's Dream" also serves as the philosophical centerpiece of the book, articulating the novel's central question of what constitutes a meaningful life: activities and accomplishments or a peaceful life of repose, food, and friends. The novel proposes two answers to this question in its depiction of the two marriages that conclude the book: that of Ilya Ilych Oblomov's childhood friend, Andrei Stolz, to Olga Ilyinskaia (the erstwhile fiancée of Oblomov himself) and that of

Oblomov to Agafya Matveevna, the housekeeper of his Vyborg-side lodgings. Olga and Stolz are the perfect match of intelligence and industry, beauty and business. Oblomov and Agafya, on the other hand, represent a retreat into an Oblomovka idyll, only shorn of the poetry of Oblomov's dreamed reconstruction of it. Agafya's household moves in Oblomovka fashion from one rich meal to another, marking time by seasonal changes and the succession of Church feast days (Shrovetide, Easter, Trinity Sunday, St. Ivan's Day, and St. Ilya's Friday are mentioned) until death's intrusion into Oblomov's ersatz paradise. Death, it turns out, is one of the novel's important themes, for, while both couples are well matched and happy, neither marriage nor the outlooks they embody are ultimately able to answer the one metaphysical challenge of the book: how to acknowledge the end that awaits all living things without falling into despair.

Olga in particular is prone to doubts in this regard, suffering bouts of depression at the thought of "mankind's common infirmity" (509). Stolz calls this "retribution for Promethean fire," but has no answer for her, save the platitude that such thoughts "force you to look again at life with even greater love" (508). For his part, Oblomov, in failing health from inactivity and overindulgence, fears his imminent death and falls into spells of weeping before passing away from a stroke while in bed. Thus the novel, in which Church holidays are acknowledged as an important feature of everyday life in Russia, is absolutely silent on the ability of the Christian faith to answer the questions the novel itself poses about the meaning of life and death. Clearly, for Goncharov Russian Orthodoxy is simply part of the world his characters inhabit, not the means by which they cope with the trials of their lives.

This paradoxical outcome is not surprising, given the literary context of the day. Progressive ideology, not Christian theology, occupied writers, and works were judged based on how relevant they were to current sociopolitical debates. This was how *Oblomov* was read, too. In his famous essay, "What is Oblomovitis?" (1859), Nikolai Dobroliubov analyzed the novel as the diagnosis of a malady infecting Russian society: inaction and passivity. Oblomov, Dobroliubov argued, was but one of a series of heroes from Onegin and Pechorin to Ivan Turgenev's Rudin who failed to use his talents for the betterment of society. In this context, the novel's Christian milieu was nothing but a textual marker of cultural backwardness. Christianity did not have the answers to society's problems, the new socialism did.

For his part, Ivan Turgenev understood literature's new role very well, describing both the clash of generations in Russian society and the evolving political realities of the day in a series of novels—*Rudin* (1856), *On the Eve* (1860), *Fathers and Sons* (1862), *Smoke* (1867), and *Virgin Soil* (1877)—that established his reputation as a writer of prose that addressed social, not spiritual, questions. Like Belinsky, Herzen, and other intellectuals of his generation, Turgenev was secular to the bone. A believing Christian as a young man, Turgenev lost his faith as he grew older, though he seemed to admire sincere religious faith and occasionally regretted his own inability to believe. Never an outright atheist, he remained an agnostic throughout his life. He would, however, attend church with his illegitimate daughter Paulinette and even defended himself against accusations that he had "taken God away from her." "I would never permit myself such an assault on her liberty," he wrote in 1862, "and if I am not a Christian—that is my private affair, my private misfortune."[27]

Turgenev's agnosticism, however, did not keep him from treating religious sentiment in his works. Indeed, strong religious undertones pervade *A Nest of Gentlefolk* (1859), whose heroine, Liza, takes the veil at the conclusion of the story to atone for an unhappy love affair. But Liza, like *A Nest of Gentlefolk* itself, is something of the exception that proves the rule. Like nearly all of Turgenev's strong heroines, she leads a life of sacrifice and dedication but, as Avrahm Yarmolinsky points out, "she does so on the religious plane" while her successors are "secular-minded."[28] Secular-mindedness characterizes Turgenev's outlook as a writer and promoter of Western values in Russia. Turgenev disapproved of "religious trappings, serfdom, and sentimental attachment to traditional 'old Russian ways,'"[29] a mindset reflected in his novels.

In attitude and outlook, Turgenev thus anticipates Anton Chekhov, whose short stories and plays marked the end of realism in fin-de-siècle Russia. The grandson of a serf who had managed to purchase his own freedom and that of his family, Chekhov had ample reason to believe in progress and, indeed, as a doctor with scientific training in medicine, he knew the value of education and the importance of knowledge in all spheres of learning. Like Turgenev, he viewed religion warily, which was perhaps the outcome of coerced participation in family prayer sessions and his father's church choir. At the same time, he retained a love of Church music and liturgy throughout his life, and many of his stories reference Orthodox liturgy, icons, scripture, feast days, and saints' lives, often as part of the milieu of his characters' lives but also, as some critics have argued, as important imbedded Christian subtexts.[30] Chekhov also admired Tolstoy's reinvention of the Christian faith in the last two decades of the century, a faith reconfigured as a set of moral precepts shorn of ritual, dogmas, or priests. "I am not a believer," Chekhov wrote in January 1900, "but of all beliefs I consider his the closest to mine and most suitable for me."[31]

While the writer's attitude toward faith is more complicated than his declarations of unbelief imply, at the same time it is clear that for Chekhov, morality was not governed solely by religion. "I am neither liberal, nor conservative, nor gradualist, nor monk, nor indifferentist," Chekhov wrote to Alexei Pleshcheyev in an 1888 letter that would later be identified as the writer's credo. "My holy of holies is the human body, health, intelligence, talent, inspiration, love and the most absolute freedom imaginable, freedom from violence and lies, no matter what form the latter two take."[32] One does not have to believe in God to believe in these virtues, so it is not surprising that Chekhov was not bothered by the decline of religion in Russia. In a 1902 letter to Sergei Diaghilev, Chekhov wrote that the educated segment of Russian society was "moving away from religion and is moving farther and farther away from it, whatever people may say or whatever philosophical and religious societies may be formed."[33]

This growing decline in faith among the educated classes was no secret. All of Dostoevsky's post-Siberian exile works respond to it in one way or another and it is a prominent theme in Nikolai Leskov's *The Cathedral Clergy* (1872) and Tolstoy's *Anna Karenina* (1875–1877), where belief in God and Jesus Christ is viewed as incompatible with a modern, educated outlook. Father Savely in *The Cathedral Clergy* bemoans "the general indifference spreading throughout Russia that a cultivated person 'should be ashamed to believe in God.'"[34] In *Anna Karenina*, Levin struggles with belief in God throughout the novel and the artist Mikhailov, laboring over his painting of Pilate's confrontation with Christ, flatly declares that "for an educated person the question can no longer exist" whether Jesus was divine.[35] For many in the novel, "religion was just a bridle for the barbarous part of the population" that had nothing to do with the rest of society who, like Anna's brother, Stepan Oblonsky, "could not even stand through a short prayer service without aching feet and could not grasp the point of all these fearsome and high-blown words about the other world, when life in this one could be so merry."[36]

Stepan's attitude is typical of the upper classes in Russia, many of whom, as Hugh McLean points out in his biography of Leskov, "ceased to have any but casual contacts with the church." McLean calls the "widespread religious indifference" of the upper classes and civil authorities a "more serious threat to the church than the avowed atheism of the radicals" at this time.[37] To a lesser extent in his *Cathedral Clergy* and more overtly in works that followed it, Leskov also identifies as a threat to genuine belief in Russia the failings of Orthodoxy itself, from poorly educated, corrupt priests and an inflexible hierarchy to Orthodox liturgical and sacramental rituals that smacked of magical incantations and were divorced from a more pragmatic and robust spirituality, such as that promoted by certain strains of Protestantism and Tolstoy's own idiosyncratic Christianity, both much admired by Leskov.

A loss of faith in Orthodoxy, however, does not necessarily mean the collapse of the desire to believe. Leskov's admiration of non-Orthodox and unorthodox Christianities reminds us that when people became disaffected with the Church, they often sought alternatives to it.[38] One need only to recall Pierre Bezukhov's fling with Freemasonry in *War and Peace*; Tolstoy's description of the interest in table turning, spiritualism, mediums, and Pietism in *Anna Karenina*; or the growing interest in evangelical Protestantism in *Resurrection* (1899) to get a sense of the changing landscape of belief in nineteenth-century Russia. Orthodoxy—still the dominant religion—was nevertheless challenged as much by a growing heterodoxy as by an ever-increasing secularization.

If, however, Tolstoy's assertion in *Resurrection* is true that most Russian believers—and not just the educated elite—were unreflective about the articles of their faith and simply "believed that this belief had to be believed in,"[39] then it is not difficult to understand how it was possible for the Bolsheviks to discredit and marginalize Orthodoxy with such efficiency after the revolution. But to say that the nineteenth century was a century of unbelief is nevertheless to make more of a polemical argument than a factual assertion, partly because the historical reality is quite complicated and partly because labeling writers as "secular" or "religious" is a somewhat dubious undertaking that can only take us so far. After all, authors write not only as their times might incline them but as their unique preferences lead them. What is more important to the present study and what the idea of the century of unbelief helps make clear is the peculiar anxiety provoked in Russian writers by the intertwined questions of belief and the meaning and significance of Jesus. Calling the nineteenth century a century of unbelief is one way to seek a label for that anxiety.

THE CHRIST OF FAITH IN THE CENTURY OF UNBELIEF

If the century of unbelief in Russia is a product of the Enlightenment, then the anxiety surrounding belief in Jesus addressed here can be traced to the

Enlightenment's contribution to biblical scholarship: the historical critical school of biblical study. To fully understand this anxiety, one must first examine the two images that confronted Russian writers in the century of unbelief: the Jesus of history and the Christ of faith.[40]

The Christ of faith was ubiquitous in nineteenth-century Russia: he stared out from icons in houses and churches and was the object of worship at Divine Liturgy. He was the *Pantokrator*, the Almighty, the ruler of the universe, whose stern face looked down from within the highest cupola of Russian churches. He was also the merciful Savior, who humbled himself by assuming human form. He was the humiliated God, crucified on the cross. The Jesus of history, by contrast, was someone entirely different, according to the two most influential works of the historical critical school of biblical study to appear in Russia in the nineteenth century. In David Friedrich Strauss's *The Life of Jesus Critically Examined* (1835), he was the "creator of the religion of humanity,"[41] who, though himself not divine, revealed the divinity that resides in the human race. In Ernest Renan's *Life of Jesus* (1863), he was a "sublime person," provincial, mortal, non-miraculous, a sinner like the rest of us and "the one who has caused his fellow-men to make the greatest step toward the divine."[42] The impact these two works had on the century of unbelief in Russia is hard to overstate. Indeed, the historical critical method did as much to change how Jesus was understood in the nineteenth century as the ecumenical councils of Nicaea (325 CE), Constantinople (381 CE), Ephesus (431 CE) and Chalcedon (451 CE) did in the early church.

Both the councils and the scholars of the historical critical school sought to settle the question about the true identity of Jesus and both labored to prove one point in particular: that Jesus was fully human. The historical critical school argued that Jesus was merely a mortal man. The councils decreed that Christ's divinity and his humanity were both complete. This assertion has immense implications not only for understanding Jesus, but also for understanding our own personhood and our relationship with God. Early church councils grappled with competing notions about the relationship between Jesus's divinity and his humanity, discrediting and rejecting some ideas (subsequently designated as heresies) and affirming others. Heresies inevitably were given labels such as Docetism (Jesus's humanity was a mere illusion masking his divine nature); Arianism (Jesus was a created being subordinate to God, something less than God, but more than a human being); Nestorianism (Jesus was merely a human being joined to the divine person of God's Son); and Monophysitism (Jesus's humanity was entirely subsumed by his divine union with the Son). These banned conceptions of Jesus provided valuable clarifying moments for the early church, which, while professing a divine Christ, nevertheless did not want to deny or diminish the humanity of Jesus. In confronting the inadequacies of each rejected Christology, the councils arrived at the understanding preserved in Christian profession today, that Jesus was "true man and true God," fully human and fully divine, with the human and divine natures sharing equally in all things, even Jesus's suffering and death.

All Russian writers knew this Jesus. The God-Man Jesus Christ as the intersection of the human and the divine could be glimpsed not only in the icons that Russian writers grew up with but also in the very structure of any Russian church. Each church was a liminal place where earthly and divine realities touched, with the iconostasis demarcating the boundary: earthly nave on one side, holy sanctuary on the other. Entering a Russian Orthodox church was not only a feast for the senses, but a theological lesson, where every architectural and sacramental element told the story of God incarnate. The icons ubiquitous in Russian churches played a particularly important role in telling this story.

Icons, after all, are the very image of God made visible, fully human and fully divine. As Leonid Ouspensky reminds us, "the image is necessarily inherent in the very essence of Christianity, from its inception, since Christianity is the revelation by God-Man not only of the Word of God, but also of the Image of God."[43] "He that hath seen me hath seen the Father," Christ declares in John 14:9. The Greek letters in the nimbus surrounding Christ's head spell this out in no uncertain terms. At the top of the nimbus is the Omicron, the article "the" in Greek. To the left of Christ's head is the Omega, to be combined with the Greek letter Nu on the opposite side. The resultant phrase translates as "the existing one" or "I am that I am," the words with which God revealed himself to Moses in the burning bush (Exodus 3:14). The only conclusion left to draw is that the figure before us is the same as God.

As liminal space, however, the icon is as much a marker of separation as it is reconciliation. It is like the iconostasis, the screen "dividing the Divine world from the human world," which in the context of the church interior itself "unites the two worlds into one whole in an image which reflects a state of the universe where all separation is overcome, where there is achieved a reconciliation between God and the creature, and within the creature itself."[44] The believer seeking reconciliation must participate in the reality being depicted in the images on the iconostasis. In looking at an icon of Christ, she must do the same as the saints before her: follow in the path of the God-Man who points the way to union with God.

These aspects of iconography are worth dwelling on, as they inform how Russian writers understood the image of Christ as God-Man. Icons, after all, teach a kind of imitation of Christ that is distinct from typical Western practice. If *imitatio Christi* in the West is often construed as doing as Christ would do,[45] in the East, believers imitate Christ by aspiring to be like Christ not only in thoughts and in acts, but also in body. Like the glorified Christ of the Transfiguration and the resurrection, they, too, are to become transfigured, spiritualized, deified. It is this spiritualization of the body to which the Eastern Church aspires and for which icons are aid and model. Jesus Christ is not only the Son of God and the second person of the Trinity, but he is also the "deified prototype" whom believers seek to imitate and who reminds them they they are created in the image and likeness of God.[46]

It is important to note, however, as the Eastern Church Fathers point out, that these terms "image" and "likeness" do not mean the same thing, a distinction implied in Genesis, where God proposes to "make man in our image and likeness" but then creates him only "in the divine image," without further mention of divine likeness (Genesis 1:26, 27). Orthodox tradition holds that image and likeness are thus two different things. The image of God, according to Pavel Florensky, is "the spiritual ground of each created person."[47] It is a permanent part of our identity; "however sinful we may be, we never lose the image."[48] The likeness to God, however, is "the potentiality to attain spiritual perfection."[49] It is to be accomplished "by the action of the grace of the Holy Spirit, with the free participation of man himself."[50] Indeed, Jesus's incarnation is dramatic affirmation of this part of our relationship with God. As St. Irenaeus expressed it, "God made himself man that man might become God."

Therefore, to understand the image of Christ in icons is also to acknowledge our call to make ourselves "like" him so that our human state—body and personality—can be spiritualized. This process—known as *theosis*—is at the center of the theology of icons and the teaching of the Orthodox Church. "The beauty of an icon is the beauty of the acquired likeness to God," Ouspensky writes, "and so its value lies not in its being beautiful in itself, in its appearance as a beautiful object, but that it depicts Beauty."[51] Beauty here acquires a theological meaning, for Beauty is an epithet describing God. And the icon is not just a representation of Beauty, but also a means of achieving it. The role of the icon, therefore, is not static depiction but rather dynamic creation.

Given the centrality of *theosis* in Orthodox spirituality, it is little wonder that Russian religious thought is so intensely personalist, and, with it, Russian philosophy and literature. The call to deification is an invitation to share in the divine life of Christ and to join in "a personal and organic union" with God, a constant theme of the Gospel of John and Paul's epistles. In becoming "partakers of the divine nature" (2 Peter 1:4), however, we "retain our full personal integrity."[52] Human beings do not merge with God but remain distinct from him, for Christ's revelation as God Incarnate affirms the absolute value of human personhood (*chelovecheskaia lichnost'*), creating an ontological commonality between humanity and God.

The influential Russian religious philosopher Vladimir Solovyov, whose famous 1878 lectures on Godmanhood were attended by both Dostoevsky and Tolstoy, makes this point when he argues that union with God would be impossible "if the divine principle were purely external to humanity, if it were not rooted in human personhood itself. If it were not so rooted, our relationship to the divine principle could be only one of involuntary, fateful subordination." Personhood is thus a key concept for understanding both human beings and God. The human person "has absolute, divine significance," Solovyov notes, for she can "unite with the divine principle freely" and in this way "participates in Divinity." God, on the other hand, is "both a person, a possessor of personal being, and the absolute content, or idea, that fills that personal being."[53]

These concepts, emerging from Orthodox doctrine about icons, *theosis*, and the Trinity and further elaborated by Solovyov, are developed into a full-blown theory of personalism by the Russian twentieth-century religious philosophers Nikolai Berdyaev and Sergius Bulgakov. In his work *The Divine and the Human* (1947, *Ekzistentsial'naia dialektika bozhestvennogo i chelovecheskogo*), Berdyaev, following Solovyov, argues that the incarnation revealed not only "the human in God" but also "the divine in man," elevating the concept of "humanity" and "humanness" (*chelovechnost'*) in the process.[54] "Humanness is not what is called humanism or humanitarianism," Berdyaev argues, "it is the God-manhood of man" (112). It is not "self-sufficiency" or "self-deification" but a recognition that "human personality" is "the highest value" (115–16). And it is the highest value only because personhood is bound up with the image and likeness of God, who affirms this link between the divine and the human in Christ's incarnation and who models personhood in the mystery of the Trinity. Thus, human-ness is "the revelation of the fullness of human nature," according to Berdyaev, because "human-ness is divine; it is not man that is divine, but human-ness" (125–26).

This understanding of personhood ultimately derives from the Trinitarian nature of God, which, as Sergius Bulgakov argued, must be understood as a personalistic phenomenon. The Triune God, in whom the three persons of Father, Son and Holy Spirit "'dwell' in the other two by virtue of a perpetual movement of love,"[55] models the relational aspect of personhood and the irreducibility of the notion of personhood to the idea of the individual. The individual is merely an autonomous unit of society, an object, not a religious or philosophical subject. Personhood, however, is a theological concept, for it is inextricably linked to the image and likeness of God. Fully realizing our personhood is not the same as fully realizing our individuality, for personhood involves a radical turning to God and a fundamental overcoming of division and disunity. Human beings are relational, Bulgakov writes, both within themselves and between themselves: "The revelation of oneself through the other, the knowledge of oneself as the other ... such a relationship in which every one exists only for the other and in the other, identifying oneself with him: such a life in the other is love. Love as reciprocity and mutual self-negation is the substantial relationship of the triune subject."[56]

The personalism that emerges from Orthodox teachings on *theosis* was influential not only in the formation of Russian religious thought but in that of European humanism as well. Greek patristic concepts of *theosis* made their way to Europe, influencing Renaissance thinking on the subject of the human person, then back to Russia in the mid-nineteenth century in vernacular translations undertaken by the empire's four theological academies.[57] These concepts thus traced a path from religious to secular sources, leaving their mark along the way and influencing important nineteenth-century writers and thinkers of both the Slavophile and Westernizer camps, each of whom emphasized the centrality of human personhood.[58] D. S. Mirsky notes a distinct "philanthropic" mindset in Russian literature of the nineteenth century that gave rise to "a sympathetic attitude to human beings, without distinction (not only of class but) of intrinsic moral significance." This attitude became a "principal characteristic of Russian realism," particularly in the works of Dostoevsky, where "the torture of self-consciousness is the torture of the ultimate and absolute value of a human personality, wounded, unrecognized, and humiliated by other human personalities."[59] Dostoevsky's personalism in turn influenced later religious thinkers as well as Mikhail Bulgakov and Boris Pasternak.

The danger here, of course, is that the strongly articulated idea of personalism attending the Orthodox concept of *theosis* can lead to unexpected outcomes.

If the idea of the sanctity of personhood is reduced to a mere humanism, for instance, it is quite easy to do away altogether with the need for Christ, that is, to extol man over God. This is precisely what happened in Russia in the mid-nineteenth century when intellectuals like Alexander Herzen and Vissarion Belinsky preached a radical philosophy of the individual, but one not based on the idea of the human person created in the image and likeness of God. Rather, theirs was a strictly materialist philosophy, which found in human beings the source and summit of all dignity and value.

"The fate of the subject, the individual, the person is of more importance to me than the fate of the whole world," Belinsky declared in 1841.[60] To defend the individual personality and raise him up through reason and science, however, the first and most necessary task was to oppose Christianity, which, as Herzen writes in *From the Other Shore* (1850), recognized "the infinite worth of the individual, as if only for the purpose of destroying him all the more solemnly before Redemption, the Church, [and] the Father in Heaven."[61] For this reason, it was absolutely necessary for the materialists (in Dostoevsky's words) "to destroy Christ's teachings; to label them false and uniformed philanthropy, proscribed by contemporary science and economic principles."[62] The God-Man had to be renounced to make room for new role models.

THE JESUS OF HISTORY AND THE NEW PROTOTYPE

In renouncing Christ, Russian secular humanism follows Strauss and the historical critical method. In his *Life of Jesus Critically Examined*, Strauss rejects the divinity of Jesus as something implausible and unnecessary for the confirmation of humanity's divinity. He writes: "In an individual, a God-Man, the properties and functions which the Church ascribes to Christ contradict themselves; in the idea of the race, they perfectly agree. Humanity is the union of the two natures—God become man, the infinite manifesting itself in the finite." The individual cannot be perfect or divine, but humanity can, for "pollution cleaves to the individual only, and does not touch the race or its history." Strauss's view is essentially anthropocentric: it is humankind that "dies, rises, and ascends to heaven" in successive generations, ever proceeding toward "a higher spiritual life," a "union with the infinite spirit of the heavens." By thus "kindling within him the idea of Humanity," Strauss concludes, "the individual man participates in the divinely human life of the species."[63]

Strauss's book, which circulated in Russia shortly after its publication, was
hugely influential. It was quickly translated into the major European languages and had a profound impact on Belinsky, in whose circle, according to
Dostoevsky, Strauss's name was spoken of "very reverently."[64] *The Life of Jesus
Critically Examined*—not the first venture into the historical school of biblical
criticism, but, alongside Renan's *Life of Jesus* thirty years later, the most important in Russia—came at a critical juncture in Russian culture. Dominant ideas
imported from the West, such as German Romanticism or French utopian
socialism, were waning. Strauss and other Left Hegelian thinkers like Ludwig
Feuerbach (in his book *The Essence of Christianity*, 1841) stressed the "anthropological essence of religion," preaching that man's salvation lay in his own
hands, through reliance on empiricism and reason. Human beings were to orient themselves, as Patrick Lally Michelson notes, "not toward a supernatural or
transcendental authority" but rather "toward an anthropological ideal of 'rational man' and 'purified personality.' Humanity could attain authentic freedom
only after man became conscious of the world-historical fact that he was his
own supreme being."[65]

The historical critical method played a particularly important role in this
process of dethroning Christ for it challenged the indisputability of the Gospel
texts themselves.[66] Together with what Charles Taylor calls the modern "cosmic imaginary"—the understanding introduced by advances in science in the
nineteenth century that the universe is too vast to be contained or explained by
the Christian narrative—the historical critical method called into question the
explanatory authority of Christianity itself.[67] No work of the historical critical
school accomplished this task better in Russia than Ernest Renan's revisionist
biography of Jesus. When it was published in 1863, Renan's *Life of Jesus* was
almost immediately translated into over a dozen languages, including Russian,
and went through thirteen editions in its first two years.[68] Most importantly,
Life of Jesus appeared during a decade when materialist outlooks were making important inroads into middle-class consciousness.[69] With its ability to
make the discoveries of the historical critical method both comprehensible and
attractive, Renan's book was particularly influential. Renan translated the dense
intellectual debates of revisionist academic Christology into the clear, lyrical,
and simple story of a charming Galilean preacher who introduced a new way
of worship and of imaging God in first century Judea. In so doing, according
to Albert Schweitzer, he summed up "in a single book the result of the whole

process of German criticism,"[70] radically changing how Christ was imaged wherever it was read.

Renan draws his biography of Jesus from the four Gospels, each of which he admits is "authentic" even as all are "in part legendary."[71] In keeping with the historical critical method, Renan rejects any miraculous origins or deeds in Jesus's life, sometimes offering his own rational explanations for out-of-the-ordinary events. Renan theorizes, for instance, that Jesus's raising of Lazarus may have simply been a stunt concocted by the sick man and his two sisters in order to convert unbelievers, an occasion when "the ardent desire of silencing those who violently denied the divine mission of Jesus carried his enthusiastic friends beyond all bounds" (184). As for Jesus's many healings—by far, the majority of his miracles—Renan offers a historical explanation:

> Jesus had no more idea than his countrymen of a rational medical science; he believed, like everyone else, that healing was to be effected by religious practices, and such a belief was perfectly consistent. [...] Healing was considered a moral act; Jesus, who felt his moral power, would believe himself specially gifted to heal. Convinced that the touching of his robe, the imposition of his hands, did good to the sick, he would have been unfeeling if he had refused to those who suffered a solace which it was in his power to bestow. (140)

Provincial and minimally educated, Jesus "knew nothing beyond Judaism" (42). His acquaintance with the scriptures "made much impression upon him" (43) and fired his particular genius with a vision of the messianic destiny of the Jewish people, fostering an apocalyptic mindset (44). Early on, Jesus developed the "profound idea of the familiar relations of man with God" (46). This idea led to Jesus's theology of "God conceived simply as Father" (61). No longer "the partial despot who has chosen Israel for His people," he is, instead, "the God of humanity" (62), accessible through a "pure worship, a religion without priests and external observances, resting entirely on the feelings of the heart, on the imitation of God, on the direct relation of the conscience with the Heavenly Father" (64–65). These beliefs brought Jesus into conflict with the Jewish religious hierarchy in Jerusalem and led to his demise: crucifixion on the cross. His body was buried and then disappeared, giving rise to reports of his resurrection, the outcome, Renan argues, of "the strong imagination of Mary Magdalen," which "played an important part in this circumstance" (215). Perhaps, Renan speculates, "always credulous" enthusiasm among his grieving followers gave rise to the stories of "a resuscitated God" (215).

In the end, Jesus—the "highest summit of human greatness" (222)—laid the "foundation of true religion," which is yet to be developed and rendered fruitful in this world (220). He is someone who is still imperfectly understood, whose interpreters, thinking to raise him with their Christology of divine sonship, have in reality only lowered him (223), for he never "gave utterance to the sacrilegious idea that he was God" (61). In this sense, he is still something of a stranger who must be encountered outside of the traditional Christian profession, a point with which the four subjects of this book agreed in their own approaches to imaging Christ. On one point, however, Renan is in agreement with Orthodox Christian teaching: "that among the sons of men there is none born who is greater than Jesus" (227). With this, he concludes his slender volume.

The reception of Renan's book in Russia was stormy. The 1864 Russian translation of *Life of Jesus*, published in Dresden, was banned by the minister of the interior, P. A. Valuev, for its blasphemous and heretical content.[72] This prohibition, predictably, only heightened its allure. "If Strauss and Renan had not been banned," Dostoevsky lamented in an unpublished note, "who would know about them in our country?"[73] Both printed and hand-copied versions of the book circulated widely and were read in intellectual and popular circles. It was virtually mandatory reading among the intelligentsia, and *Life of Jesus* soon took its place alongside the works of Western materialists and Russian radicals as part of the required curriculum for aspiring progressives, especially after 1905, when censorship was relaxed and the work could be published legally in Russia.

In a case of perfect timing, Renan's *Life of Jesus* appeared the same year as the other most influential text of Russian secular humanism in the nineteenth century: Nikolai Chernyshevsky's novel, *What Is to Be Done?* The two works together struck a double blow for secularism in Russia in the century of unbelief: Renan's in its replacing of the God-Man Christ with the mortal Jesus, and Chernyshevsky's in its proposal of a new prototype for humanity: idealistic "new people" (*novye liudi*—Chernyshevsky's term), who perfect themselves not in order to aspire to the likeness of Christ, but in order to bring about a new society based on reason and scientific knowledge. A whole generation of educated commoners or *raznochintsy* gathered around Chernyshevsky, uncompromising, eager for action, and willing to sacrifice themselves for the cause. Together with Chernyshevsky, they maintained that one could take a scientific approach to moral questions.

To promote his ideas, Chernyshevsky wrote his 1863 novel *What Is to Be Done?* while incarcerated in the Peter and Paul Fortress awaiting trial for inciting unrest. A tendentious political tract thinly disguised as a novel, *What Is to Be Done?* emerged as the single most inspirational work of the revolutionary movement in Russia, giving voice and direction to thousands of converts to the new cause of revolutionary action and materialist philosophy. The novel also marks a crucial moment in the movement from sacred to secular iconography in its promotion of a new, non-divine role model. Although of all of the major characters in the novel he occupies the least textual space, the most important character of *What Is to Be Done?* is arguably the enigmatic revolutionary Rakhmetov, the first of the "new people" to have ascended to a superior level of political purposefulness, ideological commitment, personal self-sacrifice, and physical self-mortification. Rakhmetov is, in the chapter title that introduces him, "an extraordinary man" (*osobennyi chelovek*), and the two chapters devoted to him in the novel are at once a kind of saint's life and a verbal icon, whose likeness readers were to assimilate in their own lives.

The novel gives Rakhmetov's biography in reverential tones, relating facts that no one knew "while he lived among us."[74] Like Christ's, his genealogy is venerable, as he is descended "from one of the oldest families not only in Russia but in all of Europe" (275). At a young age, Rakhmetov devoted himself to study and physical fitness, working at common labor to boost his physical strength. Toward that end, he eats prodigious amounts of "almost raw" beef and sets off to wander around Russia, working as barge hauler, plowman, carpenter, and common laborer. During these peregrinations, he meets one of the "new people" and has a quasi-religious conversion to the revolutionary cause. He reads political literature for eighty-two hours straight, swears off women and wine, refuses to eat anything the common people cannot eat, and begins to live a Spartan life, sleeping on a strip of felt and devoting all his waking hours to the cause. At the age of seventeen, he thus surpasses his teachers, who begin calling him "an extraordinary man." He starts supporting poor university students financially, engages in underground political agitation in Petersburg, and then departs for Europe, where he continues his revolutionary activity. The narrator alludes to mysterious gaps in his biography and relates various wonder stories about him, such as the time he slept an entire night on a bed of nails as a test of self-mortification. He is an unbelievable amalgam of self-confidence, moral purity, high expectations, and steely resolution whose only fault is a love of cigars.

As improbable as this portrait and the stilted narrative that surround it were, the novel was received rapturously by the Russian public. Its appearance, made possible through a series of blunders by the censors, was itself a kind of miracle. It soon became a secular New Testament, "a true positivistic Gospel."[75] While Rakhmetov and the novel's "new people" inspired a generation of revolutionaries, no single individual better personified Chernyshevsky's ideals than the leader of the revolution itself, Vladimir Lenin, who himself took Rakhmetov as a prototype. Lenin reread *What Is to Be Done?* after his brother was hanged for plotting the assassination of Alexander III and the novel had a formative influence. Chernyshevsky, he later recalled, "ploughed me up more profoundly than anyone else."[76] As a tribute, he named his 1902 work on the role and organization of the Bolshevik Party after the novel. He also behaved much like Rakhmetov in his disregard for personal comfort, his modesty, self-confidence, single-minded dedication to the revolution, work ethic, and expectation that others follow his example.

Both Chernyshevsky and Renan offered a secular role model for their readers, and each of these role models, in turn, reflects one of the two chief anxieties of the century of unbelief in Russia. Renan's compelling portrait of Jesus represents the rationalist overthrow of the God-Man. Chernyshevsky's hagiography of Rakhmetov announces the advent of the new Man-God of scientific materialism. Henceforth, all Christological battles had to be fought on two fronts in Russia: that of the historical critical method that reduced Jesus to a mere man; and that of the materialists, who dumped Jesus from the ship of modernity altogether and replaced him with a different sacred prototype—the devoted revolutionary destined to usher in a just age under the banner of science and progress. It is on these two battlefields that Russia's greatest novelist-Christologists—Fyodor Dostoevsky and Leo Tolstoy—would wage their own "holy wars."

Dostoevsky, Tolstoy, and the Anxiety of Belief

Both Dostoevsky's and Tolstoy's response to Chernyshevsky and Renan is paradoxical. Dostoevsky answered *What Is to Be Done?* with his underground man's rebellion of whim and spite, an irrational antidote to the rational excesses of Chernyshevsky's utilitarian Utopia but one, curiously, that does not include direct mention of Jesus Christ. As for *Life of Jesus*—"a book filled with unbelief"[77]—Dostoevsky responded with his novel *The Idiot*, written in the years immediately following Dostoevsky's first acquaintance with Renan. But here, too, critics note a paradox, for Prince Myshkin seems to share many of the very traits prominent in Renan's Jesus: "His sweet, poetic nature. [...] His naiveté; the powerful attraction of His gaze and His smile; His lack of familiarity with the sciences; His ignorance of how the higher strata of society lived; His enjoyment of time spent with children and women, who understood and valued Him most of all; His own childlike nature; His weakness and doubts; and His struggle 'with the demon who lives in the hearts of every man.'"[78] It is as if in responding to Renan, Dostoevsky could not avoid falling under his spell.

Tolstoy, too, shares fundamental views with both Chernyshevsky and Renan, even as he rejects what they advocate. Ever the dualist, Tolstoy did not agree with Chernyshevsky's exclusive emphasis on the power of human reason and rational egoism as both the essential nature of human beings and the only path to improve the conditions of society. As Donna Orwin reminds us, Tolstoy "believed in the existence of both rational self-interest and an inner spiritual principle that allowed human beings to direct or even contradict it."[79] His 1864 play *The Infected Family* is a thinly veiled response to Chernyshevsky's novel in which Tolstoy pits the emotions and spontaneity of his aptly named heroine, Liubov' (Love), against the petty egoism of her nihilist suitors, whose rationalism prevents them from really loving her.[80] At the same time, as A. N. Wilson points out, Tolstoy "absorbed much of the extreme radicalism of Chernyshevsky, Herzen and Proudhon," whose influence can be marked in positions Tolstoy would take on questions of land ownership and the government in later years. As for *Life of Jesus*, although Tolstoy famously ridiculed Renan's supposed interest in Jesus's biological functions, like Renan, Tolstoy would also argue for a non-divine Jesus in his own study of the Gospels and the Christian faith.

Two things were central to both authors' opposition to the Man-God and the non-God-Man: the conviction that Chernyshevsky and Renan were wrong but also a distinct anxiety about what their proper response should be. Clearly, for Tolstoy and Dostoevsky the challenges Jesus Christ presented for their age and for the well-being of humanity were of utmost importance. Indeed, the last decades of each writer's life were devoted to little more than the articulation of their understanding of Jesus and his message to a readership increasingly hostile or indifferent to it. In the century of unbelief, each writer was like a voice crying out in the wilderness, "Prepare ye the way of the Lord." And like John the Baptist, each writer in his own way points to Christ, albeit one of his own making. What image of Christ they reveal is the subject of the following chapters.

CHAPTER TWO

CHRIST OUTSIDE THE TRUTH

Negative Christology in *Demons* and *Brothers Karamazov*

A complete atheist stands on the next-to-last step to the most complete faith.

Demons, "At Tikhon's"

DOSTOEVSKY'S SYMBOL OF FAITH

Paradox is at the center of Dostoevsky's engagement not only with Christ but also with matters of faith throughout his career. In his famous March 1854 letter to the Decembrist wife Natal'ia Fonvizina he declares, "I am a child of this century, a child of doubt and disbelief, I have been and shall ever be (that I know), until they close the lid of my coffin." At the same time, he nevertheless singles out a potent "symbol of faith" in his life "in which all is clear and sacred." He writes: "This symbol is very simple and here is what it is: to believe that there is nothing more beautiful, more profound, more sympathetic, more reasonable, more courageous, and more perfect than Christ; and there not only isn't, but I tell myself with a jealous love, there cannot be. More than that—if someone succeeded in proving to me that Christ was outside the truth, and if, *indeed*, the truth was outside Christ, I would sooner remain with Christ than with the truth."[1]

All of the writer's future artistic method is on full display here: the writer's love of hyperbole and contradiction, his use of assertion through negation, his allowing of unexpected outcomes, and perhaps most of all, his reluctance to make a straightforward, earnest declaration of faith. After all, a declaration of faith in a Christ "outside the truth" is hardly an affirmation of the Christian profession of Dostoevsky's native Orthodoxy, for if Christ is not the truth, then what becomes of Orthodoxy? Is Dostoevsky's credo, then, perhaps even a tacit admission of a possible atheism on the writer's part? Or is he instead using unbelief as a paradoxical way of affirming belief, by making a negative formulation serve a positive end? Or, finally, is Dostoevsky's symbol of faith ultimately meant to present an unresolvable contradiction, allowing for both possibilities at once, faith *and* unbelief, like the metaphysical gambits of the writer's later works, where readers can find as many reasons *not* to believe as to believe. "What a terrible torment this thirst to believe has cost me and is still costing me," Dostoevsky writes in his letter, "and the stronger it becomes in my soul, the stronger are the arguments against it."[2]

If doubt is faith's constant companion, then for Dostoevsky it is also a kind of dangerous but necessary goad. Indeed, unbelief is so strongly and convincingly articulated in his works precisely because it is also capable of revealing faith both dramatically and compellingly. Readers often learn the most about faith in Dostoevsky's works apophatically, that is, by discovering what it is not. Dostoevsky's letter to Fonvizina alerts us to such possible paradoxes when the writer speaks about belief. The letter is thus important not only because it speaks to the writer's state of mind about faith, but also because it anticipates his future methodology, for it is one of his first written provocations in which he probes given truths and seeks affirmation in seeming refutation. But does *all* apparent refutation of belief by Dostoevsky serve as a covert affirmation of faith? Or, like his statement about Christ "outside the truth," does the apophatic impulse in his novels lead as easily to unbelief as to belief? Why does unbelief loom larger than belief in so many of Dostoevsky's works? These questions are at the heart of two of the writer's most important Christological novels: *Demons*—in which Dostoevsky actually quotes the paradoxical credo from his 1854 letter—and *The Brothers Karamazov*, in which the writer's apophatic approach is more pronounced than in any other novel.

MAN-GOD VERSUS GOD-MAN: CHRIST "OUTSIDE THE TRUTH" IN *DEMONS*

Though intended as a "pamphlet novel" in which he vowed to lay bare all of his opinions "fervently" and "to the last word" about the political issues of his day,[3] *Demons* is as much about Dostoevsky's metaphysical preoccupations as it is about his political concerns. Indeed, the two are connected. In an 1873 article responding to critics of *Demons*, Dostoevsky links his own involvement in a radical political society—the Petrashevsky Circle—to questions of belief in God. He first makes clear that, while *Demons* was based on the story of the revolutionary and conspirator Sergei Nechaev[4]—whose ruthless murder of one of his collaborators, I. I. Ivanov, and eventual arrest in 1869 received sensational coverage in the Russian press—his intention in his novel was not the "literal reproduction of the Nechaev story" but an attempt to explain how such a phenomenon "could arise in our society."[5] Dismissing the notion floated in the press that only the "idle and underdeveloped" could be so radicalized, Dostoevsky uses his own life story to suggest that the opposite is more likely; that "diligent, ardent young people who were in fact studying and who possessed good hearts" are the very ones most likely to turn into "Nechaevs" and "Nechaevists" (279, 283). Indeed, Dostoevsky declares that this is what happened to him. "I myself am an old 'Nechaevist,'" he pronounces in his article. "I also stood on the scaffold condemned to death, and I assure you that I stood in the company of educated people" (284).

Dostoevsky's point is that if the "utopian socialism" à la Charles Fourier of his youth could have given birth to the radical materialists of the present day, then any ideal is susceptible to sudden and extreme change—a theme worked out explicitly in *Demons*. As if to emphasize this point, Dostoevsky reveals that he himself came from "a family that was Russian and pious" who "knew the Gospels virtually from our earliest childhood" (289). While he blames "all these [John Stuart] Mills and [Charles] Darwins and [David Friedrich] Strausses" for leading today's educated youth astray with their marked secularism (287) and rails about the "amazing lengths" the human mind can go "having rejected Christ" (288), the fact remains that Dostoevsky was nevertheless living proof of the possibility that someone piously raised on the Gospels could still become "an old Nechaevist." He is thus confirming a cardinal truth of his own works: that the most ardent faith may turn, suddenly and dramatically, into the most passionate atheism.

In the censored chapter from *Demons*, Dostoevsky actually articulates this relationship, although the other way around. The Orthodox bishop Tikhon tells Nikolai Stavrogin, "A complete atheist stands on the next-to-last step to the most complete faith," thus advocating the quasi-apophatic view that the more convinced people are of the impossibility of the divine, the more complete is the negative place from which they may grope their way back to God. They "may or may not take that step," Tikhon acknowledges, but complete faith is never-theless within their grasp. [6] At first glance, this seems to be the case in *Demons*. While Dostoevsky's political conspirators plot against God as much as against Russian autocracy, they also cannot quite do without God, as seen in the beliefs of Stavrogin, Aleksei Kirillov, and Ivan Shatov. In practice, however, belief only seems to beget unbelief in the novel, thus inverting the apophatic impulse artic-ulated by Tikhon and reducing God to a shadowy presence glimpsed only at the edges of the novel's metaphysical discourse.

A patchwork quilt of genres—now political satire, now gothic grotesque, now metaphysical drama—*Demons* is a novel that relies on mystification, inversions, doublings, and misdirection, in its plot and in its Christology. Stavrogin, who Dostoevsky claimed was the center of the novel and its "real hero,"[7] is also cen-tral to its metaphysical inquiry. Christological associations attach to him and his two "disciples," Kirillov and Shatov. The Greek word for "cross"—*stavros*—is inscribed in his name and, in a textual variant of the unpublished chapter "At Tikhon's," the narrator describes Stavrogin's confession as expressing "the need for the cross in a man who does not believe in the cross."[8] He is an object of fas-cination, worshipful adoration, and ultimate revulsion. Kirillov and Shatov are his one-time ardent admirers and exist almost exclusively as the embodiments of his cast-off ideologies. Pyotr Verkhovensky, too, is in awe of him and seeks to make him the center of his revolution: "You are a leader, you are a sun, and I am your worm," he exclaims, rapturously (2:8:419).

Verkhovensky's interest in Stavrogin, however, is ultimately self-serving: Stavrogin is to be his "Ivan the Tsarevich," his imposter, who will help him bring about his anarchic plans. The relationship between Stavrogin and Kirillov and Shatov is much deeper and more complicated. Stavrogin is, for them, a kind of god who has brought them into being. Shatov declares as much about Kirillov: "He's your creation," he tells Stavrogin (2:1:6:248). For his part, Shatov harbors a kind of religious faith in him, exclaiming: "Stavrogin, why am I condemned to believe in you unto ages of ages?" (2:1:6:255). Both men are tied to Stavrogin by their convictions and their very identities. Richard Peace calls them "the two halves of his divided self."[9] Indeed, when Stavrogin visits them in the long "Night" chapter, it is as if he is visiting two sides of his former self. They are dou-bles of him and inverse doubles of each other. But these doublings and inver-sions are themselves diabolical in nature: they all turn back upon themselves. Their chief feature is nullity, and in this way they help describe the void at the center of the novel: Stavrogin himself.

"Night" is one of the pivotal chapters for the novel's Christology, where Stavrogin pays a visit to each of his protégés in succession, something that is not hard to do as they live in adjacent quarters. The ostensible reason for Stavrogin's visit to Kirillov is to ask him to act as his second at his duel with Artemy Pavlovich Gaganov, which is itself a hint at their twin natures. The conversation quickly takes a philosophical turn, as Stavrogin inquires whether Kirillov is still intent on taking his own life—a plan that is part of Kirillov's metaphysical game of "chicken" that he is playing with the idea of God. He desires, as he later explains to Pyotr Verkhovensky, to "proclaim self-will to the fullest point" as a way of proving the non-existence of God: "If there is God, then the will is all his, and I cannot get out of his will. If not, the will is all mine, and it is my duty to proclaim self-will" (3:6:2:617). Kirillov's suicide would demonstrate that there is nothing greater than human volition, freeing humankind from the need to believe in God.

Kirillov's act takes on a quasi-messianic character.[10] "I will begin, and end, and open the door. And save," he tells Verkhovensky (3:6:2:619), sounding like the Christ of Revelation.[11] Stavrogin picks up on this in his conversation with him. When Kirillov proclaims that all people are good despite their committing the vilest of crimes, Stavrogin mutters, "He who taught that was crucified." Kirillov, however, does not attribute this idea to Jesus Christ, the God-man (*bogochelovek*), who, in any case, never made such a statement.[12] As Stavrogin finds out, he is referring to Christ's opposite, the "Man-God" (*chelovekobog*) (2:1:5:238), the human being now raised higher than God, which Kirillov believes he will become through his act of supreme self-will—the outcome, Dostoevsky seems to be warning, of the secular humanists' desire to exclude God from the definition of human personhood. "If there is no God, then I am God," Kirillov tells Verkhovensky (3:6:2:617).

But Kirillov is full of contradictions, as Stavrogin discovers. He believes in eternal life, but not in an eternal power. He plays with children and loves life, but is intent on suicide. He lights his landlady's icon lamps and prays "to everything," but swears he is an atheist. Stavrogin is unconvinced, suspecting Kirillov of an unacknowledged theism: "If you found out that you believe in God, you would believe; but since you don't know yet that you believe in God, you don't believe" (2:1:5:239). Indeed, he predicts that Kirillov will be a believer the next time he sees him, while Pyotr Verkhovensky accuses him of believing "even more than any priest" (3:6:2:618).

They are right to be skeptical. If Kirillov deploys affirmations in the service of negation (his declarations that he loves life and that everything is good are, paradoxically, part of his justification for suicide), Kirillov's negations can also conceal an affirmation. In his conversation with Verkhovensky, for instance, he cites the story of Christ's crucifixion as confirmation of the deceitful nature of belief in God. "If the laws of nature did not pity even *This One*, did not pity even their own miracle, but made *Him*, too, live amidst a lie and die for a lie," he argues, "then the whole planet is a lie, and stands upon a lie and a stupid mockery." And yet, the language he uses to describe Jesus—a "miracle," "the highest on all the earth," who "constituted what it was to live for," without whom "the whole planet with everything on it is—madness only" (3:6:2:618)—is also strong affirmation of the exalted nature of Christ. Kirillov's argument for unbelief thus also gives us reason to believe. It has a whiff of apophaticism to it. But it is also characteristic of the novel's device of doublings and inversions. Outwardly, Kirillov extols humanity over God. Inwardly, he may secretly believe in God. He thus embodies an impossible contradiction.

Shatov suffers from a similar incongruity: he believes in Christ but not in God. Actually, he is obsessed with the idea of the Russian Christ. And he is upset that Stavrogin, from whom he first learned of the messianic qualities of the Russian people, no longer believes in Christ. "But wasn't it you," he asks Stavrogin, "who told me that if someone proved to you mathematically that the truth is outside Christ, you would better agree to stay with Christ than with the truth? Did you say that? Did you?" (2:1:7:249). Stavrogin does not reply. Shatov, who seems to have succumbed to Stavrogin's temptation that Christ and the truth—presumably, the Godhead—can be separate things, desperately needs Stavrogin to confirm that such a faith is possible. Here, the lines from Dostoevsky's letter take on quite a different tone. Whereas Dostoevsky's Christological formulation in his letter is ostensibly used in the service of a desire to believe, Shatov's question to Stavrogin points in the opposite direction, toward unbelief. But he is terribly conflicted in his convictions. In this, he resembles Stavrogin, about whom Kirillov says: "If Stavrogin believes, then he does not believe that he does believe; but if he doesn't believe, then he doesn't believe that he doesn't believe" (3:6:2:616).

Kirillov's characterization of Stavrogin also sums up the book's metaphysical indeterminacy. Belief shades into unbelief and unbelief into belief, but no one seems able to commit to either belief or unbelief entirely. The metaphysical landscape is as unstable as the political one. Indeed, Kirillov and Shatov seem to espouse philosophical views that actually subvert themselves. Kirillov's atheism seems to allow for the possibility of belief in God, while Shatov's belief in a messianic Christ is built on an atheistic foundation.[13] Contradiction, it turns out, is the reigning spirit of the novel. There is no better example of this phenomenon in *Demons* than Shigalyov's speech. A member of Pyotr Verkhovensky's group and the novel's chief theoretician of socialism, Shigalyov shares his vision of the "social organization of the future society" only to discover that his idea leads him to the exact opposite position from which he started. "I got entangled in my own data, and my conclusion directly contradicts the original idea from which I start," he declares. "Starting from unlimited freedom, I conclude with unlimited despotism" (2:7:2:402).

Stavrogin, too, epitomizes contradiction, the perfect state for a man who appears to stand for nothing at all. Indeed, contrariness is central to his concept of self, as his erratic behavior confirms.[14] It is a product of the negation that he claims "pours out" of himself. But even that negation is "shallow and listless," he confesses (3:8:676), amounting to nothing more than a kind of lukewarm indifference. He thus fits the description of the passage from Revelation 3:15–16, which Sofya Matveevna opens at random and reads to Stepan Verkhovensky at the end of the novel: "I know your works: you are neither cold nor hot! Would that you were cold or hot! So, because you are lukewarm, and neither cold nor hot, I will spew you out of my mouth" (3:7:2:653).

The passage from Revelation confirms the importance of the vital polarities in Dostoevsky's own examination of belief: absolute doubt and absolute faith. Either is preferable to a tepid conviction that hedges, for each in their extreme certitude conceals a revelatory potential (the possibility that atheism might illuminate faith or faith, atheism) and potential reversal (from belief to doubt or unbelief to faith). Stavrogin professes no such strong conviction. Our hero whose name is inscribed with the cross thus turns out to be a rather poor guide for our *via negativa* toward Christ, despite what Rowan Williams calls all of his "messianic resonances."[15] Unlike his two disciples, he professes nothing at all. He thus represents not so much a negation of Christ as supreme indifference to him. He neither "believes in the cross" nor articulates any alternative to it. He is merely lukewarm.[16]

The most distinct Christology that emerges from the novel's doublings and inversions, it turns out, is the parodic one played out in Kirillov's suicide,[17] a death, like Christ's, that is meant to "save" humanity. But Kirillov's suicide will "save" humanity by proving the non-existence of God and, concomitantly, the non-divine nature of Christ, thus setting mankind free not from the shackles of sin and death but from the throes of superstition. It is thus a mockery of Christ's crucifixion, a fitting outcome for a novel that seems to affirm only a Christ who is "outside the truth." Inversion and negation are the ruling spirits of the novel's metaphysics—the absent Godhead is more strongly articulated in this novel than anywhere else in Dostoevsky's work. Whether this aspect of the novel produces an apophatic darkness from which to glimpse the transcendence of God, however, is debatable. Are Dostoevsky's characters on the next-to-last step to the most complete faith, as Tikhon puts it, by novel's end, or are they drowning in a sea of unbelief? By all indications, the latter outcome seems to be the case. Kirillov's parodic inversion is not so much a kind of apophaticism as it is a negation in the service of unbelief (there is no God, I am the Man-God). Similarly, Shatov's faith in a Christ "outside the truth" is not so much inversion as it is perversion: it does not bring us closer to a union with the Godhead but rather distances us from it (I believe in Christ, but I do not yet believe in God).

One thing is certain: the gloom—more darkness than apophatic ignorance—is thick in this "darkest of Dostoevsky's novels,"[18] with its five murders, two suicides, and two untimely deaths. Even Stepan Verkhovensky's deathbed conversion at novel's end does little to lift the mood or enlighten the novel's spiritual quandaries, for it is unclear whether he is actually declaring unequivocal belief in God or merely articulating his "Great Thought" that human beings must always be able to bow down before the "immeasurably great" (3:7:3:664). Typical of the novel's refusal to grant clarity in spiritual matters, it is never made clear whether Stepan's "Great Thought" is meant to be equated with God. The narrator himself is skeptical about Stepan's conversion, wondering whether he "had really come to believe" or whether "the majestic ceremony" of taking the Holy Sacrament on his death bed had simply "shaken him and aroused the artistic receptivity of his nature" (3:7:3:662). Stepan, after all, is one of Dostoevsky's great unreliable speakers, as he himself admits, summing up the novel's philosophy of contradiction: "My friend, I've been lying all my life. Even when I was telling the truth" (3:7:2:652).

THE ABSENT CHRIST

If *Demons* fails to provide a Christ narrative that may redeem its protagonists, it does remind us of one paradoxical aspect of Dostoevsky's Jesus: it is his absence that most intrigues us about the writer's image of Christ. Nabokov may have complained about the number of characters "sinning their way to Jesus" in Dostoevsky's novels,[19] but in truth, Christ is an elusive figure in the writer's works. He is all but absent from Dostoevsky's fiction before 1860, when *Notes from the House of the Dead* (1860–1861) was published with its marvelous descriptions of the convicts' celebration of Christmas and Easter. There, the image of Christ fleetingly asserts itself in the midst of the monstrous brutality of penal servitude. But even in those post-1860s works where the idea of Christ is central, it is Christ's absence that is most striking. This is one reason why one may find unbelief to be as strongly or even more strongly expressed in Dostoevsky's works than belief, for Dostoevsky's Christ is often articulated as an absence.

Notes from Underground (1864) is one striking example. Written in response to the scientific materialism of his day, which reduced human beings to biological entities bereft of a spiritual nature and ruled entirely by environment, *Notes* was supposed to make a case for the necessity of Christ. It was to do so by showing the failure of both the underground and the Crystal Palace as socio-philosophical destinations of mankind. The Underground Man's attempts to undermine the rationalist foundations on which radical materialism rests by asserting an extreme irrationalism were meant to be as ridiculous as they seem when readers first encounter them. The idea was to move from the Underground Man's hell of arbitrary whim, spite, and self-lacerating solipsism to a higher notion of irrationalism embodied by Christ's sacrificial love—the subject of the novel's tenth chapter. The escape route proposed by Dostoevsky from both the dead end of the underground and the fraud of enlightened egoism was to be faith. But the censors got in the way. "It really would have been better not to print the next-to-last chapter at all (the most important chapter, in which the main idea is expressed), than to publish it as it is, i.e., with sentences chopped out, which distorts the meaning. But what can be done!" he complained to his brother. "The censors are a bunch of pigs—those places where I mocked everything and occasionally employed blasphemy *for the sake of form* they allowed to stand; but when, from all that, I deduced the need for faith and Christ, they took it out."[20]

Instead, chapter 10 is the shortest in the novel. But it does raise the issue of a better alternative to both the underground and the Crystal Palace: "Show me something better and I'll follow you," the Underground Man declares. "Can it be that I was made this way only in order to reach the conclusion that my entire way of being is merely a fraud? Can this be the whole purpose? I don't believe it."[21] Curiously, however, Dostoevsky never attempted to restore his novel's tenth chapter. Either he did not relish asking the censors to reverse their ruling or he was not that interested in restoring a work that failed to make a splash when it appeared.[22] Or perhaps he realized that the space where Christ was meant to be was still there, that his absence was as potent as his presence, perhaps even more so.

When the prostitute Liza throws her arms around the Underground Man in a spontaneous act of selfless compassion after being insulted and abused by him for having come to visit, she commits an act that makes her what in theological parlance is called a "type" of Christ. She is not Christ but in her actions affirms and illuminates him, perhaps doing so more effectively than any speech the Underground Man may have made in chapter 10 of part 1. Dostoevsky himself may well have sensed this, hence his disinclination to restore the censored chapter. Liza had, in a sense, already articulated "the need for faith and Christ."[23] What is left unsaid about the Godhead may serve better to illuminate him than what is articulated.[24] If Christ is silent, absent, parodied, or otherwise distorted in the writer's mature works, it is because Dostoevsky may well have understood the danger of trying to articulate Christ's meaning in words. Say too much or the wrong thing and you may diminish that which you seek to elevate. Much of what drives the narrative of *The Idiot* seems to stem from this apprehension. By contrast, an apophatic approach can be a powerful tool by which to define the indefinable.

Olga Meerson, Carol Apollonio, Tatyana Kasatkina, and Malcolm Jones over the last twenty years have recognized the importance and applicability of apophatic theology in the writer's works. There are two reasons for this development. First is the realization that all of those characters in Dostoevsky's works who live in the liminal state between belief and nothingness are, intentionally or not, striking textual embodiments of the spiritual state of apophatic seekers of God. Second is a growing appreciation for how much Dostoevsky's contact with Russian monasteries influenced him, where among other things he observed the prominence of hesychasm in the Russian Church—the attempt to know God through prayer "that is stripped, so far as possible, of all images, words and discursive thinking."[25] Here, the apophatic strain in Orthodox prayer is strongly pronounced and easily observable.

Paradox is key in Dostoevsky's literary apophaticism, where states of unbelief may become markers of apophatic darkness leading to belief, where negation may work to affirm on some level, and where untruths can be deployed in the search for the truth. As Dmitrii Prokofych Razumikhin in *Crime and*

Punishment explains: "I like it when people lie! [...] If you lie—you get to the truth! Lying is what makes a man. Not one truth has ever been reached without first lying fourteen times or so, maybe a hundred and fourteen, and that's honorable in its way" (3:1:202).[26] While lying does not constitute an apophatic exercise, Razumikhin nevertheless summarizes here an apophatic principle: truth, like God, is best revealed along a negative path. He also, of course, summarizes the whole movement of the novel: Rodion Romanovich Raskolnikov must also lie his way to the truth.

In no work is Dostoevsky's apophatic approach more apparent than *The Brothers Karamazov* (1879–1880). In this novel as in no other Dostoevsky explores how negative assertions about the Godhead constitute a kind of seeking after belief, whether it actually leads to belief or not. While in *Demons* Dostoevsky shows how unbelief only begets more of the same, in *Brothers Karamazov* he tests the extent to which a discourse of unbelief can actually illuminate a way to faith. In the analysis that follows, three arguments are made. The first is that, contrary to popular consensus, *The Brothers Karamazov*, like *Demons* but for different purposes, is primarily a book about unbelief rather than belief. The second is that it is Ivan Karamazov, not Alyosha, who is the novel's important seeker after faith. And the third is that Ivan seeks God precisely along a negative path, that is, from the position of an atheist. His journey, and the main movement of the novel, thus describes a *via negativa* or apophatic quest.

Ivan Karamazov as Apophatic Quester

D. H. Lawrence famously called Ivan Karamazov "the greatest of the three brothers, pivotal," for whom the "passionate Dmitri and the inspired Alyosha" are "only offsets."[27] Though he had previously declared his atheism when asked by his father, Ivan is, in fact, desperately in search of God. But Ivan can only search for God from a position of doubt and skepticism. Indeed, when they meet in a tavern to get acquainted, Ivan asks Alyosha where they should begin their discussion. Alyosha advises: "Begin with whatever you like, even 'from the other end.' You did proclaim yesterday at father's that there is no God" (5:3:234).[28] Alyosha's urging to begin "from the other end," that is, from an atheistic perspective, nicely anticipates the negative path that Ivan will traverse in his poem about the Grand Inquisitor, which is an apophatic text par excellence.

But can Ivan truly be understood as an apophatic quester after God? In one crucial aspect, he can. First and foremost, he bases his rebellion against God on the premise that the human mind can never comprehend God—the starting point for all apophatic inquiries. The Godhead by definition cannot be comprehended; hence the need for apophaticism in the first place. Ivan explains his position mathematically: human minds can only understand Euclidean geometry with its three dimensions of space. The idea put forward by non-Euclidean geometry that parallel lines might meet somewhere in infinity is beyond our ability to understand. "If I cannot understand even that," he tells Alyosha, "then it is not for me to understand about God" (5:3:235).[29]

And yet, Ivan sincerely wishes to embrace God and esteems the idea of God highly. What intrigues him is not that man should have invented God, but that "such a notion—the notion of the necessity of God—could creep into the head of such a wild and wicked animal as man—so holy, so moving, so wise a notion, which does man such great honor" (5:3:234–35). Ivan goes even further. He confesses to Alyosha: "I believe in order, in the meaning of life, I believe in eternal harmony, in which we are all supposed to merge, I believe in the Word for whom the universe is yearning, and who himself was 'with God,' who himself is God, and so on, and so on and so forth, to infinity" (5:3:235). Here, Ivan sounds like any Orthodox Christian. What gets in his way, however, is reason. And, though he admits that reason "is a scoundrel" that "hedges and hides" (5:3:236), he proceeds to base his rebellion against God and his world precisely on reason, namely the incomprehensibility of a God who would allow innocent children to suffer. He wants to understand how this could be or, failing that, to reject God altogether. He does not, however, understand the terms of his own apophaticism. God cannot be comprehended; on the contrary, human beings must renounce reason "in order to be able to attain in perfect ignorance to union with Him who transcends all being and all knowledge," as Vladimir Lossky notes. One must "draw near to the Unknown in the darkness of absolute ignorance."[30] This is the apophatic lesson that Ivan must learn in the novel.

Father Zosima is the first person who seems to glimpse something apophatic about Ivan's atheism. In particular, he sees how Ivan's notion that "there is no virtue if there is no immortality" (1:6:70) hides an affirmation in its negative formulation. On the one hand, it proposes that, in the absence of God, "nothing would be immoral any longer, everything would be permitted, even anthropophagy" (2:6:69). It is thus a provocation: if you cannot prove the existence of God, then you cannot insist on virtue. On the other hand, Ivan's formula can be read in the opposite fashion, as a negative affirmation of God, as Zosima hints when he tells Ivan: "You are blessed if you believe so, or else most unhappy!" (1:6:70). Ivan is unhappy if he truly does not believe in virtue, God, and immortality. He is blessed, however, if he is using this negative formulation as a way of journeying toward God. Zosima's optimistic take goes something like this: God must exist, for I see that people are not devouring each other. There is virtue, so there must be God. In his response, Zosima reveals Ivan's negative formulation as something that can affirm belief.

The most dramatic and weighty example of apophaticism in the novel is Ivan's "poem" of the Grand Inquisitor. D. H. Lawrence characterized it as "the final unanswerable criticism of Christ," a "deadly-devastating summing up" of how Jesus has failed humanity.[31] Dostoevsky himself called Ivan's poem "a powerful denial of God" in a diary entry.[32] And yet, if there is any doubt that this bitter critique of Christ and Christianity, with its blasphemies, clever temptations, and damning indictments, can somehow be understood as an apophatic affirmation of Christ, one has only to listen to what Alyosha Karamazov says when his brother Ivan finishes narrating: "But . . . that's absurd! Your poem praises Jesus, it doesn't revile him" (5:5:260). Alyosha's reaction is astounding, given what he has just heard in Ivan's poem, and it is remarkable that so few critics have dwelt on its seeming inappropriateness. How does Ivan's Grand Inquisitor poem, intended to be a damning denunciation of the incomprehensible and unfulfillable expectations of Christ's teachings, wind up praising Jesus? It cannot, unless it does so apophatically, by articulating that which is *not* Christ.

Malcolm Jones mentions Alyosha's reaction but does not connect it to apophatic theology.[33] Joseph Frank also quotes Alyosha's response, but provides the more conventional explanation that rebuking Christ for proclaiming mankind's radical freedom is "in effect to praise Him for protecting the very foundation of man's humanity as Dostoevsky conceived it."[34] Wil van den Bercken recognizes the negative theology at work in Alyosha's statement, but argues that it leads to a cataphatic outcome. He declares this moment in the novel "the climax of apophasis: minus becomes plus, an explanation meant as a rejection turns out to be a defense."[35] But though he discerns the apophatic impulse of Alyosha's response, Bercken does not identify the Grand Inquisitor text as a "traditional apophasis." Rather, he argues that the Grand Inquisitor winds up making positive statements about Jesus and faith: "[E]verything the prelate denounces and criticizes in Jesus is exactly what Jesus wants to disseminate. [. . .] The Inquisitor's indictment against Jesus is really an explanation of the nature of the Christian faith."[36] In so doing, however, Bercken actually undermines his apophatic analysis and replaces it with an argument that is much harder to support: that the Grand Inquisitor unwittingly preaches an Orthodox Christology. And yet, judging by what the Grand Inquisitor says about the devil's three temptations of Christ (which the Inquisitor describes as containing "the entire future history of the world and mankind" [5:5:252]), he is actually distorting Christ's pronouncements almost beyond recognition, and in the process, presenting a false Christ.

The idea in the first temptation that Christ rejected earthly bread and demanded of humanity only heavenly bread—that is, strict obedience to the word of God—is not, in fact, an explanation of Christ's teaching but a misrepresentation of it. As Robin Feuer Miller points out, Christ's answer that "man shall not live by bread alone, but by every word that proceeds from the mouth of God" (Matthew 4:4) is not an either/or proposition: the precedence of the word of God does not make bread unimportant. Both are necessary, but God more so.[37] The Inquisitor distorts this relationship. The Inquisitor's interpretation of the second temptation—that Christ rejected miracles as an aid to faith—is also untrue. Jesus performed miracle after miracle during his earthly ministry and all of these miracles did, indeed, inspire or deepen the faith of those who witnessed them. The fact that these miracles did not ultimately make all human beings believe he was the Son of God or prevent his followers from lapsing in their faith is more a statement on human nature and the difficulty of belief than on the efficacy of miracles to aid faith. Again, the Inquisitor oversimplifies and, in so doing, misrepresents and misleads.

Finally, the Inquisitor's assertion that Jesus's rejection of earthly power (the third temptation) has created the circumstances in which only an elect few can possibly be saved is another distortion of Christ's teaching. When the disciples, dismayed by Christ's pronouncements about the difficulty of entering the kingdom of God, ask Jesus, "Who then can be saved?" Jesus answers: "With man this is impossible, but with God all things are possible" (Matthew 19:25–26). Christ's teachings may be hard and even unfulfillable, but with God's grace, even the most unworthy may attain the kingdom of God. Semyon Marmeladov in *Crime and Punishment* articulates this idea well in his drunken speech to Raskolnikov about Christ on Judgment Day:

> And when He has finished with everyone, then He will say unto us, too, "You, too, come forth!" He will say. "Come forth, my drunk ones, my weak ones, my

shameless ones!" And we will all come forth, without being ashamed, and stand there. And He will say, "Swine you are! Of the image of the beast and of his seal; but come, you, too!" And the wise and the reasonable will say unto Him, "Lord, why do you receive such as these?" And He will say, "I receive them, my wise and reasonable ones, forasmuch as not one of them considered himself worthy of this thing ..." And He will stretch out His arms to us, and we will fall at His feet. (1:2:23)

Marmeladov, it would seem, understands a lot more about the Christian faith than our Grand Inquisitor. Through God's grace, all can be saved, even the most unworthy. It is thus difficult to see in any of the Inquisitor's readings of the three temptations anything but a falsification of Christ's teachings, not, as Bercken claims, an explanation of them. Falsifying Christ's teachings, he falsifies Christ himself.

Alyosha recognizes this fact. What the Grand Inquisitor says about Christ is nothing like the Christ of the Gospels, nor can it be. His Christ is a negative distortion. "Miracle, mystery, and authority"—the pillars on which the Grand Inquisitor has created his deformed and perverse church—have nothing to do with Jesus, as the two acts Jesus performs in the poem remind us, an instance where Ivan seems to have sabotaged his own argument. Healing and forgiveness—Jesus's raising of the dead child and the kiss he bestows on the Grand Inquisitor—are the essence of the Jesus of the Gospels and they help us to distinguish the real Christ from the false one of the Inquisitor. The "church" created by the Grand Inquisitor's atheistic cabal—where the masses are bribed with bread, manipulated with "miracles," and kept in blissful ignorance of the death of God— more closely resembles Shigalyov's "unlimited despotism" than the "unlimited freedom" offered by Christ and decried by the Grand Inquisitor as an ideal too high and hard for humanity to accept. Alyosha grasps all of this immediately in his excited reaction to his brother's poem: "Your poem praises Jesus, it doesn't revile him." The negative portrait of Jesus and his message in Ivan's poem only serves to set off in vivid contrast the virtue of Christ and the Gospel he preached. Readers are meant to recognize this along with Alyosha. The Grand Inquisitor has declared not what Christ is, but what he is not. And in doing so, he has paradoxically revealed Christ in all of his goodness. He has given us a negative path toward Christ, who is to be found paradoxically in his absence.

Perhaps on a subconscious level Ivan actually realizes this, for he seems to slip into his anti-religious poem the dynamite capable of blowing it up, namely, the opposite of reason: the power of irrational love. The power of irrational love can be glimpsed first in the poem's preface, where the Virgin Mary begs God to forgive even Christ's tormentors (a potent example of the divine love of forgiveness of enemies that Christ himself taught) and later in the poem itself in Jesus's acts of healing and forgiveness. If that were not enough, Ivan subsequently even renounces his poem in his discussion with Alyosha, calling it "nonsense" and "the muddled poem of a muddled student who never wrote two lines of verse" (5:5:262), as if acknowledging the dead end to which reason has brought him. Later in his hallucinatory interview with the devil, he forbids mention of the poem (11:9:648). He is ashamed because his apophatic poem has revealed an uncomfortable truth: his desire to believe despite the incomprehensibility of belief.

Even if Ivan's poem is a negative path toward the Godhead, however, it is not yet a declaration of belief. He is still struggling with belief and does so until the end of the novel. But so, for that matter, is Alyosha, who confides to Lise at one point that he might not truly believe in God (5:1:220). Indeed, all of the Karamazovs, from father to sons, seem to embody opposing beliefs, an ability seemingly bred into them, as the prosecutor reminds us in his closing speech. Dmitry, he argues, personifies the "broad, Karamazovian nature [...] capable of containing all possible opposites and of contemplating both abysses at once," that of "lofty ideals" and that of "the lowest and foulest degradation" (12:6:699). What Ivan and Dmitry exemplify here and throughout the novel, however, is that these extremes do not necessarily cancel each other out, but may, in a sense, actually heighten the apprehension of their opposite. In other words, unlike in *Demons*, where doublings and opposites end in diabolical inversions or tend to undo themselves, in *Brothers Karamazov* opposites are capable of enabling the realization of that which opposes them. This is an important point to remember and one that, while not apophatic in and of itself, contributes to the apophatic discourse in the novel.

Nowhere is this principle exemplified better than in Dmitry's conflicted relationship with Katerina Ivanovna Verkhovtseva. When he relates how he forces Katerina Ivanovna to visit his room to ask for the 4,500 rubles she needs to restore her father's honor, Dmitry admits to Alyosha that he looked at her with "the kind of hatred that is only a hair's breadth from love, the maddest love!" (3:4:114), echoing Tikhon's statement about the proximity between complete atheism and complete faith. While Katerina's love/hate relationship with Dmitry is a kind of "laceration" (*nadryv*—wounding oneself in order to wound others, wounding others to wound oneself[38]), Dmitry's is precisely a hatred that is linked inextricably with love, a hatred that describes the paradoxical negative space from which the most complete love can be suddenly realized. It is thus a textual reflection of the apophaticism so pronounced elsewhere in the novel.

The apophatic impulse in *Brothers Karamazov* is so prominent partly because the novel makes so much use of irony and paradox to illuminate its moral and thematic subtleties and its image of Christ. While apophaticism is not a theology of opposites, it *is* a theology of paradox: you draw closer to God when you distance yourself from concepts of him. You may know God only when you do not *know* God. Perfect ignorance is a state that enables perfect knowledge of God, that is, union with him. There is an apophasis at work in apophaticism, a denial that we say or do what we say or do.[39]

Negative theology, however, has its own risks. In emptying oneself of all concepts of God, one may lose God as well. Like Dostoevsky's paradoxical credo, apophaticism contains the seeds of its own undoing. If *The Brothers Karamazov* is an apophatic novel, then it, too, may lead us to a negative space from which it may be difficult to return. That is, indeed, where Dostoevsky leaves Ivan. His state of unconsciousness at novel's end is symbolic of the state of apophatic darkness he has reached, but Dostoevsky does not say whether he will emerge from this state a convert to faith or a confirmed atheist. This tension underscores his special role in the novel and reminds us that it is Ivan, not Alyosha, who is the book's key metaphysical quester. The novel's greatest seeker of faith is actually its greatest skeptic.

Readers are so conditioned by what they read in the author's preface about how Alyosha is the novel's hero that they forget that all the seeking after God in the novel is on his brother Ivan's part, not Alyosha's. Alyosha may have a crisis of faith over his beloved elder's conspicuously decaying body, but it is Ivan who undertakes a torturous search for God throughout the novel and suffers a mental collapse from the strain of it. In fact, rather than a hymn to the triumph of faith, *The Brothers Karamazov* is actually a book about the difficulty of believing. Doubt haunts all of the Karamazov brothers. Ivan rejects a God who would allow innocent suffering. Dmitry listens to Mikhail Osipovich Rakitin's lectures about the French scientist Claude Bernard and declares that he's sorry to lose God since all life boils down to chemical reactions. Pavel Fyodorovich Smerdyakov reads the sayings of St. Isaac the Syrian as if repenting his parricide, but then commits suicide as a kind of ultimate rebellion against God. Even

Alyosha has doubts about God's existence. Unbelief permeates Dostoevsky's apophatic inquiry.

It is not surprising, then, that while the ending of *Brothers Karamazov* seems to point to the ultimate victory of good figured in the joyous cries of "Hurrah for Karamazov!" that the boys shower upon Alyosha, in truth, Dostoevsky leaves important questions unresolved, especially about faith—a fitting outcome given the prominence of the book's apophatic impulse. Dostoevsky does not say whether Dmitry will attempt to escape or serve out his sentence as an exercise in innocent suffering for the sake of the starving baby of his dream. Nor does he disclose whether Ivan will survive his brain fever and, if he does, whether he will turn away from his unbelief. Dostoevsky also does not say what will become of Alyosha or his own struggle with faith or whether he will marry Lise. Indeed, Alyosha's warning to the boys that they or even he may need to be rescued from some great evil in the future by their shared memory of how they buried Ilyusha casts a slight pall over the novel's conclusion. If speculation is true that Dostoevsky intended Alyosha to lose his faith in the novel's sequel and make an attempt on the tsar's life, it could confirm that Alyosha's warning to the boys is well founded.[40] The character in the book who seems most sure in his faith, Alyosha, may actually be poised on the threshold of unbelief, an opportunity for Dostoevsky to affirm the inverse of Tikhon's formulation from *Demons* and investigate how faith may lead to unbelief, how a true believer actually stands on the next-to-last step to the most complete atheism.

Thus, instead of a conclusion that would definitively resolve the novel's narrative and metaphysical questions, everything—most of all, the question of belief—is left up in the air. And yet, Dostoevsky's reticence at the end of *Brothers Karamazov*, his reluctance to let faith have the final say, is, itself, characteristic of his apophatic approach to Christ and the Godhead. Ever fearful lest he say too much because "a thought once uttered is untrue," Dostoevsky may well have thought it best to "be patient, humble, hold thy peace," as Dmitry himself resolves, quoting the poet Fyodor Tyutchev (9:4:469), who warns us of the inadequacy of language in the task of true cognition. Dmitry finds out how easy it is for others to turn his own words against him in his interrogation by the police and subsequent trial. His lesson is one readers may apply to the text of the novel, where reticence on metaphysical matters emerges as one of the themes of the novel itself. If parody, paradox, and inversion have any kinship with the apophatic way in Dostoevsky's works, it is in how they prevent us from drawing definitive conclusions about the workings of divine love, the meaning of Christ, or the nature of the Godhead. The most eloquent pronouncement on these things is sometimes silence, as Ivan's Christ shows us in his response to the Grand Inquisitor. Dostoevsky leaves the important conclusions for his readers to intuit.

Dostoevsky admits as much in a July 1876 letter, in which he explains the danger of fully disclosing one's thoughts: "Deploy any paradox you like, but do not explain it completely and everyone will think it is witty and subtle and comme il faut. But follow some risky pronouncement to its very end, declare, for instance, directly and without beating around the bush, 'This is exactly what the Messiah is' and no one will believe you precisely because of your naiveté, precisely because you disclosed your idea fully and said what you meant down to the last letter." For this reason, Dostoevsky writes, "I have never allowed myself to spell out *certain* of my convictions or have my full say in my writings."[41] His implication is clear: better the negative way of disclosure than the explicit; the apophatic, not the cataphatic. Better a book where unbelief predominates, the better, perhaps, to glimpse belief.

This quality is especially apparent in the most Christocentric of all of his novels, *The Idiot*, in which Dostoevsky attempted to portray the nearest thing to Christ himself: Prince Myshkin, a "positively beautiful person" and the most important Christ figure in the writer's oeuvre. In this instance, Dostoevsky's apophaticism derives from an unexpected source: the writer's use of comedy, which both conceals and reveals a distinct Christology. One might well ask, how can there be a comic Christology? Christ, after all, is not comic or ridiculous to any but unbelievers. And yet Dostoevsky's exploration of the "ridiculous man" Myshkin can be looked at as an exercise in negative Christology par excellence. Comedy—always a fixture of the writer's works—becomes in *The Idiot* the unexpected vehicle for a quite serious exploration of the nature and challenges of belief. How does Dostoevsky's comic Christ figure serve as a *via negativa* that strips Christ of the conceptual language by which he is usually described? How does the ridiculous, comic or absurd aid true discernment of Christ?

CHAPTER THREE

A NARROW ESCAPE INTO FAITH

Dostoevsky's *Idiot* and the Christology of Comedy

"What a comedy!"

Ippolit Terent'ev, part 4, chapter 5

"You're a good fellow, but you're comical."

Princess Belokonskaia to Prince Myshkin, part 4, chapter 7

THE IDIOT AND COMEDY

The Idiot (1869) is often singled out as one of Dostoevsky's most tragic novels. In this respect it rivals *Demons*, which followed it two years later. What makes *The Idiot* so grim is not the number of murders or suicides it contains, for there is only one: the murder-suicide of Nastasia Filippovna at the end of the novel. The source of the novel's pall of gloom is, as Sarah Young argues, that "*The Idiot* ends with fewer hints of spiritual regeneration or the possibility of new life than Dostoevsky's other novels," with "no truly redemptive figure to offset its many ambivalences"[1]—this despite the fact that its hero, the sickly Prince Myshkin, is identified by Dostoevsky in three separate places as a Christ figure in his note-books for the novel.[2] At the same time, *Demons* and *The Idiot* contain some of the most humorous scenes and outsized characters Dostoevsky would ever compose. Joseph Frank speaks of scenes in *Demons* of "irresistibly funny broad comedy,"[3] while Gary Rosenshield claims "there are more comic episodes in *The Idiot* than in any of the other major novels."[4]

Tragedy and comedy, of course, are not exclusive categories.[5] In point of fact, the two are related in Dostoevsky's universe. Petr Bitsilli speaks of Dostoevsky as the author of the "novel-tragicomedy"[6] and Dostoevsky scholarship has long recognized that "the comic element underpins his entire artistic world."[7] But how does comedy enter into the interpretive matrix of *The Idiot*? After all, in his endeavor to depict a "positively beautiful man," Dostoevsky not only endowed Myshkin with obvious Christ-like qualities,[8] but also identified him as the embodiment of Christian love.[9] This complicates the matter somewhat, for, as Rosenshield argues, "If the prince were comic, he could hardly serve as the embodiment of the Christian idea."[10]

And yet the comic and Christian worldviews have long been linked in world literature—something Dostoevsky himself comments on in a letter to his niece about *The Idiot*. The real question is whether the comic elements of the novel or a comic Prince Myshkin shed new light on the question of faith or on Dostoevsky's own religious convictions. How might a submerged comic discourse in the novel function and how might it explain why "the comic is an integral part of the novel"?[11] To date, very little has been written about comedy in *The Idiot*[12] and even less connecting the novel's comic vision to its Christian themes.[13] A comment Dostoevsky made some six years before beginning *The Idiot*, however, indicates that he might have resorted to humor in the novel as a vehicle for communicating ideas that might otherwise themselves be ridiculed. "The moment you wish to tell the truth [*istina*] according to your convictions, you are at once accused of uttering copybook maxims," Dostoevsky writes. "Why is it that if in our age we feel the need to tell the truth, we have more and more to resort to humor or satire or irony in order to sweeten truth as if it were a bitter pill, or to present one's convictions to the public while pretending to be a shade haughtily indifferent to them or even with a certain shade of disrespect for them—in short, with some mean little concession?"[14]

The truth, Dostoevsky implies, must be asserted indirectly (through humor, satire, and irony), or even negatively ("with a certain shade of disrespect"), an attitude that suggests that comedy in *The Idiot* may perform a similar function. More specifically, the ostensibly negative aspects that attach to Dostoevsky's comic Christ figure may actually constitute a kind of apophatic discourse that reveals Christ anew to an unbelieving public, both in the novel and among the novel's readers. In this reading, comedy serves a serious Christology in *The Idiot*, one that changes how the novel's conclusion must be understood.

PRINCE MYSHKIN AS RIDICULOUS MAN

The first task of a comic apophatic analysis of the novel is to address Myshkin's status as a "ridiculous man" (*smeshnoi chelovek*). If it is true, as one critic argues, that "any interpretation of *The Idiot* has to be first and foremost an interpretation of Prince Myshkin,"[15] then our reading of the novel will change rather dramatically if Prince Myshkin is a comic hero. The Russian adjective *smeshnoi*—translated variously as comic, ridiculous, absurd, or silly—is consistently used throughout the novel to describe the prince, by Myshkin himself as well as by others. When the prince acknowledges that in proposing to Nastasia Filippovna he expressed himself "very comically" and was "comical" himself (1:16:178),[16] he may be trying to explain his awkward behavior, but he is also revealing a deeper truth about his character.

In a later and more revealing confession about his comicality, Myshkin links his perceived ridiculousness to his idiocy. He states: "There are ideas, lofty ideas, of which I must not begin to speak, because I would certainly make everyone laugh [...] I have no graceful gestures, I have no sense of proportion; my words are inappropriate to my ideas, which devalues those ideas. [...] I know (in fact I'm certain) that after twenty years of illness, something is bound to remain so that people can't help laughing at me" (3:2:359).[17] Aglaya promptly reinforces this image of Myshkin when she vows not to marry "such a ridiculous/comical man" (3:2:360) and declares that she "blushes with shame for his absurd/comical character" (3:3:378). Earlier, her sister Alexandra also calls him "a little ridiculous/comical" (1:7:82). Other important characters—Ippolit Terent'ev and Princess Belokonskaia—use the same epithet to describe Myshkin in part 4, as does Myshkin himself, thus activating the word in our consciousness as an important interpretive reference late in the novel.[18]

Prince Myshkin is not the only significant *smeshnoi chelovek* in Dostoevsky's oeuvre. The otherwise nameless protagonist from his 1877 short story "Dream of a Ridiculous Man" ("Son smeshnogo cheloveka") is another incarnation of this character type. Although temperamentally his opposite in many respects, the Ridiculous Man shares Myshkin's cardinal qualities, and by sharing them, confirms their significance. Both men are called "holy fools" (*iurodivyi*) by others;[19] both exhibit Christ complexes; both privilege the heart over the head;[20] and both lose the ability to reason at the end of their narratives (Myshkin is reduced to idiocy, the Ridiculous Man "loses command of words"[21]). There are, of course, differences between them as well. At the beginning of his story, the Ridiculous Man is a solipsistic misanthrope with a persecution complex and a boundless pride.[22] He changes after a crisis one night in which he resolves to kill himself but instead experiences a dreamlike visit to an Edenic other world whose innocent inhabitants impress him with their perfectly selfless love. When our hero unwittingly corrupts the inhabitants of this paradise, he is conscience-stricken and begs them to crucify him, even showing them how to build a cross (thus literalizing his Christ complex). Upon awakening from his dream journey, however, he is a changed man, and vows to devote the rest of his life to preaching one of Christ's central edicts: loving others as oneself (Mark 12:31). Thenceforth, he is no longer proud, but happily "ridiculous," a voice crying in the wilderness.

Though critics disagree on whether the Ridiculous Man's story is a parable or a parody,[23] it nevertheless strongly affirms the connection between the figure of the comic man and the figure of the God-Man Jesus Christ in Dostoevsky's literary imagination and, in so doing, it also confirms a link between Dostoevsky's Christian worldview and his comic vision. Myshkin is not a Christ figure just because Dostoevsky calls him "Prince Christ," but also because of his status as a "ridiculous man," an epithet the author would later link to a veiled comic Christology. Ridiculousness in Dostoevsky's works is often a litmus test for humility, and humility is the essence of the Russian Christ.[24] Ridiculousness is also the quality which, initially loathed by the Ridiculous Man, ultimately becomes his way of life, the only way he can point people to the greater truth of Christ's utopian commands.

Critics have largely mentioned the comic sides to Myshkin's character in passing, if at all, and none has linked him to Dostoevsky's Ridiculous Man.[25] Discussions of Myshkin's comicality are most often linked to his affinities with the *iurodivyi* or holy fool, a role suggested for him by Parfyon Semyonovich Rogozhin in the novel's opening chapter.[26] But holy foolishness does not address the function of comedy in *The Idiot* or exhaust the interpretive possibilities of Myshkin's "ridiculousness," though it may explain why so little attention has been paid to Myshkin's comic identity. This dearth of analysis may be due as well to the fact that Myshkin is not the only or even the most obvious comic character in the novel. Other humorous characters—and the book is full of them— tend to displace Myshkin as a comical figure, just as other characters (Nastasia Filippovna, Ippolit, even Rogozhin) supplant him as the central tragic figure.

The most conspicuous comic figures in the novel are Lukyan Lebedev and General Ivolgin, the novel's central buffoons who form a comic duo as unforgettable as they are indispensable to the comedic formula. They are as much linked by their comic recitals, dubious assertions, and humorous gestures as they are by their inferior position in society, a circumstance that seals the strange bond between them. Lebedev and General Ivolgin are joined by other minor clowns, such as the hanger-on Ferdyshchenko who serves as court jester at Nastasia Filippovna's name-day party, and the pugilist and one-time feuilletonist Keller, who growls and twirls his mustaches comically at moments of *skandal* (understood by Dostoevsky as any deeply wounding and dramatic public confrontation). Lizaveta Prokof'evna Yepanchina is the novel's most endearing comic figure. Her attempts to manage her headstrong girls are as amusing as they are ineffective and no matter how many times she loses her temper, she is quick to acknowledge her faults and to restore peace. Most importantly, she has the last word in the novel, thus affirming its hidden comic vision.

All of these characters extend the novel's humorous tenor across the entire comic spectrum, from the broad and burlesque of General Ivolgin's incredible tall tales and Lebedev's comic scheming and miming, to the "black comedy, anticipating Beckett" of the reading of Ippolit Terent'ev's "Necessary Explanation,"[27] to the farcical and absurd in the scene with Antip Burdovskii's crew and the reading of Keller's newspaper article, and the gently humorous in the scenes with Mme. Yepanchina and her girls. Of all of the characters, Lebedev's comicality is the most theatrical. As early as the opening chapter, he cringes, mugs, offers to walk on his hands and dance for Rogozhin (1:1:9) and is nearly beaten by him, only to attach himself permanently to his company by exclaiming, "If you thrash me, it means you're not rejecting me" (1:1:13).

Myshkin certainly cannot compete with the likes of Lebedev in terms of comic performance. His comicality is of a different order and stems from his conspicuous incongruities, what Mikhail Bakhtin calls the "constant *inappropriateness* of his personality,"[28] announced by his name Lev (lion) Myshkin (from *myshka*, "little mouse") and confirmed by his split identity as prince and idiot. And yet it is this inappropriateness of personality—what makes Myshkin "ludicrous" or "comic"—that also draws people to him and softens them.[29] In part 1 Myshkin charms everyone he meets, even as he stands out as an absurd figure. He arrives in Russia underdressed for the weather in European clothes, takes no offense at Rogozhin's and Lebedev's insinuations while on the train to Petersburg, and speaks on equal terms with General Yepanchin's servant about, of all things, capital punishment, a topic he inappropriately returns to at lunch with Madame Yepanchina and her daughters, where he even suggests an execution scene as the subject of daughter Adelaida's next painting.

Like the clown who keeps wandering into danger, Myshkin inexplicably finds himself at the center of two family dramas involving Nastasia Filippovna, even—in the best tradition of the clown—taking a blow Gania Ivolgin meant for his sister in a family row. Finally, our idiot prince willingly lets himself be duped out of twenty-five rubles "on a carnivalistic tour of Petersburg with the drunken general,"[30] then crashes Nastasia Filippovna's name-day party and proposes marriage to her, and all of this within his first twenty-four hours in St. Petersburg. Throughout, Myshkin is laughed at and referred to as an idiot some dozen times.[31] The last comic incongruity of part 1 is realized when, after seven attempts to draw attention to a letter his Swiss doctor received announcing he had inherited millions of rubles from a distant aunt,[32] Myshkin is able finally to produce the document and have its contents verified, moving from impoverished distant relation to most eligible bachelor in a single instant. Thus transformed from comic prop to magic wand, the letter sets the stage for a decidedly different kind of novel: the comic novel of the marriage plot.

The classic formula for the so-called New Comedy is as familiar as any Shakespeare play or Jane Austen novel. A couple in love seek to marry but are opposed by other characters with greater power, wealth, or social position until, late in the story, a plot device reverses the unjust situation and a new comic society forms around the freshly united couple in the establishment of a more sensible order of things.[33] Blocking characters occupy much of the plot interest and, in the ironic or realistic comic tradition, can even triumph, crushing the hero in frustration and despair.[34] Misalliances are common as, through magic or mischief, couples are wrongly aligned, only to right themselves by comedy's end, or, as in the darker comedies of Chekhov, to remain permanently estranged.

In Dostoevsky's novel, the latter outcome obtains. Blocking characters triumph, discord and disunity reign, and none of the romantic couples unite by novel's end, as Myshkin's inheritance fails to serve as the plot device ensuring a happy ending. Quite the contrary ensues, as no romantic partnering survives. When the novel opens, Gania Ivolgin is betrothed to Nastasia Filippovna, but has designs on Aglaya, instead. Aglaya rejects Gania's advances and appears to be ready to marry Myshkin. It turns out, however, that she loves Myshkin only as the embodiment of an ideal, and when that ideal fails, she ends up marrying a shady Pole instead whose nobility of soul proves too great for her impressionable character to resist. For his part, Myshkin falls in love with Aglaya and sincerely wants to marry her, but instead honors his earlier marriage proposal to Nastasia Filippovna after a dramatic confrontation between her and Aglaya.

Nastasia Filippovna in turn abandons Myshkin at the altar for Rogozhin, but rather than marrying her as he has wanted throughout the novel, Rogozhin murders her. As Richard Pearce points out, instead of a wedding and a happy ending, the novel instead produces "a travesty on the marriage ritual that ends traditional comedy."[35]

Pearce argues that this travesty is the "ultimate subversion, for it turns comedy against itself." As such, it is an affirmation of the novel as tragedy.[36] But is the comic impulse in the novel actually so neatly defeated by its tragic conclusion? Or do the novel's comic elements—and indeed, its passing similarity to the New Comedy itself—argue for a more complex and contradictory outcome? These are critical questions, especially if the various comic tropes in the novel are to support an underlying apophatic Christology. One thing is certain: the link between a ridiculous central protagonist and Christian themes was on the writer's mind as he composed the novel, as this passage from a letter Dostoevsky wrote to his niece, Sofya Ivanova, suggests.

> The main idea of the novel is to portray a positively beautiful person. There's nothing more difficult than that in the whole world, and especially now. [...] There's only one positively beautiful person in the world—Christ, so that the appearance of this measurelessly, infinitely beautiful person is in fact of course an infinite miracle. (The whole Gospel of John is in this sense; he finds the whole miracle in the incarnation alone, in the appearance of the beautiful alone.) But I've gone too far. I'll just mention that of the beautiful people in Christian literature Don Quixote stands as the most complete. But he is only beautiful because he's ridiculous [*smeshon*] at the same time. Dickens's Pickwick (an infinitely weaker idea than Don Quixote, but still an enormous one) is also ridiculous [*smeshon*], and effective in fact because of that. Compassion appears for the beautiful that is mocked and does not know its own value, and therefore, sympathy appears in the reader too. That arousal of compassion is in fact the secret of humor.[37]

For his part, Dostoevsky did not originally mean to make Myshkin a comic figure. In his notebook for part 2 of the novel he writes that Quixote and Pickwick are "charming to the reader" because "they are comical [*smeshni*]," whereas "the hero of this novel, the prince, is not comical [*smeshon*] but [...] *innocent*."[38] And yet Myshkin is referred to as a comical or ridiculous man throughout the novel, even as characters (ironically or otherwise) hail him as one "sent from God."[39] His time in Russia is marked by his involvement in one comic spectacle after another.[40] Moreover, comic characters like Lebedev and General Ivolgin constantly surround him, and their frequent comedic performances in his presence constantly inscribe him into mini comic narratives throughout the novel.

Perhaps the ultimate confirmation of Myshkin's comic persona is Dostoevsky's own allusion to Don Quixote on two separate occasions: first when Aglaya places a note from Myshkin into a volume of *Don Quixote* for safekeeping (laughing afterward at the appropriateness of her choice of books); and later when Pushkin's poem "The Poor Knight" is discussed and Quixote's name is linked to the poem and, through the poem, to Myshkin himself.[41] In thus associating his hero with Quixote, Dostoevsky not only affirms Myshkin's comic identity but also hints at a possible link between his comicality and a Christian worldview like that of Don Quixote, whose hallmark is "faith, compassion, suffering, a tendency toward humiliation, foolishness, and being childlike."[42] These qualities of Christ in both heroes—made strange, ridiculous, or foolish—bind the Christian ethos to the comic worldview common to each novel.[43] Myshkin may follow Christ, but he does so, like Quixote, first and foremost as a "ridiculous man." He thus articulates and unites in his character and actions the novel's comic and Christian worldviews.

THE COMIC WORLDVIEW IN *THE IDIOT*

As the greatest comic Christian protagonist in Russian literature, Myshkin embodies two kinds of comic discourse: the comic as the ridiculous, and comedy as a worldview that emphasizes positive values, perseverance, reconciliation, and harmony. The former establishes the novel's comic apophaticism; the latter helps establish generic affinities between comedy and the Christian worldview generally. The former provides a negative path toward Christ; the latter affirms the power of the comic vision throughout the novel, even in the most trying and chaotic of circumstances.

A case in point is the night Nastasia Filippovna abandons Myshkin at the altar and flees with Rogozhin intent on throwing herself upon his knife. Our comic hero returns home, where Keller and Lebedev try to chase away a crowd of curiosity seekers and scandalmongers, who insist on crashing the post-nonnuptial festivities, including the doctor whom Lebedev had originally engaged in order to commit Myshkin to an asylum. Rather than drive them away, however, Myshkin invites them in and for the next hour, entertains them with tea.

The scene teeters on the brink of the farcical. One of the guests expounds at length about property he doesn't own and others try in vain to request champagne. And yet, to the surprise of the reader and of Keller and Lebedev themselves, the evening ends "cordially and noisily" and quite sanely (4:10:631). The guests depart in orderly fashion, Vera Lebedeva cleans up after the reception and Myshkin even sleeps through the night. Tragedy is answered by comedy—not by a celebration of the absurd, but precisely by the comic spirit, which promotes affirmation in place of negation, perseverance in place of rejection, and hope in place of despair. Our "ridiculous" prince responds in a way fully in keeping with the comic vision, which, as Nathan Scott observes, "is not dedicated to the ludicrous" but rather "to the telling of the Whole Truth."[44] The whole truth here is not just Nastasia Filippovna's tragic action, but also Myshkin's refusal to despair. Thus comedy proves itself capable of blunting the novel's tragic impulses. Tragedy insists on tears and death; comedy counters with tea and sleep.

This juxtaposition of the tragic and the comic is at the center of *The Idiot*, whose themes and metaphysical inquiry align themselves along a central opposition pitting death (the tragic arc) against resurrection (the comic arc). In the first category belongs the novel's apocalyptic vision (Myshkin's execution stories, Lebedev's interpretations of Revelation, Nastasia Filippovna's death wish, and Rogozhin's knife). Here also belong the Holbein painting of the dead Christ; Ippolit's revolt against a meaningless universe; and the life-killing materialism, egoism, and utilitarianism of Rogozhin, Gania, Afanasy Totsky, Burdovskii's crew, and others. In the second category (the comic arc) are the prince's intimations of happiness in the present (the idea, attributed to Myshkin, that "beauty will save the world"; his marriage proposal to Aglaya; and his faith in the Pavlovsk trees to cure Ippolit of his existential despair). Here also belong the prince's parables of Christian love and faith;[45] his belief in a meaningful universe; and his generosity, humility, and compassion. This tension between the tragic and comic arcs constitutes the drama and dynamic of the novel, impelling the narrative forward in a dialectic in which the "*gloomy, infernal*" atmosphere that surrounds Nastasia Filippovna is countered by the "*bright*, almost *joyful*" atmosphere attaching to Myshkin.[46]

If, as Dostoevsky notes in his letter to his niece, the most beautiful heroes in Christian literature are comic, it is because the comic and Christian worldview are so compatible. There is, as Conrad Hyers notes, "a special affinity between later Christian themes of crucifixion, resurrection, ascension, and paradise and kindred themes of comic art—themselves derived from earlier Easter rites."[47]

Indeed, Christ's birth, life, death, and resurrection are, according to Dominic Crossan, but "the Christian delineation of the full comic arc in the ancient Greek rituals."[48] The Christian imagination and the comic worldview meet on the frontier between the sacred and the profane, where the distance between what is holy and what is worldly is lessened insomuch as comedy brings the holy down to earth while Christ's incarnation reveals the earth as a holy place. Here, as Scott points out, the comic imagination's "deeply affirmative attitude toward the created orders of existence" and "the profound materialism of its outlook" summarize "an important part of the Christian testimony about the meaning of human life."[49] Christian belief in the creation and the incarnation means that the materiality and finitude of life are not in themselves evil. Rather, the Christian imagination celebrates the quirks and idiosyncrasies of life and does so in a way that aligns well with the comic vision.[50]

These shared features of the Christian and comic outlook take on a heightened importance in a novel in which the material world is represented as something corrupt and corrupting and doomed to pass into nothingness and decay. This is especially true with regard to Myshkin, whose comic and Christian identity is bound up with his naïve (and thus ridiculous) faith in the beauty of creation and the goodness of people (here, Dostoevsky's own pronounced personalism can be glimpsed). In his study of the comic in Dostoevsky, A. E. Kunil'skii situates Dostoevsky's humor in close proximity not just to his Christian faith, but also to faith as an affirmation of the present beauty and joy of life.[51] One function of comedy in the novel and of Prince Myshkin as a "ridiculous man" clearly lies here. Myshkin, like Christ, affirms the goodness of creation.

In this context, it is not surprising that the novel's anxieties over death-haunted material existence are answered by a very materialist metaphysics. Indeed, contrary to our expectations, Dostoevsky's Christ figure—like any comic hero—is everywhere firmly grounded in the here and now, a source of some exasperation for the consumptive nihilist Ippolit Terent'ev. In his "Necessary Explanation" Ippolit recalls accusing Myshkin of speaking "like a materialist" only to have Myshkin reply "with that smile of his that he had always been a materialist." Ippolit concludes, "As he never lies, these words must have some sort of significance" (3:5:408), and indeed they do. The issue is a critical one for Ippolit, who has but weeks to live and whose revolt against God is premised on the very finitude of material existence, with its laws of entropy, decay, and death, most famously figured in a copy of Hans Holbein's painting of the dead Christ in the tomb that Ippolit sees in Rogozhin's house:

the very image of the impossibility of resurrection and victory over death. "Looking at that picture," Ippolit recalls,

> one has the impression of nature as some enormous, implacable, dumb beast, or more precisely, much more precisely, strange as it might seem—in the guise of a vast modern machine which has pointlessly seized, dismembered, and devoured, in its blind and insensible fashion, a great and priceless being, a being worth all of nature and all her laws, worth the entire earth—which indeed was perhaps created solely to prepare for the advent of that being! The picture is, as it were, the medium through which this notion of some dark, insolent, senselessly infinite force to which everything is subordinated is unwittingly conveyed. (3:6:430–31)

For Ippolit, therefore, Myshkin's materialism is incomprehensible; what is there in the material world that is not subject to corruption and decay? How will beauty save the world? And yet, the novel is built on such paradoxes, and with good reason. As Scott reminds us, "The great difference between the tragic man and the comic man" has to do with "their different ways of dealing with the burden of human finitude." Nothing wounds the tragic man more (in this case, Ippolit) than to be reminded that "life is a conditioned thing" over which "pure intellect or pure will" cannot ultimately triumph. The comic man, however (our Myshkin), "has no sense of being under any cruel condemnation; nor does he have any sense of desperate entrapment within a prison."[52] When Ippolit asks Myshkin what would be the most virtuous way for him to die, Myshkin does not answer with platitudes about the other world. On the contrary, like any materialist, he answers in the context of this one: "Pass us by and forgive us our happiness" (4:5:552).[53] Yet, like any Christian, he is also affirming the goodness of the created world in this statement: the beauty and joy of life always outweigh the pain of death. Myshkin thus confirms comedy's "very 'realized' eschatology. 'Paradise' is to be experienced *now*, in the midst of the turbulence of life."[54] Indeed, Prince Shch. accuses Myshkin of just that: trying to establish paradise on earth (3:1:358).

This paradisiac impulse is at the very heart of our comic hero and his actions throughout the narrative, but it is constantly misunderstood, such as when Myshkin satisfies dubious and even non-existent claims on his distant relative's estate from all sorts of riff-raff just because he feels sorry for them (2:1:192) or when Myshkin assures Radomsky at novel's end that all would be well if only they would let him love both Aglaya Yepanchina *and* Nastasia Filippovna. "Do come to your senses!" Radomsky replies (4:9:617), confirming what is becoming increasingly clearer in the book: such thinking as Myshkin's is not of this, but the other world—that of comedy. Indeed, one of the central functions of comedy is its intimation of a better world order just outside our grasp but tantalizingly close by, which the forces of the "real," fallen world constantly oppose. Myshkin's function as a comic character helps establish this contrast of worlds. The comedic performances of the novel's overt clowns (Lebedev and Ivolgin) enact the real world's absurdity; Myshkin's "ridiculousness," however, gestures toward the better world order of the Christian comic vision and, obliquely, to Christ himself.

Like Radomsky, Ippolit fails to grasp Myshkin's meaning. He laughs dismissively at his advice to "pass by and forgive," taking it for the metaphysical dodge it, at first glance, appears to be. As so often happens in the book, Myshkin's comic vision is laughed away as something ridiculous, and it is easy to see why. If the comic impulse is to triumph in the novel and, moreover, affirm a saving Christology, it must ultimately overcome seemingly insurmountable obstacles. It must first confront the Holbein painting and everything it stands for: the finality of death, the failure of Christ, and the hopelessness of faith.[55] But comedy must also transcend the dark events that conclude the novel: the tragic murder-suicide of Nastasia Filippovna and Myshkin's own regression back into idiocy at novel's end. As it turns out, these tasks are linked. If comedy can triumph over the tragedies that close the novel, it may also plot an escape route from the spell of unbelief cast by the Holbein painting. That escape route, paradoxically, is linked to Myshkin's transformation from ridiculous man to idiot, a development that lays bare the comic Christology associated with his character and completes the negative path toward Christ charted by our comical Christ figure.

FROM RIDICULOUS MAN TO IDIOT

At lunch with the Yepanchin family the day he arrives, Prince Myshkin declares, "I look closely at faces now" (1:6:80). Faces are important in *The Idiot*,[56] both as markers of the distinct personalism at work in Dostoevsky's fiction, where they affirm the uniqueness and worth of every human being, and also for what they reveal about the novel's Christology. If the face of the dead Christ in Holbein's painting is central to the novel and its thematic concerns, then two other faces must also be mentioned: that of Nastasia Filippovna, which haunts Myshkin throughout the novel, and that of Myshkin himself, unseeing and bereft of all reason at the end of the novel, the face of the "idiot" announced in the book's title. In fact, the face of the dead Christ in Holbein's painting points to the function of the other two faces. They, too, are tests of faith, because both Myshkin and Nastasia Filippovna, in their names and their fates, are tied to the novel's Christological themes. Moreover, as embodiments of the novel's comic and tragic plot trajectories respectively, they bring into conflict and ultimate resolution the themes at the heart of this analysis.

When Myshkin first glimpses Nastasia Filippovna in a photograph his first day in St. Petersburg, he remarks: "An astonishing face! … I do hope she's good! It would redeem everything!" (1:3:37). When he views the photo again four chapters later (1:7:85), he kisses it reverently, thus confirming its iconic qualities. By the end of the novel, however, he tells Radomsky that he can no longer bear to look at her face. Radomsky later ponders: "What did that *face* mean, that he was so much afraid of, and yet so loved?" (4:9:618, emphasis in the original). As it turns out, "that *face*" belongs to a woman morbidly bent on her own self-destruction. Myshkin is right to be afraid of it, for Nastasia Filippovna Barashkova, both in her name and her actions, is key to Myshkin's own fateful *imitatio Christi*. Like Myshkin's, her name alludes to the central tenets of Christian belief. If the name Lev Myshkin alludes to Christ as the meek "Lion of Judah" who can open the seven seals in Revelation 5:5, the book of the New Testament so important in the novel, then Christ as the slain lamb who is resurrected is conspicuously inscribed in the name Nastasia (from the Greek *anástasis*, "resurrection") Barashkova (from the Russian *barashek* or "lamb"), as commentators have pointed out.[57] On the surface, the Christological allusion inscribed in her name is ironic. While her death at the hands of Rogozhin activates the meaning of sacrificial lamb hinted at in her last name, it also pointedly negates the resurrection hidden in her first name, for Rogozhin must wrap her corpse in oilcloth and surround it with four opened bottles of antiseptic precisely to mask the smell of her already decaying body. As with Holbein's Christ, it appears there can be no resurrection here.

And yet Nastasia Filippovna as a Christ figure provides a clue to deciphering the novel's macabre climactic scene, which, as critics have noted, eerily evokes the Holbein painting.[58] Like Holbein's dead Christ, Nastasia Filippovna's murdered body lies in a state of decay, while Rogozhin and Myshkin hold vigil a few feet away. Here, "that *face*" invites comparison with the face of the Holbein

Christ described by Ippolit Terent'ev. Now shrouded by oilcloth, it is a blank space on which may be inscribed the features of the dead Christ, the "face of a person *just now* taken down from the cross," still preserving "a great deal of the warmth of life" but "not spared in the slightest" (3:6:430). Like Christ in the Holbein painting, Nastasia Filippovna is the very image of suffering and sacrifice.[59] Whereas Christ offers himself as an innocent sacrifice for the sins of all men, Nastasia Filippovna's death can be viewed as an innocent sacrifice for the sin of one man: Totsky, who molested her when she was a teenager. The problem, however, is that ultimately Nastasia Filippovna herself rejects this narrative. Throughout the novel, Nastasia Filippovna seeks to punish herself for her past with Totsky, but in seeking out Rogozhin's knife,[60] she is also seeking to hurt others. Unlike Christ's sacrifice, her death is a lashing out, a punishment aimed at Totsky as much as herself. It is thus a laceration: a self-inflicted wound meant to wound others.[61]

Not so, Myshkin's sacrifice. The "complete destruction of the reasoning faculties" (4:12:650) that Dr. Schneider of the Swiss Clinic diagnoses as a result of Myshkin's vigil with Rogozhin over Nastasia Filippovna's body is at once the medical description of his relapse into idiocy as well as a sign of the *imitatio Christi* that Nastasia Filippovna's death makes possible. If Nastasia Filippovna is ultimately revealed as a failed Christ figure, her death nevertheless serves to point us back to the novel's true Christ figure, whose transformation from ridiculous man to idiot precisely mirrors the Christ-like complete and unconditional destruction of the self in service of others that Dostoevsky describes in his famous notebook entry written on Holy Thursday, 1864, upon the death of his first wife: "To love a person, *as oneself*, according to Christ's commandment, is impossible. The law of the self is binding on earth. The *I* stands in the way. Only Christ was able to, but Christ was the eternal ideal of ages. [...] The highest use to which man could put his self and the full development of his *I* is to destroy that *I*, to give it away in its entirety to each and everyone, completely and unconditionally."[62]

Myshkin's relapse into idiocy, if understood as an *imitatio Christi*, appears to be just such a relinquishment of self for the sake of others. Though it costs him his sanity, Myshkin follows Christ's commandment, loving the murderer Rogozhin as he would himself, staying with him and comforting him through the night, compassion being, according to Myshkin, "the most important, perhaps the sole law of human existence" (2:5:242). (Dostoevsky called compassion "the whole of Christianity" in his notebooks to the novel.[63]) Idiocy is thus both the price Myshkin pays for this compassion and a sign to others of his imitation of Christ.

Where some see faith, however, others see pathology.[64] Steven Cassedy argues that Myshkin is "led to his moment of dissolution by his morbid condition, therefore *against* his will."[65] Myshkin's epilepsy, Cassedy argues, entails its own kind of relinquishment of self similar to that which Dostoevsky describes in his Holy Thursday comments. It is, thus, a false indicator of a higher spiritual reality, as Myshkin himself speculates in part 2. What if all of these "lightning flashes of heightened self-awareness, and hence also of 'higher existence,'" he ponders, are "nothing more than the illness itself?" (2:5:237). And yet, epilepsy does not explain what happens to Myshkin at the end of the novel for the simple reason that Myshkin does not have an epileptic fit at Rogozhin's that fateful night, *despite Rogozhin's fears that he might* (4:11:643–44). Thus epilepsy with the "destruction of personality" that accompanies it[66] is pointedly rejected by Dostoevsky as the reason behind Myshkin's relapse into idiocy. The triggering event must be sought elsewhere.

As idiocy is linked to Myshkin's comic makeup ("after twenty years of illness something is bound to remain so that people can't help laughing at me" [3:2:359]), one explanation may be found in the novel's submerged comic vision and its intersection with the Christian worldview. R. P. Blackmur has argued that idiocy in the novel is the "condition of the great divestment."[67] It is thus, in Christological terms, a kenosis: a humiliation or emptying (from the Greek, *kenoûn*). In loving the murderer Rogozhin all through the night, Myshkin, the novel's "ridiculous man," performs his most absurd and humiliating stunt: he empties himself of all ego and all reason. But in so doing, he reveals their opposite: pure heart. And as Mme. Yepanchina reminds us early in the novel, "the heart is the great thing, the rest is nothing" (1:7:86).[68]

This kenosis is, on one level, not surprising, given Myshkin's constant placing of others' needs before his own. Indeed, it is dramatically anticipated and distinctly prepared for in the scene in which Aglaya confronts Nastasia Filippovna some three chapters earlier. This confrontation is a clarifying moment both for Myshkin's *imitatio Christi* and for the resolution of the conflict between eros and agape in the novel. The marriage plot begun when Myshkin proposes to Nastasia Filippovna at the end of part 1 and complicated by his marriage proposal to Aglaya Yepanchina in part 4 must be resolved if Myshkin's role as a Christ figure is to be illuminated. While it would seem that only an idiot would propose to two women at the same time, in truth our ridiculous man has very nicely articulated for us the novel's central quandary: how must one love?

If Dostoevsky were writing a Jane Austen novel, Myshkin would marry the favorite of the Yepanchins' three daughters and live happily ever after. That Aglaya represents for Myshkin the object of his romantic love is clear to everyone in the Yepanchin household and their circle, and the unorthodox courtship that takes place between them is both touching and amusing. Only Myshkin seems to be in denial over it,[69] but even he, deep down, seems to understand. He is romantically in love with Aglaya and it is a lover's love—eros—that he experiences, one that starts with physical attraction and seeks physical as well as spiritual intimacy. The object of Myshkin's love, however, is another story. Aglaya is clearly *not* in any kind of romantic love with Myshkin. She admires his mind, not his heart.[70] She sees Myshkin as an ideal, a means toward fulfilling her wish of sacrificing herself for some cause. She has a very immature understanding of what marriage between them might mean.

Nastasia Filippovna understands that Myshkin is in love with Aglaya and she even writes Aglaya letters in which she tells her as much. Though she rejected Myshkin's marriage proposal to her in part 1, his affirmation of her as an honest woman that night made a deep impression on her. She may have left with Rogozhin and even glibly advised Myshkin to marry Aglaya on her way out the door (1:16:179–80), but she never quite overcomes the feelings Myshkin's sincere declaration evoked in her. By part 4, she looks at Myshkin differently, even though his love for her has changed. Myshkin now only feels compassion for her. He pities her and loves her, but it is not romantic love. It is a spiritual kind of love (agape)—the very love Nastasia Filippovna most craves at this moment. It is for this reason that Nastasia Filippovna allows herself to be killed by Rogozhin the night of wedding: marriage—eros—is not what she is seeking.

Eros and agape are thus in conflict with each other, as the confrontation between Aglaya and Nastasia Filippovna dramatizes in no uncertain terms. Aglaya's goal in confronting her rival is as simple as it is adolescent: to put Nastasia Filippovna in her place by asking Myshkin to choose between the two women. But when Myshkin reproaches her instead for her harsh words, Aglaya rushes mortified from the room, leaving Myshkin to comfort Nastasia Filippovna, who faints into his arms. Myshkin spends the rest of the evening stroking her head and face with both hands and comforting her. Myshkin's ministrations, his stroking of Nastasia Filippovna's face, the laughter, tears, and incoherent delirium of the scene are all significantly repeated later in Dostoevsky's description of Myshkin's night with Rogozhin. But while Myshkin's self-abnegating act of compassion toward Nastasia Filippovna costs him his relationship with Aglaya, this same act of love for Rogozhin later will cost him much more dearly.

Myshkin's first reaction to what he sees in Rogozhin's study is literally one of fear and trembling. In fact, Myshkin's trembling is so bad at first that he cannot get to his feet (4:11:645). Eventually he collects himself and begins to ask Rogozhin about the murder, even at one point requesting the playing cards Rogozhin and Nastasia Filippovna used to pass the time. It is only then that Myshkin understands that "he had not been saying what he ought to have been saying, not doing what he should have been doing" (4:11:647). This is a critical moment, for it signifies Myshkin's awareness that a different, more difficult response is required, one foreshadowed when he and Rogozhin exchanged crosses in part 2, chapter 4. Indeed, the exchange of crosses made them brothers, as Myshkin pointed out at the time (2:4:232) and as Rogozhin confirmed when he took Myshkin to his mother directly afterward, asking her to bless him "as if he were your own son" (2:4:233). Significantly, Rogozhin addresses Myshkin as "brother" twice in this final scene as well (4:11:645). The implication is clear: the demands of the cross and Christian fraternity must be answered. Myshkin is his brother's keeper and thus Rogozhin's cross must become his own.

Myshkin accepts this burden, responding to Rogozhin's act of murder with unconditional love. When Rogozhin begins to rave, Myshkin seats himself beside him on the cushions Rogozhin had arranged on the floor and comforts him, "pass[ing] his trembling hand gently across his hair and cheeks, as though caressing and soothing him," "a totally new sensation of infinite anguish [...] oppressing his heart" (4:11:648). Myshkin passes the rest of the night lying next to Rogozhin, pressing his face against his brother's, his tears flowing from his eyes onto Rogozhin's face. These tears bind the two together as surely as the crosses they exchanged and, in light of these crosses, become a striking metaphor for Myshkin's kenosis, his self-emptying: through his tears, Myshkin symbolically pours himself—his heart brimming with anguish—into Rogozhin until there is nothing more left of himself to give.

Myshkin's acts of kenotic sacrifice—first with Nastasia Filippovna, then with Rogozhin—do not by any means come easily to him. In each instance, he hesitates, but in neither case does he shrink from the demands of a higher kind of love. Like the Ridiculous Man of Dostoevsky's eponymous short story, he learns that "the main thing is to love your neighbor as yourself."[71] This he does fervently, an action that exacts a terrible price. Ultimately, Myshkin's act of compassion at the expense of his sanity is both the sign of his imitation of Christ and a decoding of the novel's title. Idiocy, the reader learns, is revealed as something intricately tied to the novel's comic and Christological themes, for it is what makes Myshkin both "ridiculous" and Christ-like at the same time. Fulfilling the expectation raised by the title of the novel, Myshkin becomes an idiot, but he does so in a way that challenges how that term is understood. Idiocy, it turns out, is a condition associated with the heart, not the mind. The cushions Rogozhin arranges for him and Myshkin to lie on throughout the night do not constitute a wedding bed, the site of eros. The wedding bed is already conspicuously occupied by the body of the dead Nastasia Filippovna, thus symbolizing the dead end of self-centered, possessive love. On the contrary, the cushions on which Myshkin loves Rogozhin are the site of agape—unconditional, selfless, active love. It is a divine, unmerited love, an affirmation of the absolute value of the human being, be they murderer or victim. Through his self-negating acts of love, Myshkin acknowledges the primacy of personhood: Nastasia Filippovna's as well as Rogozhin's.

If idiocy is the ultimate deciphering of the novel's ridiculous hero, then it also reveals the Christian basis of his comic identity. The face of the idiot at the end of the novel has become iconic, the sign of a higher love. With his unseeing eyes, Myshkin's face is like the Holbein Christ's because it, too, is the face of Christ crucified, the humiliated God.[72] But, unlike the face of the Holbein Christ or Nastasia Filippovna, Myshkin's face does not cause people to lose their faith, as the novel's concluding chapter implies. In his mute and transformed state at novel's end, Myshkin has become a living icon of sorts, a reminder of the sacrifice required of all who follow Christ. Our comic Christ figure has led us on a seemingly negative path straight toward the Christian ideal.

Ultimately, Myshkin's act of love in imitation of Christ accomplishes in deed what his words about Christ could not. This is especially apparent at the Yepanchin's party in part 4, where Myshkin delivers a manic, anti-Catholic rant about Rome as the source of atheism and the need to show the world "our Christ" instead. Just as Dostoevsky often puts his most cherished beliefs into the mouths of characters whose worldview discredits these beliefs, here he puts into Myshkin's mouth views very close to his own knowing that Myshkin will render them utterly ridiculous.[73] The effect is intended. This is Myshkin's last comic performance, as his smashing of an expensive Chinese vase at the apex of his zeal, just as Aglaya had predicted, confirms—a late reaffirmation of the novel's comic vision at a crucial point in the plot.

In reality, Myshkin's speech about the Russian Christ contains truths that are only apprehended later, in the speech he delivers *after* he breaks the vase, when he, like the Ridiculous Man, shares his "utopian vision of a world ruled by love"[74] and affirms the goodness of creation "that even the most desperate man finds beautiful" (4:7:585). This speech, in which Myshkin identifies his Petersburg high society interlocutors as being "comical" or "absurd" like him ("*smeshny*," he repeats the word four times), also underscores the link between the comic and Christian worldviews. "Being absurd [*smeshnym*] is actually all right some-times," Myshkin states, "better than that in fact: it makes it easier to forgive one another and be properly humble" (4:7:584).[75] Humility and forgiveness, of course, are the essence of the Russian Christ.[76]

Equally importantly, in this second speech to those gathered at the Yepanchin household Myshkin also alludes to the apophatic function of his own ridicu-lous/comic state. Being absurd, he argues, identifies us as "good material" for ultimate perfection. "You don't take offence because I tell you to your face that you're absurd, do you?" he asks the company around him. "And if that's the case, then you are good material aren't you? [...] One can't understand everything in a flash, after all, you can't start off with perfection! To attain perfection you have to start off by being ignorant of many things! If we understand things too quickly we may not understand them properly" (4:7:584). Myshkin here is teaching an Orthodox truth: humility is an essential state for the seeker of God. Being *smeshnoi* makes it easier to be humble and to forgive. It also helps one recognize one's state of ignorance—the proper starting point for true discern-ment in the apophatic exercise. In this way, Dostoevsky's literary apophaticism (Myshkin as a negative index of Christ) intersects with apophatic theology, which links the apophatic state with the process of *theosis*. Perfection—the goal of Orthodox believers (*theosis*)—is possible only after first emptying oneself of knowledge. Myshkin thus confirms the link between the comic and Christian worldview, between being absurd, comic, *smeshnoi*, and traveling a *via negativa* toward Christian enlightenment.

Unfortunately, Myshkin's words fall on deaf ears and, in any case, an epileptic fit interrupts his "inspired discourse."[77] The point is that words are ultimately inadequate to describe the Russian Christ. Only Myshkin's sacrifice of self at novel's end can reveal Christ to the world. Myshkin even says as much in apol-ogizing for his overzealous speech. "I know it's wrong to talk: better to show an example," he says, alluding to the example he himself will later set (4:7:585). In this important narrative sequence, Myshkin moves from comic "gesticulating automaton" at the engagement party to someone revealed to be "more valuable and fragile than the vase he smashes."[78] Indeed, the smashing of the vase is but the comic foreshadowing of the shattering of Myshkin's sanity during his night vigil comforting Rogozhin.

BEYOND THE POOR KNIGHT

Initially, Myshkin seems doomed to fulfill the destiny of Pushkin's Poor Knight, to whom he is likened by Aglaya earlier in the novel, and live out his life "prey to grief," eventually dying "like a madman" (2:2:265). And yet the novel does not end with Nastasia Filippovna's murder and Myshkin's idiocy, in seeming tragedy. Its real conclusion is still to come, in the next and final chapter, where the novel's comic vision reasserts itself, fleetingly but forcefully, and at the very last moment. The "Poor Knight's" deeds, it seems, may not have been in vain. If the New Comedy must close with a wedding and the Christian comic vision must at least hint at resurrection, then these things are to be found in the book's last chapter, where the "permanent trace" Myshkin left behind him[79] is revealed in those gathered around him at the Swiss Clinic in the last pages of the novel. It is curious, but understandable, that so little attention has been paid to this, the novel's actual conclusion (this despite the fact that Dostoevsky actually titles it *zakliuchenie*, "conclusion"—no other chapter in the book has a title). A mere few pages, it can hardly compete with the shocking murder scene described in the chapter that precedes it. And yet the developments summarized in this last chapter considerably deflect the tragic tenor of the novel and conclude it, instead, on a much more ambivalent note.

The reader learns that, somewhat paradoxically, it is Radomsky who sees to Myshkin's care, arranging for Dr. Schneider at the Swiss Clinic to take his patient back and even frequently visiting him there. During one of those visits, he is joined by Mme. Yepanchina and two of her daughters, Alexandra (now married to Prince Shch.) and Adelaida. Radomsky is a changed man. Formerly the cool voice of reason in the novel, he now "has a heart" (4:12:650), as demonstrated by his care of the prince and his correspondence with two unlikely pen pals: Kolya (Gania Ivolgin's little brother and a devoted disciple of Myshkin) and Vera Lebedeva, Lebedev's oldest daughter. Besides Aglaya's fate (her elopement and conversion to Catholicism), the most surprising development in the months since Myshkin's relapse into idiocy is the romantic attachment that has developed, largely through their correspondence, between Radomsky and Vera Lebedeva. The narrator is at a loss to explain it, except that it all began in connection with "what had happened to the prince" (4:12:650).

This development is noteworthy. First, in this novel of characters with significant names, Vera means "faith," thus hinting at an impending marriage in the novel between Reason (in the person of Radomsky) and Faith (in the person of Vera). This romance, in turn, also calls to mind the special relationship once shared between Vera Lebedeva and Prince Myshkin. In many ways, she—and not Aglaya or Nastasia Filippovna—is the most suitable love interest for Myshkin. The novel's Christ figure, after all, is best matched to Faith. Dostoevsky's symbolism is direct here—raising her baby sister, Liubov' (Love), in place of their dead mother, Vera is an obvious image of "Faith nursing Love" in the novel.[80] As Myshkin's housekeeper at Lebedev's dacha, Vera is in close contact with the prince, takes care of him, and has an obvious affection for him. Myshkin, too, is somewhat taken with her. He thinks of her inexplicably and at odd moments, such as when he confesses his fear of Nastasia Filippovna's face to Radomsky (4:9:617) or during his final search for Nastasia after she abandons him at the altar (4:11:638).[81] When he takes leave of her for the last time, he kisses "her hands" and then kisses "her herself" on the forehead (4:10:632). Indeed, she is one of only two women whom he actually kisses in the novel.[82] Her sudden appearance on the novel's final stage—even if only virtual, through her letters—puts her (and Kolya, for the same reason) in a select company gathered around Myshkin one last time.

With the exception of Radomsky, these are all the people who most cared about the prince during his brief time in Russia, and even Radomsky seems to look at the prince differently. He now views the prince under the influence of Vera. The implication is that the prince, "in his sick and humiliated state" (4:12:651), cannot be understood through reason alone; one must be aided by faith. There is the suggestion here of a "new society" forming around the prince, one that has been influenced and changed by him and one that stands in opposition to the dark forces of murder and destruction that hover menacingly over the novel.[83] This company of friends constitutes the comic society of the New Comedy whose unity is symbolized by the impending marriage of Radomsky and Vera. Their wedding both reveals the significance of the comic marriage plot and links it to the novel's comic Christology, for in Radomsky, Vera, Kolya, and Mme. Yepanchina readers can glimpse that "accidental family" that so fascinated Dostoevsky—one bound together not by blood but by belief.[84]

As in every New Comedy, the establishment of a more sensible order of things is in the offing, one hinting at a resurrection—the regeneration of Russia itself (a topic very much on Dostoevsky's mind while he wrote the novel), where the ideal of the Russian Christ in the sacrifice of the idiot prince will be preserved and promoted by this nascent "accidental family." As one of the novel's outsized comic characters, Mme. Yepanchina fittingly brings the novel to a close both with a confirmation of the common sense that reasserts itself at the end of comedies and an implied affirmation of Russia itself. "There's been enough getting carried away with things," she declares, "it's time to listen to common sense. And all this, and all this abroad, and all this Europe of yours, it's all just an illusion, and all of us abroad are nothing but an illusion . . . mark my words, you'll see!" (4:12:652). Murray Krieger, in an article otherwise very critical of the novel and Myshkin in particular, correctly points out that these words of Mme. Yepanchina ("one of Dostoevsky's most magnificent creations") are spoken "beyond the tragic vision" of the novel.[85] He is right. Comedy gets the last word.

"Comedy is an escape," Christopher Fry assures us, "not from truth but from despair: a narrow escape into faith."[86] A narrow escape into faith is what the company gathered here at the end of the novel quietly implies. Myshkin, our "Prince Christ," points the way in his total relinquishment of reason in an act of pure agape. Radomsky, Myshkin's greatest former skeptic, follows his heart and not his head and aligns himself romantically with that "wonderful girl" (Myshkin's words, 3:9:463) Vera, whose very name declares the escape route from tragedy proposed by the novel: "faith." Ultimately, readers face the same choice as Radomsky, Mme. Yepanchina, and the others at the end of the novel. Do they see vacant idiocy in Myshkin, the equivalent of Holbein's dead Christ? Or is Myshkin's "sick and humiliated state" the face of the humiliated God, an icon-like marker of the Russian Christ, and hence an affirmation of faith, a reason to believe in the midst of tragedy? Dostoevsky, characteristically, does not choose for us. Indeed, he makes belief a hard choice, just as it had always been for himself.[87] Myshkin's function as an apophatic index of Christ together with the narrative's submerged comic vision, however, suggest one way that the novel's tragedy may be subtly subverted, making the novel of the failure of belief a narrative about the overcoming of unbelief.

MYSHKIN AND STAVROGIN

The comic Myshkin is arguably Dostoevsky's most interesting image of Christ. The ridiculous figure of the idiot prince in Dostoevsky's comic apophaticism affirms the Jesus of the Gospels in striking fashion, as the Christian concepts of the comic worldview explored here and their link to the New Comedy have helped to show. Having grappled with comedy's apophatic function in *The Idiot*, readers may be in a better position to understand Dostoevsky's novel in a more positive light. They are also better prepared to understand not only the hero of Dostoevsky's "Dream of a Ridiculous Man" but, interestingly enough, Stavrogin as well.

Marina Kostalevsky makes a compelling case for an "intentional correlation" between Myshkin and Stavrogin based on a number of interesting parallels: they each arrive from Switzerland and either return or intend to return there; they each preach—or formerly preached—a Russian messianic vision; each is referred to as a prince; each has a pseudo-romantic relationship with a woman named Maria; both are slapped in the face; both are involved "in complicated relationships with competing women," and so on.[88] The fact that Dostoevsky wrote *Demons* after completing *The Idiot* may account for some of these similarities. All the same, the parallels are illuminating, especially one that is not on Kostalevsky's list. Both Myshkin and Stavrogin must confront the consequences of being ridiculous.

When Stavrogin makes his confession to Tikhon, the bishop has two main concerns. The first is whether Stavrogin would be able to endure not the hatred but the pity of those who would read his confession should he go through with his intention to publish it. His second concern, which takes Stavrogin completely off guard, is whether he would be able to withstand the public's *laughter*. The idea that he might come off as a "very comical character" (*komicheskoe litso*) unnerves Stavrogin, who nevertheless assures Tikhon he had anticipated that, too. But Tikhon persists, saying that there "will be horror on all sides, and, of course, more false than sincere," but the laughter "will be universal." At this point, Stavrogin insists that Tikhon show him what precisely makes him "ridiculous" (*smeshon*) in his manuscript. This epithet "ridiculous" repeats four more times: when Tikhon assures Stavrogin that "even the form of this truly great repentance has something ridiculous [*neshto smeshnoe*] in it"; when Stavrogin asks whether it is just the style of his confession that is ridiculous; when Stavrogin assumes that he "made quite a ridiculous figure" when he kissed "the dirty little foot" of his child rape victim; and when he gets angry at Tikhon for presuming that it is precisely the ridiculous aspect of his confession that he won't be able to endure (709–10). But Tikhon is right to zero in on this aspect of Stavrogin's confession. Of all of the outcomes of his confession, looking ridiculous, comical, or absurd would be the hardest thing for Stavrogin's pride to endure. Indeed, the reason Tikhon wants Stavrogin to put off publishing his confession is that Tikhon suspects that it is pride that is driving Stavrogin to confess, rather than the need for real repentance.

At the midpoint of the novel, Liza Tushina exposes the same weakness in Stavrogin. In a conversation the morning after she comes to him at Skvoreshniki, she tells him that she had long suspected "that there is something horrible, dirty, and bloody" on Stavrogin's soul, and at the same time something that makes him "look terribly ridiculous [*stavit vas v uzhasno smeshnom vide*]." "Beware of revealing it to me, if it's true," she warns him, "I'll ridicule you. I'll laugh at you all your life" (3:3:1:524). Liza has discerned the same weakness as Tikhon. If there is one thing Stavrogin cannot endure, it is laughter and ridicule. He cannot endure the idea that he might be comical. And it is precisely here that he parts ways with Myshkin, for whom "being ridiculous" is key to his ability both to imitate Christ and to reveal him in negative fashion. Stavrogin cannot bear such a cross, and so his story ends not in the redeeming light of comedy, but in the despairing darkness of tragedy.

CHAPTER FOUR

LOVING THOSE WHO HATE YOU

Toward a Tolstoyan Christology

... not the love that loves for something, for some purpose, or for some reason, but that love I experienced for the first time when, as I lay dying, I saw my enemy and yet loved him.

Prince Andrei, *War and Peace*, volume 3, part 3, chapter 32

The negative theology charted up to this point in Dostoevsky is even more pronounced in the life and works of Leo Tolstoy. Unlike Dostoevsky, Tolstoy was not fascinated by the person of Christ as the incarnation of God, but rather by Christ's teachings and what they reveal about God. In particular, he was taken with Christ's commandment to love your enemies. What began in his two great novels as a fascination with the idea of divine love understood as loving those who hate you became in his later writings the expression of an apophatic approach to discerning God, one predicated on the denial of Jesus's divinity. This movement from the concept of divine love imaged negatively to a negative imaging of Jesus himself is the subject of this and the next chapter. In this chapter, Tolstoy's treatment of divine love is examined both for its importance in illuminating the strong divide between earthly and heavenly kinds of love in his works but also for the significance Tolstoy ascribes to love of enemies as its basis. Tolstoy's exploration of divine love as love of those who hate you influenced both Bulgakov's and Pasternak's Christ novels in substantive ways. Paradox is key here for Tolstoy. Divine love and Christ are not what people suppose them to be, Tolstoy argues. The former requires the violation of societal expectations surrounding the proper object of love; the latter must be understood only as the non-divine bearer of this teaching, whose non-divinity actually serves as assurance that such hard ideals are achievable here on earth. These aspects are essential elements of Tolstoy's idiosyncratic Christology. The implications of divinely loving one's enemies will find their ultimate reflection in Tolstoy's final novel, *Resurrection*, where Dmitry Nekhliudov learns to give up love in the romantic sense in order to devote himself to the well being of others, even those whom he hates. This topic and a treatment of Tolstoy's apophaticism in his religious writings will be the subject of Chapter 5.

CHRIST AS PROVOCATION

Like that of his great contemporary, Tolstoy's quest to believe carried him well into the regions of unbelief, at least as far as traditional Christianity goes. If Dostoevsky once vowed to remain with Christ even if he were "outside the Truth," Tolstoy declared that Jesus was neither the incarnate Son of God nor the second person of the Trinity precisely because the hero he declared he loved "with all the power of my soul" at the end of his 1855 story "Sevastopol' in May"[1]—the Truth—demanded that he do so. And if the truth demanded that he reject the Orthodox understanding of Christianity in favor of the Christianity he came to reinvent, then so be it. "I began by loving my Orthodox faith more than my peace," he wrote in his 1901 "Reply to the Synod's Edict" of excommunication from the Orthodox Church, "then I loved Christianity more than my Church, and now I love truth more than anything in the world. And up to now truth for me corresponds with Christianity as I understand it."[2]

In their hyperbolic statements about Christ, both Dostoevsky and Tolstoy arrive at seemingly contradictory conclusions. On the one hand, Dostoevsky's "symbol of faith" is so radically Christocentric that it is capable of acknowledging a non-divine Christ if necessary, thus potentially making his Christ no different from Tolstoy's. Tolstoy, on the other hand, is so Christophobic as to divorce Christ from his message altogether. In *What I Believe* (1884) he goes so far as to confess that it seemed to him "that if Christ's teaching, with the Church teaching which has grown out of it, had not existed at all, those who now call themselves Christians would have been nearer to the truth of Christ."[3]

As different as these positions are, they both confirm a shared truth, that at the heart of each writer's image of Christ is a provocation. Dostoevsky's novels are bound up with the search for God and the need of Christ but give as many reasons not to believe as to believe. Tolstoy tells us Christ is not needed for salvation and has even gotten in the way of the Christian message, and yet professes that Jesus's teachings are the surest way to understand what God demands of us. At the same time, for all of the differences in their respective images of Christ, each writer arrives at expressions of faith—whether in fiction or elsewhere—that are at times in remarkable accord with each other. Tolstoy's faith, for instance, is in places as ecstatic as Father Zosima's in *The Brothers Karamazov*, whose rapturous love for plants, animals, and every living thing[4] is shared by Tolstoy, who likewise preached a love "for every living creature."[5] For Tolstoy, "birds, horses, dogs, and monkeys" are as much neighbor to us as our fellow human beings. "Do not ask who is the neighbor," he wrote in 1910, "but do for everything living what you want to be done for you."[6] There is also scarcely any difference between Zosima's claim that "each of us is undoubtedly guilty on behalf of all and for all on earth" and his injunction not to judge others unless "you are able to take upon yourself the crime of the criminal who stands before you"[7] and Dmitry Nekhliudov's discovery at the end of *Resurrection* that "the only sure way of salvation [. . .] was for people to acknowledge that they are guilty before God and therefore disqualified from punishing or correcting other people" since you cannot "correct evil while being evil."[8]

Although both authors arrive at similar conclusions about what it means to follow Jesus, they do so through very different concepts of Christ. Tolstoy may well have agreed with Dostoevsky that there was nothing more "beautiful, profound, loving, wise, courageous and perfect" than Christ, but only in as far as Christ expressed best in word and deed how to live one's life. "For me the chief question was not whether Jesus was or was not God, or from whom the Holy Ghost proceeded and so forth, and equally unimportant and unnecessary was it for me to know when and by whom each Gospel was written and whether such and such a parable may, or may not be, ascribed to Christ," Tolstoy wrote in the preface to his *Gospel in Brief*. "What was important to me was this light which has enlightened mankind for eighteen hundred years and which enlightened and still enlightens me."[9]

In his "Reply to the Synod's Edict," Tolstoy articulates his credo in no uncertain terms: "I believe in God, whom I understand as Spirit, as Love, as the Source of all. I believe that he is in me and I in him. I believe that the will of God is most clearly and intelligibly expressed in the teaching of the man Jesus, whom to consider as God and pray to, I esteem the greatest blasphemy."[10] Thus Christ for Tolstoy is but the bearer of the means of salvation; he is not salvation himself.

It is what Christ said, not what he did or who he was, that is important. Least important of all is the claim that Jesus was resurrected from the dead. "What do I care if Christ was resurrected?" Tolstoy once remarked to the family tutor I. M. Ivakin, a Greek scholar whom he consulted while translating the Gospels. "So he was resurrected—God bless him! What's important to me is the question of what I am to do, how I am to live."[11]

Like Dostoevsky's, Tolstoy's image of Christ had its roots in something he wrote as a young man. If Dostoevsky described his "symbol of faith" in his March 1854 letter, Tolstoy made a similarly important declaration in a March 1855 diary entry:

> Yesterday a conversation about divinity and faith inspired me with a great idea, a stupendous idea, to the realization of which I feel capable of devoting my life. This idea is the founding of a new religion appropriate to the stage of development of mankind—the religion of Christ, but purged of beliefs and mysticism, a practical religion, not promising future bliss but giving bliss on earth. [...] *Consciously* to work towards the union of mankind by religion is the basis of the idea which I hope will absorb me.[12]

While it would take Tolstoy some thirty years to undertake the realization of his dream, he had already grasped its essence at the age of twenty-seven. Like Dostoevsky's letter, whose ironic affirmation of Christ over the Truth anticipates the metaphysical paradoxes that would pervade his major novels, Tolstoy's diary sets the tone for all of its author's own religious questing.

Tolstoy's Christian enterprise begins in earnest after *Confession* (1879–1880, published 1884 abroad, 1906 in Russia), a powerful autobiographical piece in which he describes being overcome by depression and suicidal thoughts shortly after finishing *Anna Karenina* (1873–1877), sparking a crisis of faith. By the end of the work, he surmounts his thoughts of suicide by rededicating himself to a search for God and the task of discovering what is true and what is false in the Christian teaching handed down to him. But questions of belief and the existence of God figure prominently in *War and Peace* (1863–1869) and *Anna Karenina* as well. Indeed, Gary Saul Morson calls them the "only two books in world literature" that have attempted to depict "in a way that is psychologically convincing" a conversion to Christian love, understood "in the full sense of actually loving one's enemies."[13] It is in incorporating into his two great novels Christ's most difficult commandment from his Sermon on the Mount that

Tolstoy takes his first steps toward exploring what it means to act according to Christ's moral teachings, that is, what it means to image Christ in this world.

Morson argues that Christian love in *Anna Karenina* ultimately leads to "moral disaster" because it "cannot be reconciled with ordinary life."[14] Love of enemies in *War and Peace* presents a similar challenge to the demands of daily living. And yet, in his writings that postdate these novels, love of enemies is but one of five commandments that Tolstoy viewed as both reasonable and achievable *precisely in one's ordinary life.* "It would be possible to believe that the fulfillment of Christ's teaching is difficult and terrible and tormenting," he writes in *What I Believe*, a work he began a few years after finishing *Anna Karenina*, "if the fulfillment of the world's teaching were easy, safe, and pleasant. But in fact the fulfillment of the world's teaching is much more dangerous and tormenting than the fulfillment of Christ's teaching."[15] In his last novel, *Resurrection*, Tolstoy attempts to show just this—how it is the world's teaching, not Christ's, that leads to unhappiness. But he also probes this idea in the two great novels that precede it. Indeed, it is in the tension between ordinary life and extraordinary love in *War and Peace* and *Anna Karenina* that Tolstoy's serious Christological inquiry begins, with all of its paradoxes and provocations.

The ability to love those who hate you is the ultimate expression of divine love (*liubov' bozheskaia*) in these novels. It is also the kind of love that in Russian corresponds with agapic love. It is an apophatic expression of love, because Christ demands that we use hatred as a means of measuring our ability to love like God. If God is not hate in the apophatic exercise of discerning the divine, then hatred as a measure of our ability to love like God in Christ's commandment serves a similar end. There is an apophatic quality to divine love thus defined that endows the metaphysical quests of Tolstoy's heroes with a paradoxical complexity. Their grappling with Christ's hardest commandment is both a heretofore-underappreciated theme at the heart of each novel's religious and philosophical inquiries and a concept that helped reveal where the writer's own radical imaging of Christ would lie: not in the person of Christ, but in his demanding and lofty teachings.

Agapic Love in *War and Peace*

The conversions to Christian love that Morson speaks of refer to two moments: the moment when Prince Andrei Bolkonsky forgives his rival and enemy

Anatole Kuragin at a field hospital where Andrei is mortally wounded and Kuragin is having his leg amputated; and the moment when Aleksei Karenin forgives his unfaithful wife while she is lying mortally ill after giving birth to her lover's child. Andrei calls this "divine love" because only with that kind of love is it possible to love one's enemies (3:3:32:921).[16] Both scenes are significant if not key to each novel's themes and yet neither constitutes the philosophical center of Tolstoy's novels, at least in most critics' assessments, where the forms of earthly—not divine—love are more often identified as the subject of Tolstoy's writing.

Our first problem in addressing the meaning of divine love in *War and Peace* is that, as commentators have noted, there is very little actual talk of God in the novel. To be sure, Princess Marya Bolkonskaya has her devotion to the Gospels and her pilgrims in the first half of *War and Peace*; the Russian troops pray to God and venerate the icon of the Smolensk Mother of God; Natasha Rostova prays to God for forgiveness at the Razumovskys' chapel and listens reverently to the prayer for the deliverance of Russia from hostile invasion at the Divine Liturgy; and Platon Karataev evokes God in his prayers and parables. But God is mentioned almost everywhere primarily in passing and certainly never, as Edward Wasiolek points out, as "a litany of conventional Christian beliefs."[17] The God most frequently encountered in *War and Peace* is less the deity of the Judeo-Christian tradition and more the image of some impersonal and implacable force, simultaneously remote from humankind but also penetrating all corners of the universe.

As for the second person of the Christian Trinity, there are even fewer mentions of Christ in *War and Peace*. They can be counted on two hands. Indeed, Inessa Medzhibovskaya claims that Christ earns "no more than five fleeting mentions in the whole corpus of Tolstoy's imaginative fiction and personal writings" before *War and Peace*.[18] As for *War and Peace*, two important references to Christ—important, because they are so few in the novel—occur at the very beginning and end of the book. At one point late in the novel, Christ is described as the source of "the measures of good and bad" (4:3:18:1071) in Russian society—a characteristic Tolstoyan invocation of Christ as the embodiment of moral teachings, not as Savior or incarnation of divine love. Elsewhere, Christ is mentioned by the most devout character in the novel, Princess Marya, as a teacher and symbol of divine, agapic love.

In a letter to Julie Karagina, Marya writes that Christian love is "the love of one's neighbor, the love for one's enemies," thus defining agapic love as something "more meritorious, sweeter, and more beautiful" than the romantic love (eros) about which her friend writes (1:1:22:94). She thus sets up an important opposition between the two kinds of love in *War and Peace*: the one that leads to "blessings that last a moment" and the one taught by "Christ, the Son of God" (2:3:26:486). And yet, just one page later, having determined to flee her home and become a pilgrim in search of God on the dusty roads of Russia, Marya comes to the abrupt realization, upon seeing her father and her little nephew, that she actually loves them more than God. As it turns out, she needs and craves earthly love more than divine love. Her deepest dream is actually of eros, not agape. She wants a future family and is so desperate to see that dream come true that she even contemplates the possibility of marriage to the dissolute Anatole Kuragin. Moreover, when she ultimately realizes this dream with Nikolai Rostov, the reader, like Marya, clearly sees that this life is truer to her authentic self than the one she would have had living for the Gospels.

Elsewhere in the novel, the same choice between eros and agape will confront her brother Prince Andrei, who conceives of God as "the great all or nothing," "an indefinable, unfathomable power" (1:3:19:293). An educated man of his age, Andrei cannot bring himself to believe in the God professed by the Russian Orthodox Church. Divine love seems to him to be as remote and inaccessible as the possibility of earthly love, either on the part of Andrei's first wife Lise, who dies in childbirth, or Natasha Rostova, who accepts his marriage proposal but then attempts to elope with Anatole Kuragin. Having given up on God, Andrei also gives up on romantic love, returning to active service in the army, vowing to find Kuragin and challenge him to a duel. In finding his rival, however, Andrei also discovers that most elusive thing of all: divine love.

Badly wounded in the Battle of Borodino, Andrei is taken to a medical station, where he witnesses doctors amputating Kuragin's leg. Suddenly, Andrei's desire to kill his enemy Kuragin in a duel is transformed into the understanding that he actually loves him. But it is a love he has never experienced before. To his own surprise and despite his earlier conviction that forgiveness of enemies was merely "a woman's virtue" (3:1:8:631), he now experiences "compassion, love for our brothers, for those who love us, love for those who hate us, love for our enemies—yes, that love which God preached on earth" (3:2:37:814). Andrei later elaborates on this understanding of agapic love and how it differs from eros: "Not love which loves for something, for some quality, for some purpose, or for some reason," he recalls. It is, rather, "that feeling of love which is the very essence of the soul and does not require an object" and that allows one "to love one's neighbors, to love one's enemies, to love everything, to love God in all His manifestations. It is possible to love someone dear to you with human love, but an enemy can only be loved by divine love" (3:3:32:921).

Later, reunited with Natasha but dying, he understands that such love is impossible for the living. He realizes that "to love everything, everybody, always to sacrifice oneself for love, meant to love no one, meant not to live this earthly life" (4:1:16:982). A paradox thus obtains: the very nearness to God that Andrei experiences on the verge of death makes his new understanding of love inapplicable to human relationships. Earthly love—the love that loves for some quality or for some reason—opposes, even hinders, agapic love, as Andrei apprehends when he sees Natasha again, "whom of all people in the world he most wanted to love with that new, pure, divine love which had now been revealed to him" (3:3:32:922). But Andrei soon realizes that he cannot love her this way. Eros and agape appear to be mutually exclusive types of love. Earthly love and living for oneself—the kind of love and living most celebrated in the novel—are not compatible with divine love, understood as love of those who hate you. Indeed, disinterested love and love of enemy are concepts that are not achievable in this world, a fact that Andrei's death seems to underscore.

Pierre, too, must grapple with eros and agape. And, as with Andrei, it is a member of the Kuragin family who plays a role. In Pierre's case, it his ill-fated marriage to Anatole's sister, Helene Kuragina, that provokes a crisis of love. Helene, beautiful and voluptuous, is the perfect object of eros, but she also embodies the unreliability of romantic love: she attracts other admirers. After fighting a duel with his wife's purported lover, Pierre separates from Helene and leaves for Petersburg. At the Torzhok posting station he ponders his situation and begins to ask himself the so-called cursed questions: "What is bad? What is good? What should one love, what hate? Why live, and what am I? What is life, what is death? What power rules over everything?" And to all of these questions, he finds only one answer: "You will die—and everything will end. You will die and learn everything—or stop asking" (2:2:1:348).

At the Torzhok posting station, however, he also happens to meet the Freemason Iosif Bazdeev and undergoes his first "conversion" in the novel. Pierre repudiates a life of sensuality and unbelief and joins the Masons, devoting all of his energies to philanthropic endeavors. Like Princess Marya, he seems to choose living for God—the great "pre-eternal architect of the world" (2:2:4:359)—over living for the self. Freemasonry, however, ultimately proves in practice to have more to do with living for the self than with living for God, even though it, too, preaches a divine love of enemy. "Forgive your enemy," Pierre is told by a brother Mason during his initiation ceremony, "take no revenge upon him, unless it be by doing him good" (2:2:4:361). Love of enemy, however, is hardly practiced by his fellow Masons, for most of whom the fellowship is merely a means of social advancement (2:3:7:434). Disappointed in his new devotion, Pierre slips back into a life of stupefaction of the senses, drinking heavily and spending time in various "bachelor circles" (2:5:1:535). His former agnosticism reasserts itself, as does his fear of death.

All of this changes after the French invade Russia and Pierre is taken captive and nearly executed. Pierre is brought to his lowest point yet, utterly losing his faith in humanity, his own soul, and in God. He is ultimately resurrected and rediscovers meaning in life through his conversations with Platon Karataev. Indeed, through Karataev, Pierre discovers a different kind of love and philosophy of life that seem to hold the answers Pierre has been seeking. Karataev, Pierre realizes, "had no attachments, friendships, or love, as Pierre understood them; but he loved and lived lovingly with everything that life brought his way, especially other people—not any specific people, but those who were there before his eyes" (4:1:13:973). Platon's philosophy of "loving the one you're with," even your enemies, receives its ultimate illustration in his tale of the merchant wrongly accused of murder, who forgives the man responsible for sending him to hard labor for over ten years (4:3:13:1062–63; this tale is later retold by Tolstoy as a separate story titled "God Sees the Truth, but Waits").

But Pierre soon discovers a peculiarity about Platon. He senses that, "despite all his gentle tenderness towards him," Karataev "would not have been upset for a moment to be parted from him" (4:1:13:974). Loving the one you are with for Platon means not dwelling on the one you are without. On the one hand, as Wasiolek asks, "What kind of self-sacrificial Christian loves no one in particular, has no friendships and attachments, and feels affections for another only when he is in his presence?"[19] On the other hand, there is nevertheless a divine quality to that kind of love, a love that shows no gradation of affection or distinction between love objects.[20] Indeed, love of "this man here before me" is, according to Nikolai Berdyaev, "the highest idea of humanity and personalism" and, consequently, "the Christian attitude to man."[21] Platon is thus the supreme embodiment of the personalist view of humanity, as Russian religious philosophy would come to understand it. At the same time, as Pierre notices, in loving all without distinction, Platon loves no one in particular. In this regard, he demonstrates how divine love can be practiced between human beings (thus

correcting Andrei's supposition), but fails to show how personal human relationships can be sustained by it. Platon's philosophy is perfectly suited to captivity or life in the army, where human relationships are fluid and changing. But
how do you maintain a committed relationship to another when, in Platon's
particular vision of divine love, all must be equally worthy of your love?

Ultimately, you cannot, at least if the reader judges by Pierre, who, after his
captivity, follows Karataev's philosophy of loving everyone without cause, but
only temporarily. Love overflows his heart and, "loving people without reason,
he discovered the unquestionable reasons for which it was worth loving them"
(4:4:19:1124). Indeed, the "legitimate peculiarity of each person, which formerly
had troubled and irritated Pierre, now constituted the basis of the sympathy
and interest he took in people" (4:4:13:1107). Here, Pierre's personalism is at its
zenith: everyone is equally worthy and equally deserving of attention. Suffused
with divine love, Pierre sees the divine basis in every human being around him.
Such a state of "insanity" (Pierre's own epithet, 4:4:19:1124) cannot endure,
however. Shortly after marrying Natasha, Pierre abruptly breaks off his practice
of universal love. Eros is a jealous love, and Natasha seems intent on keeping
Pierre firmly "under her heel," as the narrator puts it (Epilogue:1:10:1156; also,
Epilogue:1:15:1172). Agapic love—as Andrei or Karataev understood it—must
give way. Pierre's love for Natasha is a selfish, self-interested love. Divine love,
the love taught by Christ, the love measured by love of enemies, is more or less
forgotten by novel's end, though it reappears significantly in Tolstoy's next novel.

EROS VERSUS AGAPE IN *ANNA KARENINA*

If *War and Peace* celebrates a very earthly and selfish love—the love of couples
and of family—then it is not surprising that Tolstoy should probe precisely the
limits of both of these kinds of love in the tale of Anna Karenina's adulterous
affair with Aleksei Vronsky and in the story of Konstantin Levin's marriage and
family life. How to reconcile this opposition of love of self and love of the other
is one of the driving themes of the novel. If adultery, divorce, and suicide are
potent symbols of human estrangement and the objects of divine judgment in
Anna Karenina, then divine love—figured as love of enemies—becomes the
ultimate expression of human relatedness in the novel and thus the novel's true
subject as well as the next step in Tolstoy's own Christology.

Tolstoy addresses the theme of agapic love at length only once in the novel, in the scene where Aleksei Karenin visits his wife on her sickbed and experiences a transcendent moment of love of enemies. This theme of love of enemies, however, is arguably the principal theme of the book. Of all the forms of love explored in the novel, it is the greatest—the form of love most at stake in the book but the one seemingly least scrutinized. In a novel where husbands are set against wives and sexual rivals square off against each other, the inadequacies of romantic love (eros) are plain for all to see. Agape, precisely as a love of enemies, is the only love capable of restoring harmony and order.

The opening pages of the book set the stage by depicting the novel's chief device for exploring divine love: a family made unhappy by adultery. Stiva Oblonsky, the reader learns, has cheated on his wife Dolly and that is why "all was confusion in the Oblonskys' house." Within the next one hundred fifty pages, however, the Oblonskys' problem becomes that of the Karenin family. Karenin warns Anna about paying too much attention to Vronsky, not knowing that she is already betraying him. Vronsky, in his turn, betrays Kitty Shcherbatskaya, the young lady whom everyone thought he would marry and with whom Levin is in love, in order to pay court to Anna. Levin, whom Kitty rejects in favor of Vronsky, develops an instant dislike for him. Immediately, characters pair off into "enemy camps": Dolly and Stiva, Anna and Karenin, Karenin and Vronsky, and, to a lesser degree, Levin and Vronsky and Kitty and Anna. The central estranged couple—Anna and Karenin—are, of course, at the heart of the novel's inquiry into adultery and family happiness, but the underlying theme of forgiveness and love of enemy permeates the dramas of all of our enemy pairs.

Underscoring the centrality of this theme, Karenin's epiphanic moment at his wife's bedside when "the joyful feeling of love and forgiveness of his enemies filled his soul" (4:17:413)[22] occurs almost exactly at the mid-point of the novel. Karenin, who had just moments before been coldly thinking of how Anna's death "would resolve at a stroke all the difficulty of his situation" (4:17:410), is suddenly overwhelmed by pity and forgiveness, which bring about "a blissful state of soul" and "a new, previously unknown happiness" (4:17:413). He not only forgives Anna, but Vronsky, too, telling him: "I want to turn the other cheek, I want to give my shirt when my caftan is taken, and I only pray to God that He not take from me the happiness of forgiveness!" (4:17:414). Here, Christ's teaching, if not the image of Christ himself, is placed center stage. Karenin's hatred of Anna becomes, in quasi-apophatic fashion, both a means of loving divinely and a measurement of divine love as he suddenly understands Christ's command to love those who hate you and whom you might hate yourself.

As with Pierre, however, Karenin's practice of divine love soon wanes. While this fall from grace may be ostensibly attributed to the influence of Countess Lydia Ivanovna, who introduces Karenin to the "new explanation of Christian doctrine that had lately spread in Petersburg" (5:22:511)—an amalgam of Pietism, with its eschewing of ritual and reliance on inner prayer, and spiritualism, the newest vogue that included table-turning and mediums—Karenin's change of heart also stems from the same difficulty of maintaining an attitude of divine love in everyday life that Tolstoy explored in *War and Peace*. Karenin discovers that his forgiveness of enemies and his love for "his sick wife and another man's child"—both outcomes of the feeling of agapic love that has changed his life—earn a perverse reward in the world of Petersburg society, where he finds himself "alone, disgraced, derided, needed by none and despised by all" (5:21:505).

In such a hostile environment, Karenin's conversion falters. Maybe, as Vladimir Alexandrov argues, Karenin is simply too weak to embody "the Christian ideal in its purest form for any length of time."[23] Or perhaps the problem with divine love is deeper, as Morson suspects. Morson argues that agapic love may be possible but it also ultimately "may not be a good thing" for it can lead to "destructive results."[24] At fault, according to Morson, is the utopian impulse at the core of the Christian notion of love of enemies, a concept that "defies human nature and everyday practices." Any utopian impulse that, "like Bolshevism, sets out to change human nature entirely," is bound to lead to failure, suffering, and even evil, Morson maintains.[25]

In place of divine love, Morson argues that Tolstoy advocates the prosaic love exemplified by Dolly Oblonskaya, who adheres to a less "superhuman" doctrine of forgiveness: that of overcoming "feelings of resentment so that one can forgive injuries."[26] But perhaps Morson undervalues Dolly's act of forgiving her husband, for she herself seems to associate it precisely with Christ's hard command to love our enemies when she advises Karenin to follow her example and forgive Anna. "I forgave, and you must forgive," she tells Karenin, and, when he says he cannot, she whispers to him "shamefacedly," "Love those who hate you" (4:12:395). Dolly cites the Gospels (Matthew 5:44 and Luke 6:27) to Karenin so simply and so self-effacingly that it is easy to underappreciate the very "superhuman" nature of the agapic love that she is affirming here. Karenin certainly does, immediately dismissing her advice as something that "could not be applied in his case" (4:12:395). And yet, a mere twenty pages later, he abruptly does just as she advises and loves his enemies at Anna's sickbed.

The close proximity of these two scenes suggests a link between them and underscores the importance Tolstoy attaches to love of enemies as the moral compass of *Anna Karenina*. Dolly Oblonskaya is the first to enact this kind of love in the novel and she, significantly, passes on the moral charge to arguably the most unheroic character in the book. And it is precisely because he is so unheroic that readers take such notice when Karenin is so utterly transformed by his experience of divine love. Karenin's betrayal of the principle of agapic love, however, does not render it a dangerous ideal unachievable in reality. Dolly's example alone would argue against such a judgment. It is just that Karenin's failure carries a much greater thematic charge, tied as it is to the plot trajectory culminating in Anna's tragic suicide. His failure to adhere to the love of enemy he discovers at Anna's bedside foreshadows her failure to achieve any semblance of love of enemy as well.[27] Indeed, her suicide is the emblem of this failure. It is the opposite of divine love—a rejection of love of enemies in favor of retribution. Anna lashes out at her enemies—Karenin, high society, even Vronsky, whom she wishes to punish for their recent quarrels—and, true to the novel's epigraph, she exacts her vengeance, but her retribution ultimately falls on her own head as well.

The failure to love one's enemies so dramatically enacted in the Anna Karenina plot line has the potential to overshadow those instances—less noticeable because less dramatic—celebrated elsewhere in the book where such love *is* achieved. Dolly and Stiva represent one instance where an enemy pair is undone through forgiveness. Three other important but muted instances occur late in the book, all involving other lesser "enemy pairs" in the story. All of them complete and deepen in subtle but crucial ways the notion of divine love that Tolstoy promotes in the novel, and all of them contribute to our understanding of the novel's ending, which significantly does not conclude with Anna's death, but rather with Levin's awakening to faith.

Our first enemy pair reconciled late in the novel is Vronsky and Levin. Rivals for Kitty's hand early in the novel, Vronsky and Levin remain on unfriendly footing until shortly before Anna's suicide. Levin has a hard time hiding his feelings of animosity toward his former rival. At the same time, Levin is bothered by these feelings. "It's so tormenting," he tells Kitty, "to think that there's a man who is almost an enemy, whom it's painful to meet" (7:1:674). After an awkward encounter with Vronsky at the Kashin provincial elections, Levin seizes upon an opportunity arranged by Stiva to make up with Vronsky at their club. This reconciliation, however, is somewhat superficial. It is more of a "cessation of hostilities" (7:8:694). As such, it is not so much an embodiment of divine love of enemies as a distant echo of it.

As in *War and Peace*, the discovery of love of enemies seems to be possible only in states of altered consciousness and intense subjectivity. Andrei finds divine love on the threshold of death, after being gravely wounded at the Battle of Borodino. Pierre comes to an understanding of divine love after the physical and mental trials of war and captivity.[28] So, too, in *Anna Karenina*. Divine love discloses itself to Karenin only under the powerful influence of his "inner disturbance" (*dushevnoe rasstroistvo*, literally, discomposure of the soul) at the sight of his dying wife, a feeling that leads to a "blissful state of soul" in which he experiences total and genuine love of enemies (4:17:413). Levin feels no such transport in reconciling with Vronsky. But the relinquishment of enmity that Levin's superficial reconciliation brings does lead unexpectedly to a more meaningful brush with forgiveness of enemies for Levin and the only meeting in the novel between its two main characters, when Stiva insists on taking Levin to see his sister, Anna, shortly after Levin's rapprochement with Vronsky.

This encounter, too, is significant, for it extends and modulates the theme of forgiveness and love of enemy indistinctly raised in Levin's meeting with Vronsky. In a typical Tolstoyan inversion of scale, the significance of this meeting and its dramatic potential are belied by the scene's brevity. Levin's visit to Anna occupies all of a half-dozen pages in chapters 9 and 10 of part 7. As the only meeting between the novel's two main characters, however, the scene is integral to the novel's concerns and, as always with Tolstoy, is open to multiple interpretations. Flush with wine from his evening at the club and relieved over his reconciliation with Vronsky, Levin accompanies Stiva to his sister's house, twice wondering if he is doing the right thing (7:9:694, 696). He even wonders whether he is drunk when he glimpses his red face in the mirror in the entrance-way of Anna's house, though he immediately assures himself he is not.

At first, it appears that Tolstoy is signaling that Levin is making a mistake in visiting Anna. The question of whether he has had too much to drink is especially significant. If Levin is drunk, then the decision to visit Anna and the feelings of "tenderness and pity" he experiences upon meeting her (7:10:700) could be ascribed to impaired judgment. Such is Levin's own later explanation to Kitty when he realizes how upset his wife is by news of his visit. Levin assures her that his "feeling of pity, along with the wine, had thrown him off guard and made him yield to Anna's cunning influence." Now, in the face of Kitty's distraught reaction, Levin "knew that he should not have done it" (7:11:703).

It would seem no more need be said about the subject, and yet Tolstoy's description of Levin's confession to Kitty suggests that Levin may be hasty or acting under the duress of Kitty's emotional response when he decides he should not have visited Anna. After all, it takes Levin and Kitty until three o'clock in the morning before they are "reconciled enough to be able to fall asleep" (7:11:703). It is possible that that Levin is not telling the whole truth when he calls the visit a mistake. Moreover, attributing all of the emotions he feels that night to Anna's "cunning influence," as Levin does, is both a gross oversimplification of Levin's encounter with her and an unfair judgment of Anna's character as well, which is more complicated than that of a woman who, as Alexandrov argues, is merely interested "in her own power to awaken love in a chance caller."[29] Tolstoy seems to allow for another truth here, one that is central to the novel's theme of divine love.

In point of fact, Levin's flushed face as he enters Anna's house *is* significant, but not for the obvious reason. Rather than impairing his judgment, Levin's mild inebriation may actually allow him to make a better moral assessment than he could have achieved through sober reason alone. As he does elsewhere in the novel and in *War and Peace*, Tolstoy may actually be implying here that Levin sees Anna more truly because he views her from a state of altered consciousness—a state of heightened emotional receptivity and subjectivity—brought on by the wine he has consumed at the club. Throughout his visit, Levin reflects how "simple and pleasant" it is to be with her (7:10:697). He sees her "intelligence, grace, [and] beauty," and discovers "truthfulness in her," someone who does not attempt "to conceal from him all the difficulty of her situation" (7:10:700). Surely these impressions are not simply the deceitful workings of "Anna's cunning influence," as he later claims (7:11:703). They are, rather, truths disclosed to him precisely because he has let his guard down, because the wine has allowed his emotions, and not just his reason, to guide his perception. *In vino veritas*, as the saying goes; Levin sees truly here *because* of the wine he has drunk.[30]

Having expressed disapproval of "fallen women" over lunch with Stiva in part 1 (1:11:41), Levin might well be expected to judge Anna harshly. And, indeed, he does so later, when he sobers up during his confession to Kitty. But for us readers who have, in the course of the novel, compared the fates of the two main characters, Levin's encounter with Anna confirms what the entire novel up to this point has been showing us about her: that she is charming, sympathetic, and altogether appealing. The reader cannot easily condemn her, even when she behaves badly and even when the narrator later states that Anna had "*unconsciously* done everything she could to arouse a feeling of love for her in Levin, and [...] had succeeded in it" (7:12:704, my emphasis). Anna, as the narrator informs us, clearly does not deliberately manipulate Levin. That is just Anna's way—she cannot help charming those she meets. It is part of her nature.

The real truth of the encounter is not calculated manipulation but spontaneous forgiveness, as Tolstoy so eloquently informs us at the end of chapter 10: "And he who had formerly judged her so severely, *now, by some strange train of thought*, justified her and at the same time pitied her, and feared that Vronsky did not fully understand her" (7:10:701, emphasis added). This "strange train of thought" is precisely the estranged perception Levin's mildly inebriated state allows him access to. It is the "true vision" he achieves in his encounter with Anna. When Levin leaves Anna's house feeling "a tenderness and pity for her that surprised him" (7:10:700), these sentiments inevitably communicate themselves to the reader. The reader, too, participates in Levin's unexpected economy of divine forgiveness. More importantly, readers, too, get a foretaste of the divine love exemplified in love of enemies.[31]

Pity is a key ingredient to divine love. Prince Andrei pities Anatole Kuragin and in his pity, realizes he loves him. Levin pities Anna and in that pity he feels tenderness toward her and even justifies her.[32] Earlier in the novel, pity and forgiveness are linked with the image of Christ himself in the painting by the Russian artist Mikhailov, whom Anna and Vronsky visit while in Italy—the only instance in the novel where Tolstoy gives us any image of Christ at all beyond what is implied in his teaching on love of enemies.[33] The painting is of Pilate's judgment of Christ. In Christ's expression there is "pity, [...] love, unearthly peace, readiness for death and an awareness of the vanity of words" (5:11:474). Pilate, by contrast, has the vexed face of a bureaucrat "who knows not what he does" (5:11:473). Here, of course, is the novel's second overt depiction of the concept of divine love of enemies so much at the center of *Anna Karenina*'s themes.

The painting is emblematic, as Mikhailov acknowledges when he observes how he had painted "the expression of a functionary in Pilate and of pity in Christ, because one embodied carnal and the other spiritual life" (5:11:474). Clearly, one could make an analogy between Pilate's carnal life and Anna's, just as one could argue that Levin is linked to Christ in that he lives more for his spiritual self.[34] And yet it is Anna who remarks on Christ's "astonishing" expression and correctly identifies Christ's pity of Pilate as the most meaningful aspect of the painting (5:11:474). She, too, knows what agapic love of enemies looks like, having just witnessed it in her husband's forgiveness of her just a few months and some sixty pages earlier. She also singles out the one quality of Christ most important for her own situation in life and that she most needs from others, including Levin: compassion. Thus Tolstoy's distinction between eros and agape, so important to his later works, is here complicated and challenged. While Anna has clearly chosen eros over agape in her own life, at the same time she never loses sight of a higher spiritual love.

Recognizing a higher spiritual love and practicing it, however, are, two different things. When Anna encounters Kitty the very day she will commit suicide, Kitty, though jealous of Anna and still harboring resentment towards her, follows her husband's example and instantly and sincerely forgives Anna for being the cause of Vronsky's abrupt cessation of his courtship of her. Though she had struggled with feelings of "animosity towards this bad woman," Kitty cannot help but feel sorry for her at this encounter and she looks at Anna with sympathy (7:28:759). She thus embodies our third example of love of enemies in the novel. Anna, however, cannot reciprocate. "We all hate each other," she thinks on the way home from the meeting. "I Kitty, Kitty me. That's the truth" (7:29:760). It is in this state of mind that she conceives of the notion to kill herself and indeed before the day is through she carries this feeling of hatred with her to the very moment when she throws herself under the train. She cannot bring herself to love her enemies, whether Karenin, Kitty or, after they quarrel, Vronsky. Failing this test of love, she also fails the novel's primary metaphysical challenge. Hatred as a paradoxical measure of divine love has been turned upside down by Anna's anger. Love of those who hate you has become its opposite: hatred of those who love you.

Unable to feel agapic love, Anna is unable to forgive or be forgiven. She tells Levin when they part that in order to forgive her, "one must have lived through what I have lived through" (7:10:701). Readers know that this is not true, for they witness how both Levin and Kitty forgive Anna, despite their feelings of animosity toward her and without having gone through what Anna has experienced. These small examples of love of enemies affirm the essential connection between the two plotlines of the novel. In both the Anna Karenina storyline and that of Levin, everything ultimately turns on this concept. Divine love—returning love for hate—in turn reveals the beginning of Tolstoy's imaging of Christ.

The reason why *Anna Karenina* does not end with Anna's suicide is because Tolstoy must affirm the triumph of agape over eros. Dolly's advice to Karenin to "love those who hate you" and Karenin's temporary realization of that love shortly afterward are the prefiguration of a deeper knowledge of God that Levin discovers himself only when he, too, has practiced divine love in his own way. That Levin's discovery of divine love takes place precisely in part 8 and comprises the novel's actual conclusion underscores the importance of this concept in *Anna Karenina*. When the peasant Fyodor tells Levin how another peasant "lives for the soul" and "remembers God," he provides the catalyst for a chain of thoughts that brings Levin, our former atheist ("He could not believe, yet at the same time he was not firmly convinced that it was all incorrect," 5:1:439), to a new understanding of God and faith (8:11:794).

This idea of faith is simple and links seamlessly with the novel's concept of agapic love, for Levin arrives at it unaided by his reason but rather propelled by his own experience of love of others. "Where did I take it from?" he asks himself. "Was it through reason that I arrived at the necessity of loving my neighbor and not throttling him? I was told it as a child, and I joyfully believed it, because they told me what was in my soul. And who discovered it? Not reason. Reason discovered the struggle for existence and the law which demands that everyone who hinders the satisfaction of my desires should be throttled. That is the conclusion of reason. Reason could not discover love for the other, because it's unreasonable" (8:12:797). Levin goes on to reject "the stupidity of reason. And, above all—the slyness, precisely the slyness, of reason. Precisely the swindling of reason" (8:12:797). In rejecting reason, Levin echoes Ivan Karamazov, who tells Alyosha: "Reason hedges and hides. Reason is a scoundrel."[35]

Like Ivan, Levin thus reveals the distinct apophatic thrust of his quest for knowledge of God, in which "it is necessary to renounce both sense and all the workings of reason" in order to attain "union with Him who transcends all being and all knowledge."[36] Here also the reader glimpses a distinct reflection of the truth behind Levin's encounter with Anna: one cannot reason one's way to divine love of the other—one must feel one's way to it, just as one must grope one's way toward faith, something Levin discovers in the novel and Tolstoy discovered in life.

That divine love figured as love of enemies should occupy such a significant though underscrutinized place in both of Tolstoy's masterpieces marks it as an important concept in the development of the writer's thinking about Christ and God. One key here is Tolstoy's fascination with the moral *ideal*, not with the one who taught it. In neither of Tolstoy's novels does Christ as redeemer or even as a person occupy any significant textual space. Golenishchev may criticize the painter Mikhailov's rendition of a non-divine Jesus in *Anna Karenina* (5:9:467), but nowhere in that novel or in *War and Peace* does Tolstoy offer any other image of Christ. Rather, Tolstoy is taken by Jesus's moral teachings, and the more difficult and paradoxical they are, the more Tolstoy seemed to pay attention. Divine love understood as love of enemies was as much a revolutionary moment in the writer's thinking as it was a moral test for the protagonists of his two famous novels. Love measured by its opposite, negation leading to affirmation, contradiction giving rise to clarity—these were the sorts of things that drove Tolstoy's theological method. For the next thirty years, he spent nearly every waking moment pursuing the paradoxes and contradictions of his own Christian vision, one that took negation as its starting point and, one might argue, its ending point as well. "There is no Christianity without love for those who hate us," Tolstoy would write in 1907, "precisely for those who hate us."[37]

CHAPTER FIVE

"CAN THIS BE FAITH?"

Tolstoy's *Resurrection*

> If I exist, there must be some cause for it, and a cause of causes. And that first cause of all is what men have called "God." And I paused on that thought, and tried with all my being to recognize the presence of that cause. And as soon as I acknowledged that there is a force in whose power I am, I at once felt that I could live. But I asked myself: What is that cause, that force?
>
> Tolstoy, "A Confession"

TOLSTOY'S APOPHATIC GOD

The theme of love of enemies as the measure of divine love in his two great novels marks an important moment for Tolstoy, who made of this and four other equally paradoxical commandments from Christ's Sermon on the Mount the centerpiece of his new faith. Like love of enemies, each of these moral precepts sets standards of behavior that are seemingly impossible to meet. In his sermon, Christ equates lust with adultery, anger with murder, oath-taking with lying, and resisting evil with abetting it, all in an attempt to teach human beings about the nature of divine love. For Tolstoy, there was no greater revelation of what divine love must be than these teachings. But like his fictional characters, he came to this realization about the nature of divine love and faith only gradually and with difficulty.

When Konstantin Levin gropes his way to belief at the conclusion of *Anna Karenina*, he asks the question Tolstoy himself asked while writing the novel:

"Can this be faith?" (8:13:800). The question is not entirely a rhetorical one, for what Levin has discovered is less a belief in God per se and more the conviction that the "sole purpose" of humankind is "serving the good instead of one's needs" (8:13:799). For Levin, however, this is as close to belief in God as he gets. By novel's end, Levin acknowledges two things: that this feeling—"faith or not faith—I don't know what it is" (8:19:817)—has changed his life and that, try as he might, he cannot "express this knowledge by means of reason and words" (8:19:816). A few years later, Tolstoy will come to similar conclusions in his *Confession* (1879). Tolstoy, too, was "seeking a faith," but he also understood that he could not seek "the explanation of everything." He writes: "I know that the explanation of everything, like the commencement of everything, must be concealed in infinity. But I wish to understand in a way which will bring me to what is inevitably inexplicable. I wish to recognize anything that is inexplicable as being so not because the demands of my reason are wrong (they are right, and apart from them I can understand nothing), but because I recognize the limits of my intellect."[1]

In speaking of the "inevitably inexplicable" and the "limits of [the] intellect" in his search for God, Tolstoy was acknowledging that God, if God exists, must be beyond the limits of human comprehension and the ability of Tolstoy's native Christian profession to explain. In fact, traditional Christian concepts of God interfere with our proper understanding of divine reality. For Tolstoy, the idea of God as a separate entity who created the universe and to whom one may pray already limited the limitless deity in a way that violated his reason, even as he acknowledged that reason alone is inadequate in understanding God. "A God of whom one can ask things and whom it is possible to serve is an expression of weakness of mind," Tolstoy wrote in his diary in 1860. "He is God precisely because I can't imagine to myself His whole being."[2] Tolstoy thus charts a course away from his native Orthodox Christian faith and yet, at the same time, employs language and assumes a theological position that strongly evokes apophaticism, the *via negativa* that refuses to form concepts about God, since conceptualization diminishes the divinity.

This apophatic God is Tolstoy's God. It is the same God who haunted and eluded Prince Andrei, the "indefinable, unfathomable power" that one "not only cannot address," but "cannot express in words" (1:3:19:293). It is the *panenthe-istic* God (God is in everything but is not limited to everything[3]) Pierre apprehends in captivity "not through words, not arguments, but though immediate sensation"; the God that is "here, right here, everywhere" (4:4:12:1103). It is

Levin's God, "whom no one can either comprehend or define" (8:12:795). It is the unprovable God Tolstoy had been pursuing since an 1853 diary entry, for whom he cannot "find a single sensible piece of evidence" but in whom he believes and of whom he asks for help "to understand Him."[4] "God is for me that after which I strive," he would later write, "that the striving after which forms my life, and who, therefore, *is* for me; but he is necessarily such that I cannot comprehend or name him."[5]

For Tolstoy, to strive after God is to perfect oneself. He writes in *Confession*: "I now see clearly that my faith—my only real faith—that which apart from my animal instincts gave impulse to my life—was a belief in perfecting myself."[6] In later years, this program of self-improvement became a full-blown "theology of perfection"[7] with Christ's teachings at its center. God may be essentially unknowable, but through Christ one at least has a notion of how one must proceed. "Man never attains perfection, but only approaches it," Tolstoy wrote in a letter to the American minister and pacifist Adin Ballou. "As it is impossible to trace in reality a mathematically straight line and as every such line is only an approach to the latter, so is every degree of perfection attainable by man only an approach to the perfection of the Father, which Christ showed us the way to emulate."[8]

But Christ shows us the way not because he is the Messiah or the Son of God. On the contrary, after *Confession* Tolstoy rejects Jesus altogether as God incarnate and is indifferent to and at times even dismissive of Jesus as a specific, historically real person. "I was led to Christianity neither by theological nor historical investigations," he writes in his preface to his *Gospel in Brief*. What is important is that this person "Jesus Christ" passed on teachings that "gives us the meaning of life."[9] For Tolstoy, neither theological arguments about Jesus's divinity nor historical claims about his life and times have any relevance. On the one hand, "the Epistles, the decrees of the Councils and the decisions of the Fathers" only lead us away from Christ's message and, worse yet, darken it with obscure doctrines "that God is three persons, that the Holy Ghost descended upon the apostles and was transmitted to the priesthood by the laying on of hands; that seven sacraments are necessary for salvation; that communion should be received in two kinds, and so on."[10] On the other hand, the ascendancy of secular studies of Jesus in the nineteenth century—particularly Strauss's *Leben Jesu* and Renan's *Vie de Jésus*—are as harmful as claims for Christ's divinity, and, like those claims, miss the point altogether. The adherents of the historical critical method, according to Tolstoy, are so intent on teaching that Jesus was not God that they ignore altogether what he taught and why this message has endured for so long.

Tolstoy's Christology thus proceeds from a double negation: first, that Jesus is not divine, but rather his teachings are; and second, that among those teachings, the greatest is love even of those who hate you, which is the best expression of divine love that human beings know, a definition of love derived from a negative reference point. In this way, Tolstoy charts his own course toward understanding the meaning of Christ and his message. But however much Tolstoy criticized or deviated from the Church, his own ideas and thinking about Christ and God were nevertheless distinctly influenced by his native Orthodox faith.[11] Adopting the methodology of apophatic theology in his thinking and writing about God is one way Tolstoy reveals his dependence on Orthodox ideas. In his emphasis on self-perfection as a way toward God, Tolstoy also evokes the Orthodox notion of *theosis* or deification.[12] Both of these concepts are central to Tolstoy's understanding of Jesus Christ and what it means to follow him, an outcome hardly surprising given the link between apophaticism and *theosis* in Orthodox theology. Tolstoy's adaptation of these concepts in his writing about God, Jesus Christ, and the construction of personhood, however, ultimately lead to conclusions quite at odds with Orthodox theology.

Tolstoy believed his revolt against received notions of faith, God, and Christ offered the possibility of achieving paradise on earth, the fulfillment of his youthful dream of founding a practical religion for the scientific age. Tolstoy set out the basic features of this new religion in four works that he intended to be read together as parts of a larger composition. The first was *Confession*, which, as mentioned above, chronicles his crisis of unbelief, his struggle to find God and faith, and his inability to do so within the beliefs and practices of his native Orthodox Church. It was to serve as a preface of sorts for his *Critique of Dogmatic Theology* (1880–1884, published 1891), where he next systematically dismantles—with indignation, rage, and sarcasm—all the tenets of Orthodox doctrine and practice as being in fundamental disagreement with what Christ taught in the Gospels. His *Harmony and Translation of the Four Gospels* (1880–1884, published 1892), written while he labored over his *Critique*, seeks to restore Christ's true teachings by separating the "pure water of life" from the "mud and slime" that obscured it in the Gospels as they are handed down to us.[13] To do this, Tolstoy combined all four Gospels, removing miracles and downplaying social and historical references, in order to reveal "a very strict, pure, and complete metaphysical and ethical doctrine, higher than which the reason of man has not yet reached."[14] Finally, in *What I Believe* (1884) Tolstoy lays out a catechesis for his new faith in which he distills the great intellectual, emotional, and physical labors over his previous three works into one succinct and sustained apologia for his new faith of reason and enlightenment.

So great was Tolstoy's desire to separate Christ from his teaching that Jesus as a person almost disappears entirely from his harmonized Gospels. Having spurned the "Strausses and Renans" for their insistence on placing Jesus in a specific historical reality and for stressing his humanity (in particular, how he "sweated and went to the lavatory," as Tolstoy scornfully complained in a letter to Nikolai Strakhov[15]), Tolstoy makes his Jesus a disembodied figure distinctly displaced from any concrete historical reality. As Ani Kokobobo argues, "in the later portions of the *Harmonization* he ceases being a fleshy person" altogether and instead "grows into an abstraction, a mere personification of his teaching."[16] At the same time, this "abstract" Christ is certainly not a divine being. Rather, he is, as David Matual argues, "the most eloquent and most authoritative spokesman of the Tolstoyan message."[17] Simply put, the Gospels afforded Tolstoy the best material with which to articulate his own long-held beliefs. Indeed, in an 1884 letter to Vladimir Grigor'evich Chertkov, Tolstoy calls his Gospel "the best manifestation of my thought." It was, he declared, the "one book" he had been writing all of his life.[18]

It is little wonder, therefore, that Tolstoy could not resist bending his translation of the Greek to suit his own needs, employing "pedantic literalisms, lexical rarities, and inflated definitions" as necessity dictated.[19] In his unpublished memoirs, the family tutor I. M. Ivakin reports how Tolstoy would run to him with passages in Greek that he wished the tutor to translate. When he did, Tolstoy would be disappointed that they would often correspond with the existing Church translation. "But couldn't one give it such-and-such a meaning?" he would ask.[20] Tolstoy himself admitted in an August 1887 letter to M. A. Novoselov that there were "many places [...] where the meaning is strained and the translation artificial." But, he adds, "This happened because I wanted as far as possible to depolarise, like a magnet, words of an ecclesiastical interpretation."[21] Two years later, Tolstoy admitted in his diary that the experiment had not been entirely successful: "Read the Gospels, my own exposition, with Ivin, and there was a lot I didn't like: a lot of unnecessary strained interpretations. It would be good to revise it, but I doubt if I can now. And I doubt if it's necessary."[22]

Not surprisingly, then, Tolstoy's Gospel very much bears the mark of its author, and the Tolstoyan Christ met there is rather like Tolstoy in the last three decades of his life: speaking out against wealth, property, and society, criticizing nearly all human institutions, and preaching a life of the spirit over the flesh. His Christ is at once an ordinary man and an extraordinary visionary, but lacking, of course, any miraculous qualities or powers. In his biography there is no virgin birth, no wedding at Cana, no walking on water, no exorcisms, no supernatural healings, no transfiguration, and no resurrection. In place of miracles there are explanatory narratives, either in his prefaces to each Gospel chapter or in the Gospel text itself. These narratives both reveal the prosaic events that the evangelists later embellished as miracle tales and also elucidate the rational principal of Christ's teaching, as Tolstoy understood it.

For instance, Jesus never heals the crippled man at the pool of Bethesda, but simply tells him: "Do not expect to be cured by a miracle, but live according to your strength and do not mistake the meaning of life."[23] Likewise, Jesus feeds the five thousand not through multiplication of loaves, but through communal sharing of food: "And Jesus said: That is how you should always act. It is not necessary for each man to obtain food for himself but it is needful to do what the spirit in man demands, namely to share what there is with others."[24] Elsewhere, the healing of the blind man is, in fact, no literal healing at all, but rather a figurative one. In his retelling, Tolstoy substitutes for *slepoi* the word *temnyi*, literally, "dark," here, however, understood as "ignorant," a translation far better suited to Tolstoy's message:

> And Jesus explained to the ignorant man that he was a son of God in the spirit, and on receiving this teaching the ignorant man was conscious of light. Those who had known him previously did not recognize him. Though resembling what he had been, he had now become a different man. But he said: I am he, and Jesus has shown me that I am a son of God, and the light has reached me, so that now I see what I used not to see.[25]

These examples could be multiplied. The point is that in each instance, Christ's teaching is emphasized over his acts and this teaching is everywhere an expression and elucidation of the *razumenie* ("understanding," "knowledge," "enlightenment") that, in Tolstoy's cosmology, takes the place of Logos, the word of God. It is *razumenie* (with its root, *razum*, "reason") that, in Tolstoy's Gospel, existed "at the basis and beginning of all" and "gives true life," which "the darkness cannot extinguish" and which "in the person of Jesus Christ manifested itself in the flesh." And it is the teaching of Jesus that "is the full and true faith" because it is "based on the attaining of knowledge [*razumenie*]."[26] This knowledge Tolstoy sums up in the five commandments he took from the Sermon on the Mount: do not be angry; do not lust; do not swear any oaths; do not resist evil; and love those who hate you.[27] These five commandments are the centerpiece of chapters 4 and 9 of Tolstoy's Gospel and constitute the core of his own reimaged Christian profession. According to Tolstoy, the fulfillment of these "very simple definite commands" would soon "establish the Kingdom of God" on earth—the goal he had envisioned in 1855.[28]

One may legitimately object that these, of course, are hardly simple commands, nor are they entirely reasonable, for that matter. Renan called Christ's commandments impossible ideals and exaggerations.[29] For one thing, Tolstoy, like Jesus, is demanding that people behave in a way that goes against human nature. For another thing, he is asking us to live by the lofty and hard ideals of Christ but without any recourse to the concept of Christ's grace (so important in Dostoevsky's fiction) to help us out. In this aspect, he reveals his own radical faith, not in Christ, but in the power of human reason. For Tolstoy, however, there was never any question of the unreasonableness of Christ's teachings, and everywhere in his writings he emphasizes that those teachings appealed precisely and primarily to his reason.

At the same time, though, Tolstoy's belief in the powers of reason and his demand that a distinction be made between the divinity of Christ's teaching and the non-divinity of Christ himself led the writer to acknowledge that Jesus could not be the only agent of divine revelation. Other religious traditions also must offer viable paths to true meaning in life. Levin articulates this idea in *Anna Karenina* when he wonders why the truth should be "limited to the Christian Church alone" and not include "Buddhists" and "Mohammedans" (8:14:814). Particularly in the last decade of his life, Tolstoy often lumped Christ's name, virtually without qualification, together with such moral teachers as Buddha, Socrates, Confucius, and others who "believed in reason and served it" for it is on the basis of reason that Tolstoy builds his metaphysics.[30]

To anyone who has read Tolstoy's writings on religion, his privileging of reason as the basis of faith should come as no surprise. Here, he parts ways with apophatic theology as such, with its emphasis on a transrational approach to communion with God. Though he acknowledges the incomprehensibility of the Godhead, the negative path toward God that he charts takes reason as its starting point, reason being essential in obtaining "the understanding of life" (*razumenie*), which is God and which is "manifested in the flesh" in Jesus.[31] This, too, is the lesson of Tolstoy's most sustained fictional treatment of his new faith, his final novel, *Resurrection*, published in serial form in 1899. In this, his sunset novel, Tolstoy reveals with impatience and moral indignation the institutional evils assailing Russia and the remedies offered by reason, whether expressed in his own "religion of Christ" or in the writings of progressive thinkers like Herbert Spencer, Henry George, and Karl Marx.

The Christ of *Resurrection*

The true story on which the novel is based was told to Tolstoy by the prominent lawyer Anatolii Koni. A prostitute, destitute and suffering from typhus, was on trial for theft. Incredibly, one of the jurors recognized in her the young woman he had seduced years ago when she was a servant in his parents' house. Driven from the home when she became pregnant, the woman (Rozalia Oni) soon became a prostitute. Later accused of stealing one hundred rubles from a client, she was put on trial, where she was recognized by her first seducer. Guilt-ridden over how he had caused her downfall, the nobleman visited her in jail and offered to marry her, but she died before her four-month sentence expired.[32]

Tolstoy worked on the novel in spurts from 1889 to 1899. Over the course of the decade, the original story evolved from a tale of sexual seduction and guilt to a broader indictment of the institutions of so-called "civilized society," including the criminal justice system, government bureaucracy, the Orthodox Church, and the class structures that perpetuate social inequality and unequal treatment before the law. These aspects of the novel made it a sensation when it was published, and it easily became Tolstoy's most popular work in Russia. Anton Chekhov read it in one sitting, pronounced it a "remarkable work of art," and praised in particular Tolstoy's depiction of the princes, generals, peasants, prisoners, and prison wardens in the novel. In other words, it was Tolstoy's pitch-perfect rendering of the flawed social reality of tsarist Russia that intrigued, not the tale of Nekhliudov's relationship with Katerina Maslova, which Chekhov called the novel's "least interesting aspect." Tolstoy's attempt to integrate his favorite Gospel passages into the narrative was also singled out by Chekhov for criticism.[33]

While *Resurrection* with its overtly religious title seemed to have succeeded more on the level of social criticism than spiritual revelation, it is nevertheless a late and important articulation of Tolstoy's views on the nature of belief, the identity of Jesus Christ, and the meaning of God. Indeed, *Resurrection* implies its own distinct Christology, one drawn directly from Tolstoy's arduous study of the Gospels and his own idiosyncratic religion "purged of beliefs and mysticism." While one might assume at this point in Tolstoy's career that his idiosyncratic Christology would drive and, indeed, enable the novel's social critique, in actuality, the relationship is the other way around: it is the novel's social critique that drives its Christology. This outcome results in a much more radical Christology than even Tolstoy likely intended. Tolstoy's apophaticism—negating Christ in order to discover God in his teachings—has the unintended consequence of absenting God altogether from the lives of the people Tolstoy is attempting to resurrect in the novel, thus unintentionally undermining his Christ project.

This project is very much at the heart of *Resurrection*, which was written not only to unmask the evils of society but to suggest, in the actions of the selfish and depraved Nekhliudov, how those evils might be overcome: through the teachings of Jesus Christ. In a novel prefaced by epigraphs comprised of four of Christ's sayings from three Gospels and concluding with extensive citations from the Gospel of Matthew, Tolstoy is clearly saying that the message of Jesus Christ is as central to the text as the novel's social message and that the two are, in fact, entwined. Indeed, the novel may be read as an extended elaboration of the parable of the rich young man from the Gospels (Mark 10:17–31 and Matthew 19:16–30), a parable that is, paradoxically, never mentioned in the novel. Like him, Nekhliudov is faced with the same challenge by Christ to achieve a higher degree of holiness than merely keeping the commandments. He is challenged to be perfect. "Jesus said to him, 'If you wish to be perfect, go sell what you have and give to the poor, and you will have treasure in heaven. Then come, follow me'" (Matthew 19:21). This is what Nekhliudov attempts to do in the novel. He wishes to divest himself of the riches that separate him from his fellow man and to perfect himself in the way of Christ. *Resurrection* does not show us Nekhliudov's attainment of perfection, but it does chronicle the first steps he takes on the path toward self-betterment.

Like Pierre Bezukhov in *War and Peace* and Konstantin Levin in *Anna Karenina*, Dmitry Nekhliudov in *Resurrection* is on a quest for God, and like them he is at first but dimly aware of it. His quest is brought about by the extraordinary guilt he feels over the fate of Katerina Maslova, whom he seduced and impregnated while she was a servant at his aunt's house, causing her dismissal and her inevitable slide into prostitution and ruin. Here, Tolstoy's story matches that told by Koni, including Nekhliudov's service as a juror at a trial featuring

Maslova. Unlike Rozalia Oni from Koni's story, however, Maslova is accused of murdering one of her clients. Thus Tolstoy raises the stakes of his story, for Maslova is on trial for her very life.

On the level of theme, however, Maslova is not being judged for her culpability in the death of a merchant. The trial is emblematic in a different way. When asked to give her name in court, Maslova uses her professional name, "Liubov'" (Love), rather than her real name. Tolstoy's point is clear, as Gustafson argues: "'Love' is on trial."[34] By love, several meanings are implied. Certainly sexual love (eros), the fixation of Tolstoy's later years and the frequent target of his ire, is being judged. But so, too, is the whole meaning of love between a man and a woman, as is evident in the extended flashbacks dealing with the past relationship between Nekhliudov and Maslova and as developments in the rest of the novel also make clear. Perhaps most importantly, both God and Jesus Christ as the expression or personification of divine love (agape) are also very much on trial, not least because both are implicated in what is going on in the court room and in what took place between Maslova and Nekhliudov ten years ago.

Nekhliudov meets the seventeen-year-old Maslova while he is spending the summer with his aunts in the countryside. A third-year university student, Nekhliudov has sought the peace and quiet of the country in order to complete his thesis on the ownership of land. At this stage in his life, he is a young idealist and a follower of both Herbert Spencer's idea that private ownership of land is unjust and Henry George's theory of a single tax on land, which would work to abolish land as private property. He is so convinced of the justice of Spencer's and George's conclusions that he gives away to the peasants on his parents' estate the land due him as an inheritance from his father. He also decides to write his dissertation on this topic. His political idealism at this juncture in his life coincides with his personal lack of worldliness. The nineteen-year-old Nekhliudov, the narrator declares, is "a completely innocent young man," a state that extends to his views on sex: "If he thought of a woman, it was only as a wife" (1:12:51).[35] It is in this state of innocence that he first meets Maslova.

Their relationship is chaste and joyful, the very personification of the beauty of their Edenic surroundings, but Nekhliudov leaves without realizing he has fallen in love. Three years later and now a newly commissioned officer, Nekhliudov returns to his aunts' estate, thoroughly debauched from his time serving in the Guards. He arrives, symbolically, on Good Friday, for it will be during the conclusion of Passion Week and the celebration of Easter that Nekhliudov's own fatal passion for Maslova will be awoken. The irony is intended, for Tolstoy wishes to

link Christ's triumph over the flesh through resurrection with Nekhliudov's succumbing to the weaknesses of the flesh in his seduction of Maslova. The chaste
kiss of Christ the two exchange at the Easter Vigil is subverted by Nekhliudov's
forced kiss on Maslova's neck just a few hours later, a reminder of the flesh/spirit
dichotomy at the center of Tolstoy's own life and spiritual struggles, and a sign
of what he sees as the flawed nature of the Orthodox Church's understanding
of Christ and Christian living. That Nekhliudov could be capable of forcing his
attentions on Maslova on Easter day and seducing her that very night already
indicates that all of the ritual and ceremony of the beautiful Easter Vigil service
have not effected an inner conversion. Indeed, it is the Church's emphasis on
exterior rites to the exclusion of interior states that constitutes what is wrong
with organized religion, according to Tolstoy.

This is a subtle point at this juncture in the novel, but the condemnation of
Orthodox doctrines and dogma soon becomes a shrill polemic, as does Tolstoy's
attack on the body and living what he calls an "animal life." The two are, in fact,
implicitly linked. Orthodox faith in God incarnate as Jesus Christ is tantamount
to reducing the spirit to the flesh, to limiting the limitless God. Tolstoy's point
is that God must remain ineffable, Christ must be distinguished from God,
and both must be divorced from the enterprise of the body and bodily living.
Christ's triumph is precisely that he overcame the temptations and desires of the
flesh in order to serve the spirit, and in this he points the way for the rest of us,
who must also deny our animal selves in order to live according to the spirit.
Here, the contrast between types of love is strongly drawn. Love of the flesh and
sexual love in general—eros in our use of the term—is corrupt and corrupting
in *Resurrection*; only through agapic love—disinterested, unconditional, sacrificial love; the love of enemies—may one discern the nature of God's love and the
source of true life.

In the novel, Tolstoy makes this spirit/animal, agape/eros dichotomy clear
early on in chapter 13's description of Nekhliudov, who has just returned to
his aunts' house as a newly commissioned officer. He is a "completely different
person" from his summer days as a student writing his dissertation: "Then, he
had considered his true self to be found in his spiritual being; now he found
his real ego in a joyous and red-blooded animal existence" (1:13:55). Tolstoy
emphasizes this point a few pages later, explaining how Nekhliudov, "like all
people, consisted of two persons": one spiritual, "seeking benefit for himself only
if it would be a benefit to others": the other, animal, "seeking benefit only for

himself" (1:14:61). On the afternoon of Easter day, the animal self wins, and Nekhliudov, tormented by his lust for Maslova, resolves to seduce her.

Throughout the novel, Tolstoy repeatedly equates satisfying one's physical appetites with living for the animal self, such as when the father of Nekhliudov's fiancée eats with gusto, his face flushed, with "podgy jowls" and "sensual, guzzling lips" (1:26:104). The body as the vessel of the animal self is the source of all evils, Tolstoy proclaims. This truth is asserted most insistently with regard to Maslova. Maslova's full bosom and shapely curves inflame Nekhliudov's passion and continually bring her unwanted attention from lustful men throughout the novel. In an early passage, her body is marked grotesquely as the site of "debauchery with all and sundry" by a Homeric catalogue of all who have sampled her fleshly charms: "young men, middle-aged men, boys just out of childhood and old men disintegrating, married and unmarried, merchants and clerks, Armenians, Jews and Tartars, rich men, poor men, the able and the lame, drunk and sober, boorish and charming, soldiers and civilians, students and schoolboys—men of every class, age and character" (1:2:4). There seems to be no one who has not contributed to Maslova's depravity.

It is hardly a coincidence that shortly after Nekhliudov's recollected seduction scene, both the body and Orthodox conceptions of an incarnate God are the subject of attack by Tolstoy. The attack on the body continues shortly after the flashback when an autopsy report of the internal and external organs of the "bloated and decaying body of the horribly huge, fat merchant" is read out in court—a document as oversized as the poisoned merchant himself. A fitting companion to the catalogue of the grossly used and misused body of Maslova herself, it takes over an hour to read and consists of a gruesome inventory of body parts suffering the effects of poison and decay. Excerpts provided to the reader—"Orifices (nose, both ears and mouth) oozing frothy serous liquid, mouth half open" (1:20:80)—are intended to repulse, for the scene is clearly emblematic. As John Bayley observes, the stench of the merchant's corpse "poisons the air of the whole novel."[36]

To emphasize the connection between the merchant's corpse and Maslova's debauched body as markers of the worst transgression of living for one's animal self—sex—Tolstoy offers us the image of a third body where death as the inevitable consequence of the wages of the flesh is unmistakably linked to sexuality. This image is that of the body of Nekhliudov's mother in a painting in his drawing room:

The painter had made much of her bosom, with a marked cleavage between her breasts, and the dazzling beauty of her shoulders and neck. It was totally vile and mean. There was something revolting, even sacrilegious about this depiction of his mother in her glamorous semi-nudity. It was made even more revolting by the fact that in this same room three months ago that woman had lain here, as desiccated as a mummy and yet emitting a sickening stench which nothing could dispel as it filled not just the room but the whole house. He almost felt he could still smell it. (1:28:115)

The semi-nudity of the portrait immediately reminds Nekhliudov of his fiancée Missy, whom he had seen "in a similar state of near nudity only a day or two ago" when she modeled her new ball gown for him (1:28:115). The memory, like the smell of his mother's dying body, nauseates him.

Throughout the novel, Nekhliudov's chief failure and main temptation is sex—that is, erotic love. His seduction of Maslova is, of course, the raison d'être of the novel and the catalyst for his own conversion process. Like Tolstoy, Nekhliudov discovers that sex is the one aspect of human nature that presents the gravest impediment to moral living. Significantly, Nekhliudov believes that the biggest factor in favor of marrying Missy is that his sexual cravings would have a legitimate outlet: "marriage would put an end to the irregularity of his sex life and create the possibility of living a moral life" (1:4:22). Certainly Missy makes it clear that she is his for the taking. But Nekhliudov's recent encounter in the courtroom has changed him and he cannot look at Missy as anything but a symbol of the power and privileges of his class, a class responsible for the plight of people like Maslova. As a result, he finds himself drifting away from her and her family.

But even as he dedicates himself to helping Maslova and other prisoners similarly wrongly incarcerated (an exercise in agapic love in service of others), Nekhliudov must be on his guard. At his aunt's house, he meets Mariette Chervyanskaya, the wife of an influential prison official known for his harsh punishment of prisoners. Nekhliudov needs Mariette to intercede with her husband on behalf of Lidiia Shustova, a woman incarcerated for her ties to revolutionaries. Mariette is sympathetic, but she is also a coquette, and early in the course of their acquaintance, she and Nekhliudov exchange smiles that betray their attraction to each other. When Mariette comes to visit after her husband has obtained the release of Shustova, the two of them flirt and Nekhliudov is taken in by "the radiant look and glittering eyes which accompanied the words of this elegant and beautiful young woman." An instant sexual tension develops between them: "The real question in their eyes, as they gazed at each other over the murmur of the conversation, was, 'Could you love me?', to which the answer was, 'Yes, I could,' while sexual desire at its most stunning and dazzling drew them together" (2:24:330–31).

After a sleepless night troubled by his attraction to Mariette, Nekhliudov wakes up feeling like he had committed some "foul deed" the night before (2:25:32). He rededicates himself to his activism. Later, seeing Mariette again at the theater, Nekhliudov realizes that she "had nothing to say to him; all she had wanted was for him to see her in all the grandeur of her evening finery, shoulders and mole included, and he felt simultaneously delighted and disgusted" (2:28:346). Leaving the theater that night, Nekhliudov realizes that Mariette is no different from an attractive prostitute he sees strolling down the street, her "whole body exuding an awareness of the despicable power she wielded" (2:28:347). The connection is plain: thus can sex and sexuality make all women into prostitutes, for eros in Tolstoy's universe is the love of seduction and dissipation. Worse still is the fact that society has made of this kind of sexuality an ideal. "Man's animal nature is revolting," Nekhliudov muses. When it "hides itself under a thin cover of poetic charm and pseudo-aestheticism and demands an attitude of worship," it will "swallow you up, and you can't tell good from evil" (2:28:347–48).

Of course, the harsh lessons of depraved sexuality and the perils of living for the animal self are most dramatically played out in Maslova's life. Maslova and her fate in the novel make it clear that sex is an act that is connected to all the evils that afflict humanity. Within very little time, her trade as a prostitute coarsens her and perverts her view of the world. She tells herself that "the greatest blessing for all men, without exception, old and young, schoolboys, generals, educated and uneducated, is sexual intercourse with attractive women, so, though they may pretend to be otherwise occupied, in fact they want this and nothing else." Indeed, "the whole world appeared to her as a collection of men consumed by lust." The conclusion she draws, however, is that "far from being the lowest of the low, she was actually a very important person," as she was the one all of these men wanted the most (1:44:175). It is not until she falls under the influence of imprisoned revolutionaries that she comes to see the error of her understanding. The lesson she learns is one the reader is meant to learn as well: The body is a dead end, whether figured as Maslova's dissolute body, the merchant's corpse, the indecently exposed bodies of Mariette, Nekhliudov's mother, and his fiancée, or, to return to the novel's Christology, even the body of Christ on the crucifixes that hang in public institutions. It, too, is a dead end, for reasons Tolstoy soon makes clear.

Early in the novel, the corpus of Christ on crucifixes or his image in icons or paintings is conspicuously visible where the teachings of Jesus are most disobeyed: in the courtroom where Maslova is being judged (part 1, chapter 7); in the cell where Maslova and other women are being held (part 1, chapters 30 and 32); and in the entrance to the prison itself (part 1, chapter 41). Looking at a huge painting of a crucifix in a prison alcove, Nekhliudov is struck by its inappropriateness: "He couldn't help associating the image of Christ with setting people free rather than locking them up" (1:41:164).

An even greater incongruity regarding the *corpus Christi* is exposed during the Divine Liturgy attended by Maslova and the other prison inmates, where bread and wine are turned into the body and blood of Christ and then consumed. The whole scene is an exercise in Tolstoy's favorite literary device of *ostranenie* or "making strange."[37] Readers are meant to see the Divine Liturgy in the "enstranged" way Natasha views the opera in *War and Peace*, where the suspension of disbelief that is required of the observer is replaced by a naïve, literalist viewpoint: Natasha sees only fat singers in tight stockings warbling and waving their arms in front of two-dimensional stage props. The point of Tolstoy's estrangement device is to see the underlying reality that our "automatic perception" prevents us from seeing. This is how readers are to view the Divine Liturgy, where the narrator similarly refuses to "suspend disbelief" and, like Natasha, reports everything from the perspective of what Donna Orwin aptly calls a "terrible simplifying gaze":[38]

> The essential meaning of the service was the idea that the pieces of bread cut up by the priest and put into the wine would, after special handling and special prayers, be turned into the flesh and blood of God. The special handling involved the priest raising both hands on high, despite being hampered by the brocade sack that he was dressed in, holding them up and then, rhythmically, dropping to his knees and kissing the table and everything on it. But the main action occurred when the priest took hold of a napkin with both hands and wafted it, rhythmically, in one smooth movement, over the dish and the golden chalice. The supposition was that at this moment the bread and the wine became flesh and blood, which meant that this part of the service was invested with a special solemnity. [...] The priest removed the napkin from the dish, cut the middle piece of bread into four, and

put it first into the wine and then into his mouth. He was assumed to have eaten a small piece of God's body and drunk some of his blood (1:39:155–56).

Children, too, receive communion while the deacon sings "a cheerful song" about "eating God's body and drinking his blood." Later, the priest "drank all the blood that was left over and ate up all the bits of God's body," then "scrupulously sucked his moustaches dry" (1:39:156)—the very image of Missy's father eating steak and drinking wine.

Tolstoy's contempt in his depiction of this most sacred moment in the Divine Liturgy is plain—it is, as a matter of fact, what led the Orthodox Church to excommunicate him. This revulsion over the body and its functions, established in the grotesque inventory of the swollen corpse of the dead merchant and linked to the sex act itself, is reaffirmed in his description of "eating God's body" in the Eucharist, a kind of unseemly cannibalism that finds its gruesome reflection in stories Nekhliudov later hears of escaped tramps who resort to cannibalism to survive in the taiga.[39] As with all of Tolstoy's writing, readers are meant to see the pattern of linkages by which sense is made in his fictional universe. In this instance, Tolstoy plainly implies that cannibalism is cannibalism, whether it is tramps in the taiga or Orthodox believers at Divine Liturgy who are committing the act. Tolstoy's Christology simply cannot accept the idea that Jesus is God whose body believers must consume, even mystically.

In truth, Tolstoy's anxiety over the body and his insistence that Christ is a man who triumphed over the flesh in order to serve the spirit are linked and point to the same solution: the renunciation of carnality. To follow Christ is to deny our bodies and live for the spirit, an idea that comes not so much from Jesus Christ as from St. Paul, who develops this notion at length in Romans 8:1–13 and Galatians 5:13–26. When Paul warns "if you live according to the flesh, you will die, but if by the spirit you put to death the deeds of the body, you will live" (Romans 8:13), he is anticipating the philosophical and theological thrust of Tolstoy's own harmonized Gospels, though Tolstoy himself would have been loath to admit it. Tolstoy blamed Paul for distorting Jesus's teachings by linking them with "the pharisaical tradition and by extension all the teachings of the Old Testament." "This very teaching on tradition, this principle of tradition," Tolstoy asserts, "was the main reason that the Christian teaching was distorted and misread."[40] In this way, Tolstoy joins a long list of other thinkers and skeptics who likewise accuse Paul of misrepresenting Jesus's teachings or "inventing" his own Christianity, one that mythologizes and deifies the historical man, Jesus.[41]

Such mythologization is superfluous in Tolstoy's view, for Christ is already an ideal model for perfecting the self, overcoming the flesh, and following God's will; he does not need to be made into a god himself. In perfecting the self and triumphing over the flesh, however, Tolstoy certainly did not have in mind the idea of the divinization of the body, as in the Orthodox concept of *theosis*. This kind of transformation of the body in imitation of Jesus's own transfiguration on Mount Tabor was an idea as fantastic and repulsive as that of the resurrection of the body. Tolstoy's Jesus exemplifies a quite different task. Rather than *divinizing* the flesh, he shows how one must *discipline* it. Thus Tolstoy's Christ, especially in his *Gospel in Brief*, must be more spirit than flesh, even as he is as mortal and non-divine as the rest of humanity.

The task of disassociating the Christ of Tolstoy from that of the Church or traditional Christianity—that is, distinguishing the disembodied Tolstoyan Jesus from the embodied Christian Christ—is undertaken in apophatic fashion in the novel: readers discover who Christ is in the novel by understanding what Christ is *not*. Christ is not to be found in the Jesus preached by the evangelical English missionary who appears late in the novel and whose idea of following Christ is disseminating copies of the Gospel to largely illiterate prisoners. Christ is not to be found in the lives of the privileged classes or the unwashed masses who, if they retain any faith, do not actually *believe* in Christ but rather "believed that this belief had to be believed in" (1:40:160). Finally, Christ is not to be found in the crucifixes, icons, and paintings in courtrooms, prisons, and churches, for Christ in *Resurrection* is neither the God-Man worshiped by Christians whose body and image are so prominently displayed where his teachings are so systematically perverted, nor is he the mortal Jesus of history—the first century Jewish itinerant teacher and philosopher. Christ, it becomes clear in the novel, is not a body in the physical sense at all; he is, rather, the body of teachings that everyone reads but no one follows, "the logos, the understanding [*razumenie*]" as Tolstoy would put it elsewhere.[42] It is this body of teaching that readers encounter in the epigraphs to the novel and that Nekhliudov discovers reading the Gospel of Matthew in his hotel room. This is Tolstoy's Christ—not a God-Man, but a divine preaching.

To follow this Christ, you must first understand that if there is any divinity in Jesus it is in his teachings, not his person; and, second, you must follow this divine teaching, this *Christ*, literally. You must, for instance, do as Christ dictates in Matthew's Gospel: deny yourself, take up your cross and follow him, for as Christ says in Matthew 16:25, "whoever wishes to save his life will lose it, but whoever loses his life for my sake will find it." Nekhliudov is certainly learning this lesson, which is at the very heart of Tolstoy's novel. In losing his life—that is, in renouncing his property and life of privilege and leisure in order to serve God and his fellow human beings—Nekhliudov has surely found it. He has, as the novel's title proclaims, been "resurrected." But his resurrection, of course, is purely figurative, being the marker of his new understanding of his life and how to live it. The notion of resurrection most associated with Christ—that of the body—is, of course, alien to Tolstoy. Thus the novel's title is purposefully ironic. Belief in Christ does not lead to resurrection of the body, for there is no resurrection of the body either in Tolstoy's novel or in his Christianity. There is only renunciation of it.

This renunciation of the body is most bound up with Tolstoy's critique of sexual love, which is, significantly, at the center of the novel's plot, for it is the "love / liubov'" that is, after all, on trial in the novel. Here, again, the opposition between eros and agape is felt acutely and it is a foregone conclusion which kind of love will win out in the novel. The spirit must conquer the body. The ultimate expression and resolution of the theme of sexual love in the novel are figured in the political prisoners Vladimir Simonson and Marya Pavlovna Shchetinina, who both hold sex in contempt. Simonson, who pursues a chaste relationship with Maslova, believes that "propagation is only the lower function of man, his higher function being to serve all life that already exists" (3:4:423–24). For her part, Marya Pavlovna "looked upon it [sex] as something incomprehensible and at the same time repulsive and offensive to human dignity." In fact, a "shared loathing for sexual love" (3:3:422) helps seal the friendship that develops between Marya Pavlovna and Maslova who, in a predictable and thoroughly emblematic move, eventually agrees to a platonic married life with Simonson, turning down Nekhliudov's own marriage proposal to do so. Thus Tolstoy resolves the novel's anxiety over sexual love by renouncing it altogether, freeing Nekhliudov from his own sexual guilt just in time for his spiritual rebirth. Maslova gives up her professional name "Liubov'" for love by another name: agape. In this way she is "resurrected" in the novel. So also must Nekhliudov now seek resurrection by supplanting eros with agape in his own life.

Admittedly, Tolstoy never actually uses the term "resurrection" to describe either Nekhliudov's spiritual transformation or, for that matter, the alteration that takes place in Maslova. Besides the title, it figures only in chapter 39 of part 1, in the satirical description of the Divine Liturgy, where the resurrection of Jesus Christ is mentioned as part of a litany of ridiculous assertions from the Gospel of Mark and the Acts of the Apostles that believers are supposed to believe in. In his *Harmonization of the Gospels*, Tolstoy translates the word as an "awakening to life" (*probuzhdenie zhizni*)[43] and a "restoration to life from death" (*vostanovlenie k zhizni ot smerti*).[44]

And yet there is a problem with the purely metaphorical idea of resurrection in the novel. If Christ is neither the Jesus of history nor the incarnate God but the "understanding of life" (*razumenie zhizni*) of Tolstoy's *Harmonization* and *Gospel in Brief*[45]—that is, a body of divine teachings but not a divine body—then what is to distinguish Christ's teachings from Herbert Spencer's positivist political theory or Henry George's theory of land value tax, both of which formed the basis of Nekhliudov's world outlook in his youth and both of which play a role in his "resurrection"—the awakening of his forgotten self—ten years later? Their role in his resurrection is arguably as big as that which the Gospel of Matthew plays, perhaps bigger, given how transformative Spencer's and George's writings are in Nekhliudov's life. Tolstoy does not indicate how the Gospel of Matthew may change Nekhliudov's life, for the novel ends with Nekhliudov's reading of it. The narrator only says that "a totally new life" is now dawning for Nekhliudov (3:28:510), but whether the Gospel of Matthew is now the center of his life or merely one more "progressive text" spurring on his social and political activism is unclear. Indeed, given the novel's rather positive depiction of political activists and socialist philosophy, it may well be more accurate to conclude that it is actually the spirit of Marx and not Matthew that truly presides over the book's conclusion.

This question is not an idle one, for in the stories of political activists like Simonson, Kryl'tsov, Markel Kondratyev, Nabatov, Marya Pavlovna, and Vera Bogodukhovskaya (ironically, "Faith God-Spirit") in part 3 of the novel, Tolstoy introduces us to characters who have achieved their spiritual "resurrection" through purely political means, without recourse to Christ or the Gospels. "The thing that set the revolutionaries apart," Tolstoy writes, "was their insistence on higher moral standards than those of ordinary people. Abstinence, a spartan lifestyle, honesty and altruism were taken for granted, as was their readiness to sacrifice everything, even life itself, for the common good" (3:5:429). Maslova, too, significantly completes her spiritual transformation "without [ever] reading the Gospels," as Viktor Shklovsky points out.[46] In fact, it is the political activists who most influence her, not Nekhliudov and certainly not Christ. She calls them "wonderful people" and thanks God for the prison sentence that has brought her into contact with them (3:3:420).

The point is, it is not surprising that the novel's scripture citations at the beginning and the end of the book have a "tacked on," superfluous feeling to them (as Anton Chekhov pointed out[47]), for Maslova and Tolstoy's "good revolutionaries" are people who live in an enlightened state of "resurrection" or *razumenie* that has nothing to do with the Gospels or Christ at all. To be sure, Tolstoy does not hide his disdain for "bad" revolutionaries like the power-hungry Novodvorov, who is narrow-minded and vain and whose "moral quality" is "well below average" (3:15:458–59). But the majority of the revolutionaries described in the novel are either tragic victims of tsarist oppression or admirable idealists.

By the end of the novel, then, Tolstoy has painted himself somewhat into a corner. His disdain for the "animal self" has become a fear of the body. The body must be disciplined in order to avoid the terrible fate that awaits it, emphasized grotesquely by the merchant's bloated corpse and the stinking mummified body of Nekhliudov's dying mother—the end point of all who live for the body, be they indecently exposed mothers and daughters, fornicating prostitutes, or bestial men eating red meat and seducing women. One must forsake living for the body, take up the cross and follow Christ instead, who, now revealed through the novel's apophatic theology, is neither the Jesus of history nor the incarnate God but a body of divine teachings. And yet, as a body of divine teachings, the Gospels are hardly different from other "sacred" documents in the novel, such as Marx's *Das Kapital* or Herbert Spencer's political philosophy. They are all writings that are apparently equally capable of bringing one to the kind of personal enlightenment Tolstoy celebrates in his novel.

Thus Tolstoy's apophaticism is problematic. If Christ is not God and God is but a vague feeling of well-being and moral rightness that comes over Nekhliudov in moments when he lives in accord with his conscience, then there is not only room in the novel for other moral compasses but the distinct possibility of doing away with God altogether. Moreover, if it is Nekhliudov's "socially acquired structure of desires"[48] that is to blame for his serving the animal self, then the environment in which those desires are structured must be altered, hence the novel's flirtation with Marxism. Building the Kingdom of God, in the novel and elsewhere in Tolstoy's writings, means not only changing yourself but ultimately changing society as well. Thus, in the end it is not just resurrection, but insurrection (not *voskresenie* but *vosstanie*) that is necessary, or so Tolstoy comes close to saying by novel's end. Here the novel's apophatic theology is unexpectedly cast upon the hard rocks of radical materialism in a way that threatens to undo it.

An endorsement of Marxist revolution was, of course, hardly Tolstoy's intention in writing *Resurrection* but it was certainly on his mind as he wrote. In the years he was composing the novel, Tolstoy left an ongoing record of his reflections on socialism, revolution, Marx, Spencer, and George in his diaries and letters. Generally speaking, Tolstoy was wary of the possibility of real political change. In a February 26, 1889, diary entry, he wrote: "There can be no political change of the social system. The only change can be a moral one, within men and women."[49] Furthermore, in a diary entry nine years later (August 3, 1898), Tolstoy expresses his doubts about Marxist revolution with uncanny prescience: "Even if what Marx predicts were to happen," he wrote, "then the only thing that would happen would be that despotism would be transferred. Now the capitalist are in power; then the workers' bosses would be in power."[50] Be that as it may, shortly after the events of 1905 and half a decade after completing *Resurrection*, Tolstoy seems to exhibit a change in his thinking about revolution. In a letter to Ernest Crosby, he writes (in English): "As to the disturbances that are going on now, they are only the precursors of the great revolution which I hope will begin at once everywhere and will consist in the annihilation of state power."[51] Thus six years after publishing *Resurrection*, Tolstoy actually seems to be sympathetic to the idea of revolution.

Regarding Nekhliudov's other guiding influences—Herbert Spencer and Henry George—Tolstoy expressed differing assessments. He liked George but did not care for Spencer. "I'm not an admirer of Spencer," he wrote in a 1904 letter, citing a lack of any *"grandes pensées"* (great thoughts) in his work.[52] To Nikolai Strakhov in 1891 he complained that Spencer is "wasted on me. I'd quite forgotten the effect Spencer makes on me, but in trying to read this pamphlet through I felt many times what I used to feel: not boredom, but depression, dejection and the physical impossibility of reading a single page more."[53]

Tolstoy was of an entirely opposite opinion of Henry George, whose single tax system he promoted in life as in his novel. "The more I know of him, the more I esteem him," he wrote in an 1894 letter to Crosby, "and am astonished at the indifference of the civilized world to his work."[54] Nekhliudov's desire to institute a single tax system on his estates in part 2 of the novel is surely an attempt on Tolstoy's part to further George's ideas in Russia.[55] Here the reader discovers one reason why Nekhliudov's "resurrection" is as much a political awakening as it is a spiritual one, for Tolstoy clearly intended his novel to be a vehicle for the airing of his own views on the problems ailing his country and the various ways—political, social, and spiritual—those ills might be cured. *Resurrection* as a novel was never intended to be solely a disquisition on Tolstoy's religious views.

Thus readers expecting to find a "resurrection" in a religious sense or an encounter with the Christ of faith discover, instead, that the novel is also a *political* conversion story as well as an encounter with economists and materialist philosophers. Rather than explicating the "practical religion which does not promise future happiness but gives happiness on earth," Tolstoy's final novel at times comes close to being a political tract in novel form. The reason for this outcome is not hard to discover. Into the empty apophatic space of Tolstoy's search for Christ and God, other figures rush in, as in a vacuum: Karl Marx, Herbert Spencer, and Henry George. Nekhliudov may be reading the Gospel of Matthew at novel's end, but the writings of Marx, Spencer, and George also distinctly attend his resurrection. The Gospel, it turns out in Tolstoy's last novel, is as much a radical political document as Marx's *Das Kapital*, which the revolutionary Markel Kondratyev devours so voraciously in the novel. While Tolstoy may not have realized it, his novel's apophatic theology had managed to inscribe Jesus Christ into the revolution, albeit some two decades ahead of the fact. When Alexander Blok put Christ at the head of a rag-tag band of Red soldiers in his poem "The Twelve," he was but completing the gesture Tolstoy had unwittingly begun in his sunset novel, *Resurrection*.

THE CENTURY OF BELIEF
Christ in Twentieth-Century Russian Literature

And so they keep a martial pace
Behind them follows the hungry dog,
Ahead of them—with bloody banner,
Unseen within the blizzard's swirl,
Safe from any bullet's harm
With gentle step, above the storm,
In the scattered, pearl-like snow
Crowned with a wreath of roses white,
Ahead of them—goes Jesus Christ.

Alexander Blok, "The Twelve," January 1918, trans. Maria Carlson

The growth of secularism in Russia had its dramatic crowning moment in the 1917 revolution, the ultimate confirmation of the triumph of unbelief in Russia. The fascinating thing about this outcome is that it happened in a nation with a unified national Orthodox creed and a nearly thousand-year history of belief—the confirmation, perhaps, of Dostoevsky's premise that the line between fervent faith and militant atheism is very fine indeed, that the conditions that foster belief can just as easily give rise to a virulent atheism in sometimes sudden and unexpected ways. Looking at the Soviet century, however, it is tempting to make the opposite argument: that militant atheism eventually gave rise to a resurrected faith in the USSR among intellectuals and writers pushing back against an increasingly totalitarian government. Indeed, one might even argue that the Soviet Union as an officially atheist state where the Church was persecuted and belief was ridiculed actually became the perfect negative space from which, in apophatic fashion, writers could discern anew the nature of faith in the absence of positive cultural conceptualizations of belief. In truth, of course, the relationship between belief and unbelief in the Soviet century is more complex than such a neat formulation might imply. For one thing, the Soviet government soon made a state religion out of ideology complete with sacred foundational narratives and a gallery of secular saints. For another, the teachings and life of Christ himself helped to inspire adherence to the revolutionary cause, as Alexander Blok confirmed when he put Jesus Christ at the head of twelve Bolshevik revolutionaries in his famous poem.

The path that led to the appearance of Jesus Christ there began in the waning years of the century of unbelief, a period in Russian culture enigmatically referred to as *bezvremen'e*—literally, "timelessness," but here designating a period of cultural and social stagnation. Blok chose this word as the title for one of his first prose articles in 1906, a meditation on Russian society and culture at a crossroads. Where before "nature, art and literature" had been valued and protected, Blok writes, now people had given up on the muses, devoted all their time to work and petty pursuits and, "proceeding along a path of languor, gradually lost first God, then the world and finally themselves."[1]

Blok's indictment of his age is both the summation of a fin-de-siècle malaise afflicting Russian society and the anticipation of some kind of cataclysmic rupture. Thus, the century of belief in Russian literature was born amid a sense of social and cultural collapse and impending apocalypse, the culmination of the last fitful decades of the century of unbelief. Society had lost its faith in both Orthodoxy and literature as repositories of the answers to life's questions. The Church was beset by rival heterodox belief systems—including Tolstoy's anarchic Christianity, various Orthodox sects (Skoptsy, Khlysts, Dukhobors, Molokans) that persisted into the twentieth century, as well as different strains of Protestantism—and was under assault from radicals and materialists who pronounced the death of God and railed against clerical indifference to social inequality and injustice.

As the giants of Russian realism either died (Dostoevsky a month before Alexander II's assassination in 1881, Turgenev two years later) or absented themselves from the literary scene (Tolstoy after *Anna Karenina*), new authors appeared responding to the demands of an increasingly more literate society for works of a popular, diverting nature. Small genres—short stories, sketches, and novellas—proliferated, while thick idea novels addressing the cursed questions disappeared from the scene. According to the critic Mikhail Menshikov in an 1891 article, literature in the last decades of the nineteenth century lost "its former significance as a guider of souls." Russians now read mainly to be distracted.[2] The close of the century of unbelief was a time of the "redundancy of old forms" and the "madly pressured search for new ones" capable of "moving society forward" and bringing about "its rebirth through prophetic supplication."[3] Realism was no longer adequate to the tasks at hand. A different, more exalted art was needed, and its first herald was the forefather of Russian Symbolism, Dmitry Merezhkovsky, who, in a series of lectures, helped plot the path back to Jesus Christ.

The Symbolists and Jesus Christ

Merezhkovsky's 1892 lectures titled "On the Reasons for the Present Decline and the New Tendencies in Contemporary Russian Literature" marked the beginning of what would soon become the Symbolist movement in Russia. Often called the first manifesto of Russian Symbolism, Merezhkovsky's essay is a wide-ranging appraisal of how the dominant strains of positivism and materialism in society had brought Russian literature to a crisis. It is against this materialism that Merezhkovsky aims his essay. The main ailment of Russian literature and Russian society is one and the same, according to Merezhkovsky, and it is essentially a spiritual ailment. Merezhkovsky identifies the philosophical battle lines as between "the most extreme materialism and also the most passionate idealism. [...] The supreme demands of religious feeling are colliding with the recent findings of empirical science." Or, as he puts it a few sentences earlier: "Never before have people so felt in their hearts the need to believe and understood with their minds the impossibility of belief."[4]

In Merezhkovsky's assessment, it was Dostoevsky and Tolstoy who lent Russian literature its mysticism (540). Here, Merezhkovsky sees the "beginning of a new idealism" in Russian literature, thanks to which a "mystical feeling has invaded the bounds of precise empirical experimentations" (535–36). According to Merezhkovsky, this new idealism is already blossoming in French symbolism, whose language of allusion, symbolic elements, and air of inaccessibility point the way toward a mystical, revelatory art capable of disclosing spiritual truths. The poet was no longer just a writer, but a high priest and seer.

Merezhkovsky cites the famous line from Fyodor Tyutchev's 1830 poem "Silentium"—"a thought expressed is a lie"—as a reminder of the limits of language in the new idealism and the need for a heightened impressionism. Valery Bryusov advanced this idea—and the cause of the fledgling symbolist movement—in his own early writings, declaring that the poetic language of Pushkin was no longer adequate to the realities of fin-de-siècle Russia. Though the poems he published in three volumes in 1894 and 1895 under the title *Russian Symbolists*—his own and others'—were better known for their shock value than their poetic mastery, Bryusov's intent was to create a new kind of poetic language and, along the way, to found a new literary movement. In his seminal 1904 article "The Keys to the Mysteries," he laid out his theory of art as a method of cognition in which the artist records the fleeting insights granted by moments of nonrational epiphany. Though he criticized the mystical aspects of Symbolism as early as 1894, he nevertheless set as the task of art the revelation of the "concealed essence" of the artist's soul,[5] thus revealing the Symbolist interest in an "inner or transcendent, Ideal realm" that "betrays a continued yearning for religious or quasi-religious belief."[6]

In truth, a mystical tendency characterizes both early and later phases of Russian Symbolism and its practitioners, just as an interest in decadent self-absorption, pessimism, and perversion—characteristic of the first generation of Russian Symbolists (roughly, 1894–1906)—can be found in the works of the second generation (1906–1917). Russian Symbolism, never a uniform movement, was a gathering place for those highly diverse and talented artists who rejected the "reign of positive science" and the conventions and morality of bourgeois society of the dying century in favor of a transcendental world just beyond the five senses.[7]

In responding to their age, the Russian Symbolists veered from decadent or morbid meditations on debased urban life to evocations of a higher spiritual reality or expressions of apprehension over a future cataclysmic event in Russia's history. Apocalypticism dominated the turn of the century in Russia, and often took the form of an anticipated catastrophic conflict between Europe and Asia, with Russia as the central battlefield. Vladimir Solovyov's 1894 poem "Pan-Mongolism" was the first to image the apocalypse in Russia as another Mongol conquest. Bryusov and Blok followed suit with their own versions of an Asian-themed invasion, Bryusov writing "The Coming Huns" under the influence of political unrest in 1905 and Blok composing "Scythians" a few months after the October Revolution in 1917.

Fellow Symbolist writers Dmitry Merezhkovsky and Andrei Bely shared similar eschatological preoccupations, but responded in different ways to the impending Armageddon: Merezhkovsky, by championing a kind of apocalyptic Christianity; Bely, by turning to a Solovyovian theosophy that later gave way to the anthroposophy of Rudolf Steiner. For his part, Blok—the least philosophical of the three—promoted an eclectic mysticism that was soon replaced by a gloomy and misanthropic view of a world out of joint.[8] All three of them represent a turning away from the century of unbelief on some level even as two of them—Bely and Blok—embraced the revolution that would eventually install the first officially atheist state in the world.

Belief, however, can be understood in more ways than one, as the esoteric spiritual quests of the Symbolists or the utopian visions of the revolutionary movements in Russia made clear. Bely insisted that there was a religious aspect to the Bolshevik Revolution itself and he was far from alone in holding that conviction. For his part, Merezhkovsky saw in political upheaval the opportunity for a "religious revolution," one that would usher in a post-apocalyptic Christian anarchic society without government, laws, or violence.[9] Blok understood the imminent destruction of the Old World intelligentsia in the fires of the revolution as a kind of moral and mystical atonement for past sins—part of Holy Russia's self-immolation necessary for its purification and rebirth. Certainly there were no greater true believers than the architects of the new Soviet order. Their revolution replaced religion with a new secular mythology that in the span of some fifteen years produced the cults of Lenin and Stalin, whose lives, ideas, and place in history were raised to a quasi-divine status. Thus the revival of spiritual, idealist, and religious thought in fin-de-siècle Russian modernism prepared the ground for a century in which belief as such was very much in the air. Indeed, Blok and Bely responded to the revolution with poems that grappled with the image of Christ, seeking in the chief figure of the Christian apocalypse a means for expressing the essence of the apocalypse of their times.

Bely wrote his long poem "Christ Is Risen" in April 1918, during the time between the February and October revolutions when hopes for a better future were highest. Comprised of some twenty-four stanzas, it is a treatment of Jesus's life, beginning with his baptism in the river Jordan and ending with his crucifixion and resurrection. At the same time, however, Bely also inscribes scenes from contemporary revolutionary Russia into his Christ narrative. Beginning in stanza 15, Russia appears as a trampled-down country, but one hearing the tidings of its imminent resurrection: the revolution. In the next stanza, steam engines, rain showers, and telegraph ribbons all proclaim: "Long live the Third International!" (a full year before it was even constituted). In following stanzas, the dry crackling of revolver shots sound out over the words of the "enfeebled intelligentsia"; steamships sing about the brotherhood of nations; machine guns fire their rounds; and the revolution enacts its great mystery. By poem's end, Russia is likened to the woman clothed with the sun from the book of Revelation, and the baptism of Jesus with which the poem opens now breaks upon the heads of "all of us." In the wake of this baptism, the fierce storms of spring—in place of the Holy Spirit—breathe God's favor on everyone, and a voice cries out: "Beloved sons, Christ is risen!"

Bely's poem reflects its author's revolutionary and religious messianism, which saw in Russia's sufferings a Golgotha necessary for the ultimate salvation of the country. Christ was resurrected in Russia in the guise of the revolution, which proclaimed a "new Gospel amid storm and blood."[10] Blok's poem, by contrast, was a brilliant, innovative, and controversial evocation of the times, far superior to Bely's but much more ambiguous in its declarations, whether on the revolution, Jesus Christ, or the relation of one to the other. Stylistically, the poem is an impressive amalgam of urban street slang, revolutionary rhetoric, Church archaisms, and folk ditties (*chastushki*), punctuated by moments of elevated poetic diction. Thematically, it is a collision of seemingly disparate subjects. It is at once an ideological caricature of the remnants of the Old World (a potbellied priest, a rich lady in furs, a long-haired writer, a down-at-the-heels bourgeois and his mangy dog); a depiction of a love triangle that ends in murder (the Katka-Vanka-Petrukha story); an allegory of the elemental storm of the revolution figured in the image of an all-encompassing blizzard; and a parable that ends with an affirmation of Jesus Christ, who enacts a kind of second coming in the retributive violence of the revolution.

The central action of "The Twelve" focuses on the love triangle. A ragtag band of twelve Red Army Guardsmen are marching through Petrograd in a blizzard, reveling in their liberation from the bonds of Church and state and intent on defending the revolution by "putting a bullet into Holy Rus." Almost immediately they get sidetracked by news that their comrade Petrukha's girl, Katka, has taken up with Vanka, a soldier for the other side. Seven of the twelve cantos of the poem relate the story and aftermath of the violent confrontation between Petrukha and Vanka in which Katka gets shot through the head by a stray bullet from Petrukha's rifle. Vanka escapes, and the band of soldiers continues its march through the streets, the violent act rationalized as a trivial event in the context of the cause they serve and, indeed, even emboldening them to continue their lawless looting of the capital while on patrol. As the poem ends, the soldiers continue their patrol night and day, with the storm intensifying at every step, both hiding and revealing a figure in the swirling snow ahead of them, who is waving a red banner. Attempts to get the figure to halt by threat or rain of bullets are of no avail and so the soldiers are forced to continue marching behind the figure, who is revealed by the narrator in the poem's last line to be none other than Jesus Christ, "crowned with a wreath of roses white." Thus in one stroke the squad of soldiers is ostensibly transformed from a gang of twelve looters into a brotherhood of twelve disciples.

Blok's poem was greeted with indignation on both ends of the ideological spectrum. Believers considered the late insertion of Christ into the poem blasphemous; Bolsheviks deemed Jesus's appearance there superfluous and dangerously retrograde. While the controversy the poem evoked was inevitable, Jesus's association with the Bolshevik Guardsman was hardly a startling Christological development. Belinsky had insisted a half century before Blok's poem that Christ's allegiance, were he alive, would be to the cause of socialism. Many Russian revolutionaries of the second half of the nineteenth century—Andrei Zheliabov, Vera Zasulich, and Vera Figner, to name a few—drew inspiration from the life, teachings, and self-sacrifice of Jesus Christ, even as they renounced his divinity and the Church that taught it.[11] At his trial in 1881 for helping to organize the assassination of Alexander II, Zheliabov defiantly evoked Christ in his defense: "I deny Orthodoxy, though I affirm the essence of the teachings of Jesus Christ. The essence of his teaching was my primary moral incentive."[12] Egor Sazonov, who assassinated Minister of the Interior Vyacheslav von Plehve in 1904, declared that his "revolutionary and socialist beliefs became fused with [his] religion" and that "socialists are continuing the cause of Christ, who preached brotherly love among people and died for the people as a common criminal."[13] Thus, Christ or his image were never far from the revolutionary cause in Russia.

For his part, Blok had no doubts about his decision to include Christ in his poem, asserting in a March 10 diary entry six weeks after finishing "The Twelve" that the fact that "Christ is with the Red Guardsman" should be clear to anyone who has read the Gospel and thought about it: "I merely stated a fact: if one looks into the columns of the snowstorm *on this path*, one sees Jesus Christ."[14] In truth, the image of Christ had been on Blok's mind in the weeks preceding the composition of his poem as he contemplated a new drama about Jesus.[15] When he depicted his own Jesus in "The Twelve," however, he was not entirely happy with the outcome, confessing in his March 10 diary entry that he sometimes deeply hated "this feminine phantom" he had created.

Blok's conflicted attitude toward his image of Christ reflects the ambiguity of the poem itself. What, after all, is Jesus's place there, in the poem and in the revolution? Does the idea of "Christ with the Red Guardsmen" represent an image of a Renanian Jesus: a mortal paragon of moral authority fighting for human justice, in other words, Jesus as a political activist? Or is Jesus "crowned with white roses" merely a metaphor for the sanctification of the upheaval and suffering Russia is experiencing along the lines of Bely's poem? Why does Blok or the revolution even need Christ?

JESUS, LENIN, AND THE REVOLUTION

In his 1924 study *Literature and Revolution*, which devotes an entire chapter to Blok, Leon Trotsky—Marxist theorist and founder and first leader of the Red Army—suggests an answer. "Christ belongs in no way to the Revolution, only to Blok's past," he writes.[16] "The Twelve" is "not a poem of the Revolution" at all, but "the swan song of the individualistic art that went over to the Revolution." And the appearance of Jesus in the poem is simply an attempt by Blok "to save the artistic image of Christ by propping it up with the Revolution" (119). Blok, Trotsky explains, "gravitated in two directions, the mystic and the revolutionary," unable to commit to either (118). Therefore, he concludes, "Blok is not one of us, but he reached toward us" (125).

The same might be said of Jesus. Though Lenin famously stated that belief in God was a kind of necrophilia,[17] there was nothing preventing prominent Bolsheviks—among them, Alexander Bogdanov and Anatolii Lunacharsky, the first commissar of enlightenment—from claiming the Jesus of history as a distant forerunner of the present revolution.[18] Lunacharsky called Jesus "a unique leader of the proletarian masses of Galilee, a proletarian hero, a teacher of great love and also of great hatred," a position he seems to have adhered to from 1908 to 1927, when his views on the subject changed dramatically.[19] Indeed, it was Bogdanov, Lunacharsky, and Maxim Gorky who in the inter-revolutionary years sought to add a metaphysical aspect to Marxism by attributing divine aspects to the proletarian program.

Known as "God-building" (*bogostroitel'stvo*), the idea was a product of the Orthodox culture against which these thinkers agitated and of the Promethean impulse of Bolshevism that had been growing in the decades before the revolution. Rather than strive toward the divinization of the body in imitation of the God-Man Jesus Christ, the God-builders sought to instill in people a belief in the perfectibility of human beings through non-supernatural means. The movement was a reaction to the "God-seekers" (*bogoiskateli*) who gathered around Merezhkovsky and his wife, Zinaida Gippius, at the turn of the century, advocating a new religious consciousness. Lunacharsky hoped to channel what was good about religion—its emotional resonance, inspirational qualities, moral emphasis, and sense of higher purpose—into his own secular variant that would grant the revolution a distinct religious character. God incarnated as Jesus Christ no longer pointed the way to eternal life; the Man-God would achieve immortality through scientific and collective means.[20]

The belief that human reason and science could serve as the means by which all of humanity's problems might eventually be solved was a common article of faith among radical materialists in the nineteenth century and it became the dominant vision of the Soviet century as well. Traditional religion and belief in God were incompatible with human reason and the new Bolshevik state. Almost immediately after the revolution, therefore, the Bolsheviks launched a campaign against the Church that resulted in the confiscation and defacement of Church property, the arrest and execution of priests (by the 1930s, the number reached into the tens of thousands), the prohibition of the publication of religious materials, and the closing of seminaries and monasteries.

At the same time, however, and somewhat paradoxically as Mark Steinberg points out, the conditions of the revolution itself "nurtured religion and a religious spirit," due largely to the "revolutionary enthusiasms, expectations, and vision stimulated by the revolution and by Bolshevik radicalism."[21] That the cause of revolution should be perceived as a kind of religion was a truth that dated back in Russia to Alexander Herzen, and those who pursued it often did so with the fervor of true believers. Some of the religious feelings associated with the revolution were a direct outcome of the apocalypticism that accompanied the turn of the century and the mystical dread it inspired. The persistence of the religious spirit was also quite prominent in the peasant and working classes, who still felt the need for ritual and sacred symbols in their lives, especially in light of all the upheavals that revolution had brought.

The state responded to the vacuum left by the suppression of organized religion with the trappings of its own faith. "Octobering" rituals were developed to replace baptisms. Red weddings and red funerals were established to take the place of church ones. State holidays replaced religious feast days in the Soviet calendar. The role of religion in regulating personal conduct was supplanted by an increasing emphasis on physical hygiene and moral conduct in posters, newspapers, and official pronouncements. Streets and cities were renamed, establishing a new pantheon of Soviet heroes, martyrs, and saints. Religious metaphors were often deployed in revolutionary contexts (references to the cross, crucifixion, and Golgotha being the most prominent).[22] And a growing cult of Lenin developed, well before his early demise in 1924.

The father of the 1917 revolution and its protector during the ensuing Civil War, Lenin was not just respected and admired, but loved and praised. His fiftieth birthday in April 1920 was a national celebration, complete with portraits, posters, new biographies (one in a massive edition of 200,000 copies), and poetic odes. Vladimir Mayakovsky read his poetic tribute honoring Lenin on April 28, 1920. It was first published in *Krasnaia gazeta* on November 5, 1922, and established the quasi-religious tones that would soon be used to describe Lenin: "Who can restrain himself / and not sing / of the glory of Ilich? [...] / Kindling the lands with fire / everywhere, / where people are imprisoned, / like a bomb / the name / explodes: / Lenin! / Lenin! / Lenin! [...] / I glorify / in Lenin / world faith / and glorify / my faith."[23]

The religious language here is not at all unexpected. There was always the sense that the socialist cause was the one true holy cause of humanity. The influence of religious forms and themes can be readily seen in posters and leaflets of the Civil War period, many of which evoked old Russian icons in their compositions.[24] Similar feelings were stirred by Lenin himself. As Nina Tumarkin reports in her study on the Lenin cult, the assassination attempt on Lenin in 1918 provoked the first wave of overt myth-making.[25] By 1920, the writer Maxim Gorky noted that Lenin was becoming "a legendary figure" who in a previous epoch of religious fervor "would have been considered a saint." For Gorky, however, this was a good thing, for "the domain of civil activity has always produced more truly saintly people, if by saintliness we understand honest and fearless service in the interests of the people, of liberty, and truth."[26] Three years later, as Lenin recuperated from his first major stroke but well before his death, the first "Lenin corner" (*Leninskii ugolok*) modeled on the icon corner of the Russian home appeared, aimed at supplanting this traditional place of honor that still existed in many peasant homes and instilling in the peasant an attitude of reverence toward the leader. Efforts to bolster the leader's image during his slow recovery soon devolved into blatant cult making, over the objections of Lenin's family.

Lenin's death in January 1924 became the defining moment in the cult that had grown up around him. Not only were there proposals and demands that various institutions and the city of Petrograd itself take the name of Lenin, but the religious rhetoric used to describe the leader heightened dramatically. The editor of the newspaper *Izvestiia* (News) declared that Lenin's name had "entered the church calendar."[27] The poet Mayakovsky invoked the form of the Christian Mystery of Faith— "Christ has died, Christ is risen, Christ will come again"—in a poem published on the occasion of Lenin's death, proclaiming: "Lenin lived, Lenin lives, Lenin will live."[28] A poster with this communist "mystery of faith" written next to an image of a prophet-like Lenin soon became one of the most ubiquitous icons of the leader. As Richard Stites puts it, after his death, Lenin provided "the missing face of the workers' God."[29]

Over the objections of Lenin's widow and prominent Bolsheviks such as Trotsky, Lev Kamenev, and Nikolai Bukharin, Lenin's funeral took on such qua-si-religious aspects (including palm branches adorning the hall where he lay in state) that, according to Jay Bergman, it was hard not to miss "the suggestion that the founder of the Soviet state bore at least some resemblance to the founder of Christianity."[30] The defining moment in the canonization of the leader, however, was the decision to preserve Lenin's body and keep it on permanent display in a specially built mausoleum on Red Square. While a mummified body is not the same thing as a divinized one, the idea to put Lenin's body on display does have a corollary in the Russian Orthodox Church, which held that the miraculous incorruptibility of the body of a saint was an important marker of sanctity. Joseph Stalin seemed to hint at this connection when he suggested that Lenin be buried in a "Russian" manner, taking up Leonid Krasin's idea to preserve and display the body.[31]

For Krasin, there was more than just a symbolic reason to preserve Lenin's body. Like Gorky and Lunacharsky, Krasin had at one time been an outspoken adherent of God-building and, whether the idea of displaying Lenin's body was intended as such or not, Lenin's death provided a perfect opportunity for a very public articulation of the God-building impulse in the young Soviet state. Krasin went further, however. To his God-building, he added the belief—based on the ideas of Russian "Cosmist" philosopher Nikolai Fedorov—in scientifically based resurrection of the dead. Krasin's hope was that Lenin's body could be preserved until such time as science could figure out a way to reanimate or "resurrect" him.[32] As late as 1921, Krasin declared, "I am certain that the time will come when science will become all-powerful, that it will be able to recreate a deceased organism [...] to use the elements of a person's life to recreate the physical person."[33] As George Young notes in his study of the Russian Cosmists, "If Christ was the firstborn of the mythical resurrection, Lenin, waiting in his glass coffin, would be the first resurrected by science."[34] Though Krasin's Funeral Commission reconstituted itself as the Immortalization Commission, no reanimation was attempted. Instead, some seven months after Lenin died, the Immortalization Commission announced that they had successfully preserved Lenin's body. On August 1, 1924, the grand opening of the Lenin Mausoleum was held. The century of belief had begun in Soviet Russia.

While the Lenin cult was temporarily eclipsed by the cult of Stalin, it presided over nearly the entire history of the Soviet state. Lenin was communism's symbol and its saint. Lenin busts small and massive, Lenin portraits, photos, and posters, Lenin badges, and Lenin's words constituted the forms and catechism of a new state religion. The paradox, of course, is that this state religion was based not on the one who believers claim was resurrected and lives, but on the one whose plainly dead body was on permanent public display in Red Square. Though turned into a sacred relic, Lenin's body nevertheless marked the heart of Soviet power as a grave.[35] And that ultimately is a problem, especially for the iconography of Lenin. At worst, Lenin had been turned into an inanimate object and trivialized by the mass reproduction of his image in kitschy artifacts, the epitome of the dead end of the materialist philosophy of the Soviet Union. At best, he had been made into a mere abstraction, the symbol of the ideas and ideals of communism but as unreal as the heroic renditions of him that increasingly departed from photographs of the short, unremarkable looking man.

Paradoxical as well is Lenin's presence in Soviet literature. Even as a cult figure and the founding father and symbol of Soviet communism and despite the associations made between him and Christ, Lenin never seemed to appeal to the creative imaginations of Soviet writers the way Jesus continued to do, well into the Soviet period. The overpowering personality cult of Stalin, which originated in celebrations of his fiftieth birthday in 1928–1929 and flourished until his death in March 1953, certainly played a pronounced role in curbing and controlling Lenin's legacy and his prominence. While Stalin cited Lenin liberally during his rise to power and afterward to promote his own political fortunes, it soon became clear who the object of active veneration truly was: Stalin himself.

Lenin's image, writings, and legacy, though ubiquitous and foundational, were equaled if not superseded in significance by the ongoing quasi-deification of Stalin over the next twenty-five years. In the meantime, the image of Christ glimpsed at the head of Blok's Red Guardsmen continued to haunt Soviet literature, even as attempts to put Lenin and Stalin in his place in the minds of the populace continued apace.

CHRIST IN SOVIET LITERATURE TO *DOCTOR ZHIVAGO*

Given the religious ambience of the two decades preceding the revolution and the pseudo-religious aspects associated with the revolution itself, it is hardly surprising to encounter literary references to Jesus Christ in the first decade of the Soviet state. Mark Steinberg describes pervasive references to Christ and Christian imagery among pro-Bolshevik proletarian writers in the years immediately following the revolution. Typical images in the creative visions of the revolution that he describes include "the crucified people, a promise of deliverance from suffering, an apocalyptic final battle, a reunion between the living and the dead, and the coming of a new age."[36] The only sustained literary Christology—Bulgakov's *Master and Margarita*—would not be written until the 1930s and then not published for nearly three decades thereafter. However, Jesus figures importantly if fleetingly in works by some of the most important authors of the 1920s.

Not surprisingly, references to Jesus in works written after the revolution are almost uniformly parodic. Evgeny Zamyatin's imaging of Christ is a case in point. Heresy was Zamyatin's holy writ as well as the reason for his rebellion as a young man against the Church and its doctrines and dogmas (he later published scathing satires of Orthodoxy after the death of his father, a parish priest and teacher of religious education). His heretical inclinations are also what made him problematic in the eyes of the Soviet state. He quit the Communist Party shortly after the revolution and was arrested twice, in 1919 and 1922, on suspicion of involvement in counterrevolutionary activity. Partly for these reasons, his novel *We*, completed in 1920, was not allowed to be published in the Soviet Union until 1988 (an English translation in 1924 constituted its debut).

If a heretical outlook is a core element of the writer's personality, it is also the central theme of *We*, which chronicles the attempts of a band of revolutionaries fighting the oppressive One State of a distant future Russia ruled over by a godlike Benefactor. The revolutionaries—known as the Mephi (from Mephistopheles, the tempter in the Faust legend)—try to recruit the main engineer of the government's *Integral* project, a rocket ship meant to subjugate the inhabitants of distant worlds to the "beneficent yoke of reason" and "compulsory happiness" of the One State (1).[37] The Mephi want to seize the *Integral* for their own purposes. The central conflict in the novel pits the mathematically regulated but dead "perfection" of the One State against the unfettered freedom of the lightly furred denizens living beyond the Green Wall. The whole story is told through the diary entries of the engineer, D-503, a true believer from whom readers learn about the One State's laws, rituals, and principles but whose allegiance to the government is sorely tested.

Though scientific socialism, war communism, and the rationalization of labor are the overt targets of Zamyatin's satire, Christianity is also singled out for criticism as a distant precursor of the One State. D-503 calls Christians his "imperfect predecessors" and gives them credit for the collectivist precept so cardinal to the One State: "'We' is from God, and 'I' from the devil" (128). Elsewhere, I-330, the revolutionary agent in charge of recruiting D-503, identifies herself and her fellow revolutionaries as "anti-Christians" (165). As if to underscore the extent of the correspondence between Christianity and the One State, D-503 likens the annual Day of Unanimity (in which the Benefactor is unanimously reelected as leader) to Easter. It is the most important day of the year, in which the Benefactor is celebrated as "the new Jehovah" (140–41) and the One State is likened to "the Church, one and indivisible" (137). Indeed, at one point the Benefactor even reveals to D-503 the secret meaning of Christ's crucifixion. According to the Benefactor, the God who allowed his own son to be put to death and who consigns to the fires of hell all of those who do not submit to his laws is a cruel God. In being a cruel God, however, he confirms for the Benefactor that the "true, algebraic love of humanity is inevitably inhuman" (213), a lesson D-503 must learn himself if he is to play the role of the "obedient son" of the One State.

This theme is supported by D-503's status as an unlikely Christ figure himself, whose Christological associations are easy to spot.[38] His forty diary entries chronicling his temptations by I-330 are like the forty days Jesus spends in the desert. Like Christ, he is thirty-two years old at the time of his own metaphorical "crucifixion"—the fantasiectomy that removes the part of the brain responsible for imagination. He also makes references to Christ's crucifixion and resurrection. "Let me nail or let me be nailed—perhaps it's all the same" (216), he writes at one point, wondering whether he is the one who helps execute the Messiah or, on the contrary, is the Messiah who is being executed. Zamyatin clearly implies the former, for in agreeing to undergo the "great operation" and thus betraying the revolution, D-503 actually reverses the Christian salvation story. He does not sacrifice himself to set others free—he simply reverts to his former true believer self of his pre-diary days.

Ironically, the act of Christ-like sacrifice in the novel is reserved for the "anti-Christian" rebel, I-330. Captured by the Guardians and tortured under the Bell, she faces execution as the novel ends and dies bravely while refusing to betray her comrades. Since D-503 twice remarks that her face is "marked with a cross" (53, 143), readers can see in her willingness to die for the sake of others an unlikely evocation of Christ and his self-sacrifice. The rebel leader thus paradoxically articulates a faint but positive Christology in a novel that otherwise views Christianity very negatively.

Like Zamyatin, Yuri Olesha also makes use of overt Christological references in his 1927 novel *Envy* about the clash between the old world and the new in Soviet society. These references are all connected to Ivan Babichev, a self-styled wonder-worker and prophet who sounds the death knell of the passing age. The Christological references in *Envy*, however, are all pointedly inverted. Instead of turning water into wine, for instance, Ivan turns wine into water (91).[39] Instead of being king of the Jews, Ivan declares that he is "the king of the vulgarians [*korol' poshliakov*]" (93). And though he is symbolically crucified in the novel's penultimate chapter while his disciple Nikolai Kavalerov, sounding like the apostle Peter, shouts, "Teacher! I shall die with you!" (149), no such crucifixion actually takes place, and the whole incident, like others in part 2 of the novel, is but an alcohol-induced hallucination. Ivan neither performs any redemptive act nor imparts any moral teachings. The few so-called miracles attributed to him are either tricks or mere legends. Indeed, Christ as the second Adam sent by God to undo the sin of the first Adam is quite superfluous in the novel. This role has been supplanted by Volodya Makarov, the ward of Ivan's brother, Andrei.

Volodya and Valya (Ivan's daughter) are the true Adam and Eve of Soviet literature of the twenties. They exemplify the Soviet idea of the New Man (*novyi chelovek*), for whom Soviet reality is the new Garden of Eden: a utopian paradise in which human beings have been restored to their perfect state of physical health and absolute belief. This is the image of the two formed by Ivan and Kavalerov—the two representatives of the Old World in the novel—when they spy on Volodya and Valya practicing gymnastics in a courtyard. Volodya is a "nearly naked" specimen of physical perfection while Valya, in sports shoes and "very bare" legs (130), is to be "an incubator" for "a new breed" of people who will populate the "new world" of the great Soviet experiment (89). It is Ivan's brother, Andrei, who presides over this dream of a new world. He takes Volodya under his wing and attempts to save Valya from her father by aligning her with Volodya, whose goal, outlined in a letter to Andrei, is to become "a man-machine" (63), thus answering the call of the Promethean spirit of the Soviet age by professing belief not in God but in man and machines—the materialist approximation of God in the new era. (Ivan calls the machine "the divinity of these coming men" [115].) While Christ, together with Ivan and his "disciple" Kavalerov, seem to be reduced to serving as mere symbols of a passing era, Olesha does not mock them, for Ivan and Kavalerov are also champions of feelings that will soon be extinct in the new age, such as "pity, tenderness, pride, jealousy, love" (94). They thus signal the author's anxiety over the shape of the New Jerusalem, one reason *Envy* fell into disfavor in Soviet criticism.

Like Olesha, Isaak Babel also had difficulty accommodating his art to the demands of his times. His 1926 *Red Cavalry* collection about Semyon Budyonny's First Cavalry Army features striking evocations of Christ in stories treating the ethnic, religious, and political antagonisms of the Civil War that followed the revolution. The narrator of these stories, Kirill Liutov, is a thinly disguised stand-in for Babel himself who, like his fictional creation, was a Jewish intellectual from the south of Russia serving with the notoriously anti-Semitic Cossacks of Budyonny's cavalry. Since much of the fighting takes place in Polish territory, Liutov is brought into contact with Catholic priests and churches, and he is fascinated by the Christ he meets there, whether in paintings or stories or, elsewhere, personified by individuals. If Christ in *Envy* is a marker of the passing age, in *Red Cavalry* he is often an emblem of meekness and compassion in brutal times, but imaged in unexpected ways that emphasize a very earthly—even earthy—humanity. In three stories in particular, the essence of Jesus's humanity is affirmed in a rather unorthodox fashion: through the act of sexual intercourse.

The first association between Christ's humanity and sexual intercourse occurs in a story told by the eponymous hero of "Pan Apolek." Pan Apolek is an itinerant painter who inserts the ordinary faces of his village clients into his depictions of biblical scenes and saints, including Christ himself, thereby incurring the wrath of the local religious authorities. When Liutov meets him, Pan Apolek tells him the story of how "Jesus, the son of Mary, was married to Deborah, a maiden of Jerusalem, and of common birth."[40] According to Apolek, Deborah was engaged to a young Israelite seller of elephant tusks. On her wedding night, however, she is so overcome with fright at the sight of her husband approaching their nuptial bed that she vomits the contents of their wedding feast all over the bed. Taken aback, her bridegroom promptly gathers together all of the wedding guests in order to mock her publicly. Jesus, present at the wedding and witnessing this, has such pity on "the woman who yearned for her husband and feared him" that he "united himself with Deborah as she lay in her vomit." Vindicated, Deborah shows herself to the guests and announces what had happened. Jesus, unobserved by the guests, slips away to "a deserted region east of Judaea, where John was awaiting him" and Deborah bears his son nine months later (111).

No wedding at Cana, this story—as provocative as Apolek's religious paintings—achieves a similar goal: it affirms the ontological significance of an ordinary sinful person. It does so blasphemously, by having Jesus perform an act inconceivable of the Son of God: out-of-wedlock intercourse, and in the most debased and revolting setting possible. Shocking and offensive as the story may be (a bystander warns that Pan Apolek "will not die in his own bed" for telling it [109, 111]), it also all the more dramatically affirms Christ's kinship with the most humiliated ranks of humanity, thus revealing his moral beauty in a new if scandalous way. This was doubtless Pan Apolek's intention all along, and one reason that the narrator is drawn to him. "I took a vow that day that I would follow the example of Pan Apolek," Liutov remarks, crediting the painter with revealing to him "a gospel that had been sheltered from the world" (104).

A similar association between the humanity of Christ and the act of sexual intercourse is made in two other stories, "Sashka the Christ" and "The Song." In the first story, a fourteen-year-old public herdsman in a Cossack settlement and his stepfather contract syphilis from a beggar woman who visits them while they are toiling in a city work cooperative. When they return to their village in the spring to resume their summer peasant work, the stepson asks to be allowed to be a herdsman, in part because he cannot bear to watch his syphilitic stepfather sleep with his mother. After threats and refusals, the stepfather eventually agrees. From that time onward, Sashka's simpleheartedness brings him fame throughout the district, earning him the nickname "Sashka the Christ." People visit him to unburden their souls and no one is ever angry with him "because of his love and because of his disease" (143). He thus attains a kind of holiness. Indeed, the syphilis that he contracts becomes the means of his *imitatio Christi*. As in "Pan Apolek," Jesus is made visible thanks to a profane act of sexual intercourse.

Eventually, Sashka is called up for service and lands in Liutov's detachment, where the narrator strikes up a friendship with him, drawn by his meekness. He reappears in "The Song," one of the last stories in the collection, where he makes peace between Liutov and the widow in whose hut Liutov is billeted. Liutov is upset because he discovers that his landlady had fed her son cabbage soup with meat but did not save any for him. Sure she is hiding what remains, Liutov threatens the woman with his gun. Sashka arrives at this moment and plays them songs on his concertina to calm Liutov down. Liutov softens, but the woman continues to complain, worn out from her lot in life and the war. So Sashka the Christ takes pity on her. He offers to do her "a courtesy" and lies down with her in her bed, thus reenacting the story of Christ and Deborah and affirming for a third time in the collection a connection between physical intimacy and divine compassion.

A fourth and final instance of the linking of Christ and sexual intercourse occurs in "The Sin of Jesus," a story that predates *Red Cavalry*. In it, Jesus intervenes in the life of a hotel servant, Arina, whose fecundity and promiscuity lead to two out-of-wedlock pregnancies with the hotel janitor, Seryoga. When Seryoga is conscripted into the army, she appeals to Jesus for help and the Lord sends her an angel to be her protector for the four years of Seryoga's service. Jesus promises Arina that she will not get pregnant by the angel, "for there's a lot of fun in him, but no seriousness."[41] The very first night they spend together, however, Arina—six months pregnant with Seryoga's child—smothers the angel as they sleep together. Angered, the Lord casts her from his sight. Unprotected, she is henceforth hounded mercilessly at the hotel by "kitchen-boys, merchants, [and] foreigners" looking for sexual favors. Finally, beside herself in misery, she shows the heavens her nine-month-pregnant belly and appeals to the Lord. Jesus, seeing her suffering, asks for her forgiveness. "No," she tells him, "There's no forgiveness for you, Jesus Christ" (250). Unlike the stories from *Red Cavalry* on this theme, divine compassion is not affirmed in the unlikely context of out-of-wedlock intercourse. Instead, Jesus's refusal to seek in the disordered sex life of Arina a means of restoring harmony creates a divide between the profane and the divine that results in atomization as well as the rebuke of Jesus himself.

Babel's earthy Jesus is the most provocative imaging of Christ in the Soviet twenties. Ilya Ehrenburg's *The Extraordinary Adventures of Julio Jurenito and His Disciples*, however, provides an example of how the image of Christ could be deployed in ostensibly pro-Soviet fashion. Written in 1921, published in Berlin in 1922 and in the Soviet Union in 1928, the novel is a parodic "gospel" in which its Mexican hero (known as "The Teacher"—a satiric caricature of Christ) travels Europe gathering a band of seven disciples and mocking the evils of Western bourgeois civilization. But the novel's satire also targets aspects of the Bolshevik state. When the band of "believers" ends its journey in Moscow on the eve of the Bolshevik Revolution, Jurenito ironically praises the "iron yoke" of Bolshevism in satiric approbation of the historically necessary eradication of freedom. He later, Christ-like, perishes on his thirty-third birthday.

By the end of the twenties, references to Christ were uniformly negative. The swindler Ostap Bender in Ilya Ilf and Evgeny Petrov's *The Golden Calf* (1931), for example, is likened to Christ on two occasions in the novel, but largely in order to link the two as throwbacks to a bygone age. First, Bender claims to have been Jesus Christ "for a few days" in some God-forsaken town where he "even fed several thousand of the faithful with five loaves of bread."[42] Elsewhere, as his world crumbles around him, he laments that he has reached the age of Christ at his death and yet accomplished nothing: "I haven't created a teaching, I wasted my disciples, I haven't resurrected the dead Panikovsky" (318). In both instances, the associations with Christ are examples of politically correct negative association, and indeed are made the more ridiculous because Ostap himself is no believer, having long disliked "rabbis, Dalai Lamas, Orthodox clergy, muezzins, shamans, and other purveyors of religion" (160).

As the decade drew to its close and Stalin consolidated his power, Soviet literature had little use for Christ, the outcome of the government's anti-religious campaign over the course of the twenties, which openly discouraged any but the most disparaging depictions of Jesus or religion in general. The journal *Bezbozhnik* (The godless one), which began circulating in December 1922, ridiculed all religious belief and regularly published exposés about corrupt and exploitive priests and rabbis alongside poems, parodies, caricatures, and cartoons debunking all aspects of faith. *Bezbozhnik* and similar periodicals regularly linked the Church to the exploitive classes, the repressive tsarist government and their Western counterparts. In this increasingly shrill campaign, none but the most negative portraits of Christ were possible.

By the end of the 1920s, interest in Jesus Christ in Soviet literature was eventually supplanted by the emerging paradigm of a different kind of hero, one unique to the revolution and Soviet reality and celebrated in novels such as Dmitry Furmanov's *Chapaev* (1923), Alexander Serafimovich's *Iron Flood*

(1924), Fyodor Gladkov's *Cement* (1925), Alexander Fadeev's *The Rout* (1927), Mikhail Sholokhov's *Quiet Flows the Don* (1928–1932), and Nikolai Ostrovsky's *How the Steel Was Tempered* (1932). These novels established a model for what would eventually become socialist realism, a state-sanctioned and state-patrolled literary aesthetic formally proclaimed at the First Congress of Soviet Writers in 1934.[43] The new "positive heroes" of the socialist realist canon exemplified the values of the state, often in narratives that edifyingly described their maturation or "conversion" into models of ideological conformity; depicted their unwavering dedication to the building of socialism; or celebrated their feats taming nature with their machines, their wits, and their steely determination. These heroes embodied a different kind of sanctity—that of the ideology of the Soviet state, based on Marxist-Leninist values. The time for Christ was past; the time for new heroes had arrived. Maxim Gorky made this point clear in his speech at the 1934 Writers Congress. "Christ is the 'Son of God,' the only 'positive' type that religious literature has ever created," he declared, "and that type—that of the unsuccessful reconciler of all of life's contradictions—stands as a particularly vivid demonstration of the creative debility of religious literature."[44]

In place of Christ, Lenin became the source and summit of exalted knowledge in Soviet literature of the thirties, a role soon eclipsed by Stalin. Encounters with either Lenin or Stalin—even at several degrees' remove—constituted quasi-divine moments. In Ostrovsky's *How the Steel Was Tempered*, howling storms and blizzards attend the news of Lenin's death; strong men who had not wept in decades sob openly; and factory and train engines mournfully sound their sirens and horns to mark the magnitude of his passing.[45] But even as Ostrovsky shows the people's great love of Lenin, he is, ironically, sparingly mentioned elsewhere in the novel. Compounding this irony is the fact that Pavel Korchagin, Ostrovsky's autobiographical hero, is strangely absent in the chapter describing the effect of Lenin's death on the cadres—one of the few chapters in the book in which he does not figure. His absence there prevents Ostrovsky from making a stronger link between his self-sacrificing true-believer hero and the father of the Russian Revolution. While Lenin's death is credited by the narrator with bringing many thousands into the Bolshevik party, he is in reality hardly more than an abstract notion in the novel. His mention lends the text a kind of ideological sanctity, but little more—a paradoxical outcome for a novel so obviously intent on creating a new Soviet mythology.

Stalin's fate in Soviet literature, however, was quite different. He was eventually transformed into a living deity in the pages of some Soviet novels. A vivid example of Stalin's pseudo-divinization can be found in Pyotr Pavlenko's *Stalin Prize*–winning 1947 novel, *Happiness*. Its hero, a heavily wounded war veteran named Alexei Voropayev, is unknowingly summoned to Stalin in Yalta on the eve of the summit of the Big Three in February 1945. Voropayev has passed up a promotion to a cushy desk job in the military bureaucracy in Moscow to remain in Crimea and help rebuild the home front. Stalin has heard of this and wishes to see Voropayev for himself. But when Voropayev arrives and first catches sight of Stalin, he cannot move, paralyzed by his sudden encounter with the deity: "His legs would not obey him. *He saw Stalin*."[46] Throughout the interview, the awestruck Voropayev does his best to answer the questions put by Stalin, who eventually praises him and others from Voropayev's circle for their dedication to rebuilding. When Voropayev finally takes his leave of Stalin, the leader looks straight into his eyes, at which point Stalin's face "flashed, as if a sunbeam had passed across it" (356)—a quiet confirmation of the leader's supraterrestrial essence.

For his part, Voropayev later declares to his friends that he has "grown younger today . . . by a thousand years!" from his brush with the deity (358). Stalin has remade him. His friends, meanwhile, are stunned—and, ironically, a little horrified—when Voropayev tells them that he gave Stalin a full report of all the wonderful things they have been doing to rebuild the countryside. They worry that their names had been mentioned to Stalin and wonder aloud whether they can live up to his high expectations—or his later inquiries about their activities. As his friends all go their separate ways to ponder how their lives have been changed now that Stalin has been made aware of their existence, Lena breaks into song. For a long time "her shrill, girlish voice could be heard above the noises of the street" (369)—whether out of love for Stalin or for other reasons, Pavlenko does not say.

Bulgakov, Pasternak, and Christ

Like the fictional Voropayev, Mikhail Bulgakov and Boris Pasternak also had their brushes with the Soviet deity, only not in person. They each received a telephone call instead. Bulgakov's came on April 18, 1930, almost a month after he had written a letter to the Soviet government complaining of the harsh critical reception of his works and asking to be allowed to leave the country.[47] In his phone call responding to Bulgakov's letter, Stalin asked the writer three questions: did he really want to leave the USSR; would he accept a job at the Moscow Arts Theater; and would he like to meet sometime personally to talk. Bulgakov answered no to the first question and an enthusiastic yes to the other two (though no personal meeting was ever forthcoming). Pasternak's phone call from Stalin came four years later, in June of 1934, as the dictator contemplated the poet Osip Mandelshtam's fate. Mandelshtam had been taken into custody and sentenced to three years' internal exile, ostensibly for having written a highly unflattering poem about Stalin. Stalin asked Pasternak about the nature of his relationship with the poet and whether he thought Mandelshtam was a "master." Pasternak answered evasively: "But that isn't the point.... Why do we keep on about Mandelshtam? I have long wanted to meet with you for a serious discussion." "About what?" Stalin asked. "About life and death," Pasternak replied, whereupon Stalin hung up.[48]

Both Bulgakov and Pasternak were disappointed by their phone conversations with Stalin and both felt betrayed by the fact that their desire for an in-depth personal conversation with the dictator never came to pass. J. A. E. Curtis calls Bulgakov's attitude toward Stalin "politically naïve and even morally dubious."[49] The same can be said of Pasternak, who, according to Natal'ia Ivanova, "was fascinated by Stalin."[50] While each writer had his doubts about Stalin's beneficence, each also wrote works in praise of the dictator. Indeed, Pasternak published two poems to the leader in the January 1, 1936, edition of *Izvestiia*.[51] In the spring of that same year, Bulgakov came up with the idea of writing a play about Stalin, which was to focus on his days as a revolutionary in Batum (now Batumi), Georgia, from which the play derived its title. Bulgakov completed the play three years later at the request of the Moscow Arts Theatre so that it would be ready for the dictator's sixtieth birthday.

Clearly, for both Bulgakov and Pasternak, Stalin was a kind of "evil genius" who haunted their imaginations and exerted his power over their very lives and livelihoods. Their ultimate response to him and their times was the two works for which they are now known to the world: *The Master and Margarita* and *Doctor Zhivago*. Neither novel ever mentions Stalin by name or comments directly about him (almost all of the events in *Doctor Zhivago* occur before Stalin's consolidation of power), but each clearly alludes to him through references to Rome and Roman emperors. These references come early, within the first two dozen pages of each novel. In *Master and Margarita*, Yeshua Ha-Notsri (Bulgakov's Jesus Christ) is condemned to death by Pontius Pilate solely for violating "the law pertaining to insults to the sovereign," having declared publicly that "the kingdom of truth and justice" will one day displace all earthly Caesars.[52] This outcome contrasts sharply with the Gospels, where Pilate can find no crime against Jesus, and suggests a correlation with Bulgakov's own time, where negative comments about Stalin were punishable offenses. (Mandelshtam's satirical poem about Stalin was initially deemed "equivalent to a terrorist act."[53]) Later, when Pilate meets with the head of his secret police, they raise the obligatory toast to "Caesar, father of the Romans, dearest and best of men!" (258), calling to mind the kinds of toasts routinely raised to Stalin during his reign in both official and unofficial settings.

As for Pasternak's novel, Yuri Zhivago's uncle Nikolai Nikolaevich Vedeniapin contrasts the Gospel of Christ to the "blood and beastliness and cruelty" of "pockmarked Caligulas who do not suspect how untalented every enslaver is." The implied allusion to equally pockmarked and cruel Stalin is plain, just as Vedeniapin's comment about "the boastful dead eternity of bronze monuments and marble columns" of Rome is sure to evoke the monumentalist architecture and statuary of the high Stalinist period as well.[54] Yuri Zhivago may have died in 1929, but the whole novel on one level may be read as an attempt to understand the events that made possible the rise of a tyrant like Stalin.

To counter the great unnamable darkness of their times, each writer chose a similar path. Each chose to write a novel whose submerged subject would be Christ himself, and in doing so, they produced the two greatest Easter novels of Russian literature. Like that of Dostoevsky and Tolstoy, their Christology would be apophatic: a Christ revealed through negative means. Against the bombast of Soviet political rhetoric and Stalin's bloated cult of personality, Bulgakov and Pasternak offer images of a Christ who is purposely effaced, estranged, minimized, understated, or even unrecognizable and unheroic. This Christ appears obliquely and is elucidated dimly in the complex interrelation between inserted narratives and the novels' framing plots, on which each author's Christology depends for its ultimate deciphering. Neither Bulgakov's nor Pasternak's Christ preaches or leaves any teachings. Rather, they figure solely in each author's recounting of a single episode from Christ's life: his willing participation in the events of his Passion narrative. It is in this Passion narrative that Christ as a measure of the age is made visible.

In truth, each novel has two Passion narratives: the one about agape (Jesus's self-sacrificing love for humanity) and the one about eros (the love stories of the Master and Margarita in Bulgakov's novel, and Yuri and Lara in Pasternak's). As the chapters that follow will argue, these Passion narratives are linked in important ways. Unlike the Christ novels of Dostoevsky and Tolstoy, where eros and agape are exclusive, mutually canceling kinds of love, in *Master and Margarita* and *Doctor Zhivago* earthly, erotic love actually helps to reveal divine, agapic love, though how it does so in each novel is particular to each author. In neither instance is the connection between private, sexual love and heavenly, divine love straightforward. Instead, their idealized or exalted love stories are but the means by which an even higher and more ideal love is made visible.

The love stories of the titular characters of both novels are also closely linked with two other shared themes as well: that of the sacredness of domestic space and that of the sanctity of personhood. In this latter theme, both novels evoke the personalism so prominent in the Christologies of Dostoevsky and Tolstoy. In the former, they speak to a new Soviet reality: the problem of private space in the Soviet utopia. In actuality, the themes of sacred domestic space and personalism are linked in each novel. The assault against the dignity of the human person begins with the deprivation of the individual's private space. This deprivation of space in each novel takes the form of homelessness, a prominent theme in both novels and one that has a Christological association, for, as Jesus reminds us in the Gospels, "Foxes have dens and birds have nests, but the Son of Man has no place to lay his head" (Matthew 8:20, Luke 9:58).

Christ's homelessness echoes that of the uprooted or dispossessed heroes of both novels, establishing an important affinity between them. When readers meet the Master, he is in a psychiatric clinic, where he has turned himself in after his arrest and incarceration, having lost his beloved basement apartment to the informer, Aloysius Mogarych. In the clinic he befriends the poet whose pseudonymous last name underscores the Master's position: Ivan Bezdomny (John Homeless). For his part, Zhivago is an orphan who lives in, and is driven from, a succession of substitute homes, whether the Gromekos' house in Moscow, the Krueger estate at Varykino, the various dilapidated places he shares with his fellow refugee Vasia Brykin upon their return to Moscow (each place "uninhabitable and uncomfortable in a different way" [477]), or the apartment he lives in with his common-law wife Marina, the daughter of the Gromekos' former porter, Markel Shchapov, at the end of the novel. In these and other ways, both the Master and Yuri are Christ figures, even as their many personal weaknesses problematize their status as such.

In a 1946 letter, Pasternak said he was "settling accounts" in *Doctor Zhivago* "with Judaism, with all kinds of nationalisms (including the kind apparent in internationalism), with all kinds of anti-Christianities and their assumptions."

"The atmosphere of the thing," he states, "will be my own Christianity."[55] Bulgakov, too, was "settling accounts" in his *Master and Margarita*: with the Stalinist literary establishment, to be sure, but also with the atheism of his day and of his youth. He, too, was exploring his own kind of Christianity—unorthodox but, by all appearances, a necessary refuge for the writer from the trials of his day. In the century of belief, when communist ideology had become the new religion and Stalin its presiding demigod, Bulgakov and Pasternak articulated an alternate vision of faith, one whose symbol was Jesus Christ, but refigured for the Soviet age, a Christ very much of their own devising. Delayed though they were in reaching their readers, it is their images of Christ that nevertheless preside over the Soviet century.

CHAPTER SEVEN

"KEEP IN MIND THAT JESUS DID EXIST"
Mikhail Bulgakov's Image of Christ

And, after all, who knows whether proof of the devil is also proof of God?

Dostoevsky, *Brothers Karamazov*, 4:11:9

THE GODLESS ONE AND THE WRITER

Unlike Dostoevsky and Tolstoy, for whom the figure of Jesus Christ became a central concern of their creative lives, Mikhail Bulgakov grappled seriously with the idea of Jesus as a historical or theological entity only in his last novel, *The Master and Margarita*, completed shortly before his death, at the age of 48, from nephrosclerosis, the same disease that killed his father. He labored over the novel between 1928 and 1940, partially destroying one version of the manuscript in 1930 and reading drafts to select friends as he revised and modified his story. While Bulgakov tried out many titles for his manuscript, ranging from *The Black Magician* and *The Engineer's Hoof* to *The Great Chancellor* and *The Prince of Darkness*, one consistent feature of the various drafts of the novel, predating even the creation of the novel's titular characters, was the idea for its opening chapter.

An editor and a poet are discussing Jesus Christ when the devil appears and attests to the existence of Jesus by telling them the story of Pontius Pilate and one Yeshua Ha-Notsri, an alternate transcription of Jesus's name that Bulgakov may have first heard from Sergei Chevkin's 1922 play "Yeshua Hanotsri: An Impartial

Revelation of the Truth" ("Ieshua Ganotsri: Bespristrastnoe otkrytie istiny").[1] The story the devil tells is quite unlike the accounts from the four Gospels, featuring a Christ figure who appears to be no more than an itinerant philosopher and focusing almost exclusively on the personality and psychology of the Roman procurator. This "gospel according to the devil"[2]—enigmatically affirming the existence of Jesus but seemingly denying his divine attributes—was thus always a central part of the novel's formulation, growing from one chapter in earlier drafts to four in the final version of the novel, where it becomes the work of a nameless writer known as the Master.

Though this "gospel" is more about Pilate than Jesus,[3] its image of Christ is nevertheless remarkable, resembling neither the Jesus of the four evangelists nor that proposed by the adherents of the historical school of biblical criticism nor yet the depictions of Jesus produced by the likes of the Bolshevik poet Demyan Bedny (real name: Efim Alexandrovich Pridvorov, 1883–1945) in Russian anti-religious works published in the 1920s. Such irreverent caricatures were ubiquitous in the Communist Party's campaign against religion, for which Bedny, as the "unofficial poet laureate of the new regime," was a "principal spokesman."[4] Bedny's 1925 mock epic poem *New Testament without Defects by the Evangelist Demyan*, which parodies the Gospels and depicts Christ as a "liar, drunkard and womanizer,"[5] is one of the more prominent literary examples of the anti-religious campaign carried out in journals like *Bezbozhnik*, to which Bedny was a regular contributor. Demyan Bedny (literally, Demyan the Poor) is an obvious model for Ivan Bezdomny (Ivan the Homeless), the atheist poet from Bulgakov's novel, who was commissioned to write a poem demonstrating how Jesus could never have existed. Indeed, the whole topic of anti-religious writing not only serves as the subject of the opening chapter of Bulgakov's novel, but may also have been the inspiration for the entire book in the first place.

In a diary entry of January 5, 1925, Bulgakov records a visit he undertook to the editorial offices of *Bezbozhnik* with the express purpose of obtaining back issues of the journal. He managed to get the previous eleven issues, which he took home to read. What he discovered in their pages may very well have provided the pretext for the novel he would begin some three years later. He writes:

> When I quickly looked through the issues of *Bezbozhnik* at home that evening, I was stunned. What stings is not the blasphemy, although it, of course, is boundless, if one speaks of its external aspect. What stings is the idea that we can prove it on a documentary basis. Jesus Christ is depicted in the guise of a scoundrel and

a swindler, he of all people. It's not difficult to guess whose work this is. There is no price for such a crime.[6]

Though Bulgakov speaks of blasphemy here, his offense at Jesus's depiction in *Bezbozhnik* was more personal than for the sake of the Church. While icons hung in the apartment where he died, most commentators agree that the writer seemed "to have had only scorn for the historical church as such."[7] Here, he parts ways with his father, Afanasii Ivanovich Bulgakov (1859–1907), a professor of theology, who published prolifically in the almanac of the Kiev Religious Academy. Rejecting his father's Church, however, Bulgakov did not seem to reject his father's Christian faith. Bulgakov's third wife, Elena Sergeevna, on whom much of Margarita's character was modeled, addressed the question of his faith in 1967, shortly after *The Master and Margarita* was published in censored form in the journal *Moskva*: "Did he believe? He did, though, of course, not according to the Church but in his own way. In any case, he believed when he was ill—I can vouch for that."[8] Three diary entries in October 1923 confirm this latter assertion. Ill health plagued Bulgakov for much of his life and he would console himself by putting his trust in God.[9] Later, as he wrote the first drafts of *The Master and Margarita* in a literary environment increasingly hostile to his works, he penned on the top margin of an early version of the manuscript: "Help me, Lord, finish my novel. 1931."[10]

A distinct religious tone also pervades his first novel, *The White Guard* (1925), a sympathetic treatment of the experiences of the Turbin family during the forty-seven-day occupation of Kiev by Symon Petlyura's nationalist Ukrainian forces in 1918 and also Bulgakov's most autobiographical novel. Like *The Master and Margarita*, *The White Guard* features a vision of Jesus Christ and an atheist poet who, like Ivan Bezdomny, renounces his anti-religious poetry. Another link between the two novels is the role Bulgakov's parents played in their genesis. "If my mother served as a stimulus for the creation of the novel *White Guard*," Bulgakov records in an autobiographical note in the fall of 1926, "then according to my plans, the figure of my father is to be the starting point for another work I have in mind."[11]

If it is true that the memory of Bulgakov's father helped to motivate undertaking *The Master and Margarita*, then two assumptions can be ventured. First, given the source of its inspiration, it is rather unlikely, as David Bethea points out, that *The Master and Margarita* should be read as a "light-hearted parody or a debunking of Christian faith."[12] On the contrary, Bulgakov seems determined in his novel to rescue Christ from both the excesses of Soviet disparagement and the prescriptions of Orthodox doctrine precisely in order to affirm a renewed image of Jesus for his times. Second, the topic of theology—the subject of his father's teaching and scholarship—and its application to the themes of the novel gain in importance. Indeed, the novel's unique Christology constitutes its central subject, one that drives all other elements of the story's various plotlines.

More than a working out of the writer's ideas about the identity and significance of Christ and the nature of belief, however, Bulgakov's magnum opus is also a treatment of the difficulty and dangers of coming to definitive conclusions about Christ or faith for fear that such conclusions could be mistaken for settled doctrine. It was against religious and political dogma, after all, that the novel's pronounced satire took full aim. Neither a complete repudiation of the Christ of faith nor yet an endorsement of a non-divine Jesus of history, Bulgakov's novel proposes instead its own kind of apophatic exercise in negative Christology, one that relies on mystery and mystification to bring us to a state of truer discernment. The central mystery of the novel pertains to the identity of its two theological heroes: Yeshua Ha-Notsri and Woland—Christ and Satan, respectively. Both of these heroes are utterly unlike the Christ and Satan of Christian revelation. From biography to acts to teachings, Yeshua is a negation of the biblical Christ in nearly all ways, while Woland as determined affirmer of Jesus's existence is an inexplicably positive take on the chief villain of Christian cosmology. Nothing seems to make sense, an outcome of Bulgakov's methodology of mystification: the novel poses questions that cannot easily be answered. Instead, Bulgakov's text promotes narratological indeterminacy on all levels, with one goal in mind: to resist final interpretation, or, to put it theologically, to avoid cataphatic (i.e., positive) statements about the Godhead. Enlightenment in the novel comes from a place of ignorance along a *via negativa*. What Bulgakov reveals about the nature of belief, the identity of Christ, and the meaning of "real, true, everlasting love" (a reference to the relationship between the Master and Margarita) requires that he proceed from a negative point of departure.

Mystification, Paradox, and Ambiguity: Conversions, Christ, and Unfinished Manuscripts

Negative theology and Christology are very much what drive the opening chapters of *The Master and Margarita* and there is no better starting place for such an exercise than a conversation between two atheists and the devil about the existence of God and Jesus Christ. And while it would seem logical that the atheists Berlioz and Bezdomny and the devil should make for fine company, it turns out that they and Woland have very strong and, paradoxically, opposite views on the existence of God and Jesus Christ. Astonishingly, Woland mounts a defense of the existence of God and, regarding Jesus, states outright: "Jesus did exist. [...] No points of view are necessary. [...] He simply existed and that's all there is to it."[13]

If Woland's arguments flummox and frustrate Berlioz and Bezdomny, readers are also bewildered and intrigued. In fact, the whole point of the first two chapters seems precisely to be to mystify and astound us, to confront us with apparent contradictions and force us to sort through myriad references to ancient historians, the various gods of world mythology, and secular and religious philosophers and theologians. In this regard, chapter 1 is an annotator's dream, with passing references made to the Greek philosopher Philo of Alexandria; the Jewish historian Flavius Josephus; the Roman historian Cornelius Tacitus; Osiris, the Egyptian god of the afterlife; Tammuz, a Syro-Phoenician demigod; Marduk, a Babylonian sun-god; Huitzilopochtli, the Aztec god of war; the Greek god Adonis; the Phrygian god Attis; the Persian god Mithras; the three Magi from the Gospels; the Catholic theologian Thomas Aquinas (not mentioned by name but whose five proofs of God are cited by Woland); the German philosopher Immanuel Kant; the German poet Friedrich Schiller; the biblical scholar David Friedrich Strauss; and Gerbert of Aurillac, a theologian and mathematician who became pope in 999 under the name of Sylvester II.[14]

Equally baffling is chapter 2, in which the Gospel story of Jesus's encounter with Pontius Pilate is dramatically rewritten, complete with rich and archeologically accurate descriptions of first-century Jerusalem and a completely revisionist Jesus who calls himself Yeshua Ha-Notsri. An orphan from the city of Gamala who believes his father was a Syrian, this Yeshua wanders the countryside preaching a philosophy of peace and love, followed not by twelve disciples but only one, Levi Matvei, who writes down everything he says incorrectly. What is the reader to make of all of this, having read only the novel's first two chapters?[15]

Mystification, of course, is one of Bulgakov's chief literary devices. Ellendea Proffer calls this "desire to mystify" an "important part of Bulgakov's character," something "constantly mentioned by those who knew him."[16] His wife, Elena Sergeevna, reports that when he finished the epilogue to *The Master and Margarita* in May 1939, he held a reading of the novel for a small circle of friends that left them alarmed and puzzled.[17] But the desire to confuse or keep his audience in the dark is more than just an important literary device in *The Master and Margarita*; it is also a means toward an end. Like Berlioz and Bezdomny in chapter 1, Bulgakov's readers must be mystified before they can be enlightened. That is, they must be brought to a state in which they can recognize their own ignorance before they can begin the task of understanding where the truth must lie. Here, the distinct shape of an apophatic inquiry into the nature of God can be glimpsed. In his encounter with Woland, Berlioz perishes because he fails to understand that all of his supposed erudition is what actually hinders him from apprehending the truth.[18] Worse still, Berlioz uses his knowledge to mislead others, in this case, the poet Bezdomny.

Ironically, ignorant disbelief in the novel is actually fertile ground for spiritual conversion, an outcome Bulgakov emphasizes through Ivan, who is the first character in the novel to undergo a conversion experience. Ivan is not an intellectual. He admits as much to the Master in their first meeting (113). By all accounts, Ivan is a typical Soviet poet for the masses: shallow, poorly educated, and an ideologue. He does not believe in God or Jesus not because he has studied the question or thought it through but because Berlioz had asked him to write an anti-religious poem. Indeed, in an earlier draft of the novel, Berlioz is the editor of an atheist journal called *Bogoborets* (God-resister, someone who defies God or the divine will, a theomachist), for which Ivan is presumably writing his poem about the impossibility of Jesus's existence. The allusion to *Bezbozhnik* is unmistakable, a possible confirmation that Bulgakov's encounter with the journal in 1925 did, indeed, help beget the idea for *The Master and Margarita*.[19]

Ivan is all heart and no head, but this is ultimately a good thing in the novel. A true "disbeliever," he reacts to Woland's challenge of his atheism not with learned arguments, like Berlioz, but with heated emotion. When during their conversation Woland mentions Kant's proof of God (the postulation of the moral will, the sixth proof of God mentioned in the book, following the five offered by Thomas Aquinas), Ivan blurts out that Kant should be given three years in the Solovki prison camp for it. Later, after Woland relates what the reader will come to recognize as the first chapter of the Master's novel about Pontius Pilate, Ivan hotly declares that the devil does not exist either. And when Berlioz is decapitated by the tram as Woland predicted, Ivan hurls himself headlong in pursuit of Woland, Korovyev, and Behemoth in a wild chase across Moscow.

And yet, Ivan, our ignorant atheist, is also the first person in the novel to "believe," for he proceeds from a state of ignorance (atheism) to enlightenment (an implied acknowledgement of God's existence) along a *via negativa* (the recognition of the devil's existence, who, though not God, serves as the seventh proof of God[20]). He does so during his first meeting with the Master in the asylum where he has been committed after his mad pursuit of Woland. There, the Master, intrigued by Ivan's story of Woland and Pontius Pilate, calmly explains how it could only have been Satan that he met at Patriarch's Ponds. Listening to the Master's explanations, Ivan eventually understands and has what can only be called a conversion experience. From this moment on, he becomes a new man.[21] Indeed, during his interview with the Master, he is referred to by the narrator as "the now unrecognizable Ivan" (113).

As with all converts, Ivan has been changed. He has been set on a new path, one of repudiation of the old self (he renounces his talentless poetry to the Master) in order to awaken to new moral and spiritual realities. In Ivan's case, he not only acknowledges the existence of a supernatural realm, but he is also remorseful about the anti-religious poetry he had written. Having thus converted from *homo sovieticus* (Soviet man) to a believer in supernatural realms, Ivan's function in the novel is largely complete. He reappears only twice in the rest of the book: in chapter 17, when he is visited by the disembodied spirits of the Master and Margarita; and in the novel's epilogue, where Ivan, now a professor of history, makes a pilgrimage to the park bench on Patriarch's Ponds on the first full moon of the spring, then visits Margarita's old apartment building, after which he has nightmares of the crucifixion and, under the influence of a sedative, dreams of Pilate and Christ and the Master and Margarita, all ascending a path toward the moon. His role in the book, then, has much to do with his status as the first non-believer to convert to belief, albeit belief understood apophatically as a faith journey along a negative path (he believes in the devil but has not yet found his way to God).

Margarita is the novel's second convert and it is fitting that her introduction into the novel displaces our first convert for some two hundred pages, for her presence helps to explain his absence: his conversion story is over, hers is just beginning. When she wakes up on the morning that she encounters Woland's servant, Azazello, she prophetically utters the words "I believe"—*veruiu*—using the Russian verb *verovat'*, which means to believe in a strictly religious sense (as opposed to *verit'*, the neutral verb for "to believe"). Like Ivan's, however, her expression of faith, initially made without referent, is ultimately aimed at

Woland, as the reader soon discovers. But, as with Ivan's, Margarita's declaration of faith in the devil also, by the logic of the novel, affirms God's existence, for Woland is a proof of God. Thus, Margarita, like Ivan, testifies to God's existence without formally declaring so. Indeed, as if in confirmation of this fact, Margarita rapturously praises Woland as "omnipotent" after he reproduces the Master's previously burned manuscript, whole and intact (245). While understandable, her confusion of the proper object of such an epithet is telling. The devil has never been described as omnipotent in the Judeo-Christian tradition. Only God is all-powerful. In misdescribing the devil, Margarita actually reveals the true (though unspoken) object of her praise: God.

These two "negative conversion" stories reveal the novel's ultimate mystification, and it is apophatic in nature. Out of ignorance, disbelief, or faith in the devil, Bulgakov, magician-like, conjures up belief in God, in part by postulating the devil as the seventh proof of God and in part by strongly implying an underlying apophatic claim: "God is not the devil." This claim, like all such apophatic statements, moves us closer to discerning what God must be. The "conversions" of Ivan and Margarita thus model a *via negativa* that ultimately advances belief in God. Indeed, belief in God and in the existence of Jesus—the theme of the novel's opening chapters—becomes the hidden axis on which the entire novel turns.

But belief is also problematic in the novel, if only for the fact that it is one step removed from its proper object. Ivan and Margarita believe in the devil first and only by logical inference can be said to believe in God. Moreover, neither tells us anything about belief in Jesus Christ, even though Margarita, for one, adores the Master's story of Pilate and Yeshua Ha-Notsri. The devil may be the seventh proof of God and may even offer a kind of apophatic path toward belief in him, but God still appears to be absent from the novel and, in any case, is hardly mentioned. A similar mystery attaches to the figure of Jesus, who also seems to be absent from the novel for, by all appearances, Yeshua Ha-Notsri is nothing like the Jesus of the Gospels. If the novel, following Woland's lead, affirms belief in his existence, it also raises questions about his true identity, questions that have been debated since the novel's publication, most prominently, what kind of Jesus is he: an itinerant Jewish philosopher or divine Son of God?[22]

The question of Yeshua's identity is but one of many that the novel poses but does not answer definitively. Ambiguity is, of course, the hallmark of good literature. In the case of *The Master and Margarita*, however, part of the reason for the novel's ambiguity or its puzzling discrepancies and contradictions[23] appears to derive from the fact that the novel is, technically speaking, unfinished. Bulgakov began his final corrections of the novel in October 1939,[24] but according to his wife, Elena Sergeevna, got only as far as Margarita's conversation with Azazello at the beginning of part 2 before his health allowed him to go no further. As Marietta Chudakova reports, judging by the numerous corrections he had made in part 1, sections of part 2 might very likely have been subject to significant changes had Bulgakov not been so ill.[25]

This fact may account for "the elusiveness of a coherent theme" in the novel noted by critics like Margot Frank, who mentions the "encyclopedic sweep" of the novel's "disconnected parts" as both a liability and an asset.[26] While some critics do not view the novel's incompleteness as a liability, others, like biographer Aleksei Varlamov, claim it is one reason the novel does not rise to Bulgakov's best work.[27] Either way this question is argued, any critical interpretation of the novel must take its incompleteness into consideration. The question that must then be asked is how, if at all, the novel's status as an "unfinished" manuscript changes the way it should be read? Are the gaps, contradictions, and apparent continuity errors in various places the outcome of the manuscript's incompleteness or do at least some of them have a thematic or structural purpose? The "unfinished" state of Bulgakov's manuscript is particularly important when it comes to the questions Bulgakov poses about Yeshua, for it is unclear whether the novel about Pilate and Christ is also—for Bulgakov's readers, at least—an unfinished manuscript. After all, only four chapters of it are included in the narrative. Is there more to the Master's novel? The Master says explicitly that the novel was completed, so it would seem logical that it consisted of more than four chapters. If so, then the Master's novel also has the status of an incomplete manuscript for Bulgakov's readers, who are deprived of its other chapters—chapters that might shed greater light on the identity and nature of Yeshua Ha-Notsri.

Finally, what about the third incomplete manuscript in the novel—the one Levi Matvei is writing about Yeshua? Yeshua implores him, "For God's sake burn your parchment!" (16). But Levi Matvei does not comply with his request. On the contrary, the one thing he allows Pilate to give him when he is summoned before him at the end of the fourth chapter of the Master's novel is a piece of clean parchment, a clear indication that Levi intends to continue writing his manuscript. Burning the manuscript seems out of the question. In any case, as Woland reminds us, "manuscripts don't burn" (245), by which he means that the power of the written word and its ability to enter the world and do its work should not be underestimated. Yeshua may have said "absolutely nothing that was written there" (16), but presumably Levi Matvei finished his gospel and spread his word about Yeshua, accurately or not, or so Bulgakov implies. And if one accepts the novel's premise that Levi's manuscript is a distortion of the "real" teachings of Yeshua and agree with critics like Proffer who conclude that Bulgakov had "disdain for the historical veracity of the New Testament,"[28] then one must also be prepared to accept the fact that, by Bulgakov's own logic, this outcome merely reflects the way literature works—that is, that manuscripts have a reality and influence culture in ways that transcend questions of historical provenance or even historical veracity.

Artists like the Master "guess" the truth through the medium of their art. But art is not documentary transcription of reality. The Master folds his hands "as if in prayer" and whispers, "Oh, I guessed right! I guessed everything right!"(112) after hearing Ivan's tale of his encounter with Woland, finding in it ostensible confirmation of his own story of Pilate's meeting with Yeshua.[29] But, in truth, there is no way to know whether the Master did "guess everything right," as there is no way of knowing whether the story Woland relates to Ivan at Patriarch's Ponds is, indeed, a true eyewitness account of the meeting between Pilate and Christ (and if it is, to what extent it matches the Master's first chapter) or whether Woland is simply relating the first chapter of the Master's novel (which, of course, may not accurately reflect what really happened) or whether the two are, indeed, the same thing (as the Master's reaction implies). Thus the indeterminacy of the novel extends to issues that have little to do with its status as an unfinished novel but that are connected to matters of theme and structure. This fact, however, does not prevent either the inserted novel or the framing narrative from exerting its own cultural force or suggesting its own negative Christology.

From a Christological point of view, the novel's indeterminacy is apophatic in its thrust—a way to avoid making definitive or affirmative statements about the Godhead. Bulgakov's use of textual disjuncture and aporias enacts a similar refusal to provide conceptual language or to name things plainly on the level of plot, just as Ivan's and Margarita's "conversions" are only implied, not explicit, affirmations of God or Jesus Christ. Indeterminacy also plays out on the level of plot, where competing narrative strands, which differ dramatically in theme, style, and genre, complicate our task of making sense out of the novel or solving the riddles of its cosmology. Bulgakov, it seems, may have wanted his text to resist, not assist, interpretation. To understand Bulgakov's Christ, then, the reader must understand the nature of the novel's resistance to interpretation and what this resistance reveals about the questions Bulgakov poses about God and Jesus in his book's opening chapters and beyond.

Aporias, Aquinas, and Indeterminacy

One of the first impediments to interpretation has to do with the novel's three narrative strands, each of which is marked by its own style and genre. Critics usually identify three narrative arcs. The first is the story of the devil's visit to Moscow and its satiric deconstruction of Soviet reality. The second is the other Moscow plot—the story of the Master and Margarita—related in a romantic style with thinly veiled references to real literary personages. The final narrative strand—the Master's novel about Pilate's encounter with Yeshua Ha-Notsri in first-century Jerusalem—is told in a realistic, ornate style, with an emphasis on character psychology. Few critics can resist trying to sort out these competing narrative strands in search of artistic unity and the thematic keystone capable of integrating and harmonizing the novel's different levels of style and plot. But this task has proven elusive. Which narrative strand is the dominant plot? Which is the prevailing genre? Is the novel ultimately a comic satire? A parody? An allegory? A roman à clef? A fairy tale? An Easter novel with a distinct Christology?

For some critics, the novel's "generic instability" is its strength and allows the novel to open up "interpretive perspectives."[30] Others insist that the novel only "appears to lack unity and consistency" but actually points to a "higher order" of narrative consistency.[31] Still others suggest that the text's numerous "aporias and disjunctures" have actually led those scholars astray who attempt to synthesize the novel's disparate parts.[32] According to Gary Rosenshield, the fairy-tale world of the Master and Margarita and the Gogolian satire associated with Woland's suite come perilously close to undermining each other when read as a unified narrative and neither narrative can measure up to the psychological realism of the Jerusalem strand, hence "the novel's failure to arrive at coherent meaning(s)."[33]

But perhaps failure to arrive at one coherent meaning is an important outcome of the novel, whether or not that failure was intended or is even looked at as a flaw. On one level the novel is so appealing *because* it resists our attempts to impose any one meaning on it, a result that reflects Bulgakov's own attitude toward the question of belief and his implied polemic with the Soviet literary bureaucracy determined to do precisely that to literature: impose monolithic

meaning on it. If authority in literature is the unexplained right to final interpretation of meaning, then *The Master and Margarita* is a novel that subverts
authority, and revels in doing so. That is, the novel celebrates uncertainty, its own
and ours as readers.

Uncertainty is its main philosophical proposition, announced as soon as
Woland takes his seat on a park bench next to Berlioz and Bezdomny on that
fateful day in spring: the idea—personified by Woland himself—that things are
not always what they seem. For the next three hundred pages or so, Bulgakov
presents his readers with one puzzle after another, including Woland's identity,
the purpose of his trip, the meaning of the rewritten Gospel narrative in the
Jerusalem chapters, the identity of Yeshua Ha-Notsri, and the identities of the
title characters of our novel: the Master—who is introduced for the first time
only in chapter 13—and Margarita, whose biography is not given until over
halfway through the book. It is no wonder literary critics have long tried to solve
the novel's puzzles—readers have had to do this sort of thing since the moment
they picked up the book.

While it is true that some of the disjunctures and aporias that Rosenshield
identifies may have been mended had Bulgakov been able to finish final revisions of the book, it is also possible that the novel's central mysteries were never
intended to be fully resolved, just as the novel's competing plotlines need not be
fully integrated into one story for the novel to succeed or be enjoyed by readers.
Mystery is a central theme of the novel, whose unresolved questions lead characters and readers alike into a quasi-apophatic ignorance from which higher
truths may be glimpsed. Woland is the first and most dramatic personification
of this mystery in the novel, but he also quite conspicuously points to the novel's
other mysterious figure: Yeshua Ha-Notsri, a central figure in all three of the
novel's plotlines. Woland, then, embodies one mystery and articulates another,
and in so doing, launches all of the events that ensue in the novel.

Like Berlioz and Bezdomny, the first question readers ask of the novel is who
Woland is and why he has come to Moscow. Judging by the first three chapters,
it appears that Woland is someone who has come to Moscow for the express
purpose of disputing Berlioz's declaration that Jesus never lived and that God
does not exist either. In support of his claims, Woland offers two astonishing
pieces of evidence. The first is a narrative of Pontius Pilate's interview with Jesus,
which has almost nothing in common with canonical Gospel accounts, and
which apparently originates with Woland himself, who was present on Pontius
Pilate's balcony, thereby confirming Jesus's existence with his own eyewitness

testimony. The second piece of evidence, this time attesting to the existence of God, is Woland's status as the seventh proof of God.

Woland's proofs for the existence of Jesus and God are no mere devil's tricks. Nor are they simply plot devices intended to launch the story of our titular characters, who have yet to appear on the scene. Rather, they set the tone for the novel's very serious metaphysical inquiry. They also represent Bulgakov's first salvos against the heart of Soviet materialist ideology—the idea that human actions can be explained only by recourse to the natural sciences, with neither a spiritual realm nor a God guiding history. "Man himself is in control," Berlioz informs Woland (8). Reason reigns supreme; there is no religion, only rationality.

It is to these last points that Woland seems to direct his objections. In his metaphysical debate with Berlioz, Woland mentions the German philosopher Immanuel Kant by name and alludes to the Catholic philosopher Thomas Aquinas's five proofs of God, an allusion curiously passed over in the annotations to the two most recent English translations of *Master and Margarita* and virtually ignored in scholarship on the novel.[34] And yet Bulgakov does not bring up Aquinas lightly, for his five proofs of God not only reveal something essential about Bulgakov's theology, they also speak to the writer's cultural critique. Moreover, Woland gives these proofs added weight by counting them along with Kant's "moral will" as the six proofs that precede his own "seventh proof." Finally, and perhaps most importantly, by alluding to Aquinas's proofs, Woland draws Berlioz into a cunning contest, one in which he attempts to beat Berlioz at his own game: relying on reason as a way of apprehending the supernatural.

Aquinas's five proofs—also known as the "Five Ways"—all rely on a similar kind of logic, one that seeks to demonstrate the necessity of God through various logical premises. In his proofs, Aquinas relies on arguments from motion, causality, contingency, gradation, and governance. As Woland does not repeat them, it will help to briefly rehearse them here. The first proof is the argument from motion. It posits that if in the world, some things are observed to be in motion, then they had to have been *put* into motion by another mover. As there cannot be an infinite number of movers, there must be something that is the source of all motion, the so-called primary mover. This primary mover must be God. In his second proof, Aquinas makes a similar argument using cause and effect. Nothing is the efficient cause of itself. To be so, it would have to be prior to itself, which is impossible. Yet there is an observable order of efficient causes in the universe. As there cannot be an infinite number of causes, however, there must be a primary cause that itself is not caused by anything else but that gives rise to all other causes. This primary cause is God.

The third way is the proof of contingency. It states that if it is possible for some things to be and not to be, then that which is possible to be cannot always be—it must at some point not exist. If it were possible for *all* things not to exist, however, then nothing would exist now, which is obviously false. There must, therefore, be something which is not contingent but is, rather, a necessary being. This necessary being is God. The fourth way is the argument from gradation, which says that some things are greater than others in some quality. There cannot, however, be an infinite scale of greatness for any quality, as each gradation of quality is measured against the maximum of that quality. There must be, then, something that represents the perfection of that quality. This perfection must be what God is. Finally, the fifth way argues that even things that lack intelligence seem to act toward an end. Whatever acts toward an end must be governed by a force that moves it toward an end. That force is God. It is in these five ways that Aquinas attempts to provide a reasoned argument for God's existence.[35]

Berlioz is quick to dismiss Aquinas's proofs out of hand, insisting "reason dictates that there can be no proof of God's existence" (8). Woland points out that this was the exact response of Immanuel Kant, who found the logical flaw in Aquinas's arguments: you cannot apply observations of the physical world to metaphysical phenomena outside the boundaries of our experience. But even Kant, as Woland points out, still posited God for the moral will. Berlioz's position—that reason trumps all—is, however, a particularly Soviet one, and readers are meant to see its weakness. Berlioz seems to conceive of reason in a purely empirical fashion, something that operates only within the realm of experience or experimentation. Yet, as Kant himself argued in his *Critique of Pure Reason*, reason and rationality are not solely empirical in nature. Reason may tell us that all motion is caused, but our intellect nevertheless seeks out an explanation of the ultimate origin of that motion, even if that explanation is beyond empiricism's ability to discover. In his *Critique*, Kant tries to strike a balance between the ability of pure reason to produce knowledge outside the demands of empiricism and empiricism's claim that only experience, observation, and experimentation can be the basis of all knowledge. For his part, though Aquinas reasons his way toward God, he nevertheless attempts a kind of a leap of faith at the same time, since his proof remains in the realm of the speculative, as it must, according to Kant: science, after all, is unable to give hard answers to metaphysical questions.

This last thought is surely part of Bulgakov's cultural critique in his novel. In the anthropocentric, rational "paradise" that Berlioz praises, there is a limit to what science can tell us about the universe and an even greater limit to man's control over his life, a fact Woland demonstrates to Berlioz in the most graphic terms when Berlioz is beheaded by a tramcar after speaking with Woland. As Ivan discovers when he tries to puzzle out the mystery of Berlioz's death and as Kant affirms in his *Critique*, what one cannot explain through reason alone one must look elsewhere for the means to discover. For Ivan, this means embracing belief in the supernatural. Like Aquinas, he learns that belief may ultimately take us farther than reason.

Aquinas's proofs are important for another reason. His five ways are premised by two objections, the first of which anticipates Woland's seventh proof. This objection is the one most often raised to God's existence: that if God is infinite goodness and yet evil exists, then by definition an omnipotent, omniscient, and benevolent God cannot exist. Woland, of course, asserts just the opposite. If the devil exists (the incarnation of evil), then God must exist, too. Bulgakov's inversion of the classic question challenging God's existence—evil *proving* the existence of God, rather than disproving it—is but one of the many inversions the novel practices, many for parodic effect. At the same time, Bulgakov's inversion is thought-provoking in its own right. Where there is evil, there must also be its opposite—there must also be good. The one affirms the other and is inseparable from it, a kind of Manichean formulation often talked about in Bulgakov criticism and one that Woland himself establishes when he tells Levi Matvei in chapter 29: "What would your good do if evil didn't exist, and what would the earth look like if all the shadows disappeared?" (305). At the same time, the idea that evil might prove the existence of God has a quasi-apophatic quality to it: evil becomes the ultimate negative assertion that can be made about God (God is not evil). It therefore contributes to the apophatic exercise by which one journeys toward God.

While his five ways are not an exercise in apophaticism, Aquinas does cite Pseudo-Dionysius, the most prominent proponent of apophatic theology, numerous times in his *Summa Theologica*. However, in quoting from St. Augustine in his own response to the first objection to the existence of God in his *Summa Theologica*, Aquinas nevertheless affirms a link between good and evil that anticipates the novel's epigraph from Goethe in striking fashion. Aquinas writes: "As Augustine says (Enchiridion xi): 'Since God is the highest good, He would not allow any evil to exist in His works, unless His omnipotence

and goodness were such as to bring good even out of evil.' This is part of the
infinite goodness of God, that he should allow evil to exist, and out of it produce good."[36] Goethe, who may have had Augustine in mind, records the following exchange between Faust and Mephistopheles in scene 3 from the first
part of his drama, *Faust*: "Who are you, after all?" Faust asks Mephistopheles.
And the demon replies: "I am part of that power which forever wills evil and
forever works good." Thus Augustine, not Goethe, is the author of the premise
(announced in the novel's epigraph) that arguably drives the thematic thrust of
the novel, and Aquinas and his five proofs are the link between this sentiment
and the novel proper.

If Woland offers seven proofs for the existence of God, however, he categori-
cally refuses to do the same about Jesus, as already noted above. In fact, Woland
is adamant on this point. When he tells Berlioz and Ivan, "Keep in mind that
Jesus did exist," Berlioz concedes Woland's "great knowledge" but nevertheless
asserts "a different point of view regarding that issue." "No points of view are
necessary," Woland replies. "He simply existed, and that's all there is to it." When
Berlioz counters that "surely some proof is required," Woland repeats his assertion: "No, no proof is required." And then he begins to tell them the story of
Yeshua Ha-Notsri's encounter with Pilate.

Woland is, of course, correct. The story he tells Berlioz and Ivan is just that—a
story. It is not proof and, indeed, its source cannot be verified or even actually
identified. Only the last two Jerusalem chapters—the two that Margarita reads
from the restored manuscript in chapters 25 and 26—are undoubtedly from the
Master's novel. The first chapter told by Woland in chapter 2 and the second
chapter dreamed by Ivan in chapter 16 can only be assumed to have come from
the Master's novel by virtue of their content, style, and connected plot.[37] And yet
even if all four chapters are from the Master's novel, it is still impossible to know
to what extent it purports to tell the truth about Pilate, Jesus, and the Passion
narrative.

Indeterminacy ultimately seems to characterize the Jerusalem chapters,
though this does not seem to be the case at first glance. Bulgakov's attention
to detail in his presentation of archeological, geographic, and historical aspects
of first-century Jerusalem is universally praised by critics, who see in the writer's insistence on historical accuracy a polemic with the Gospels, the historical reliability of which has often been disparaged, especially by scholars of
the historical critical method. J. A. E. Curtis credits F. W. Farrar's *The Life of
Jesus Christ* (1874)—a work intended to provide the historical case for a divine

Jesus—as the source contributing most to the "astonishingly tangible realism" of the Jerusalem chapters.[38] From the hanging bridges, fortresses, and "utterly indescribable block of marble with golden dragon scales instead of a roof" (the temple of Jerusalem, 25) in chapter 2 to the "winged gods above the hippodrome, the Hasmonaean Palace and its embrasures, the bazaars, the caravan-series, the alleys, the ponds" (255), and the narrow, crowded streets of the Lower City in chapter 25, Bulgakov's Jerusalem is highly evocative and richly textured. Readers are meant to feel the veracity of what Bulgakov describes and its striking difference from the Gospel accounts. It seems that Bulgakov is offering a more plausible, historically sound Passion narrative.

Moreover, Bulgakov tries to further distance us from the four Gospels by defamiliarizing the names of people and places. Bulgakov's Jesus is Yeshua Ha-Notsri, a more historically authentic appellation. Yeshua is the Hebrew name from which "Jesus" is derived, meaning "the lord is salvation," while Ha-Notsri means "of Nazareth." The Sanhedrin (the Jewish Supreme Court; *sovet* in the Russian Bible) is now the Sinedrion (the Greek translation). The Head Priest Caiaphus (Kaiafa in the Russian Bible) is Joseph Kaifa (Iosif Kaifa). Judas Iscariot (Iuda Iskariot) is Judas of Kerioth (Iuda iz Kiriafa, the use of an explanatory name, after Renan). Matthew the Levite's name is russified, becoming Levi Matvei. Jerusalem (Ierusalim) is Yershalaim (a variant of the Hebrew Yerushalaim). And so on.[39] While Proffer points out that it is natural for Aramaic, Greek, and Latin to be mixed together even within a single conversation in first-century Jerusalem, Bulgakov's intention in this instance is not only realism but also estrangement, hence the unlikely Russian name for Levi Matvei.

The greatest defamiliarization, however, is the story itself. As mentioned earlier, the Jesus readers encounter is nothing like the Jesus of the Gospels. When brought before Pilate, Yeshua Ha-Notsri does everything he can to deny that he is a prophet or possesses any extraordinary abilities. Though he seems to read Pilate's thoughts and to heal him of his migraine, he explains his supposed clairvoyance by saying that he is simply interpreting Pilate's gestures. As for any healing powers, he denies that he is a physician each of the two times Pilate asks him (18, 19). Similarly, he denies entering the Shushan Gate astride a donkey and accompanied by an adoring crowd. Rather, he declares he has only one follower, Levi Matvei, who muddles everything he says, just as the crowds misunderstand him when he tells them that "the temple of the old faith will fall and a new temple of truth will be created" (17). Instead, they claim that in his assertion about the temple of the old faith, Yeshua incited them to destroy the temple in Jerusalem (the ostensible charge for which he is brought before Pilate). An orphan who does not remember his parents, he hails not from Nazareth (as his name would imply) but from Gamala (or En-Sarid, as Bulgakov notes in chapter 26—a confusion the author would likely have cleared up if he had completed his revisions of part 2). Yeshua professes belief in one God; he claims that there are no evil people in the world (he calls everyone a "good person," thus affirming a strong personalism); he believes people will change if only he can talk to them; and he is ultimately sentenced to death by Pilate for his assertion that the "power of the Caesars" will be replaced by a "kingdom of truth and justice, where no such power will be necessary" (22).

There are no miracles, no parables, no sermons, or Beatitudes. Yeshua is not crucified but simply "executed" (chapter 16 is titled "execution" not "crucifixion") on a post (*stolb*) not on a cross (*krest*), on Bald Mountain (*lysaia gora*) not at Golgotha.[40] Gethsemane is mentioned by name, but it is not the place where Jesus suffers the agony in the garden and is then betrayed by Judas. Rather, it is the olive grove where Afranius's men lure Judas and kill him. In keeping with the realist tone of the Jerusalem chapters, Yeshua's death is described with a gruesome naturalism that evokes Holbein's depiction of the dead Christ.[41] Hanging on his post, Yeshua's head is "so covered with flies that his face had disappeared beneath a black, heaving mask. Fat horseflies clung to his groin, stomach, and armpits, sucking on his naked yellow body" (151). His last words are not "my God, my God, why have you forsaken me" (as in Matthew and Mark) or "Father, into your hands I commend my spirit" (from Luke) or "it is finished" (in John), but only one word: "Hegemon," Pilate's title.

These differences between Yeshua and the Jesus of the Gospels have prompted dramatic claims about him and about Bulgakov's intent in creating him. Some critics declare that Bulgakov was attempting to rewrite the Gospels in the Jerusalem chapters, a claim that seems overstated given the fact that Bulgakov limits himself to what in all the Gospels except John's constitutes only one chapter: the interview with Pilate and the crucifixion (the Passion narrative). Similarly, though Yeshua may tell Levi Matvei to burn his parchment, to claim that because of this "Bulgakov effectively calls into question the Christian worldview" or that he "wishes the reader to believe that his narrative is more likely, more convincing, and better written than the Gospels" is to assume more than the novel can support.[42] In truth, Yeshua appears in only the first two Jerusalem chapters and says almost nothing in the second of these two. He simply says and does too little to justify the idea that the Jerusalem chapters either constitute a rewriting of the Gospels or discredit them or both, even when taking into account his seeming lack of divinity. In actuality, Bulgakov's attitude toward the biblical Jesus is more complex than it might at first appear. As a matter of fact, the story of Jesus's Passion in all but the penultimate complete manuscript version contain elements that suggest that, initially, Bulgakov might have had a much more traditional Christology in mind.

In the 1928–1929 manuscript version, Pilate's wife warns him that she dreamed of Yeshua and asks her husband to let him go, an episode straight from Matthew 27:19. In this version, Yeshua also tells the two thieves being crucified with him that they will follow him to heaven and utters "it is finished" in Greek when he dies.[43] In all but the 1938 manuscript version Woland refers to Jesus as Christ ("Keep in mind that *Christ* existed"), thereby alluding to a messianic identity, and Bulgakov uses the word "cross" (not "post") in his depiction of the crucifixion. In her reconstruction of the partially destroyed first notebooks of the novel, Chudakova reports that Bulgakov included "several Gospel episodes" as well as parts of apocryphal stories about Jesus, such as the story of Veronica, who wiped Christ's brow with her shawl on his way to his crucifixion.[44] Interestingly, the 1928–1929 version also includes a passage where Berlioz even accuses Woland of loving Jesus, thus affirming the traditional Christian notion of Jesus as love incarnate. Woland had just finished relating his version of Jesus's meeting with Pilate:

"You love him, I see," Vladimir Mironovich [Berlioz] said, squinting.

"Who?"

"Jesus."

"Me?" the stranger asked, and coughed, "Kkh-kkh," but made no answer.[45]

Woland's silence here is evocative. While this is not Dostoevsky's Christ answering the Grand Inquisitor with a silent kiss, the scene nevertheless provides one intriguing early view onto Bulgakov's Jesus as someone whom not even the devil can resist loving. That Bulgakov deleted this exchange and seems to have consciously distanced his Jesus narrative from the Gospel accounts in his final version of the novel does not mean, however, that he was entirely rejecting the Gospels as sources of knowledge about Jesus nor does it mean that he was necessarily spurning traditional Christian views of him. Rather, his estranged portrayal of Jesus may simply have better served his narrative of disjuncture and indeterminacy, for reasons explored at greater length below.

LOVE STORIES, INVERSIONS, AND APOPHATICISM

If they judge solely by the first two chapters, readers may well surmise that what they are reading is a theological novel, one that will attempt to inject the topic of God and the supernatural into officially atheist Soviet literary and cultural discourse. But just when they come to this conclusion, the novel veers into a satiric exposé of Soviet reality in which ridicule of atheist attitudes toward God and Jesus Christ is quickly supplanted by the satiric unmasking of Soviet corruption, cronyism, and philistinism in the literary and theater worlds. In these satirical exposés, the theme of the supernatural is expressed by magical stunts that displace and distance the theological inquiry with which the novel begins. Once the Master steps onto the pages of the novel in chapter 13, the book's theological themes recede even further as readers are introduced to the love story of the Master and Margarita and the sad fate of the Master's novel. With Margarita's belated arrival in the opening pages of part 2, our titular characters finally assert their centrality and a seemingly new story begins, one about "real, true, everlasting love," as our narrator informs us (185).

The introduction of Margarita in part 2 and the story of her love for the Master take the novel in an entirely new direction. Indeed, the further one reads in part 2, the more it seems that part 1 is but the preparation for part 2, that part 2 is where the novel's center is, that the novel is first and foremost a love story, in particular, the story of Margarita's fierce and self-sacrificing love of the Master and her deal with the devil to save him. And to a certain degree, this is indeed so, but with an important twist. In part 2, Woland becomes less the finger of God punishing the sinful Muscovites and more the agent who ultimately provides a happy ending for our delayed love story. In this reading, the reason for the devil's visit to Moscow is simply his annual Spring Ball of the Full Moon, while his choice of Margarita is motivated primarily by her being a native of Moscow who descends from the requisite royal bloodline.

Ivan Bezdomny, so important to part 1 of the story, is in part 2 almost nowhere to be found, as if to confirm the novel's abandonment of its opening theological inquiry, with which he was so closely linked, and to underscore instead the precedence of the love story of the Master and Margarita. All of this seems to be so right up until the unexpected appearance, from the Jerusalem chapters, of Levi Matvei and, by association, of Yeshua Ha-Notsri himself, in the narrative strands of the two Moscow stories, an event that takes our love story in a new direction. Ideally, this surprising development should bring all three plots into alignment and establish thematic and compositional harmony. In actuality, however, it only creates more aporias and raises further questions.

In his sudden appearance in the Moscow plotline, Levi Matvei conveys a request from Yeshua that Woland grant the Master and Margarita peace. And yet there is no explanation of the startling disjuncture observable between the mortal Yeshua Ha-Notsri of the Jerusalem chapters and the apparently immortal Yeshua who sends his disciple to parley with Woland. What are readers to make of this? Does Levi Matvei's appearance imply a divine Yeshua Ha-Notsri along the lines of the Christian Jesus Christ, who is deciding the fate of the Master and Margarita, thus solving the mystery of Yeshua's identity in favor of a more or less orthodox Christology? Or is this sudden, textually unmotivated quasi-divinization of Yeshua simply evidence that the novel escaped Bulgakov's control?

Here, the specter of the unfinished manuscript makes itself felt. Chapter 29, "The Fate of the Master and Margarita Is Decided," in which Levi Matvei conveys Yeshua's request to Woland, was a late addition to the novel. It is missing entirely from the penultimate version of the manuscript completed in May 1938.[46] Perhaps the revisions to part 2 that Bulgakov could not finish would have better prepared readers for this development or made clearer the connection between the Yeshua from the Jerusalem chapters and the one who sends his emissary to Woland in Moscow. Or maybe the text as it is suggests its own possible answer.

Bulgakov does, after all, provide hints that the Yeshua of the Jerusalem chapters may not be as mortal and earthly as he seems. What, for instance, is the "urgent business" in Jerusalem that takes Yeshua away so suddenly from the gardener he had been visiting in Bethany in chapter 16 and why is Matvei "hit by a sudden and terrible illness" that very evening, thus preventing him from joining Yeshua until after he had been arrested (147)? Why does this illness leave Matvei "as suddenly as it had come"? And why is Kaifa so determined that Yeshua be executed in chapter 2? What does he mean when he tells Pilate that Yeshua did "violence to their religion"? And what about Pilate himself, who, in chapter 25, refers to "the trouble caused by this messiah" whom the people have "suddenly started waiting for this year"? Are readers supposed to conclude that Yeshua was taken for that messiah, hence the trouble that overtakes him in Jerusalem?

One can only speculate. And yet it is no accident that Bulgakov should return to the questions with which he opens his novel by concluding it with the appearance of the heavenly messenger, Levi Matvei, and his request on behalf of the quasi-divine Yeshua. The question of the existence of God and the reality and identity of Jesus Christ, it turns out, are not simply a means to begin the novel but are germane to the entire narrative. Bulgakov's treatment of this theme points to an important aspect of his creative methodology. If there is a center to this novel, it is here, but it is Bulgakov's subtle treatment of this cardinal theme that gives the impression that it is of secondary importance to the story of the Master and Margarita proper.

God and Jesus Christ, after all, are not as absent from the novel as it might at first appear. By the novel's own logic, wherever Woland is, there, too, is proof of the existence of God. Woland's early interest in proving the reality of Jesus and his key link to proofs of the existence of God are thus important markers of his function in the text as an apophatic agent of belief, as is evident in the "conversion" stories of Ivan Bezdomny and Margarita, who, in opening themselves up to belief in a supernatural order, have also taken their first steps toward affirming belief in God. By the same token, it is possible that Yeshua in the Master's novel is a similar kind of negative reflection of the divine Jesus Christ, all the more so as it is the devil who first relates the story of Yeshua Ha-Notsri to our two atheists, a story which, in one of the earliest drafts of the novel, was titled "The Gospel according to Woland."[47] Edward Ericson makes such an argument, claiming that Yeshua is "only the shadow of the real Jesus Christ" viewed through "the diabolical filter" of Woland's narration, a state of affairs righted when the true, "resurrected" Yeshua "appears" at novel's end.[48] According to Ericson, the many parallels with the Gospel accounts of Jesus's Passion embedded within the Jerusalem chapters reveal how Bulgakov elaborately encodes an Orthodox theological framework into what most readers have assumed to be a heterodox work.[49]

Ericson's analysis, however, is prey to the same weakness that other quests for a unified reading of the novel suffer: it must, as Andrew Barratt points out, "explain away the ironies, ambiguities, and paradoxes that are generated at every turn by this most complex novel."[50] And yet such aporias, disjunctures, and seeming contradictions are part of the novel's appeal and contribute greatly to its subtlety and complexity. They also reflect the author's own complicated attitude toward matters of faith. Bulgakov may not be rejecting the Jesus of the Gospels so much as groping his way toward what the Christ of faith must be, in his own life and the lives of his countrymen. He is doing so, moreover, from the opposite end of the belief spectrum: from the position of least certainty and in a narrative begun by the devil and related to two atheists. The idea is to discover the true Christ in the apophatic absence of everything familiar about him from the canonical Gospels. In this regard, apophaticism harmonizes with the novel's reliance on aporias, ironies, and ambiguities because paradox and uncertainty are at the heart of its theological method. Readers are supposed to be left in a state of apophatic darkness, the better to discern the true God-Man.

The thoroughly secular Yeshua who denies any divine or magical powers, who disavows with horror the "Gospel" that Levi Matvei is apparently writing in his parchment, and who "is guilty of a cringing weakness which ill suits the Son of God"[51] is, from an apophatic point of view, everything that Christ is not. He therefore represents our first steps toward apprehending what Christ actually may be. Nor does the "offstage" appearance of Yeshua at novel's end necessarily resolve the matter of his identity, as it is unclear what position in Bulgakov's cosmology he occupies. Is he Woland's superior or equal? What is his relationship to God? Is he the Son of God and the second person of the Trinity or something else? Bulgakov's readers cannot be sure. Again, they are left in a state of apophatic ignorance, one pregnant, however, with the promise of truer discernment.

My point here is not that Bulgakov has constructed an elaborate apophatic puzzle for us to discover that neatly solves the thematic and theological issues of the novel. Quite the contrary. Few scholars believe that Bulgakov intended to affirm a traditional Christian cosmology or canonical Christ. However, it is equally clear that in his novel he is seeking, after his own fashion, answers to the same cursed questions that have vexed Russian writers before him: is there a God? Why is there evil in the world? Who was Jesus Christ? In grappling with these questions, though, Bulgakov guides us on a negative path in order to remind us of our supernatural ignorance and powerlessness, our inability, as Woland reminds Berlioz, to be in control and "have a definite plan for at least a reasonable period of time [. . .], say, a thousand years" (8). Woland is a good guide for this negative way, both because he is the perfect apophatic representation of what God is not and because he reminds us of our human limitations in divining the divine. In this context, it is clear why Bulgakov's novel depends precisely on disjuncture, aporia, and discontinuity. The pieces of the puzzle are not supposed to fit neatly together in the end. The truth—whether about the existence of God or the identity of Christ—is beyond our grasp. One can only grope one's way towards it.

In this reading, the novel's inversions serve to enact a kind of textual apophaticism, but only that. They do not propose an answer so much as pose questions, for the whole point of this textual apophaticism is the process of questioning, not the end point of answering. Ivan Bezdomny and Margarita each undergo "conversions" in the novel, but neither conversion proposes or presupposes a set of beliefs, only the marking of an initial movement toward belief in general, first in the existence of the devil and, only by implication, in the existence of God. In truth, readers learn very little of what they believe about the devil and nothing at all about what they may believe regarding God.

A similar outcome prevails in other instances of textual inversion. Let us take, for instance, the "Black Mass" inscribed into the chapter on Satan's Grand Ball, where Berlioz's severed head is made into a chalice into which is poured the blood of the murdered Soviet informant, Baron Maigel, which Woland drinks as blood, but which turns into wine for Margarita. Clearly, this scene parodies the Orthodox Eucharist, and indeed Bulgakov scholarship has long noted the "enormous semantic load of Christian iconography, much of it derived from Russian Orthodox tradition," in the novel.[52] But if this is parody, how is one to understand it? In Ericson's Orthodox reading of the novel, parody is the royal road to affirming what you negate. Thus, the Black Mass inscribes the real Eucharist into the text through a carefully supported symbolic structure.[53] And yet, Bulgakov's inversions often double back on themselves, thus complicating what might at first appear to be straightforward symbolism.

The inversion described in the chapter on Satan's Grand Ball is actually greater and more complicated than critics suppose. As queen of the Ball, for instance, Margarita experiences something of a reverse Passion: first, resurrection (the murderers, thieves, and scoundrels who come to the ball are brought back to life out of dust and corruption); then, "crucifixion" (the heavy, oval-framed picture of a poodle on a heavy chain symbolizes the heavy cross Christ must bear); then, a via dolorosa (the endless flow of guests torment her with kisses to her knee and hand that cause her excruciating pain); after which her strength fails her on two separate occasions (Christ falls three times); and concluding with the last supper (where blood is changed to wine). Readers are certainly free to see in this inversion a parodic injection into the novel of the Passion narrative, an "undoing" of the Christ story, so to speak, that also inscribes that narrative into the text.

At the same time, however, this inversion is itself reversed when the Passion story is replicated in proper order after the ball. First comes the last supper (with Woland and company after the ball—a small band of "believers" celebrating spring "Passover"); then, the via dolorosa (when Margarita is tested, fulfills her promise to release Frieda from her sufferings, fears she has lost her right to request reunion with the Master, is then reunited with him, but finds him a shell of his former self who must be revived and comforted); followed by crucifixion (when Azazello poisons them both in the Master's old basement apartment); and concluding with resurrection (they are resurrected as spiritual bodies and leave with Woland for their abode of peace). What is Bulgakov up to? Parodic affirmation of canonical religious truths, as per Ericson, or parodic inversion of them? Or is this textual play—mirrors reflecting mirrors, disjunctures, aporias—part of a strategy to estrange the readers' perception of the last supper and the crucifixion so that they may see them anew and, seeing them as if for the first time, discern Christ more truly? If so, then these inversions can be said to contribute to the apophatic thrust of the novel.

An apophatic approach provides an alternate way of making sense of the epigraph from Faust: "and who are you, after all? / I am part of the power which forever wills evil and forever works good." Obviously, like St. Augustine, Bulgakov could be suggesting here that the evils of the world can be justified as being part of God's inscrutable plan and that such an approach can be taken toward understanding Stalin's reign of terror, too. But this proposition does not hold up in the novel. Woland—the "Spirit of Evil" (Levi Matvei's words, *dukh zla*)—may restore the Master and Margarita and punish Muscovites for their pettiness, but he can hardly be said to "forever work good," even in his role as agent of their ultimate fate. Rather, evil in the novel primarily provides a negative illumination of good, thus revealing it more fully, as Woland himself implies when he tells Levi Matvei about how shadows are necessary for us to appreciate the light (305). In apophatic theology, evil would be one of the first things one would say God is not. Thus, the epigraph serves not to justify evil or even to characterize Woland but, rather, to point to the novel's apophatic impulse, one that says that an encounter with evil *can* work, apophatically, to reveal good, which is God, if only one could say so cataphatically. Evil is thus not so much a force that works good but a concept that helps lead us to an understanding of what good—and God—must be.

Woland's greatest good deed—his rescue of the Master and Margarita—is, upon closer scrutiny, hardly a good deed at all. Rather, he simply rewards Margarita for serving as the hostess of his ball and agrees to Yeshua's request to grant the couple peace. Goodness has very little to do with either act, though one may argue that he performs a good deed by default, reuniting the novel's central romantic pair and thus affirming the "real, true, everlasting love" whose story was promised at the beginning of part 2. But even here an objection may be raised, for while part 2 of the novel does indeed focus on the love story of the Master and Margarita, that love story is actually introduced in the novel in terms that set it up as a romantic cliché, thus rendering its description as "real, true, and everlasting" highly suspect. Barratt comments that the story the Master tells Ivan about how he met and lost Margarita "is replete with the sort of hackneyed clichés and melodramatic effects one associates with the very worst boulevard romances."[54] He is correct—their love story seems absolutely contrived and unmotivated. The Master tells Ivan that love struck them "instantly," "like a murderer [who] jumps out of nowhere in an alley," "the way lightning strikes, or a Finnish knife." In telling Ivan this story, the Master avails himself of cliché after cliché, insisting it was "fate" that brought them together and claiming that "they were meant to be together forever" (116–18). How can such a story describe "real, true, everlasting love"?

Some critics explain this incongruity away by relating their narrative arc to the genre of fairy tale.[55] Viewed as a fairy tale, the love story of the Master and Margarita needs no further motivation. Readers are simply supposed to take for granted, as they do in fairy tales, that theirs is a quintessential story of the power of eros—the romantic love between two people—to conquer all. But such an explanation significantly erodes the importance of their story with regard to the other two narrative arcs of the novel. How can a fairy-tale love story, after all, not only hold up to the novel's richly retold Passion narrative but somehow relate the conditions of that Passion narrative's composition in the satiric Moscow strand? Here, readers bump up against the matter of the novel's generic instability again and the question of how each plot trajectory relates to the other two, a question fraught with all sorts of difficulties, as this chapter has attempted to show. But perhaps the wrong question is actually being posed here. Maybe each narrative strand does not ultimately have to harmonize with the other two. Maybe textual dissonance is the point. After all, if the fairy-tale story of the Master and Margarita does not ultimately fit the description of "real, true, everlasting love" in the novel, then perhaps such true love is meant to be found elsewhere. And perhaps finding such true love in the novel is a task that is actually enabled by the love story of the Master and Margarita and is connected to the novel's apophatic theology.

If Woland, as an apophatic marker of God's existence, is intimately connected to the story of the Master and Margarita, then that story is itself endowed with an apophatic charge. The only problem is, while there are certainly ways in which both the Master and Margarita can point to the Godhead as possible Christ figures,[56] the affirmation of their love and their reunification at novel's end do not actually steer us to Christ or to God. Quite the contrary, as the novel makes clear, they attain peace, but not the light. Their love does not point to divine love and cannot, for neither participates in the divine love of forgiveness of enemies. Indeed, Margarita seeks to punish and harm the Master's enemies, not love and forgive them. Thus, for all of Margarita's sacrifices or all of the Master's suffering, their love remains the private, selfish, and self-interested love of any romantic plot or fairy tale. Divine love, by contrast, is not private but open to all; it is selfless and disinterested, a love not of lovers, but of enemies. There is only one love story like this in the novel—a love story of enemies. It is the story of Pilate and Yeshua.

Like that of the Master and Margarita, the love story of Pilate and Yeshua also lacks direct textual motivation. If, however, one can argue that the lack of motivation behind the Master's and Margarita's love at first sight might be explained by the fairy-tale nature of their story, the same cannot be said of the Pilate story, where the mythic contours of the Gospel have been supplanted by an ornate psychological realism. In this love story, Pilate's interest in a Jewish troublemaker and his inexplicable need to avenge his death, at considerable peril to his own position and well-being (after all, the head of his secret police, Afranius, is a dangerous coconspirator), seems to be motivated solely by the effect Yeshua has on him during their one interview. In other words, as with the Master and Margarita, it is "love at first sight," but for a radically different reason and with a dramatically different outcome. Whereas the Master and Margarita earn only peace at novel's end, Pilate follows Yeshua into the light and, presumably, eternal salvation. What do these differing outcomes mean?

On the surface, it makes no sense that Pilate earns the light; after all, he oversaw the execution of the innocent Yeshua Ha-Notsri and countless others. The Master and Margarita, by contrast, earn only peace, though they have no blood whatsoever on their hands and, indeed, can be seen as victims of the ruthlessness of Stalin's Russia. Bulgakov provides no explanation of this outcome, except in the dim outline of his novel's implied apophaticism. The novel is, indeed, a story about the triumph of love, but not the love implied by the title of the book. Rather, it is the triumph of divine love, expressed by Pilate's participation in the act of forgiveness of enemies that is at the core of agapic love. Yeshua forgives his executioner in keeping with the Master's portrayal of him as someone who believes there are no evil people. And Pilate, "the cruel fifth procurator of Judea," who is the chief protagonist of the Jerusalem chapters and the actual subject of the Master's novel, is granted the light as if to underscore how inscrutable the nature of divine love is and how central Pilate's role is in discerning it.

The eros that describes the essence of the private love between two people is shown to be inferior to the agapic love that allows the victim to forgive the executioner and the executioner to achieve salvation. This is the vision of heaven against which Ivan Karamazov rebels, where the mother of the tormented child embraces her child's tormentor and the entire heavenly host exclaims, "Thou art just, O Lord!"[57] And yet it is precisely the darkness and evil that surround Yeshua's execution that make possible our apprehension of the greatest good of all: disinterested, universal, all-forgiving agapic love, the very means by which "everything will be made right" in the world, as Woland asserts but does not explain in the novel.[58] The love between the Master and the Margarita is not divine love, but it helps point to the "real, true, everlasting love" between Pilate and Yeshua. That, it turns out, is its Christological function in the novel. Bulgakov associates Yeshua with Jesus's hardest commandment, and in showing how Yeshua loves his enemy and forgives him, Bulgakov reaffirms this act as central to his image of Christ.

Ultimately, however, the reader is not told who the quasi-divine Yeshua is at novel's end just as, Bulgakov implies, Jesus Christ must remain ineffable, like God himself. Defining the divine is tantamount to denying the divine, which is, of course, the sin with which the novel opens and for which Berlioz pays so dearly. God cannot be authored except, perhaps, apophatically. All that one can say about God is what one does not know about God in the hope that the act of divesting God of conceptual language—as Bulgakov does in his apophatic novel—will be enough to point us in the right direction, in the same way that the moonbeam ultimately leads Pilate to the light. Thus, Bulgakov's theological novel achieves its goal—it affirms the existence of God and Jesus Christ without claiming theological authority or implying divine authorship. *The Master and Margarita* remains an open, even unstable text,[59] but one that can, for that very reason, lead us into the dark apophatic space that may bring us, too, into the light. Such is Bulgakov's image of Christ, that in his utterly unrecognizable figure the reader may achieve the means of seeing more clearly and discerning more truly. In the end, Christ is revealed through negative means in three ways: via the Master's story of the non-canonical Jesus, Yeshua Ha-Notsri; through the fairy-tale love story of the Master and Margarita that points to the divine love story of Yeshua and Pilate; and through the indeterminacy of Bulgakov's text itself, which resists interpretation as a means of avoiding definitive statements about the Godhead.

CHAPTER EIGHT

"EMPHATICALLY HUMAN, DELIBERATELY PROVINCIAL"

The Christ of Boris Pasternak

But now the book of life has reached a page
More precious than the holy things of men.
And now must be fulfilled the Word ordained.
So let Thy will be done, my Lord. Amen.

"Garden of Gethsemane," *The Poems of Yuri Zhivago*,
translated by James E. Falen

If the "gospel" of Bulgakov's Yeshua is driven by a distinct personalism—there are no evil people; we must love our enemies, even our executioners; divine, agapic love is the means by which everything will be made right in the world—then Boris Pasternak makes the centrality of human personhood and the human personality the fundamental discovery and essence of Christianity itself and the core concept of his own literary Christology in his novel, *Doctor Zhivago*. Of all of the Christ novels examined in this book, *Doctor Zhivago* is by far the one most driven by a personalist understanding of human-divine relations. A pronounced personalism marks the Christian philosophy of Zhivago's uncle Vedeniapin and his disciples and helps us understand the actions of Yuri Zhivago himself, who shares his uncle's views and whose life choices are motivated by a personalist perspective. Indeed, Zhivago's relationships with three separate women and the children that he sires by them challenge how far the application of personalist insights can be used as a means of understanding his irregular love life. They also bring to the fore the opposition between eros and agape, which in this novel, more than any of the other Christ novels analyzed here, assumes a heightened Christological importance. Complicating our Christological reading are the many Christological associations attaching to Zhivago himself, beginning with his name and the private Passiontide his life story enacts and concluding with the many Christ poems Zhivago wrote that are included in the final part of the novel. To fully understand Pasternak's Easter novel, then, this chapter undertakes three important tasks: it analyzes how a personalist understanding of Christianity is deployed on the thematic and Christological levels; it assesses the meaning of Yuri's *imitatio Christi* in the novel, whether in the shape of his life or the poems he writes about Jesus's Passiontide; and it explains how Yuri's sexual indiscretions are to be understood in the context of Pasternak's unorthodox Christology. In addressing these questions, this chapter will attempt to discover the ways in which Pasternak's novel celebrates how "individual human life became the life story of God"[1]—a phrase that succinctly sums up the personalist theme of the novel itself.

Pasternak and Christianity

As was the case with Bulgakov, Pasternak's interest in Christ loomed largest in his writing at the end of his life. His biographer Guy de Mallac notes that there are only "rare references to New Testament values" in Pasternak's pre-Zhivago poetry, stating that it is only with the novel that "Christ appears as a major presence."[2] Lazar Fleishman argues that "a new concept of Christianity crystallized in the poet" in the postwar period and his work on Doctor Zhivago.[3] As evidence, he cites the February 1946 version of his poem "Hamlet," containing only two stanzas (not the four of the final version) and devoid of any reference to Christ or any Christian images.[4] By the winter months of 1946–1947, however, Pasternak had already written the first Christian-themed poems of the novel, "Star of the Nativity" and "Miracle," thus announcing the spiritual direction the novel was to take.[5] Even so, Fleishman cautions readers that Pasternak treated Christian themes "as an artist, not as a theologian, preacher or academic historian."[6]

The son of liberal Jews who did not observe the rites of the synagogue, Pasternak looked at Christianity in the context of his parents' "broad, non-denominational religiosity"[7] as well as through the unique prism of his own inspiration. Unlike Dostoevsky and Tolstoy, who each made famous pronouncements about Christ or Christianity at the beginning of their careers that determined the trajectory of their Christology, and unlike Bulgakov, whose encounter with a stack of *Bezbozhnik* back issues served as the catalyst for his own imaging of Jesus, Pasternak did not seem to have one defining moment in his own encounter with Christ that crystallized his particular religious worldview. Nevertheless, Christianity was an early and important influence, and just as it had with Yuri Zhivago, it began with the nanny who took him to church, as Pasternak himself explains in a letter to the French scholar Jacqueline de Proyart:

> In my early childhood I was baptized by the nurse who looked after me, but because of restrictions upon the Jews and particularly in a family which was exempt from those restrictions and enjoyed a certain distinction as a result of its father's artistic merits, the fact of my baptism was accompanied by various complications and remained semi-secret and private, thereby providing me with rare and exceptional inspiration rather than calm habit. But I believe this to be the source of my originality. During the years 1910–1912, when the main roots and foundation of that originality—together with my vision of things, of the world, of life—were taking shape, I lived most of my life in Christian thought.[8]

Throughout the 1920s, Christianity seemed not far from his mind despite rare mention of it in his poetry. Around 1929 Pasternak even confided to a friend of the family that at some point he "very nearly became Orthodox" and, indeed, would have, had he married an Orthodox woman.[9] Between his earlier intense interest in Christianity and his renewed attention to it in the 1940s, however, a distinct gap is detectable in the writer's religiosity, an interlude alluded to in Pasternak's poem "Dawn," from the poetry of Yuri Zhivago. The poem begins, "You were the be-all in my destiny," but then describes how war and devastation caused a rupture that lasted for "many, many years," after which the poet writes, "again your voice disturbs me":

> All night I read your testament—
> And found my consciousness returning. (17:553)

George Katkov reports that Pasternak told him that the "you" addressed in the first stanza was, indeed, Christ.[10] If correct, then, the testament the poetic narrator refers to is the New Testament, confirming this as a poem that refers to two different periods in the poet's life: his religious period before the First

World War and his newly awakened interest in Christianity later, during the Second World War.[11] Thus the poem casts valuable light on Pasternak's journey toward Christ, disrupted but resumed in time for the composition of his novel.

Bodin notes that among the relatively few books in Pasternak's library at his dacha in Peredelkino were both a complete Bible in its Synod translation into Russian and a separate edition of the New Testament. Numerous markings and underlined places in the Gospels (particularly, the Gospel of Matthew, "which especially interested the poet") indicate passages of importance to the writer, which Bodin groups in different categories by theme: Christ and his opponents; imitating Christ; Christ's active struggle; the coming triumph of Christ; Christ's parables; and the Last Judgment.[12] Pasternak also left marks and underlined places in an Orthodox hymnbook in his Peredelkino library, referring largely to Christ's resurrection and his struggle against death.[13]

There is no way of knowing exactly when Pasternak made his notations in these books, though it was most likely during his later religious reawakening and his work on *Doctor Zhivago*. While his notes on the pages of the Bible, the New Testament, and the hymnbook in his Peredelkino library are confirmation of the writer's keen interest in Christ and the Gospels, in his final years Pasternak was quite reticent about the extent of his religiosity. Within three years of finishing his Easter novel in December of 1955, Pasternak even described himself as "almost an atheist" in a conversation with German journalist Gerd Ruge, and then went on to explain "with deep emotion, his concept of God."[14] There was thus always something paradoxical about the nature of Pasternak's belief in the midst of the Soviet century. As James Billington puts it, "Pasternak was driven by religious concerns that he was unable to resolve in any conventional way."[15] So he chose unconventional means to reveal them, inscribing them into a novel whose Christology was likewise unconventional, the better to explicate it properly.

Personalism, Yuri Zhivago, and Christ

Pasternak's exploration of Christ in his novel is bound up with his hero, Yuri Zhivago, a fictional contemporary of Pasternak if not a vaguely autobiographical reflection of him. Though he grew up in the same two decades as Pasternak—1890–1910, the epoch of the *bezvremen'e* of fin-de-siècle cultural and social stagnation, which Blok described in his famous essay—Yuri Zhivago shares little else with his creator, save, of course, a talent for writing poetry. While Pasternak grew up in a loving household where a stream of writers, musicians, and artists visited—including Leo Tolstoy, Rainer Maria Rilke, Alexander Skriabin, and Nikolai Ge—Yuri Zhivago was an orphan by the age of twelve and lived in the homes of relatives. He had no parade of influential cultural figures to inspire him, with the exception of his uncle Nikolai Vedeniapin, someone who was soon "to take his place among contemporary writers, university professors, and philosophers of the revolution" (1:4:7). Although he passes care of Yuri over to first one set of relatives and then another, Vedeniapin plays an important role in his nephew's intellectual and spiritual formation.

In particular, Yuri is influenced by Vedeniapin's writings about Christ, which attract a following in the novel and also form the basis of the book's Christology. Though he admires his uncle's writings about Christ, Yuri himself never comments upon them, a function perhaps of the role Yuri assumes as a would-be Christ figure in the novel: he embodies certain virtues of Christ about which Vedeniapin can only preach. Yuri's and Vedeniapin's Christological roles are thus different and distinct. But though a minor character, Vedeniapin is an important one, expressing as he does Pasternak's own thoughts on Christ. "There never was a movement such as Nikolai Nikolaevich represents in my novel," Pasternak confessed after reading an excerpt to friends in 1947. "I simply entrusted to him my own thoughts."[16] With the exception of Yuri's poems about Jesus, Vedeniapin is the primary mouthpiece for the novel's ideas about Christ. In order to understand what *Doctor Zhivago* wishes to tell us about Christ, then, readers need to pay attention to both the nephew and the uncle: what Yuri shows and what Vedeniapin tells.

As a character, Vedeniapin is an obvious representative of the religious revival going on in Russia during the early decades of the twentieth century—the height of Symbolism and its mystical outgrowths, both rejected by Yuri's uncle. Having "gone through Tolstoyism and revolutionary idealism" (1:4:7), Vedeniapin grapples with—and largely dismisses—the mystical aspects of Symbolism, at least as they were reflected in Symbolist thought up to 1905: "a libretto in verse by the Symbolist A—to the cosmogonic symphony by the composer B—with the spirits of the planets, voices of the four elements, etc., etc." All of this, according to Vedeniapin, is "deadly" and "insufferably false." Instead, he turns to Christianity but preaches a very earthly, non-clerical Jesus, who attracts him because he speaks "in parables taken from life," explaining "the truth in terms of everyday reality" (2:10:42).

Thus, in Vedeniapin's Christology, Jesus's importance lies not in his being the Son of God or the second person of the Trinity (that is, his divine attributes), but rather in how he, in his humanity, affirms the worth of human personhood as an attribute of the divinity. Vedeniapin thereby establishes the novel's pronounced personalism as an important theme, a reflection of Pasternak's own interest in personalist philosophy at this time. In a letter to his sisters at the end of December 1945 (when his work on the novel began), Pasternak confessed that the "general spiritual picture" of the brotherhood of the English personalists—"its conceptual contours, those aspects through which symbolism and Christianity are present in it"—"coincides in surprising fashion with what is happening with me. It is dearest to me now."[17] The sanctity of the human being, the dignity and worth of the human personality, and the significance of human personhood are key components of both personalist philosophy and Pasternak's Christology in his novel.

Before Christ, Vedeniapin argues, the human person did not signify in the larger context of the movement and fate of nations. Only patriarchs, pharaohs, and kings were remembered by history, while the individual died "in a ditch like a dog" (1:5:10). All of this changed with Christ. In becoming human, God changed the scale of divine-human interaction and altered the measure of historical significance. As Vedeniapin's "disciple," Sima Tuntseva, puts it later to Lara Antipova, instead of Moses parting the Red Sea so that a nation could pass through, an ordinary girl secretly gives birth to the "universal life," Jesus Christ. God became man and personhood (*lichnost'*) was revealed as a divine attribute. In this tidal change between covenants, Christ "relegated to the past" leaders and nations and replaced them with "personhood [*lichnost'*] and the doctrine of freedom" that he himself ushered in.[18] It is in this way that Pasternak, following Vladimir Solovyov and Nikolai Berdyaev, affirms personhood as a divine trait. Or, as Tuntseva puts it (paraphrasing Vedeniapin), Christ's incarnation reveals how "individual human life became the life story of God" (13:17:413–14).

After Christ, history was no longer about the progress of nations but about the life and merit of the human person. History's task changed, too. According to Vedeniapin, the purpose of history after Christ became the "systematic exploration of the riddle of death, with a view to overcoming death" (1:5:10). Here, Vedeniapin echoes Nikolai Fedorov's "Philosophy of the Common Cause"—an influential part of the religious revival of the turn of the century—which set as its goal the overcoming of death through the actual resurrection of one's forebears. Overcoming death in the novel, however, has nothing to do with the physical restoration of one's ancestors. Rather, death is defeated through the quasi-Straussian recognition that individual extinction is meaningless in the context of the divinity of the human race itself. For Zhivago, individual immortality is expressed by the "eternal memory" (the Orthodox hymn that opens the book) into which each human life enters and remains after death. "In the crude form in which it is preached to console the weak, [resurrection] is alien to me," Yuri tells a deathly ill Anna Gromeko. "You in others—this is your soul. This is what you are. This is what your consciousness has breathed and lived on and enjoyed throughout your life—your soul, your immortality, your life in others. And what now? You have always been in others and you will remain in others. And what does it matter to you if later on that is called your memory? This will be you—the you that enters the future and becomes a part of it" (3:3:68).

According to Vedeniapin, the desire to overcome death is expressed by human activities as diverse as scientific discoveries ("mathematical infinity and electromagnetic waves") and artistic creativity ("symphonies"). But underlying all of these enterprises and essential to their success is Christ's Gospel with its message of love of neighbor and the idea of free personality (*ideia svobodnoi lichnosti*) and life as sacrifice (1:5:10). These aspects of Christ's Gospel were unprecedented in the ancient world, where "blood and beastliness and cruelty" reigned (1:5:10). As Vedeniapin explains:

> Rome was a flea market of borrowed gods and conquered peoples, a bargain basement on two floors, earth and heaven, a mass of filth convoluted in a triple knot as in an intestinal obstruction. Dacians, Herulians, Scythians, Sarmations, Hyperboreans, heavy wheels without spokes, eyes sunk in fat, sodomy, double chins, illiterate emperors, fish fed on the flesh of learned slaves. [...] And then, into this tasteless heap of gold and marble, He came, light and clothed in an aura, emphatically human, deliberately provincial, Galilean, and at that moment gods and nations ceased to be and man came into being—man the carpenter, man the plowman, man the shepherd with his flock of sheep at sunset, man who does not sound in the least proud, man thankfully celebrated in all the cradle songs of mothers and in all the picture galleries the world over. (2:10:43)

Thus, Christ affirms the dignity of the ordinary human being by affirming an ontological commonality between humanity and God. In emphasizing Christ's "deliberate" provinciality and "emphatic" humanity, though, Vedeniapin is not attempting to reduce Jesus to the mortal human being of the historical school of biblical criticism. Quite the contrary: Vedeniapin is preaching a theology of the prosaic. Human personhood as a divine attribute elevates the prosaic ordinariness of human life everywhere by connecting it to the very essence of God. Here, Pasternak is actually supporting a very Orthodox claim: Christ's incarnation reveals the worthiness of all of creation to partake in the divine life, to be transfigured.[19] However, Pasternak will test this claim in a distinctly unorthodox way through the life and loves of his hero, Yuri Zhivago. And he will articulate this theology through Yuri's uncle, someone unorthodox in his own take on Christ and Christianity.

Yuri never repeats his uncle's notions about Christ in the novel—that is left for others to do, such as Sima Tuntseva or his friend, Misha Gordon—though he does publish booklets upon his return to Moscow on various esoteric subjects including "his thoughts about religion and history (which had much in common with those of his uncle and Sima)" (15:5:476). Indeed, Lara tells Yuri that he and Sima "are extraordinarily alike" in their views (13:16:411). But Yuri never expresses any views on Christ himself in the novel. Like Prince Myshkin, he is conspicuously reticent about his Christian views, which remain "off stage" throughout the novel and can be glimpsed only in the Christ poems of part 17. Aside from various apostrophes directed to "the Lord" in moments of ecstatic gratitude for his life, Yuri mentions Jesus himself within the events of the novel on just two other occasions: when he contemplates "a Russian version of a Dutch Adoration of the Magi" (3:10:81); and when he conceives of a poem while ill with typhus about Jesus's descent into hell.

His main pronouncements about Jesus are rendered in poetry and reserved for part 17 of the novel in nine of twenty-five poems that mention or depict episodes from Christ's life and appear after the events of the novel.[20] Given his seeming reticence about Christ in the novel proper, the presence of these poems in the novel's final chapter (over a third of the entire corpus of poems) may come as a surprise to readers who have seen other characters—Vedeniapin, Misha Gordon, and Sima Tuntseva—talk about Christ, but not Yuri. Moreover, though readers are given glimpses of Yuri working on several of the other poems in part 17 in the narrative proper, they are never given any indication that he is planning a whole series of poems on Christ. They are thus somewhat unprepared for the prominence of these Christ poems in the novel's concluding part.

In contrast to the Christ poems, several of Yuri's other poems from part 17 are anticipated in the previous sixteen parts. The idea for "Winter Night," for instance, was conceived the evening Yuri saw a candle burning in Pavel

Antipov's window, behind which Lara was confessing her relationship with Viktor Komarovsky to her future husband. Later, Yuri works on this poem in part 14, "Return to Varykino," where he also completes "Star of the Nativity"—the poem in which Yuri attempts "a Russian version of a Dutch Adoration of the Magi." Paradoxically, readers are informed that these two poems and "others of the same kind" were later "forgotten, mislaid and never found again" (14:8:438), this despite their presence in part 17, "The Poems of Yuri Zhivago." Likewise, Yuri drafts "Fairy Tale" (14:9:442–43) and conceives of the preliminary images behind "Parting" a dozen pages later (14:13:454).

With the exception of "Star of the Nativity," however, there is no direct reference in the narrative to his work on any of the poems about Christ, though earlier in the novel Yuri does notably acknowledge the New Testament as a model of artistic creation. In thinking of a poem to memorialize Tonya's mother, Anna Gromeko, Yuri reflects that "all great, genuine art resembles and continues the Revelation of St. John" (3:17:90), thus alerting us to a possible Christian basis to all of Zhivago's creativity. At the same time, however, Zhivago could just as easily be reflecting the spiritual ambience of the Silver Age: Anna dies during Christmas 1911, a time still dominated by the Symbolist idea of the artist as discloser of spiritual realities and apocalyptic portents.

Compounding the paradoxical status of Yuri's Christ poetry, the one poem on a Christ theme whose genesis is given in the text never materializes. Delirious from typhus contracted during one of the harsh winters just after the revolution (1917 or 1918), Yuri dreams he is writing a poem about the interval between Jesus's crucifixion and resurrection—the so-called, "Harrowing of Hell" (*soshestvie Khrista v ad* in Russian) during which, according to Orthodox tradition, Christ brought salvation to all the righteous who had died before his coming. This poem, titled "Turmoil" ("Smiatenie"), was "to describe how for three days the black, raging, worm-filled earth had assailed the deathless incarnation of love, storming it with rocks and rubble as waves fly and leap at a seacoast, cover and submerge it" (6:15:207–8). In his delirious thinking about the poem, Yuri contrasts death, hell, and dissolution to spring, Mary Magdalene, and life. But apparently Zhivago never actually writes the poem since it is not mentioned again and does not appear in part 17. While this passage constitutes the first mention of Mary Magdalene in the novel, thus anticipating the two poems about her that make it into part 17, it also points to a revealing irony: the most sustained textual evidence of Yuri's interest in Christ as a poetic subject turns out to be linked to a poem that may never have been written and that no one ever gets to read.

This paradoxical outcome is typical of the novel's strategy of deflection and indirection when it comes to the topic of Zhivago's attitude toward Christ. Our hero is certainly no Dostoevskian spokesperson for a vision of Jesus, nor are his chief loves, Lara and Tonya. Indeed, unlike Dostoevsky, Pasternak does not at first glance seem to dramatize his Christology on the level of plot. Furthermore, those characters in the novel who *are* interested in Christ or make pronouncements about him all belong somewhat to the periphery of the novel's action and are each in their own way marginalized mouthpieces for a Christian vision.[21] Vedeniapin is an unfrocked priest, Misha Gordon is a Jew, and Sima Tuntseva is a homespun intellectual who is "a bit odd—not quite right in the head," as Lara later reports (13:16:411). None of them are official spokespersons of the Church, and their pronouncements about Christ and Christianity are somewhat unconventional. They are the active bearers of the novel's Christology, however; Yuri Zhivago is not. Thus, those seeking an explanation for Zhivago's seemingly unmotivated interest in Christ—one, moreover, that leads him to write a series of fairly orthodox poems about him—will have a hard time finding it.

Adding to this difficulty are Yuri's own secular tendencies. He is not a religious man in any traditional sense. As noted above, he confesses to Anna Gromeko on her sick bed that he does not believe in one of the central tenets of the Christian faith: the bodily resurrection of the dead. Twelve years of school and university, where he studied "the classics and Scripture, legends and poets, history and natural science," have overturned the simple faith of his childhood taught him by his nanny. Then, "the Lord God was a kindly Father" and the heavenly firmament "was close and within reach," to be glimpsed in the candles before the icons in the tiny church where he went with his nurse (3:15:87). Now, Yuri listens to the words at Anna Gromeko's funeral and expects them "to have a clear meaning," "just like any other words." Then, as a ten-year-old at his mother's funeral, he had "prayed in confusion, fear and pain"; now, at Anna Gromeko's burial (at the same church cemetery as his mother's grave) Yuri neither prays nor weeps. He "was afraid of nothing, neither of life nor of death; everything in the world, all the things in it were words in his vocabulary. He felt he was on an equal footing with the universe" (3:15:87). There is just a touch of turn-of-the-century Prometheanism here.[22]

Certainly, in this regard Yuri looks little different from any of the educated ranks of Russian society at this time: the students and intellectuals of the prewar and prerevolutionary era. Yuri's journey toward Christ, then, is one of the novel's mysteries. Neither articulated by Zhivago himself nor constituting a narrative of spiritual awakening, it must be sought out elsewhere, in the pattern and shape of the events of his life and in the Christ narrative subtly inscribed into the novel and articulated in Zhivago's poems.

Pasternak's Christ Novel

While critics have disputed the merits of a Christological reading of the novel, *Doctor Zhivago* in particular seems to cry out for it, as the novel's earliest readers were quick to understand. Writing a year after the novel was translated into English, Walter Vickery notes how Pasternak encourages the reader to identify Lara with Mary Magdalene and Yuri with Christ. For Vickery, the Christ story "has an important organizing function in the construction of the novel" and helps condition the reader's attitude toward Zhivago—"the key point on which the novel must stand or fall."[23] Others disagree. Max Hayward, who first translated the novel with Manya Harari, claimed that "Zhivago is not a Jesus-like figure" at all but rather more like "one of those disciples who could not keep awake during the vigil of Gethsemane."[24] For her part, the author's sister, Josephine Pasternak, complained about the "avid grabbing of Christologists" with regard to the novel.[25] And Guy de Mallac warns that "at times the Pasternakian Christ seems simply a conceptual moment."[26]

Yet there are ample reasons for seeking a Christological reading of Yuri Zhivago's life story. The most direct textual justification of Zhivago's status as a Christ figure comes from Zhivago himself, in his poem "Hamlet," the first of the twenty-five poems in part 17. There, the poem's autobiographical persona identifies himself both with Shakespeare's Danish prince and with Jesus Christ. Though the two figures might first seem to be nothing like each other, in actuality they each share one important quality, a quality Yuri, too, possesses: a sense of duty and self-denial. In his essay "Translating Shakespeare," Pasternak explains that "Hamlet is not a drama of weakness," for Hamlet "gives up his will in order to 'do the will of him that sent him.'"[27] Like Christ, he does the will of his father. Similarly, when the persona of the poem asks, "If Thou be willing, Abba, Father, / Remove this cup from me," he nevertheless consents to "play his part" (17:1:527).

Yuri's life, too, is a study in self-abnegation. He is continuously giving up all that is dear to him when circumstances demand, not out of weakness, but out of a sense of self-sacrifice. He breaks family ties and friendships, trades his work as a doctor for that of a menial laborer, and denies his own personal happiness in what one commentator calls a kenotic self-emptying in imitation of Christ.[28] The meaning of his life is submission to God's will, even when such submission requires that he, like Job, give up everything but his faith to the evils of the world. While the nature of Zhivago's sacrifice and the extent of his self-denial can be debated, the textual basis in "Hamlet" for identifying an *imitatio Christi* with regard to Yuri is strong.

Zhivago's name itself also has a distinct Christological quality to it. Its underlying meaning is "the living one," though its inflected ending might also suggest the translation "*of* the living one." While Pasternak once declared in an interview, "The name Zhivago has no special significance, it is just a name,"[29] it nevertheless evokes the Old Church Slavonic phrase "*Syn Boga zhivago*" ("Son of the Living God," Matthew 16:16), the term Peter the disciple uses when Christ asks him, "Who do people say that the Son of Man is?" It is also the phrase with which the angel greets Mary Magdalene and the other women coming with their spices to Jesus's tomb: "*Chto vy ishchete zhivago mezhdu mertvymi?*" ("Why are you looking for the living one among the dead?" Luke 24:5). As Marya "of the Living One," Yuri's mother evokes the Maria associated with Christ—the Virgin Mother. Indeed, Marya Zhivago's funeral occurs on the eve of the Feast of the Intercession of the Virgin. Yuri, too, is "of the Living One" and is thus also linked to Christ, who, as Sima mentions, is also called the "Life of all" (*zhizn' vsekh*, "*Zhivota vsekh*," 15:17:413).

Like Christ, Yuri is a healer (doctor) and a creator (poet). Indeed, he even chides himself after his long conversation at Anna Gromeko's sickbed that he was "becoming a regular quack—muttering incantations, laying on the hands" in Christ-like fashion. And yet the day after Yuri's visit, Anna recovers, perhaps thanks to his reassuring words (3:3:68). Furthermore, Yuri works at Krestovozdvizhenskaya Hospital—the Elevation of the Cross Hospital (6:5), the same name as that of the town Krestovozdvizhensk where the events of part 10 take place, significantly, during Holy Week. Christ-like, Yuri strives throughout his life "to love everyone, not only his family and friends, but everyone else as well" (5:15:161) and is "ready to sacrifice himself for the general good" (6:5:184). And in many ways he *does* love and serve others in Christ-like fashion, including presumed enemies, such as the Red partisans and Strelnikov himself. He even accepts a symbolic cross when he loads a big heavy beam on his back to take home for firewood in the cold, hungry days following the October Revolution in the winter of their flight to Yuriatin (6:8:194). These are only the most obvious

Christological allusions. More subtle connections between Yuri's fate and that of Jesus Christ can also be argued.

The difficult thing, however, is knowing what to make of these Christ allusions. If Zhivago is a Christ figure, then to what end? This question has challenged those critics who have attempted to answer it. Edmund Wilson says Zhivago is "simultaneously Hamlet, St. George and Jesus," but seems to confine the significance of the Christ subtext to death and resurrection, which, he claims, are the novel's "main theme."[30] Mary and Paul Rowland argue that Zhivago undergoes a "symbolic passion" that consists of "death to his former life [and] rebirth in suffering to a life of greater creativity," eventually ending in a sacrifice of self in kenotic fashion to "a long, slow death of voluntary suffering."[31] Guy de Mallac identifies "the whole of Zhivago's behavior" as a "spiritual feat" that attempts "to reenact the *podvig* [spiritual feat] of the Lord himself."[32] John Bayley argues that by his "insistence on the sacredness of the individual, Zhivago undergoes the role of savior."[33] Even the rejection letter from the editorial board of the journal *Novyi mir* (New world) turning down Pasternak's novel recognized Zhivago as a Christ figure, complaining: "Zhivago's whole life story is consistently likened to the Lord's Passion of the Gospels."[34]

The problem is, it is hard to know who exactly Zhivago is. If he is, indeed, a Christ figure, then he is a very problematic one. In any event, he is also an enigmatic character about whom it is difficult to make *any* conjectures. In his biography of Pasternak, Dmitrii Bykov asserts that Zhivago must be defined chiefly through "apophatic means": "We cannot immediately formulate who he is, because the scale of his personality, like the existence of God, 'is not proven, but shown.' We can only say what he *is not*. He is not an intellectual who has tied himself in knots, not an average man who professes the rules of middlebrow taste, not a revolutionary fanatic, not a crusader against the power structure, not a dissident, not someone with 'a good handle on life.' That is, he is not a banality."[35] Bykov also adds that Zhivago is not a Christ figure, explaining that Pasternak had merely "set himself the task of writing about a very good man as he understood him and to prove that a very good man is indeed the world's most forthright follower of Christ."[36] While "a very good man" may be the only positive (i.e., cataphatic) thing Bykov can say about Zhivago after his apophatic exercise, it hardly resolves the thorny question about all of those transparent Christological associations that suggest that he is supposed to be some kind of a Christ figure, regardless of whether Bykov or Pasternak himself says he is or not.

Perhaps, though, Bykov has the right idea about the applicability of an apophatic approach in the context of the novel. It is safest to say what Zhivago is not. However, the apophatic exercise that is needed here should ultimately illuminate Christ, the proper object of the apophatic method. That is, after all, what any Christ figure is supposed to do: illuminate through negation. Not being Christ, they nevertheless help us to know Christ, an instance where absence can reveal presence. In this regard, one of the most enlightening chapters about Zhivago as a Christ figure—and, ultimately, Christ's role in the novel—may be the only chapter in the book where Zhivago does not figure at all: part 10, "The Highway."

Located almost in the exact center of the novel, it at first seems like a digression, for no major character is present in the chapter and nothing significant happens to advance plot. Yuri has just been kidnapped by the Red partisans at the end of the previous chapter ("Varykino") while traveling home from Yuriatin where he has been carrying on an affair with Lara. He has resolved to confess everything to Tonya and never see Lara again, but has just changed his mind and turned his horse back to town when he is ambushed. For an entire chapter—the length of part 10—Yuri literally disappears, an effective literary strategy that heightens the reader's suspense over his fate. In his absence, however, Pasternak's readers learn much about the book's Christ narrative and Yuri's role therein.

Instead of following Zhivago, the narrator turns to one of a string of settlements along one of the oldest high roads in Siberia, the town of The Elevation of the Cross (Krestovozdvizhensk), where White Army recruits prepare to join the fight and revolutionary cells meet in secret. The chapter commences on the night Jesus's Last Supper is commemorated—the Thursday of Passion Week (the week before Easter)—and concludes on the third day after Easter. The nearby Vozdvizhensky Monastery (Monastery of the Elevation) is busy with Paschal celebrations. The inscription surrounding the icon on the monastery archway—"Rejoice, life-giving Cross, unconquerable victory of piety" (10:2:308)—seemingly announces that the conflict being described is every bit as religious as it is revolutionary.

The first character readers encounter in this chapter is the merchant's wife Galuzina, an observant Orthodox woman nostalgic for the old days who is apprehensive over the outcome of the Civil War. Her son has recently been recruited for the White Army. A local band of revolutionaries who have secretly gathered for a political meeting is also introduced. Among these revolutionaries are former railroad men from Lara's old Moscow neighborhood, including

Tiverzin and Pavel Antipov's father, both of whom have "become dehumanized by political conceit" (10:6:320). The leader of the band is Liberius, the head of the partisan detachment that kidnaps Yuri. New conscripts to the tsar's army are also introduced at a fête being thrown to mark their departure. When a bomb goes off there later in the evening, however, several of the half-drunk recruits panic, running away and hiding only to be later suspected of being involved in the terrorist act themselves. Among them is the merchant's son, Terentii, who now has no choice but to join the Red partisans in the forest—the same band holding Zhivago.

In certain respects, this otherwise unremarkable chapter acts as a thematic keystone of sorts, for, among other things, it inscribes the Passion of Christ into the national narrative of the Civil War. Indeed, the symbolic shading of the Civil War into a national Passion narrative in this chapter helps to motivate the presence of the Christ poems in part 17. Russia itself is being crucified, for the conflict between the Reds and the Whites is symbolically unfolding around the town of the Elevation of the Cross at Easter time. On one side of the conflict is the local monastery, with its promises of victory for those who raise the life-giving cross. On the other side are those revolutionaries "dehumanized by political conceit" in whom the image of God has been darkened. Somewhat to one side of both of these opposing forces are anarchists preaching sex and the "Liberation of the Personality" (10:7:325), the same trendy topics that Yuri rejects when he ponders how it is possible for him to be unfaithful to Tonya shortly before he is captured by Liberius's partisans: "The idea of 'free love,' terms like 'the legitimate demands of love,' were alien to him [...] nor did he regard himself as a superman with special rights and privileges" (9:16:304).

Thus in this digressive chapter important themes by which readers may understand Zhivago are articulated in his absence and against the background of the Passion story of Christ—a significant reassertion of the importance of the Christ subtext for understanding both Yuri's fate and what is happening in Russia. This chapter helps readers to see more clearly how Zhivago is located at the nexus of three ideologies: faith in the saving power of the Cross (a theme announced by the monastery; the monastery also reminds the reader that Yuri worked at Elevation of the Cross hospital in Moscow); the revolutionary rhetoric preached by the likes of Liberius and his crew; and the idea that free personality means not "life as sacrifice" or "love of one's neighbors," as Vedeniapin understands the term (1:5:10), but rather the indulging of the needs of the ego, whether in sex or other pleasures—in a word, the life of the superman. While these rival concepts receive their fullest explication in the novel through Yuri's relationship with Lara, they are importantly articulated and juxtaposed here, in a chapter that dramatizes them on the level of plot. They also shed light on the novel's absent hero, Yuri Zhivago.

What readers learn about Yuri in his absence in part 10, however, they learn apophatically, through negation. Yuri is like none of the vying forces in Krestovozdvizhensk: he is neither a practicing Christian commemorating the end of Lent and Easter who is nostalgic for the old days nor a materialist fighting for the revolution and a new world order nor yet an anarchist with utopian schemes about the restructuring of the human personality. Nevertheless, these "negative definitions"—like those in Bykov's list—all the same work to affirm: they tell us something about Yuri. In this case, they serve as a reminder that the Passion narrative that has been inscribed into the Civil War in this chapter is also a narrative into which Yuri is being drawn, as the chapters that follow confirm. Understanding this aspect of Yuri's storyline, the reader comes to see how he may, indeed, be a Christ figure of sorts, but one who inverts traditional expectations of what a Christ figure must be by his a-religious character and his relationships with three women. In this way, Yuri also challenges our preconceived notions of Christ himself.

On the level of plot, Yuri's Passiontide is most prominently dramatized in his last days at Varykino with Lara, where they flee to avoid arrest in Yuriatin after the newly installed revolutionary government begins to root out political heterodoxy. Yuri's Passiontide commences, appropriately enough, on the thirteenth day of their stay—the number for Christ (one plus twelve disciples). Running low on food and harassed at night by baying wolves, Yuri and Lara contemplate returning to town, despite the wave of arrests reaching its peak there. Lara, in particular, is anxious and orders Yuri to harness the sleigh while she packs their belongings. She changes her mind as soon as he brings the sleigh, however, and when Yuri takes the sleigh to gather wood, he is suddenly seized by a kind of "dark night of the soul":

> Although it was early in the afternoon and full daylight, the doctor felt as if he were standing late at night in the dark forest of his life. Such was the darkness in his soul, such was his dejection. The new moon shining almost at eye level was an omen of separation and an image of solitude. (14:11:446)

Here, Yuri evokes Christ, who, "troubled and distressed," takes Peter, James, and John with him into the Garden of Gethsemane and tells them, "My soul is sorrowful even to death" (Mark 14:33–34) and then goes off to pray in solitude.

When Yuri returns to the house, he finds a sleigh outside belonging to Viktor Komarovsky, the man who had molested Lara as a teenager and who is now a big official in the Bolshevik government. Standing outside the house, Yuri overhears Komarovsky characterize him as someone who is not to be trusted, someone who is "serving two masters" (14:11:447). When he goes in, Komarovsky takes Yuri aside and tells him in confidence that Lara's husband—the rogue revolutionary Strelnikov—has been executed by the Bolsheviks, thus putting Lara and her daughter in danger of imminent arrest. Komarovsky offers her and Yuri refuge with him in the Far East. Given the shady role Komarovsky played in the death of Yuri's father, there is no question of Yuri fleeing with him. But Yuri does agree to convince Lara to go with him by telling her that he will follow them shortly. She leaves, and Yuri gazes at their departing sleigh with a sinking heart, wondering what he has done in giving her up.

The textual parallels to Christ in the Garden of Gethsemane multiply. Not only does Yuri experience a "darkness in his soul," but he, like Christ, also renounces his own desires (in letting Lara go) and willingly submits to his ordeal. And if Christ is comforted in the garden by the appearance of an angel from heaven (Luke 22:43), Yuri is attended in his grief by a suddenly anthropomorphized natural world:

> The winter evening was alive with sympathy, like a friendly witness. It was as if there had never been such a dusk before and night were falling now for the first time in order to console him in his loneliness and bereavement; as if the valley were not always girded by a panorama of wooded hills on the horizon but the trees had only taken up their places now, rising out of the ground in order to comfort him with their presence. (14:13:453)

The textual evidence linking Yuri's "agony in the garden" to the Gospel account is striking and it is hardly surprising that the last poem in part 17—and the parting words of the novel—is also the "Garden of Gethsemane." But toward what end is the textual allusion to the agony in the Garden deployed in the Varykino chapter?

When Komarovsky says that Yuri has been "serving two masters," he means that Yuri refuses to choose between the Reds and the Whites. In the biblical origin of the expression, the two masters are God and money (Matthew 6:24, Luke 16:13). In Yuri's case, the two masters may actually be postulated as God and Lara—that is, what he should be doing and what he cannot stop doing: loving a woman who, morally and legally, is not his to love. In letting Lara go, Yuri is making the decision he could not make that fateful day when he was kidnapped on horseback by the Red partisans. But he is also, in a sense, choosing God, for in the dark days that follow, he relinquishes personal happiness (Lara as his "inexhaustible, everlasting joy" [14:13:453]) in order to submit to a higher calling: that is, his poetry. In Lara's absence, he gives himself wholly to his writing, which includes the important imaging of Christ in the poems that dominate and conclude part 17. This last burst of creativity, then, constitutes a kind of final poetic profession of faith, at least as far as the poems about Jesus go, for it is only in these poems that Yuri gives us some indication of his conception of Christ.

In these poems about Jesus, Yuri also establishes the importance of Christ as a narrative by which he seeks to understand his own life. "Hamlet" establishes his affinity with Christ as well as the theme of Christ's Passion so critical in understanding Yuri's life. Five of the remaining eight Christ poems also focus on the Passion narrative: "Holy Week," "Evil Days," "Magdalene I," "Magdalene II" and "Garden of Gethsemane." Thus two-thirds of the Christ poems are devoted to this one episode in Christ's life, an episode that occupies a central place in all four of the Gospels, all of which "show a remarkable unanimity" in their descriptions of it, according to New Testament scholar Luke Timothy Johnson. It was "the part of Jesus' life most requiring interpretation."[37]

Yuri's concentrated attention to Christ's Passion in his poems is thus in harmony with the earliest accounts of Jesus's life. And like the authors of these accounts, Yuri participates in spreading the news about Jesus, including the proclamation of his resurrection in the last lines of "Garden of Gethsemane": "I shall descend into my grave. And on the third day rise again" (17:563). He thus fulfills his function as a Christ figure: he is not Christ, but he points toward Christ. But more than that, he also gives us an indication of how he may understand his own life, for the Christ poems, situated as they are in close proximity to the intimate love poems and lyric nature poems, are apparently meant to tell us something not only about Christ's life, but about Yuri's as well. They are confessional in both senses of the word: they disclose important private truths but also acknowledge faith. Yuri clearly identifies with Jesus's Passion on a deep and personal level, or he would not have written his Christ poems in the first place.

The Christ poems in part 17—so tightly focused around the Gospel narrative of his Passion—provide a lens through which Yuri's life may be viewed. By the end of the book, the reader understands that Yuri, too, has undergone a kind of Golgotha and that his fate may be described using terms straight out of the essential vocabulary of Christ's Passion, terms such as sacrifice, duty, love, and self-abnegation. Naturally, these terms must be understood differently in the context of Yuri's life and fate. His sacrifice is not Christ's crucifixion for the salvation of mankind. What he sacrifices are the constituent parts of his private life: family happiness, a successful career as a doctor, and possible recognition for his writing. The duty he fulfills is to his times—his "consent to play this part" ("Hamlet") in the historical drama unfolding in Russia, which requires that he share in the martyrdom of the Russian intelligentsia. The love that he embodies is Christ-like: open and available to all, whether Reds, Whites, friends, enemies, lovers, or family. Likewise, his self-abnegation recalls Christ's "not my will, but thine be done"—a denial of the needs of the self in obedience to an external authority, in Zhivago's case, Soviet authority, which displaces and ultimately separates him from his family. Through Zhivago, then, Pasternak establishes Christ's Passiontide as the essential narrative of the Soviet century of belief, whether that narrative pertains to the fate of one man, that of the Russian intelligentsia, or the fate of the entire country.

James Billington remarks that Yuri's twenty-five poems constitute the narrative "of an *intelligent* [intellectual] feeling his way back to God."[38] Such is the feeling one gets from the religious poems, especially "Dawn," which seems to tell the story of a recovered faith. A recovered faith may be the secret theme of the novel, if not of Pasternak's life. At the same time, as Donald Davie observes, the same opening two stanzas of "Dawn" that address Christ and his New Testament can just as easily be read an address to a woman. Thus, in Davie's assessment, the poem is about both love for a woman and love for God. Nor does he see a problem with this outcome. "It would be foolish," he comments, "to think that if the poem is about the one, it cannot be about the other."[39]

Davie's point is well taken and it reminds us that if readers acknowledge Yuri's affinity with Christ and his function in the text as a Christ figure, then they must also address the question about Yuri's relationships with three women (two of them extra-marital) and how this side to his character relates to his Christological function in the text. If ten of Yuri's twenty-five poems mention Christ or address events in his life, the other fifteen do not, being love poems and meditations on nature and the seasons. Moreover, these three categories—Christ poems, love poems, and nature poems—sometimes overlap. In "Holy Week" nature is as much a participant in church services as are the worshipers inside the sanctuary. "Winter Night" inscribes Christ's cross into the passionate meeting of two lovers. Christ's encounter with the fig tree in "Miracle" is both a religious poem and a nature poem. Finally, the two Magdalene poems are both love poems and Christ poems, emphasizing again Davie's point that poems about lovers and poems about Christ are not necessarily mutually exclusive things.

The question is: does the same truth hold for the reality of our novel? Can Zhivago, for instance, be both a Christ figure and a lover at the same time? Moreover, can he be the lover of not one but three different women in the course of the novel and still remain a viable Christ figure? Pasternak's answer is not only that he obviously can, but also that this most unorthodox side to his Christ figure is precisely what best reveals Jesus's essence in his idiosyncratic Christ project. If eros and agape are mutually exclusive kinds of loves in Dostoevsky's and Tolstoy's Christologies and if Bulgakov's lovers are merely erotic echoes of the novel's true story of the agapic love between Christ and Pilate, then what role does this same opposition between eros and agape play in *Doctor Zhivago*'s Christology?

Love for a Woman, Love for God

Eros and agape are in opposition everywhere throughout the novel except, significantly, within Yuri himself, where they coexist in inexplicable balance. This eros/agape opposition is established early in *Doctor Zhivago*, when a teenage Yuri is living at the Gromekos' home, whose daughter Tonya is Yuri's age and in whose household Yuri's classmate Misha Gordon is also living. Yuri's uncle remarks what a "comical triumvirate" the three of them make, having "soaked themselves in [Vladimir Solovyov's] *The Meaning of Love* and [Tolstoy's] *The Kreutzer Sonata*" and developing "a mania for preaching chastity" (2:9:39). Tolstoy's story, of course, is little more than a tendentious tract arguing for the ideal of sexual abstinence while Solovyov's 1894 essay set as the task of human, erotic love nothing less than the "restoration of the divine image in the material world" by making "out of two infinite and perishable natures one absolute and immortal individuality."[40] If Tolstoy's story sees in sexual relations the root cause of much of the evil in the world, Solovyov sees the sexual union between two people and the offspring that issues from such a union as both "the highest flowering of individual life" (35) and "the justification and salvation of individuality through the sacrifice of egoism" (42) by which we "live not only in ourselves, but also in another" (45). To put it roughly, Tolstoy sees eros as a dangerous and flawed kind of love; Solovyov sees it as the potential means for revealing a higher order of love, even agapic love.

It is on this axis of opposing notions of love that the whole novel turns, from the moment Yuri glimpses the "mysterious and shamelessly frank" nature of Lara's liaison with Komarovsky the night her mother attempts suicide to his own sexual affair with her some fifteen years later. "Here was the very thing which he, Tonya, and Misha had endlessly discussed as 'vulgar,'" Yuri muses the night of Madame Guishárd's attempted suicide. "What had become of their childish philosophy and what was Yura to do now?" (2:21:61–62). Zhivago will spend the rest of the novel answering that question, navigating between eros and agape.

While it is tempting to agree with those critics who see in Solovyov's philosophical treatise an explanation of how eros can be channeled and ultimately transformed into something that resembles agapic love in his relationship with Lara,[41] in truth, a purely Solovyovian reading of love in the novel poses its own problems. First, it is unclear how the love between Yuri and Lara can be understood as a Solovyovian affirmation of the other and imaging of a divine unity when it entails the betrayal of the love Yuri shares with his wife, Tonya. After all, Yuri begins visiting Lara in Yuriatin while his wife is some six or seven months pregnant with their second child. One could argue that no greater symbol of disunity and fragmentation can be found than Yuri abandoning his wife, son, and future daughter. Although Yuri is tormented by his unfaithfulness, he cannot stop seeing Lara and is spared choosing between the two women only because he is kidnapped by Red partisans.

Second is the problem of the increasing illegitimacy of Yuri's couplings. If Yuri's relationship with Lara marks him as an adulterer, his common-law marriage and the two children he has with Marina, the daughter of the Gromekos' former porter, Markel Shchapov, make him a bigamist, as Yuri and Tonya (alive and well in Paris) are still legally married. How are these aspects to be fit into a Solovyovian reading of spiritual love? Do they not, instead, emphasize how far Zhivago has strayed from the Solovyovian ideal? Even if one ignores these problems, what about Zhivago's ultimate relinquishing of Lara to Komarovsky? After all, in letting Lara go with Komarovsky, Zhivago is also most assuredly surrendering her to her "moral destruction."[42] And, indeed, her life after Zhivago is tragic and results in the abandoning of her daughter Katenka and the daughter she conceived with Yuri: Tania Bezocheredeva. Ultimately, Lara is arrested and disappears, perishing "in one of the innumerable mixed or women's concentration camps in the north" (15:17:506).

Separation, not union, then, seems to be the hallmark of Yuri's relationships. While both Lara and Yuri speak in devoted tones about their spouses and vow to reunite with them as soon as they can, their actions often betray their words. When Yuri reaches Moscow in 1922, for instance, and finally has the ability to take measures "to obtain the political rehabilitation of his family and permission for them to return to Russia," he does so with a notable lack of enthusiasm. His companion, Vasia Brykin, with whom he traveled from the Urals back to Moscow, is "astonished at how lukewarm and half-hearted his efforts were. Yurii Andreievich seemed always to be in a hurry to decide that he was not getting anywhere, and he spoke with too much conviction and almost with satisfaction of the futility of undertaking anything further" (15:5:477). It is as if Yuri wants to fail in his quest to be reunited with his wife and family.

In equally inexplicable fashion, Yuri abandons Marina and their two daughters a few years into their relationship and goes into hiding in a room provided him by his half-brother Evgraf Zhivago. He informs Marina and his friends that he needs some time alone to concentrate on his affairs, among them, paradoxically, plans he and Evgraf are supposedly forming to reunite him with Tonya (who he nevertheless hopes has found someone else by now) and their two children. There is no indication of how he plans on having two wives and two families at the same time or in what way he loves all three of the women in his life: Tonya, Lara, and Marina. He dies a few months later with none of these questions resolved. Indeed, readers find themselves somewhat in the position of Evgeny Radomsky from *The Idiot*, who wonders how Prince Myshkin can possibly love both Aglaya Yepanchina *and* Nastasia Filippovna simultaneously. If Zhivago had loved the three women in his life with only a platonic, agapic love, it might be easier understand his position as the novel's hero or Christ figure or both. But Yuri loves all three women with a carnal love that produces some five children. Moreover, he seems surprisingly at peace with his abandonment of both the women he loved and the children he sired.

Yuri's three lovers and five children clearly present the biggest challenge to his status as a Christ figure. Indeed, it is easy to look at Zhivago's Christ-like qualities and his morally questionable actions and wonder how the latter do not cancel out the former. Pasternak seemed to be aware of this problem, at least to the extent that his novel seems to propose its own solution to the eros-agape opposition and its connection to the novel's hero and its Christology. Pasternak's solution has to do with the image of Mary Magdalene and Christ, the subject of two of Yuri's poems and of Sima Tuntseva's theological discourse at Lara's apartment in part 13. While that this possible solution actually fails to resolve the Christological and erotological issues both it and Solovyov raise, its failure is ultimately characteristic of the novel's thematic thrust, which does not so much disclose truths but rather serves as an index pointing to where the truth may be found.

Dmitrii Bykov remarks that "Yuri and Lara's passion is as much a religious ministry as are Yuri's poems."[43] The temptation to view their relationship in terms of the semi-erotic love Mary Magdalene has for Christ in Yuri's poems is great, especially if Zhivago is an index of Christ. Would not the love of a fallen woman—Lara, as his own "Mary Magdalene"—fit this paradigm perfectly for our Christ figure? So it would seem, especially in light of comments Sima Tuntseva makes to Lara in Yuriatin about Mary Magdalene and the two kinds of passion.

Sima makes a connection between the two meanings of the word *strast'* in Orthodox liturgy, where it refers both to the Passion of Christ as well as sexual passion. The two meanings of passion, she argues, are importantly linked in the liturgies of Holy Week (Passion Week in Russian: *Strastnaya nedelya*), especially Holy Tuesday when the Church recites the Hymn of Kassiani about the sinful woman from Luke's Gospel who washes Christ's feet with her tears and dries them with her hair. Though she acknowledges that "there is some doubt" about whether they were the same person,[44] she associates Mary Magdalene with this repentant prostitute, as Zhivago himself does in his Magdalene poems. For Sima, as for Zhivago, an important relationship is established in this encounter between Christ and prostitute. The prostitute, who burns with passion at night, anticipates the Passion of the Lord when she anoints Christ's feet with expensive perfume. At the same time, washing Christ's feet with her tears and drying them with her hair is an act of startling familiarity. It is thus a gesture of both repentance and intimacy, a linking of carnal and spiritual passion, as Sima notes. "What intimacy," she exclaims, "what equality between God and life, God and the individual [*lichnosti*], God and a woman!" (13:17:416). In her explanation of the Magdalene subtext of Passion Week, Sima brings us back to Solovyov if only in the sense that sexual passion (eros) here is joined to Christ's Passion (agape) in a way that points to a higher, divine love.

But Magdalene's love for Christ is never sexual. Yuri's and Lara's is. And though Pasternak may blur the lines between sexual and divine love in his novel, he cannot ultimately make out of sexual love a divine love, though at times he seems to try. In passages characterizing the love Yuri and Lara share, Pasternak implies that, in the right circumstances, eros and agape together create a kind of image of "absolute beauty" or an "elemental cosmic force" that is "the foundation of the universe," as he writes in a 1942 essay.[45] This is how Pasternak describes the love of Lara and Yuri. It, too, is an "elemental, cosmic force":

> Their love was great. Most people experience love without becoming aware of the extraordinary nature of this emotion. But to them—and this made them exceptional—the moments when passion [*strasti*] visited their doomed human existence like a breath of eternity were moments of revelation, of continually new discoveries about themselves and life. (13:10:396)

Their love is indeed great, even mythic. At one point, Lara likens them to Adam and Eve (13:13:404). Later, she rhapsodizes: "You and I, it's as though we have been taught to kiss in heaven and sent down to earth together, to see if we know what we were taught. It's a sort of crowning harmony—no limits, no degrees, everything is of equal value, everything is a joy, everything has become spirit" (14:7:436). As she stands over Zhivago's coffin, our narrator describes her thoughts: "They loved each other, not driven by necessity, by the 'blaze of passion' [*opalennye strast'iu*] often falsely ascribed to love. They loved each other because everything around them willed it. [...] Never, never, even in their moments of richest and wildest happiness, were they unaware of a sublime joy in the total design of the universe, a feeling that they themselves were a part of that whole, an element in the beauty of the cosmos" (15:15:504).

In such rapturous passages, it is easy to see how the quasi-spiritual amorous relationship between Yuri and Lara could evoke the quasi-amorous spiritual relationship between Mary Magdalene and Christ in Yuri's poetry. Yuri, as it were, seemingly inscribes his affair with Lara into the biblical text of the repentant prostitute depicted in the Magdalene poems he writes, thus establishing a spiritual vocabulary for understanding his sexual transgression, as Lara herself does earlier in the novel when she identifies with the poor and oppressed in Christ's Beatitudes at the height of her misery as Komarovsky's teenage lover. Listening to a priest rattling off nine of the Beatitudes, she thinks to herself: "This was about her. He was saying: Happy are the downtrodden. They have something to tell about themselves. They have everything before them. That was what He thought. That was Christ's judgment" (2:17:49). In each instance, agapic love is evoked to remedy transgressing eros: Yuri when he betrays his wife and family; Lara when she betrays her mother (Komarovsky's lover before Lara).

In the end, however, transgressing eros is a burden too great for Yuri's love relationships to bear. Rather than a symbol of cosmic harmony, Yuri's relationships with three successive women become symbols of a unity that does not hold, as if in confirmation of their inferiority to the true model of cosmic unity suggested by the novel—Christ himself. Only in Christ is cosmic unity fully exemplified and embodied, as the poems in part 17 make clear. As beautiful, elevated, and even spiritual as the love of Yuri and Lara is, it cannot ultimately resolve the eros/agape opposition established in part 2 of the novel just as it cannot survive the impossible circumstances of revolution and civil war. At best, their relationship with its spiritual/carnal nexus can only serve to point to Christ's perfect unity in the Gospels, just as the spiritual/carnal Magdalene also points to Christ in Yuri's poetry.

Yuri's poems in part 17 serve a similar function. Divided almost evenly among Christological, meteorological, and erotological themes, these poems suggest that Yuri, as an artist, is attempting to articulate in poetic terms Sima's theological discourse about the link between carnal and spiritual passion. To put it more precisely, he is putting these kinds of love into dialogic contact, inscribing them into the very weather that unites and binds all living things but, at the same time, leaving their ultimate interrelationship unresolved, just as Yuri's own relationships are left unresolved: the exalted love he shares with Lara and the more mundane love he shares with Tonya and Marina. Lack of resolution, after all, characterizes both his personality and his fate in the novel.[46] But perhaps that is part of Pasternak's point, for here the writer seems to have reached the limits of his own Christ project as well as his ability to define love— spiritual, sensual, or otherwise.

In terms of the novel's Christology, Yuri is a weak and flawed Christ figure, much like the Master in Bulgakov's novel: he illuminates more by contrast than by example. After all, how can a man who loves and abandons three women and the five children he sired with them be anything like Christ? At the same time, however, these actions do not strip Yuri of his Christological significance. He still points to Christ. If the fact that our Christ figure makes love with three different women brings to mind Babel's blasphemous Christ and Christ figures who likewise engage in fornication, then it is important to note that in

Pasternak's novel, such lovemaking must be understood in a way completely opposite of how it appears in Babel's stories. If, in Babel's stories, out-of-wedlock lovemaking functions to reflect the divine unity of the physical and spiritual, in Pasternak's novel, it serves to show how sexual union actually reflects the *inadequacy* of human attempts to mirror the unity of divine love—an outcome that rejects Solovyov's attempt to reconcile sexual and divine love.

Ultimately, the action of love that the novel explicates is complex and even, for all of the novel's personalism, distinctly impersonal. And yet, the seemingly damning impersonal aspects of the love Yuri embodies are neither as anti-personalist nor as un-Christlike as they seem. Yuri's love and, for want of a better word, ultimate disregard of Tonya, Lara, and Marina both illuminate the eros-agape opposition in the novel and reveal a distinct Christological truth: that to love like Christ is to love beyond the demands and limits of family, friends, and lovers. One must ultimately love indiscriminately, not in the service of sexual incontinence but as manifestations of non-possessive, non-exclusive, unself-interested love.

This kind of lovemaking best characterizes our passive hero, who is as attuned to absence as he is to presence; separation from the women he loves is as natural as being united with them. It almost seems as if it makes no difference to Yuri whether they are present or absent or which one he is with. Whoever he is with, that is the one he must love. (Here, he calls to mind Platon Karataev from *War and Peace*.) In this way, the love Zhivago embodies resembles the divine love Andrei Bolkonsky discovers in *War and Peace*, which does not love "for something, for some quality, for some purpose, or for some reason." It is, rather, "that feeling of love which is the very essence of the soul and does not require an object."[47] From this point of view, Zhivago emerges as a kind of universal sign of love, albeit a flawed and limited one. Zhivago's consistent personalist philosophy—his seeming inability not to love whomever he is with—and how this personalism informs the novel's pronounced eros/agape opposition (represented by Yuri's three love affairs), ultimately both challenges a reading of Yuri as a Christ figure and supports it. As Nikolai Berdyaev reminds us, "The concrete living creature, this person before me, is higher in value than the abstract idea of good, of the general well-being, of infinite progress and the like." It is this kind of love, Berdyaev notes, that "is also the highest idea of humanity and personalism."[48]

In the end, love itself is the great mystery of the novel. Neither the Gospel story so prominently written into the narrative and the poems nor the love story at the center of the novel completely describe it or fully resolve the eros/agape opposition on which plot and theme turn. Instead, eros and agape, human passion and the Passion of Christ, remain in unresolved dialogue, the better for us to discern the movement of love each represents by understanding that love in terms of what it is not. The thematic thrust of the novel is apophatic, just as Moscow's status as a "holy city" (15:5:522) at novel's end is apophatic. It is holy only insofar as it has been the site of the most unholy darkness visited upon Russian history and therefore allows us to better see what holiness entails: suffering, sacrifice, and submission to fate. These, not uncoincidentally, are the very aspects our similarly apophatic Christ figure affirms in his un-Christlike actions. When Zhivago admonishes Innokenty Dudorov and Gordon that the "only bright and vital thing" about them is that they are his "contemporaries and friends" (15:7:484), he anticipates the line from his own poem "Garden of Gethsemane," where Christ says the same thing to his disciples: "God hath granted you to live / During my days on earth, and yet you lie there sprawling" (562). He thus confirms his own function as an apophatic index of Christ.

Last Things

Ultimately, and somewhat paradoxically, "The Poems of Yuri Zhivago" in part 17 show that our unorthodox Christ figure nevertheless affirms a rather conventional Christ in the poetry he writes about Jesus. From the story of Jesus's birth ("Star of the Nativity") to the cursing of the fig tree ("Miracle") and his entrance into Jerusalem ("Evil Days") and concluding with his Passion narrative ("Magdalene I and II," "Garden of Gethsemane"), a very familiar biography is traced, one that conforms perfectly to the Gospel accounts, complete with references to the holy family's flight into Egypt, Christ's temptation in the wilderness, his first miracle at Cana, his walking on water, and his raising of Lazarus. Jesus's arrest in the Garden and crucifixion—poetically invoked as only Pasternak can render them—are also perfectly in line with Gospel norms, as is Christ's ultimate role as cosmic judge at the Second Coming: "And, even as rafts float down a river, / So shall the centuries drift, trailing like a caravan, / Coming for judgment, out of the dark, to me" (17:563).

But perhaps this is Pasternak's intention. The unorthodox Christ figure and the orthodox Christ are meant to illuminate by contrast. The flawed, philandering Christ figure estranges in the novel what is otherwise a perfectly conventional portrait of Jesus in the poems. At the same time, the Jesus of the poems testifies to the Christ-like aspects of the poet and his life journey. To put this another way, the attempt to reconcile Yuri's life and the Christological associations that attach to it creates a double vision in the novel, a lens that distorts in two directions. If Yuri is an unlikely, even contradictory Christ figure, then Yuri, in turn, endows Christ's story with an erotic charge that can be glimpsed in the Magdalene poems and in the love poems that deploy Christological imagery ("Winter Night") or that, preceding or following poems about Christ ("White Night" and "Holy Week," "Encounter" and "Star of the Nativity"), bring eros and agape into textual proximity, the better to illuminate Pasternak's own treatment of the two kinds of love and how those kinds of love play out in the relationships of the novel's Christlike hero. Pasternak thus challenges, complicates and renews the reader's image of Christ, even as he largely affirms the Christ of faith from the four evangelists' accounts.

In this way, Pasternak's Christ differs from his predecessors. His is not Dostoevsky's Christ, revealed through unbelief, nor Tolstoy's non-divine messenger of divine truth, nor yet Bulgakov's mysterious though divine stranger. Pasternak's unlikely Christ figure and poet instead reveals a Jesus who is fully human and fully divine, who walked the earth, spent time with prostitutes and sinners, witnessed the workings of earthly love, performed miracles, and died on the cross in an act of self-sacrificial love. Pasternak thus reestablishes the importance of the biblical Christ for the Soviet century of belief, and, like the believers in the early church of the first century, affirms and promotes the story of Christ's Passion as the central faith narrative of his age.

POST-STALIN AND
POSTMODERN CHRISTS

Trembling all over, I said to myself, *talitha, cumi*, rise and prepare for the end. This is not *talitha cumi* anymore, I am certain that this is *lama sabachtani*, or, as our Savior said, my God, why hast thou forsaken me. Why, oh Lord, did you forsake me?

The Lord was silent.

Venedikt Erofeev, Moscow to the End of the Line

FAITH NARRATIVES AFTER STALIN

Neither Bulgakov's *Master and Margarita* nor Pasternak's *Doctor Zhivago* were published in their homeland during their author's lifetime, appearing only decades after each author's death: the *Master and Margarita* in censored form in 1966–1967 and *Doctor Zhivago* in 1988, during Mikhail Gorbachev's policy of glasnost and perestroika. However, the centrality of the Passion narrative to their images of Christ both established Jesus's final days as the fundamental faith narrative of the Soviet century and anticipated other post-Stalin literary imagings of Christ in Russian literature, most prominently Venedikt Erofeev's *Moscow to the End of the Line* (1969, first published in the Soviet Union in 1989), Yury Dombrovsky's *The Faculty of Useless Knowledge* (1978, first published in the Soviet Union in 1988) and Chingiz Aitmatov's *The Place of the Skull* (1986). All three of these works share both Christ's Passion narrative and a glasnost-era date of publication, a reminder that even after Stalin's death, works that treated Jesus's life in a serious or positive fashion were nearly impossible to publish in the Soviet Union.

Christ, of course, was not the only controversial aspect of these works. Erofeev's work featured an alcoholic cable layer as its hero; Dombrovsky's novel dealt with Stalin's terror and the GULAG prison system; and Aitmatov's focused on hot-button issues of the glasnost era, including drug abuse, the deterioration of the family, and the exploitation of the environment. But each novel's Christ narrative would likely have been enough by itself to sideline publication in each of the decades in which the works were written, for religion and questions of faith were still taboo subjects in post-Stalin Soviet literature. The relaxation of religious prohibitions, the restoration of the Patriarchate and the curtailing of anti-religious propaganda during the Second World War along with the sta-bilization of the church during the interregnum from 1953 to 1958 changed abruptly after Nikita Khrushchev consolidated power. Beginning in 1961 and throughout the next four years, 59 of the country's 69 monasteries, 5 of its 8 seminaries, and 13,500 of its 22,000 parish churches were all closed.[1] During this time, priests were halved in number, dropping from about 20,000 to 10,000.[2] A hostile policy toward the Church continued for the next twenty years, subsiding only when Gorbachev ascended to the leadership in 1985.

In this environment, literary works featuring Jesus Christ had little hope of being published, with, of course, one prominent exception: that of the 1966–1967 publication of *The Master and Margarita* in the journal *Moskva*. The appearance of the novel—startlingly different in every regard from the usual fare appearing in Soviet journals at the time—seemed either a kind of miraculous event or a stupendous oversight on the part of the Soviet literary censors. In truth, it was actually the product of both a quiet rehabilitation of Bulgakov that was ongo-ing at the time and the literary and geopolitical politics of the day. Bulgakov's plays, collected and published in 1962, had reappeared on Soviet stages in the late fifties. His *Life of Monsieur de Molière* appeared in 1962 and his *Theatrical Novel*, based on his work with Stanislavsky's Moscow Art Theater, was published in 1965. Thus the appearance of *The Master and Margarita* a year later could be seen as but the natural next step of Bulgakov's post-Stalin rehabilitation. At the same time, however, it is also clear that for such a controversial work to be published by Leonid Brezhnev's neo-Stalinist regime, other factors had to be in play. Some have speculated that following the notorious literary trials of the poet Joseph Brodsky in 1964 and the writers Andrei Sinyavsky and Yuli Daniel a year later—trials roundly condemned in the West—Brezhnev needed some kind of cultural event to deflect the negative reputation abroad of the Soviet literary establishment. The publication of *The Master and Margarita* may have fulfilled that role.

In truth, the sudden appearance in Soviet literature of Bulgakov's Christ—so unlike the Christ of the Gospels (who was largely unknown to generations raised on official state atheism anyway)—as well as the novel's myriad references to supernatural concepts dramatically exposed how deficient Soviet culture had become in knowledge of anything spiritual. The author of the afterword to the *Moskva* publication, A. Vulis, confessed how unprepared he was for writing about a novel like *The Master and Margarita*. "My knowledge of theology on 1 July 1966 barely attained the level of a course on scientific atheism, something which was not even on the programme in my time, I might add," he admitted. "Black magic, demonology and the occult were all unfamiliar territory. [. . .] The consequence was that once again I had to sit in the Lenin Library, with my head bent over books, for ten to twelve hours each day."[3] Two-thirds of the way into the Soviet century of belief, belief in anything—be it of a religious, supernatural, or political nature—was at an all-time low. This state of affairs is reflected in stories published in post-Stalin times, where religious belief is rare and characters who have known only Soviet reality find themselves ill-equipped to deal with the sometimes sudden discovery of a spiritual void in their lives.

One of the few literary depictions of belief in the 1960s was that of Alyosha the Baptist from Alexander Solzhenitsyn's *One Day in the Life of Ivan Denisovich*, published through the intervention of Khrushchev himself in 1962. The appearance of this novel about life in Stalin's GULAG was arguably the most sensational literary event of the decade. Among the chief revelations of the novel—such as the daily horrors and deprivations of life in Stalin's work camps and the grim stories of the denunciations and abuses that brought so many innocent victims to these camps in the first place—the positive portrayal of Alyosha's quiet and persevering faith in God was a first for Soviet literature. Though a minor character, Alyosha stands out as a Soviet-era representative of a long line of kenotic saints in Russian literature—characters who live their lives in "imitation of Christ's extraordinary humility."[4] Alyosha joyfully accepts his harsh twenty-five-year term as an opportunity to suffer for his faith. He works willingly and meekly and prays ceaselessly, earning the begrudging admiration of his fellow prisoners, including Shukhov, the novel's hero, whose bunk is opposite Alyosha's.

Elsewhere in published Soviet literature of the sixties, the closest one gets to depictions of faith are the blameless old women of Russian Village Prose who, though themselves not particularly religious, embody saintly qualities of kindness, humility, and forbearance.[5] Though technically not Village Prose, Solzhenitsyn's Matryona Vasilyevna of his 1962 story "Matryona's Home" comes to mind as the earliest best example. It is a moving tale of an ailing and neglected old woman who, in the story's closing lines, turns out to be "the righteous one without whom, as the proverb says, no village can stand."[6] Margaret Ziolkowski argues that Matryona "exhibits traits associated with both the holy fool and the kenotic monk." Though her "essentially kenotic spirituality is not linked to a formal religious commitment," she is "a model of self-sacrificing service to one's neighbors."[7] Other examples of righteous women in prose about the countryside are not hard to find. Milentyevna from Fyodor Abramov's 1969 story "Wooden Horses" is another Matryona type as is Darya Pinigina in Valentin Rasputin's 1976 novel *Farewell to Matyora*. Indeed, if Rasputin is to be believed, there is a Matryona in every Russian village. As the narrator in *Farewell to Matyora* notes, "In every village of ours there always was and is one, or sometimes two, old women with a temper to whom the weak and suffering come for protection; and it is inevitable that if one such old woman lives out her days and dies, her place will immediately be taken by another woman who has grown old, strengthening her position among the others with her firm and just temperament."[8]

The presence of these righteous old women cannot, of course, compensate for the lack of a spiritual life in the Soviet Union, either in the village or the city, as the stories of writer, director, and actor Vasilii Shukshin attest. In the absence of belief, the souls of his protagonists begin to ache. Maksim Yarikov in Shukshin's 1971 story "I Believe!" tries to explain his predicament to his wife, who finds his bouts of spiritual flu exasperating: "'Say you've got everything—arms, legs, and the other organs. [. . .] Your foot gets hurt, you feel it. You get hungry, you whip up some dinner. Right? [. . .] But a person's also got something else—a soul! Right here'—Maksim pointed at his chest—'and it aches! I'm not makin' it up! I can actually feel it—it aches!'"[9] In desperation, Maksim seeks out a visiting priest—a relative of a neighbor—and asks him whether the souls of believers ache, too. The answer he gets surprises him. Not only does the priest also admit that his soul aches, but he objects to the image of Christ that the Church has "cooked up"—"kind, soft, hornless, wishy-washy: a regular calf!" He proposes, instead, a different kind of God—Life, with its Darwinian principle of survival of the fittest. In place of the Nicene Creed, the priest leads Maksim in a drunken recitation of a new profession of faith "in aviation, in the mechanization of agriculture, in the scientific revolution" and "in the cosmos and weightlessness"—the perfect liturgy for the scientific age, to be sure, but also a metaphysical evasion, as Shukshin surely knew.[10]

Shukshin seemed to understand that his ironically titled story was a dodge, for his oeuvre is crowded with characters suffering from just such a spiritual malady for whom neither the precepts of scientific atheism nor religion offered adequate answers. As Alexander Solzhenitsyn observes, "Shukshin appears to have been much agitated by the question of religion, and [in the early 1970s] was making a strenuous effort to justify himself in a way that seemed specifically hostile to religion yet was not without inner concessions to it."[11] Robert Mann reports that Shukshin "was fascinated by the story of Christ, which he knew partly from Renan's *Life of Jesus Christ*," three copies of which stood on his bookshelf in his Moscow apartment. According to Mann, Shukshin "was contemplating a work about Jesus" when he died in 1974,[12] a fact that might explain how Yegor Prokudin, the former convict hero of Shukshin's last novella and the popular movie based on it, *Red Kalina Berry* (1973), is, according to Donald Fiene, "recognizable as a Russian Christ figure" who is "marked for symbolic crucifixion."[13] In such a reading, the story of Yegor's failed attempt to leave his criminal gang and return to an honest life in the countryside is a Christian allegory of sorts. Indeed, his nickname, Gore ("woe"), calls to mind the man of sorrows foretold in Isaiah 53:3, a chapter from the prophet foretelling the sufferings of Christ.[14] Yegor visits a woman with whom he has been corresponding from prison whose name, Liubov' (Love), is also symbolic. Though Yegor propositions her on the first night they meet, their relationship remains chaste, becoming a picture of sorrow being attended by love. Liubov's brother, Petro ("Peter" from the Gospels), extends the Christological associations, as do the shots of flooded and abandoned churches glimpsed throughout the movie. When his former gang tracks him down, intent on killing him, Yegor does not oppose them and goes willingly to his own death, setting a powerful example of non-violent resistance to evil and following Christ in the Russian kenotic tradition.[15]

THREE POST-STALIN PASSION NARRATIVES

Christ, however, was not the sole object of attention in the faith narrative of post-Stalin literature. According to Margaret Ziolkowski, Pilate became more and more prominent in literary revisitations of the Passion story, a trend that *The Master and Margarita* anticipated and to which it contributed. In works appearing abroad such as Andrei Sinyavsky's *The Trial Begins* (1959), Yuli Daniel's *This Is Moscow Speaking* (1960–1961), and Yury Dombrovsky's *The Faculty of Useless Knowledge* and in delayed works published only during Gorbachev's reign such as Chingiz Aitmatov's *The Place of the Skull*, Anatolii Rybakov's *Children of the Arbat* (1987) and Yury Trifonov's *The Disappearance* (1987), Ziolkowski identifies Pilate—whether appearances by him in the form of a character or passing allusions to him—as a symbol of moral cowardice in narratives dealing with the Stalin era or "the lingering consequences of Stalinism."[16] According to Ziolkowski, references to Pilate or his infamous handwashing "provide a convenient shorthand for abnegation of ethical responsibility and reflect the peculiar congeniality of Pilate within a Soviet milieu."[17]

The most sustained Pilate/Christ narratives are those found in Dombrovsky's and Aitmatov's novels, both of which show signs of being influenced by Bulgakov's Christ story. Dombrovsky's Passion narrative is the centerpiece of part 3 of his novel. The novel's hero, Georgii Zybin, has been arrested for allegedly stealing an artifact from an archeological dig in remote Kazakhstan. The year is 1937 and so other crimes against the state are also included in the charges. Zybin, who is detained at the end of part 1 and thrown into prison in part 2, is absent from part 3 altogether, which focuses on his younger colleague Vladimir Kornilov and the complicated series of events that ensues when he is called in by the authorities to provide testimony against a former priest and coworker, Father Andrei Kutorga, so that an arrest can be made, presumably to fill arrest quotas during the height of Stalin's terror.

Kornilov initially seems to implicate Father Andrei, even turning over to the authorities the priest's 224-page manuscript *The Trials of Christ*, which Kutorga had leant Kornilov in the course of several long sessions during which the two drank and talked about the arrest and crucifixion of Jesus. With each subsequent visit to the secret police, Kornilov is put under increasing pressure to denounce his coworker. After much mental torment, however, he eventually resolves to defend Kutorga and produces a statement entirely exonerating him only to learn that Father Andrei had, in the meantime, already denounced him to the police and fled up north. Thus compromised by Father Andrei's false testimony, Kornilov allows himself to be recruited by the police and agrees to betray Zybin by providing false evidence against him, thus assuring Zybin's conviction. In this way, he also assumes the role of the second betrayer of Christ—the one, Father Andrei explains to him during one of their long conversations, needed by Jewish law to confirm a charge against Jesus. According to Kutorga, this unknown second betrayer—presumably a disciple—disappeared into history, living, as Kornilov supposes, "pretty well": "a devout life, respectable, got married and forgot all about his master. Probably blamed him for everything."[18] This, apparently, will be Kornilov's fate.

Like Bulgakov's, Dombrovsky's Passion narrative is a thinly veiled commentary on present-day Soviet realities. In Dombrovsky's novel, Jesus's arrest and crucifixion are made indistinguishable from the perversions of justice being carried out by Stalin's legal system, as the comments of one of Kornilov's interrogators confirms. When Kornilov explains how the Sanhedrin used the second betrayer to condemn Christ, the interrogator exclaims approvingly: "Yes! A good, clean job! Can't be overturned! They really put their minds to it! And you see how all the legal safeguards seemed to obtain; the court a fair one, the witnesses impartial, but if they want to get somebody, they get him, in spite of all the laws!" (266).[19] Christ, it is implied, is no different from the victims of Stalin's purges—he was arrested "on principle" rather than for any actual crimes, and convicted by the false testimony of an informer (279). Similarly, Pilate is no different from any Soviet functionary, as Father Andrei makes clear: "[W]e're up to our ears in people like Pilate. He's a typical middle-ranking official of the imperial era. Harsh but not cruel, shrewd and worldly-wise. In minor and uncontroversial matters—just, even principled; in more important matters, evasive and indecisive" (287). As such, he is like Bulgakov's Pilate, a cog in the wheel in a political system like Stalin's that depends on the law serving power.

Christ, by contrast, remains in Dombrovsky's novel the agent of humanity's redemption through whom "man was once more restored to his rights," as Father Andrei explains (243). Indeed, in order to show the depths of Christ's courage in going willingly to his death for the sake of a world that "was weary unto death and had lost its faith" (241–42), Father Andrei provides a gruesome and meticulous medical explanation of what crucifixion does to the body. Kutorga's implication is clear: even in the face of absolute evil, a moral response has always been possible, a lesson nevertheless lost on Kutorga himself and Kornilov, both of whom cooperate with the evil of Stalin's system.[20] Father Andrei's words do have an effect on Kornilov, however. Like Woland in *The Master and Margarita*, he later becomes an unlikely agent affirming to his atheist interrogators that Jesus did, indeed, exist (300). Ultimately, Jesus's Passion narrative in *The Faculty of Useless Knowledge* is not so much retold dramatically as it is debated and reimaged in the context of the excesses of Stalinism. Dombrovsky's achievement is thus to inscribe the Passion into the cycle of denunciations, lies, interrogations, and unjust imprisonments of the Stalin years in a way that is far grimmer and more sobering than Bulgakov achieved in his own novel.

For his part, Aitmatov removes the Christ narrative into the age of Mikhail Gorbachev's reforms, when revelations of the modern evils assailing Soviet society—drug and alcohol abuse, corruption, ecological neglect, the decline of moral standards—dominated journalism, literature, and film. These topics occupy Aitmatov's novel, too. *The Place of the Skull* tells three stories: that of the son of an Orthodox deacon and one-time seminary student, Avdii Kallistratov, who tries to change the world by preaching an idealistic Christian worldview to drug dealers and alcoholics; that of a pair of wolves, displaced by men who despoil and destroy their natural environment and steal their wolf cubs; and that of Boston Urkunchiev, an embodiment of enlightened Gorbachev-era attitudes toward the economy, the environment, the family, and personal self-discipline. The only link between the stories consists of two chance meetings between the wolves with Avdii (first when he is playing with their wolf cubs and later when he is tied crucifixion-style to a tree by hunters angry at his opposition to an antelope hunt) and Boston's ill-fated attempts to return the stolen wolf cubs to their parents.

Admittedly, the links holding the three stories together are weak and the novel does not entirely succeed, as critics have noted.[21] In its treatment of Avdii's encounters with drug pushers and alcoholics and in the storyline of Boston as "an updated positive hero,"[22] *The Place of the Skull* comes across at times as too topical and superficial to support its philosophical and theological pretensions. These pretensions emanate largely from its inserted Passion narrative, which focuses on Christ's interview with Pilate before he is sentenced to be crucified. It is this part of Aitmatov's novel that has garnered the most attention and that remains one of the reasons the novel is still read today.

The Passion narrative included in the novel is the product of Avdii's semiconscious delirium after being thrown from a train by drug traffickers. The scene switches from Avdii lying at the bottom of a railroad embankment to "a hot morning in Jerusalem" where a haughty and frustrated Pilate is interviewing Jesus and attempting to get him to recant his teachings and the claims made about his kingship.[23] Though trembling, with eyes as "helpless as a child's" (129), and admitting that he is "afraid of a savage death" (133)—all attributes intended by Aitmatov to emphasize Jesus's humanity—Jesus remains firm: he will not renounce the words of his heavenly father. Nor does he refuse to engage Pilate in conversation, unlike the Gospels, where Jesus either answered Pilate's questions briefly or not at all, and also unlike Bulgakov's Yeshua, who, though not as reticent as the Gospel Christ, does not speak at length. Among the Christ narratives analyzed in this book, Aitmatov's features the most talkative Jesus of them all.

The more he talks, however, the more he distinguishes himself from both the biblical Christ and Bulgakov's Yeshua (who Aitmatov admits influenced his own literary portrait[24]). And the more he says, the more he resembles the Jesus of Tolstoy's harmonized Gospel. As the interview continues, Jesus expounds at length on the Last Judgment, the Second Coming, and a vision he has in the Garden of Gethsemane. It is in these pronouncements that Aitmatov begins to reveal a distinct Tolstoyan Christology. "The Creator gave us the greatest gift of all the world," Jesus tells Pilate,

> the gift of reason [*razum*], and he gave us the will to live according to our understanding [*zhit' po razumeniiu*]. The story of human history will be the story of how we use this gift from heaven. You will not deny, Roman Governor, that the point of man's existence is his spiritual journey towards improvement and perfection: there is no higher aim in life. That is the beauty of intelligent life [*krasota razumnogo bytiia*], the daily trudge up the endless staircase towards the shining perfection of spirit. (141)

The emphasis on reason (*razum*); the idea that understanding (knowledge, enlightenment—*razumenie* in Tolstoy's use of the term) has taken the place of Logos, the word of God, as that by which humanity must live; and the emphasis on the improvement and perfection of the self are all precepts of Tolstoy's reinvention of the Christian project.

Aitmatov's Christ also echoes Tolstoy (and Bulgakov's Yeshua) when he complains about how his teachings have been distorted (142), particularly those concerning the end times. Like Tolstoy's Jesus, Aitmatov's does away with the idea that he will come back in resurrected form to judge the world at the end of all time. Instead, the idea of resurrection is to be understood metaphorically, as Tolstoy, too, interpreted the term. For Tolstoy, resurrection was "an awakening of life";[25] one cannot die when one discovers the life of the spirit by which God wants all of humanity to live. Aitmatov's Christ also says resurrection is not to be understood in personal terms: "It is not I, who have only the distance across the city to Golgotha left to live, who will return, resurrected; it is you, the human race, who will come again to live in Christ, a righteous life, in countless future generations. That will be my Second Coming" (142). Here, Aitmatov calls to mind David Friedrich Strauss, who believed that divinity resides not in Jesus but in the human race as a bearer of "the properties and functions of Christ." Strauss argues: "It is Humanity that dies, rises and ascends to heaven, for from the negation of its phenomenal life there ever proceeds a higher spiritual life; from the suppression of its mortality as a personal, national, and terrestrial spirit, arises its union with the infinite spirit of the heavens."[26] By a similar logic, Aitmatov's Jesus tells Pilate that the Last Judgment also lies in the hands of mankind. "Man himself is the creator and judge of every one of our days," he tells Pilate, for the future that humankind creates will be the judgment of our actions today (143). Like Tolstoy's Jesus, he thus diminishes his own importance and, indeed, his own divinity and promotes an image of Christ as a kind of label for divine enlightenment.

This outcome is not surprising. The inserted narrative of the meeting between Jesus and Pilate originates in Avdii Kallistratov's delirium. Like Tolstoy, Avdii begins his spiritual quest with a sincere desire to understand Orthodoxy. He even enters the seminary to pursue his passionate interest in Jesus. He is eventually expelled, however, and—also like Tolstoy—is excommunicated for his iconoclastic views. He ends up rejecting the Church altogether and instead embarks on his own evangelical mission to bring sinners to Christ. But Avdii is not a sympathetic character. He is headstrong and overzealous and, though he is an obvious Christ figure in the novel—even dying by crucifixion at the hands of drunken poachers—Aitmatov ultimately rejects him as the novel's hero.

Avdii's views on spirituality and Christ, however, are clearly meant to be taken seriously, for the inserted chapter on Jesus and Pilate is the philosophical centerpiece of the novel. It also resonates with the novel's glasnost-era concerns, including the escalation of the arms race. The last thing Aitmatov's Jesus imparts to Pilate, for instance, is a vision of a nuclear Armageddon he had while praying in the Garden of Gethsemane (147–48). This Cold War–era warning about nuclear disaster is repeated in the next chapter, when Avdii worries that "materialist science" has done away with the need for Christ even as it has brought the world to the brink of destruction: "What is a fool hanging on a cross to them, when at the touch of a button they can destroy us all, and erase even the memory of You from the face of the earth?" (155, 158).

Aitmatov's Jesus, then, is both a late Soviet-era affirmation of spiritual and humanistic values in a materialist culture and also the mouthpiece for what even in the Gorbachev period was formulaic Soviet anti-war rhetoric, delivered, according to Joseph Mozur, "in the clichéd idiom of Soviet journalism."[27] These aspects of the novel and the collapse of the Soviet Union just five years after the novel's publication have dated both Aitmatov's novel and his image of Christ. With its debts to Tolstoy and Bulgakov, however, Aitmatov's Passion narrative remains an interesting imaging of Jesus and has the added distinction of being the last significant Christ narrative written in Soviet literature.

No survey of post-Stalin Christ narratives would be complete without the addition of Venedikt Erofeev's short novel, *Moscow to the End of the Line*, a text that suggests what a postmodern Passion narrative might look like. Written in 1969, Erofeev's slender novel tells the story of how an alcoholic cable fitter who shares the author's first name sets off on a Friday for his thirteenth trip by train from profane Moscow to sacred Petushki. Along the way, he converses with God and angels, talks about his life, shares philosophical insights, and relates various events that happen on the journey. In actual fact, however, he never reaches Petushki and instead winds up back in Moscow, where he is stabbed through the throat and dies. The journey that comprises the book is thus something of an illusion, inversion, or trick. It is also a highly unorthodox imitation of Christ's Passion, references to which pepper the narration. In truth, it is hard to determine what exactly happens in the novel, for Venichka's story moves by means of inebriated association rather than chronological linearity, despite the fact that the chapter headings all correspond to train stations on the way to Petushki—a linear route that turns out to be misleading. Venichka's journey in reality describes a closed circle, one that dooms its author, who describes his own death and then declares somewhat paradoxically at the end of the novel: "And since then I have not regained consciousness, and I never will."[28]

Like the journey it describes, the text of the novel calls into question its own reliability. It is not so much authored as accumulated from disparate sources, with Venichka acting, à la Roland Barthes's theory of authorship ("The Death of the Author," 1968), as a "scriptor" whose text becomes "a tissue of quotations drawn from innumerable centres of culture." Rather than expounding a "single 'theological' meaning (the 'message' of the Author-God)," the text (Barthes's and Venichka's) instead is "a multi-dimensional space in which a variety of writings, none of them original, blend and clash" and enter into "mutual relations of dialogue, parody, [and] contestation."[29] Just as Venichka attempts to orient himself both physically (in a hostile world of sober oppressors, something that is not easy to do, as he is drunk much of the time) and geographically (as he negotiates his way through suburban train stations to the paradisiac Petushki), so, too, does he struggle to orient himself spiritually, intellectually, and culturally by means of digressive asides and myriad allusions to the Gospels, literature, history, popular culture, and political propaganda. The density of Erofeev's text is such that the annotated edition of the novel has over four hundred pages of commentary to help explain the one hundred pages of the story proper.[30] The point is that Erofeev's novel and Venichka himself constitute sites where contested texts blend and clash in varying degrees of dialogue, parody, confirmation, and refutation.

A reader seeking to understand Venichka's embedded Passion narrative is faced with numerous challenges, not the least of which are the novel's subversion of grand narratives (especially political and religious); its parodic inclinations; the leveling effect of its intertextuality; its ironic worldview and self-ironizing narrative strategies; its purposeful decenteredness; and its questioning of the very possibility of any kind of authenticity. The question for our study is what kind of Christ narrative is possible in such a literary context? It would seem that, true to its postmodern bent, there can be no single "theological" meaning to Erofeev's Passion narrative, for history—Soviet history, in particular—has exposed the fallacy of totalizing narratives, as Erofeev well knew. There is no center, no ultimate authority. The search for the authentic has revealed only simulacra. All truths have been ironized and expressions of genuine emotion are no longer possible, having been enclosed in permanent quotation marks. These are the lessons imparted by Venichka on the pages of his "New Testament," a testament made possible precisely by conditions in the Soviet Union, where the price of alcohol was kept low partly to pacify the population.

And yet, if there is truth in wine, then even Venichka's alcohol-induced odyssey can be read as a truth-imparting narrative, despite its seeming antipathy toward authoritative utterances. In a novel in which all the important elements of Jesus's life are referenced through our unlikely Christ figure, Venichka—Jesus's birth by the Virgin Mary; his relationship with his heavenly father; his temptation by Satan; his imparting of the "secrets of being" (72); his betrayal by Judas; his denial by Peter; his crucifixion, resurrection, and ascension—a central Christian truth is also conveyed: that of forgiveness of enemies, which, as the authors of this study have shown, is the essence of divine love. Time and again on his journey, Venichka acts as an agent of compassion and forgiveness. "I forgive everything," Venichka declares (76), and he means more than just the theft of a quarter bottle of Rossiskaya vodka on the train. "No one in the world is guilty," he later declares (149–50), echoing the words of Bulgakov's Yeshua. Elsewhere, Venichka affirms his own kind of personalism when he proclaims: "We must honor [. . .] the dark reaches of another's soul. We must look into them even if there's nothing there, even if there's only trash there. It's all one; look and honor it, look and don't spit on it" (94). He gives the reason for doing this two pages later: "God, dying on the cross, preached pity to us, and, not scoffing, did he preach. Pity and love for the world are one. Love and pity for every womb, and for the fruit of every womb" (95). In this final instance, Venichka lays bare his function as a Christ figure: not being Christ, he nevertheless affirms Christ, even in his inebriated state.

In fact, despite all of the awful concoctions that Venichka drinks, there is a sacramental quality to alcohol in the novel. Toward the end of the journey to Petushki, Venichka evokes Christ's words at the Last Supper, where Jesus likens the wine of the Passover meal to the blood he will shed for the new covenant: "This is my blood of the covenant, which will be shed for many" (Mark 14:24). No solemn pronouncement, Venichka's declaration nevertheless parodically reflects Jesus's words: "I'll give of myself to the last drop (because I just drank up the last drop, ha-ha!)" (143). As Mark Lipovetsky reminds us, "in Erofeev's style, the high and the low do not destroy each other and do not cancel each other out but instead form an ambivalent unity of meaning."[31] Erofeev's parodic, postmodern Christ comprises just such an ambivalent unity of meaning, suspended somewhere between tragedy and comedy, negation and affirmation, disbelief and belief. His image of Christ fittingly presides over the end of Soviet literature, when the century of belief had run its course and the narratives by which people ordered their lives fell apart, to be reassembled in post-Soviet times.

Finis

The prominence of Jesus's Passion narrative in five Soviet-era novels tells us as much about their authors' perception of the Soviet century as it does about their particular image of Jesus—a Jesus crucified, but, notably in the three post-Stalin Christ novels discussed in this chapter, not resurrected. In post-Soviet times, interest in Christ and religion has grown tremendously. Victor Terras calls the "rediscovery of Russia's and, in particular, Russian literature's, Orthodox Christian heritage" one of "the remarkable phenomena of Russian intellectual life after the collapse of the Soviet regime."[32] At the center of this renaissance is

Vladimir N. Zakharov at the University of Petrozavodsk, the founding editor of a series of volumes devoted to Christian readings of Russian literature: *Evangel'skii tekst v russkoi literature XVIII–XX vekov: Tsitata, reministsentsiia, motiv, siuzhet, zhanr* (*The Gospel Text in Russian Literature of the 18th–20th Centuries: Citation, Reminiscence, Motif, Subject, Genre*). To date, nine volumes have appeared.[33] As Zakharov explains in the first volume, "There is a need for a new concept of Russian literature, one that will take into consideration its deep national and spiritual sources and traditions."[34] For Zakharov and others reclaiming the Christian essence of Russian literature, the starting point for such a project is the exploration of what Zakharov calls "Christian realism"—a concept akin to Dostoevsky's idea of "realism in a higher sense" but one that embraces everything from the idea of *sobornost'* (the communal spirit of Russian spirituality) to Paschal themes.[35] The idea is to unpack the underlying currents of Russian spirituality in the works of writers of the past two hundred years, whether or not they or their works have traditionally been understood to be Christian per se.

This interest in Christian literary scholarship is also reflected in a series launched by the Saint Petersburg branch of the Russian Academy of Sciences in 1994, the same year Zakharov published the first volume of his *Evangel'skii tekst*. Seven volumes of the collection *Christianity and Russian Literature* (*Khristianstvo i russkaia literatura*) have appeared over the past two decades, testifying to the broad and enduring interest in Christian literary scholarship in post-Soviet Russia.[36] For many of the critics working in this new field, there is a sense of urgency to this enterprise, the need to make up for lost time. After seventy-four years of state-sponsored atheism in all spheres of life, they are anxious to reclaim Russian literature as a specifically Christian cultural phenomenon.

Writers have also been responding to this renewed interest in Christianity in the decades since the dissolution of the USSR, publishing their own stories and novels on Christian themes. One thinks of Svetlana Vasilenko's *Little Fool* (*Durochka*, 1993–1998), Elena Chizhova's *Cave Monastery* (*Lavra*, 2002), Maya Kucherskaya's *Modern Patericon: To Be Read in Times of Despair* (*Sovremennyi paterik: Chtenie dlia upavshikh v unynie*, 2004), Ludmila Ultiskaya's *Daniel Stein, Interpreter* (*Daniel' Shtain, perevodchik*, 2006), Olesya Nikolaeva's *Mene, Tekel, Fares* (2007), and Eugene Vodolazkin's *Lauras* (*Lavra*, 2012), to name a few of the more prominent examples.[37] Mikhail Shishkin's celebrated novel *Maidenhair* (*Venerin volos*, 2005) also grapples with Christian themes, albeit as a muted but important subtext. Critic Natal'ia Ivanova has gone as far as to say that there is a "theological streak" observable in "fashionable literature" of the 2010s, evidence that religious themes have made it into mainstream literature.[38]

Among the interesting entries in the field of Christian literary works is one book that stands in a category of its own: Archimandrite Tikhon Shevkunov's *Everyday Saints and Other Stories* (*Nesviatye sviatye*, 2011), in one critic's summation a "mildly ironic account of monks beset by temptation and their adventures."[39] *Everyday Saints* unexpectedly attracted a large and quality readership and was even nominated for the prestigious Big Book award. It was hailed as a true sui generis sensation, selling over a million copies worldwide in its first year of publication and proving that a book about "the radiant light of Christly faith and the meaning of what it is to be in God" still appealed to readers both in Russia and abroad.[40] Indeed, a scandal ensued when the novel, having garnered the most votes of readers and the grand jury, was nevertheless not awarded the Big Book prize.[41]

Everyday Saints and recent works on Christian themes do not, to be sure, provide the kinds of sustained Christ narratives analyzed in this study. For now, Russian writers do not seem compelled to image Christ in their fiction with the same theological intensity and on the same dramatic scale as did Dostoevsky, Tolstoy, Bulgakov, or Pasternak. Indeed, the Christ projects of these four authors continue to cast a large shadow on the writers and novels that follow them. Not likely to be supplanted or surpassed anytime soon, they will continue to exert an enormous influence on the shape and meaning of Russia's literary imaging of Christ even as their own novelistic images of Christ echo and evoke each other's. In her study of Mikhail Bulgakov, Lesley Milne notes how similar Yeshua Ha-Notsri in *Master and Margarita* and Pasternak's "emphatically human, deliberately provincial" Jesus from *Doctor Zhivago* are and how much Yeshua's personality also evokes that of Prince Myshkin in Dostoevsky's *Idiot*.[42] In truth, there is little that is surprising in her observation. Like Jesus in the four Gospels, the Christs of our four authors are different but the same: different in how they embody their creators' response to the socio-historical and spiritual realities of their day; the same in how each provokes us to see Jesus as if for the first time and encourages us to renew our concept of belief. Like the Evangelists' Jesus, the Christs of Dostoevsky, Tolstoy, Bulgakov, and Pasternak constitute four powerful "gospels" that will preside over the length and breadth of Russian literature for some time to come. With interest in Christ and Christianity enjoying a renaissance in Russian literature well into the post-Soviet period, it is safe to say that the Christ narrative in Russian literature, so beset by polemic and prohibition over the last two centuries, will continue to appeal to writers until such time as Christ himself ceases to engage the hearts and minds of humanity. In the meantime, the post-Soviet image of Jesus Christ awaits its next incarnation.

NOTES

INTRODUCTION

1. Fyodor Dostoevsky, *Notes from Underground*, trans. Mirra Ginsburg (New York: Bantam, 1974), 21–22.

2. Fedor Mikhailovich Dostoevskii, *Polnoe sobranie sochinenii* (hereafter *PSS*), 30 vols. (Leningrad: Nauka, 1972–1990), 28:1:176.

3. Charles Taylor, *A Secular Age* (Cambridge, MA: Belknap Press of Harvard University Press, 2007), 594–617 (here, 595).

4. Leo Tolstoy, *War and Peace*, trans. Richard Pevear and Larissa Volokhonsky (New York: Knopf, 2007), 1203.

5. О Сый, котораго перомъ, / Ни бреннымъ зрѣніемъ, ни слухомъ, / Ниже витійства языкомъ / Не можно описать. Wolfgang Kasack calls this "one of the most magnificent Christ poems in all of Russian literature" in his *Christus in der russischen Literatur: Ein Gang durch die Literaturgeschichte von ihren Anfängen biz zum Ende des 20. Jahrhunderts* (Munich: Otto Sagner, 1999), 25.

6. "The Mystical Theology," translated by Colm Luibheid in *Pseudo-Dionysius: The Complete Works* (New York: Paulist Press, 1987), 141.

7. Vladimir Lossky, *The Mystical Theology of the Eastern Church* (Crestwood, NY: St. Vladimir's Seminary Press, 1998), 25.

8. Ibid., 27.

9. According to Kasack, this episode from the Gospels is often cited in Russian literature. See his *Christus in der russischen Literatur*, 8–9.

10. For the purposes of my study, agape is understood in its broadest sense as unconditional, selfless, active love. It is often considered synonymous with divine love, the love of God for humankind. Eros in this study is romantic, passionate, sexual love. For an encyclopedic study of agape in Russian religious thought, see Johannes Miroslav Oravecz, *God As Love: The Concept and Spiritual Aspects of Agape in Modern Russian Religious Thought* (Grand Rapids, Michigan: Eerdmans, 2014).

11. Leo Tolstoy, *Anna Karenina*, trans. Richard Pevear and Larissa Volokhonsky (New York: Viking, 2001), 42.

12. See, for example, Luke 14:25–26: "If anyone comes to me and does not hate father and mother, wife and children, brothers and sisters—yes, even their own life—such a person cannot be my disciple." Also, Matthew 10:37: "Whoever loves father or mother more than me is not worthy of me, and whoever loves son or daughter more than me is not worthy of me."

13. *Dostoevskii, PSS* 20:173. English translation by Liza Knapp from *Dostoevsky's The Idiot: A Critical Companion*, ed. Liza Knapp (Evanston, IL: Northwestern University Press, 1998), 220.

14. Fyodor Dostoevsky, *The Brothers Karamazov*, trans. Richard Pevear and Larissa Volokhonsky (San Francisco: North Point Press, 1990), part 2, book 6, chapter 3, 316.

15. Most recently, see Jefferson J. A. Gatrall's *The Real and the Sacred: Picturing Jesus in Nineteenth-Century Fiction* (Ann Arbor: University of Michigan Press, 2014). Gatrall's work is an excellent analysis of visual rendtions of Christ described in nineteenth-century American and European literature, including the works of Dostoevsky and Tolstoy.

16. One of the best treatments of the idea of the Christ figure and the various ways that the life and person of Jesus have been deployed in world literature is Theodore Ziolkowski, *Fictional Transfigurations of Jesus* (Princeton, NJ: Princeton University Press, 1972).

17. This has already been done in Kasack's *Christus in der russischen Literatur*.

18. See part 1, chapter 6 of his *Notes from Underground*.

19. The most significant book on this topic to date is Wolfgang Kasack's chronological reference work, *Christus in der russischen Literatur*. A two-volume anthology of Russian poetry devoted to Christ and his teachings appeared in 2013: Lidiia Molchanova, *Obraz Khrista v russkoi literature* (St. Petersburg: Novoe i staroe, 2013). The work is largely devotional, containing brief contextual notes but no analysis of Russian poetic engagement with the image of Christ.

CHAPTER 1

1. Pieter N. Holtrop and C. H. Slechte, "Foreign Churches along the Nevski Prospekt: An Introduction," in *Foreign Churches in St. Petersburg and Their Archives: 1703–1917*, ed. Pieter N. Holtrop and C. H. Slechte (Leiden: Brill, 2007), 2.

2. Alexander Herzen, *My Past and Thoughts*, trans. Constance Garnett, revised by Humphrey Higgens, 4 vols. (New York: Knopf, 1968), 1:42. Cited in Joseph Frank, *Dostoevsky: The Seeds of Revolt, 1821–1849* (Princeton, NJ: Princeton University Press, 1976), 42.

3. Frank, *Seeds of Revolt*, 42.

4. V. G. Belinsky, "Letter to N. V. Gogol," in *Belinsky, Chernyshevsky, and Dobrolyubov: Essential Writings by the Founders of Russian Literary and Social Criticism*, ed. Ralph E. Matlaw (Bloomington: Indiana University Press, 1977), 86–87. Translation modified by me.

5. Ernest J. Simmons, *Chekhov: A Biography* (Chicago: University of Chicago Press, 1962), 392.

6. Anton Chekhov, "Peasants," in *Selected Stories*, trans. Anne Dunnigan (New York: New American Library, 1960), 268–69.

7. Alexander Herzen, *Childhood, Youth and Exile*, trans. J. D. Duff (Oxford: Oxford University Press, 1980), 42.

8. Ibid., 43.

9. In his 1873 edition of *Diary of a Writer*, Dostoevsky remembers Belinsky arguing that Jesus, were he to appear today, would be "the most undistinguished and ordinary of men" and "would certainly join the socialists and follow them." See *A Writer's Diary, vol. 1, 1873–1876*, trans. Kenneth Lantz (Evanston, IL: Northwestern University Press, 1993), 129.

10. Fyodor Dostoevsky, *The Brothers Karamazov*, trans. Richard Pevear and Larissa Volokhonsky (San Francisco: North Point Press, 1990), 554. Translation modified by me. The passage is in part 4, book 10, chapter 6.

11. Nicholas de Lange writes: "'Secular Judaism' is the name given to the modern phenomenon of Jews who identify with Judaism but reject its religious dimension. This tendency, whose roots are in nineteenth-century Russia, has become an established feature of contemporary Jewry." See his *Judaism* (Oxford: Oxford University Press, 1986), 33.

12. M. N. Katkov, "Starye bogi i novye bogi," *Russkii vestnik* 31 (1861): 891–904. Cited in Victoria S. Frede, "Materialism and the Radical Intelligentsia: The 1860s," in *A History of Russian Philosophy, 1830–1930: Faith, Reason, and the Defense of Human Dignity*, ed. Gary M. Hamburg and Randall A. Poole (Cambridge: Cambridge University Press, 2010), 69.

13. Frede, "Materialism," 69.

14. See Inessa Medzhibovskaya, *Tolstoy and the Religious Culture of His Time: A Biography of a Long Conversion, 1845–1887* (Lanham, MD: Lexington Books, 2008), 3–28 (here, 14).

15. Leo Tolstoy, *A Confession, The Gospel in Brief, and What I Believe*, trans. Aylmer Maude (London: Oxford University Press, 1971), 74.

16. Ibid., 5.

17. V. N. Zakharov, "Simvolika khristianskogo kalendaria v proizvedeniiakh Dostoevskogo," in *Novye aspekty v izuchenii Dostoevskogo: Sbornik nauchnykh trudov*, ed. V. N. Zakharov (Petrozavodsk: Izdatel'stvo Petrozavodskogo universiteta, 1994), 37–49 (here, 37). Cited in V. N. Zhozhikashvili, "Notes on Contemporary Dostoevsky Studies," trans. Laura Givens, *Russian Studies in Literature* 34, no. 4 (Fall 1998): 56–91 (here, 63).

18. D. S. Mirsky, *Pushkin* (New York: Dutton, 1963), 8.

19. Aleksandr Sergeevich Pushkin, *Polnoe sobranie sochinenii v desiati tomakh* (Leningrad: Nauka, 1978), 7:100. Cited in Felix Raskolnikov, "Pushkin and Religion," trans. Liv Bliss, *Russian Studies in Literature* 42, no. 1 (Winter 2005–2006), 18.

20. Raskolnikov, "Pushkin and Religion," 31. See also Svetlana Evdokimova's and Vladimir Golstein's succinct survey of recent Orthodox readings of Pushkin in their "Pushkiniana as an Encyclopedia of Contemporary Literary Criticism," in *The Pushkin Handbook*, ed. David M. Bethea (Madison: University of Wisconsin Press, 2005), 618–19. Henri Troyat characterizes Pushkin's faith at the end of his life as "very vague, to be sure, very far from any dogma, religion or church; he simply believed in God." See his *Pushkin*, trans. Nancy Amphoux (New York: Dell, 1970), 579.

21. Dmitry Likhachev asserts that Pushkin's "journey from non-belief to belief" was framed by the *Gabrieliad* of his youth and this poem. See his "Religion: Russian Orthodoxy," trans. Nicholas Rzhevsky and Rama Sohonee, in *The Cambridge Companion to Modern Russian Culture*, ed. Nicholas Rzhevsky (Cambridge: Cambridge University Press, 1998), 53–54.

22. Mikhail Lermontov, *A Hero of Our Time*, trans. Vladimir Nabokov in collaboration with Dmitri Nabokov (Garden City, NY: Doubleday, 1958), 117. The appellation comes from Pechorin's rival, Grushnitsky: "You see in everything the nasty side ... you materialist [материьялист]!" Further citations will be given parenthetically.

23. Nikolai Gogol, *Dead Souls*, trans. Bernard Guilbert Guerney, rev. and ed. Susanne Fusso (New Haven, CT: Yale University Press, 1996), 243.

24. Victor Erlich, *Gogol* (New Haven, CT: Yale University Press, 1969), 194.

25. Ibid., 198.

26. Ivan Goncharov, *Oblomov*, trans. Marian Schwartz (New Haven, CT: Yale University Press, 2008), 128. Further citations will be given parenthetically.

27. Ivan Turgenev, *Polnoe sobranie sochinenii i pisem v dvadtsati vos'mi tomakh* (Moscow: Nauka, 1964–1969), 3:53. Cited in Leonard Schapiro, *Turgenev: His Life and Times* (Cambridge, MA: Harvard University Press, 1982), 134.

28. Avrahm Yarmolinsky, *Turgenev: The Man, His Art and His Age* (New York: Collier, 1961), 161.

29. Schapiro, *Turgenev*, 59.

30. For a succinct treatment of Chekhov and faith as well as Orthodox themes in his works, see Julie DeSherbinin, "Chekhov and Christianity: The Critical Evolution," in *Chekhov Then and Now: The Reception of Chekhov in World Culture*, ed. J. Douglas Clayton (New York: Lang, 1997), 285–99.

31. Anton Chekhov to Mikhail Menshikov, January 28, 1900, in *Anton Chekhov's Life and Thought: Selected Letters and Commentary*, trans. Michael Henry Heim with Simon Karlinsky, ed. Simon Karlinsky (Berkeley: University of California Press, 1973), 374.

32. Anton Chekhov to Alexei Pleshcheyev, October 4, 1888, ibid., 109.

33. Anton Chekhov to Sergei Diaghilev, December 30, 1902, ibid., 435–36.

34. Nikolay Leskov, *The Cathedral Clergy*, trans. Margaret Winchell (Bloomington, IN: Slavica, 2010), 212.

35. Leo Tolstoy, *Anna Karenina*, trans. Richard Pevear and Larissa Volokhonsky (New York: Viking, 2001), 475.

36. Ibid., 7.

37. Hugh McLean, *Nikolai Leskov: The Man and His Art* (Cambridge, MA: Harvard University Press, 1977), 202.

38. As Mark Steinberg contends, in Russia "alienation from the established church [...] and even crises of faith often led not toward secularism and atheism but toward alternative forms of religious faith and enthusiasm." Mark D. Steinberg, *Proletarian Imagination: Self, Modernity, and the Sacred in Russia: 1910–1925* (Ithaca, NY: Cornell University Press, 2002), 227.

39. Leo Tolstoy, *Resurrection*, trans. Anthony Briggs (London: Penguin, 2009), 160.

40. This formulation is attributed to the German theologian Martin Kähler from his work *Der sogenannte historische Jesus und der geschichtliche, biblische Christus* (The so-called historical Jesus and the historic, biblical Christ, 1896).

41. This is Albert Schweitzer's characterization of Strauss's Jesus. See his *The Quest of the Historical Jesus: A Critical Study of Its Progress from Reimarus to Wrede*, trans. W. Montgomery (London: SCM Press, 1981), 80.

42. Ernest Renan, *The Life of Jesus* (Buffalo, NY: Prometheus Books, 1991), 226.

43. Leonid Ouspensky and Vladimir Lossky, *The Meaning of Icons*, trans. G. E. H. Palmer and E. Kadloubovsky (Crestwood, NY: St. Vladimir's Seminary Press, 1994), 25.

44. Ibid., 60.

45. We need only think of the popular "WWJD" bracelets of evangelical professions: "What would Jesus do?"

46. Ouspensky and Lossky, *The Meaning of Icons*, 36.

47. Pavel Florensky, *Iconostasis*, trans. Donald Sheehan and Olga Andrejev (Crestwood, NY: St. Vladimir's Seminary Press, 2000), 51–52.

48. Timothy Ware [Bishop Kallistos of Diokleia], *The Orthodox Church* (London: Penguin, 1993), 219.

49. Florensky, *Iconostasis*, 52.

50. Ouspensky and Lossky, *The Meaning of Icons*, 34.

51. Ibid., 35.

52. Ware, *The Orthodox Church*, 231–32.

53. Vladimir Solovyov, *Lectures on Divine Humanity*, trans. Peter Zouboff, rev. and ed. Boris Jakim (Hudson, NY: Lindisfarne Press, 1995), 17, 67.

54. Nicolas Berdyaev, *The Divine and the Human*, trans. R. M. French (San Rafael, CA: Semantron, 2009), 23. Further citations will be given parenthetically.

55. Ware, *The Orthodox Church*, 209.

56. Sergei Bulgakov, "Glavy o Troichnosti," *Pravoslavnaia Mysl'* 1 (1928): 66–68. Cited in Michael Aksionov Meerson, *The Trinity of Love in Modern Russian Theology* (Quincy, IL: Franciscan Press, 1998), 177–78.

57. Gary M. Hamburg and Randall A. Poole, "Introduction: The Humanist Tradition in Russian Philosophy," in Hamburg and Poole, *A History of Russian Philosophy*, 8–9.

58. Ibid., 10–11.

59. D. S. Mirsky, *A History of Russian Literature from Its Beginnings to 1900* (New York: Vintage, 1958), 179, 285.

60. Vissarion Belinsky, "Letters to V. P. Botkin," trans. Philip Rahv, in *Russian Philosophy, vol. 1, The Beginnings of Russian Philosophy: The Slavophiles, The Westernizers*, ed. James M. Edie, James P. Scanlan, and Mary-Barbara Zeldin (Knoxville: University of Tennessee Press, 1976), 304.

61. Alexander Herzen, *From the Other Shore*, in *Russian Philosophy, vol. 1, The Beginnings of Russian Philosophy: The Slavophiles, The Westernizers*, ed. James M. Edie, James P. Scanlan, and Mary-Barbara Zeldin (Knoxville: University of Tennessee Press, 1976), 370.

62. Dostoevsky, *A Writer's Diary*, 1:128.

63. David Friedrich Strauss, *Life of Jesus Critically Examined*, trans. George Eliot (New York: Gloger Family Books, 1993), 780.

64. Kenneth Lantz, "Strauss, David Friedrich," in *The Dostoevsky Encyclopedia* (Westport, CT: Greenwood, 2004), 419.

65. Patrick Lally Michelson, "Slavophile Religious Thought and the Dilemma of Russian Modernity, 1830–1860," *Modern Intellectual History* 7, no. 2 (2010): 239–67 (here, 252).

66. Heather Bailey, *Orthodoxy, Modernity, and Authenticity: The Reception of Ernest Renan's* Life of Jesus *in Russia* (Newcastle: Cambridge Scholars Publishing, 2008), 17.

67. Charles Taylor, *A Secular Age* (Cambridge, MA: Belknap Press of Harvard University Press, 2007), 323–25.

68. Theodore Ziolkowski, *Fictional Transfigurations of Jesus* (Princeton, NJ: Princeton University Press, 1972), 37.

69. Bailey, *Orthodoxy*, 16.

70. Schweitzer, *Quest of the Historical Jesus*, 181.

71. Renan, *Life of Jesus*, 16, 6. Further references will be given parenthetically within the text.

72. Bailey, *Orthodoxy*, 21.

73. Fedor Dostoevskii, "Zapisi k *Dnevniku pisatelia* 1878 g. iz rabchikh tetradei 1875–77," F. M. Dostoevskii, *Polnoe sobranie sochinenii*, 24:95. Cited in Bailey, *Orthodoxy*, 22.

74. Nikolai Chernyshevsky, *What Is to Be Done?*, trans. Michael R. Katz (Ithaca, NY: Cornell University Press, 1989), 276. Further references to the novel will be included parenthetically within the text.

75. Irina Paperno, *Chernyshevsky and the Age of Realism: A Study in the Semiotics of Behavior* (Stanford, CA: Stanford University Press, 1988). Rakhmetov as a Christ figure is discussed by V. Serdiuchenko, "Futurologiia Dostoevskogo i Chernyshevskogo," *Voprosy literatury* 3 (2001): 66–84. English translation: "The Futurology of Dostoevsky and Chernyshevsky," trans. Liv Bliss, *Russian Studies in Literature* 38, no. 4 (Fall 2002): 58–76.

76. Cited in Rufus W. Mathewson, Jr., *The Positive Hero in Russian Literature*, 2nd ed. (Stanford, CA: Stanford University Press, 1975), 82.

77. Fyodor Dostoevsky, "Old People," in *A Writer's Diary*, 1:128.

78. Karen Stepanian, "'It Will Be, but Not Until the End Has Been Achieved' (David Friedrich Strauss's *Das Leben Jesu*, Joseph Ernest Renan's *La Vie de Jésus*, and Dostoevsky's *Idiot*)," trans. Liv Bliss, *Russian Studies in Literature*, 42, no 1 (Winter 2005–2006), 40. Translation of "'Eto budet, no budet posle dostizheniia tseli ...' 'Zhizn' Iususa' D. F. Shtrausa i E. Zh. Renana i roman F. M. Dostoevskogo 'Idiot,'" *Voprosy literatury* 4 (2003), 140–58. Here, Stepanian is summarizing and then quoting from D. L. Sorkina, "Ob odnom iz istochnikov obraza L'va Nikolaevicha Myshkina," *Uchenye zapiski Tomskogo gosudarstvennogo universiteta: Voprosy khudozhestvennogo metoda i stilia* 48 (1964): 145–51.

79. Donna Tussing Orwin, *Tolstoy's Art and Thought, 1847–1880* (Princeton, NJ: Princeton University Press, 1993), 21.

80. Ibid., 20.

Chapter 2

1. Fedor Mikhailovich Dostoevskii, *Polnoe sobranie sochinenii* (hereafter *PSS*), 30 vols. (Leningrad: Nauka, 1972–1990), 28:1:176. Translation from *Selected Letters of Fyodor Dostoyevsky*, trans. Andrew MacAndrew, ed. Joseph Frank and David I. Goldstein (New Brunswick, 1987), 68.

2. Dostoevskii, *PSS* 28:1:176. Translation from Dostoevsky, *Selected Letters*, 68.

3. See Dostoevsky's March 25/April 6, 1870, letter to Apollon Maikov, *PSS* 29:1:116.

4. For a succinct account, see Kenneth Lantz's entry "Nechaev, Sergei Gennadevich (1847–1883)," in his *The Dostoevsky Encyclopedia* (Westport, CT: Greenwood, 2004), 271–72.

5. Fyodor Dostoevsky, *A Writer's Diary*, vol. 1, *1873–1976*, trans. Kenneth Lantz (Evanston, IL: Northwestern University Press, 1993). Further citations will be given parenthetically in the text.

6. All quotations from *Demons* will be cited parenthetically by part, chapter, subsection (where they exist), and page number from the Richard Pevear and Larissa Volokhonsky translation (New York: Vintage, 1994), with modifications by me where necessary. Here, the citation is from the censored chapter translated as an appendix, "At Tikhon's," (688).

7. In his notebooks for the novel, Dostoevsky writes that Stavrogin "is the hero. All the rest moves around him, like a kaleidoscope." Also: "Everything is contained in Stavrogin's character. Stavrogin is *everything*." *PSS* 11:136, 207. English translation: Fyodor Dostoevsky, *The Notebooks for The Possessed*, trans. Victor Terras, ed. Edward Wasiolek (Chicago: University of Chicago Press, 1968), 182, 269–70. Dostoevsky calls Stavrogin "the real hero of the novel" in a letter to Nikolai Strakhov, October 9/21, 1870, in *PSS* 29:1:148. English translation: Dostoevsky, *Complete Letters*, ed. and trans. David A. Lowe (Ann Arbor, MI: Ardis, 1990), 3:282–85.

8. Dostoevskii, *PSS* 12:108.

9. Richard Peace, *Dostoevsky: An Examination of the Major Novels* (Cambridge: Cambridge University Press, 1971), 184. In a similar observation, Edward Wasiolek calls Kirillov and Shatov the "twin creations of Stavrogin." See his *Dostoevsky: The Major Fiction* (Cambridge: MIT Press, 1964), 119.

10. See, for example, Rowan Williams, *Dostoevsky: Language, Faith and Fiction* (Waco, TX: Baylor University Press, 2008), 91; Peace, *Dostoevsky*, 216.

11. See, for instance, Revelation 1:8: "'I am the Alpha and the Omega,' says the Lord God, 'who is, and who was, and who is to come, the Almighty.'" Also: Revelation 22:13.

12. See Mark 10:18: "'Why do you call me good?' Jesus answered. 'No one is good except God alone.'" Also: Matthew 19:17, Luke 18:19.

13. See Peace, *Dostoevsky*, 217.

14. As Edward Wasiolek argues, "Stavrogin liberates himself from a fixed image of self by always doing the opposite." *Dostoevsky*, 124.

15. Williams, *Language, Faith and Fiction*, 101.

16. Carol Apollonio, in *Dostoevsky's Secrets: Reading against the Grain* (Evanston, IL: Northwestern University Press, 2009), argues that Stavrogin's Christological function has been consistently overlooked by critics. She sees in his story and especially his confession an attempt "to purge the world of its sins by taking them on himself—an act of *imitatio Christi* that, wrongfully directed though it may be, still is perhaps less wrong than refusing to acknowledge his own guilt or, worse, *accusing others*, the ultimate act of evil in Dostoevsky's works" (117–43, here, 141).

17. Williams describes the narrative of Kirillov's suicide as a "parodic passion narrative, with the final interview between Kirillov and Verkhovensky a 'farewell discourse' like those in St. John's gospel, and more grotesquely, Kirillov's withdrawal into an inner room to kill himself, leaving Pyotr outside, an echo of the Garden of Gethsemane." See *Language, Faith and Fiction*, 92.

18. Kenneth Lantz, *The Dostoevsky Encyclopedia*, 86. Victor Terras points out how the second epigraph to the novel—two stanzas from Pushkin's poem "Demons" that "contain no message of hope"—considerably modulates the more uplifting first epigraph from the Gospel of Luke, anticipating the dark ambiguity with which *Demons* concludes. See his *Reading Dostoevsky* (Madison: University of Wisconsin Press, 1998), 90.

19. Vladimir Nabokov, *Lectures on Russian Literature* (New York: Harcourt Brace Jovanovich, 1981), 104.

20. Dostoevsky, *Selected Letters*, 191. Dostoevskii, *PSS* 28:2:73.

21. Dostoevskii, *PSS* 5, 120–21. English translation by Michael R. Katz, from Fyodor Dostoevsky, *Notes from Underground* (New York: Norton, 1989), 25–26.

22. On the weak reception of *Notes*, see Joseph Frank, *Dostoevsky: The Stir of Liberation, 1860–1865* (Princeton, NJ: Princeton University Press, 1986), 311. On Dostoevsky's motivation for not appealing to the censors to restore the chapter in later publications, see Frank, *The Stir of Liberation*, 328.

23. In "Fear of Faith: The Hidden Religious Message of *Notes from Underground*," Carol A. Flath argues that the Underground Man's tormented existence is an example of suffering that, "like the passion of Christ," could "lead people to faith." *Slavic and East European Journal* 37, no. 4 (1993): 510–29 (here, 527).

24. Olga Meerson's article "Old Testament Lamentation in the Underground Man's Monologue: A Refutation of the Existentialist Reading of *Notes from the Underground*," *Slavic and East European Journal* 36, no. 3 (1992): 317–22, is the first to my knowledge to point to an apophatic aspect in *Notes*.

25. Timothy Ware [Bishop Kallistos of Diokleia], *The Orthodox Church* (London: Penguin, 1993), 64. On the apophatic approach to Dostoevsky, see Malcolm Jones, *Dostoevsky and the Dynamics of Religious Experience* (London: Anthem, 2005), 71–77.

26. Earlier, Razumikhin tells Raskolnikov: "Lying can always be forgiven; lying is a fine thing, because it leads to the truth" (2:4:135). Citations are from the Richard Pevear

and Larissa Volokhonsky translation of *Crime and Punishment* (New York: Knopf, 1992), and are listed parenthetically by part, chapter, and then page number.

27. D. H. Lawrence, "Preface to Dostoevsky's *The Grand Inquisitor*," in *Dostoevsky: A Collection of Critical Essays*, ed. René Wellek (Englewood Cliffs, NJ: Prentice-Hall, 1962), 91.

28. All references to *Brothers Karamazov* will be cited parenthetically in the text by book, chapter, and page number from the Richard Pevear and Larissa Volokhonsky translation (San Francisco: North Point Press, 1990), with modifications by me where necessary.

29. See also Jones, *Dostoevsky*, 123: "And is not Ivan's insistence that his Euclidian mind prevents him from solving the question of God's existence or non-existence very similar to the apophatic view that it is impossible to reach the knowledge of God by way of positive definition?"

30. Vladimir Lossky, *The Mystical Theology of the Eastern Church* (Crestwood, NY: St. Vladimir's Seminary Press, 1998), 27, 25.

31. Lawrence, "Preface," 90.

32. Responding to his detractors, Dostoevsky wrote in his 1881 diary: "These blockheads never dreamed of such a powerful denial of God as is put in the Inquisitor and the preceding chapter." *PSS* 27, 48.

33. Jones, *Dostoevsky*, 122.

34. Joseph Frank, *The Mantle of the Prophet, 1871–1881* (Princeton, NJ: Princeton University Press, 2002), 616.

35. Wil van den Bercken, *Christian Fiction and Religious Realism* (London: Anthem, 2011), 88–89.

36. Ibid., 87.

37. Robin Feuer Miller, *The Brothers Karamazov: Worlds of the Novel* (New York: Twayne Publishers, 1992), 68.

38. See Wasiolek, *Dostoevsky*, 159–60. See also Robert L. Belknap, *The Structure of The Brothers Karamazov* (The Hague: Mouton, 1967), 37–39, and Miller, *The Brothers Karamazov*, 49.

39. This is the original 1657 definition of apophasis in the Oxford dictionary. From http://www.odlt.org/ballast/apophasis.html. A rhetorical device, apophasis derives its name from the same Greek root as apophaticism: *apophemi*, "to say no."

40. See James L. Rice, "Dostoevsky's Endgame: The Projected Sequel to *The Brothers Karamazov*," *Russian History/Histoire Russe* 33, no. 1 (Spring 2006), 45–62; and Igor Volgin, "Alyosha's Destiny," in *The New Russian Dostoevsky*, ed. and trans. Carol Apollonio (Bloomington, IN: Slavica, 2010), 271–86.

41. Dostoevsky, *PSS* 29:2:102, 101.

CHAPTER 3

1. Sarah Young, *Dostoevsky's* The Idiot *and the Ethical Foundations of Narrative: Reading, Narrating, Scripting* (London: Anthem, 2004), 1–2.

2. In his notes for part 2, Dostoevsky writes "Kniaz' Khristos," either "Prince Christ" or the "Prince is Christ." See *PSS* 9:246, 249, 253. English translation: Fyodor Dostoevsky, *The Notebooks for* The Idiot, trans. Katharine Strelsky, ed. Edward Wasiolek (Chicago: University of Chicago Press, 1967), 198, 201, 205.

3. Joseph Frank, *Dostoevsky: The Miraculous Years, 1865–1871* (Princeton, NJ: Princeton University Press, 1995), 477. See also 492. Kenneth Lantz calls it a novel "full of dark humor" despite "politically inspired murders and social chaos" (*The Dostoevsky Encyclopedia* [Westport, CT: Greenwood, 2004], 86). See also Dennis Patrick Slattery, "Idols and Icons: Comic Transformation in Dostoevsky's *The Possessed*," *Dostoevsky Studies* 6 (1985): 35–50.

4. Gary Rosenshield, Afterword to *The Idiot*, by Fyodor Dostoyevsky, trans. Henry and Olga Carlisle (New York: Signet, 2002), 651.

5. As Walter Kerr observes, "Comedy seems not only to follow tragedy, but to derive from it." Kerr, *Tragedy and Comedy* (New York: Simon and Schuster, 1967), 22.

6. P. M. Bitsilli, *Izbrannye trudy po filologii* (Moscow: Nasledie, 1996), 504.

7. Natalia Ashimbaeva, "Comedy between the Poles of Humour and Tragedy, Beauty and Ugliness: Prince Myshkin as a Comic Character," trans. Sarah Young, in *Reflective Laughter: Aspects of Humour in Russian Culture*, ed. Lesley Milne (London: Anthem, 2004), 50. See A. E. Kunil'skii, *Smekh v mire Dostoevskogo* (Petrozavodsk: Izdatel'stvo Petrozavodskogo universiteta, 1994), 5–22; M. L. Spivak, "Mesto i funktsiia smekha v tvorchestve F. M. Dostoevskogo," *Vestnik Moskovskogo universiteta, Seriia 9: Filologiia* 5 (1986): 71; R. L. Busch, *Humor in the Major Novels of F. M. Dostoevsky* (Columbus, OH: Slavica, 1987); Alla Zlochevskaia, "Stikhiia smekha v romane *Idiot*," *Dostoevskii i mirovaia kul'tura* 1 (1993), 47; I. I. Lapshin, "Komicheskoe v proizvedeniiakh Dostoevskogo," in *O Dostoevksom: Sbornik statei*, ed. A. L. Bem (Prague, 1933), 2:31–50; Ronald Hingley, *The Undiscovered Dostoevsky* (Westport, CT: Greenwood Press, 1977), 111.

8. The most detailed treatment of Myshkin as a Christ figure is Liza Knapp, "Myshkin through a Murky Glass, Guessingly," in *Dostoevsky's* The Idiot: *A Critical Companion*, ed. Liza Knapp (Evanston, IL: Northwestern University Press, 1998), 191–215. See also Frank, *Miraculous Years*, 318–22, and Victor Terras, *The Idiot: An Interpretation* (Boston: Twayne Publishers, 1990), 75–80.

9. On March 12, 1868, Dostoevsky wrote in his notebooks: "*Three* kinds of love in the novel: 1) Passionate and spontaneous love—Rogozhin. 2) Love out of vanity—Gania. 3) Christian love—the Prince." See *PSS* 9:220. English translation: *The Notebooks for* The Idiot, 170.

10. Rosenshield, Afterword to *The Idiot*, 651.

11. Ibid.

12. Zlochevskaia's article is the most detailed treatment of comedy in the novel. It identifies and catalogues various kinds of humor—satire, buffoonery, parody, social ridicule—but concludes, somewhat disappointingly, that "humor is always a form of the existence and depiction of the tragic" ("Stikhiia smekha," 25–47, here, 45). Ashimbaeva's "Comedy between the Poles of Humour and Tragedy" reads Myshkin as "the image of the principle of 'co-existence and interaction'" of disparate plot and thematic elements, ranging from the farcical to the tragic (56). "Comedy and the comic," Ashimbaeva argues, "most frequently arise in *The Idiot* in contexts where they emphasize far from comic circumstances" (53). See also Busch, *Humor*, 44–49, and Hingley, *Undiscovered Dostoevsky*, 111–14. Kunil'skii does not address comic aspects of *The Idiot* at all in his *Smekh v mire Dostoevskogo*. Spivak's "Mesto i funktsiia smekha" mentions *The Idiot* only briefly, as does Lapshin's "Komicheskoe v proizvedeniiakh Dostoevskogo." Richard Peace, in "Dostoevsky and the 'Golden Age,'" *Dostoevsky Studies* 3 (1982): 71, refers to Myshkin as "the comic man himself," but does not elaborate.

13. A notable exception is Olga Meerson's "Ivolgin and Holbein: Non-Christ Risen vs. Christ Non-Risen," *Slavic and East European Journal* 39, no. 2 (1995): 200–213, which connects General Ivolgin's comical story about the "resurrected" Private Kolpakov with the Holbein painting of the dead Christ, arguing the story and the painting taken together constitute an apophatic affirmation of the need for Christ.

14. Dostoevskii, *PSS* 18:53. English translation: *Dostoevsky's Occasional Writings*, ed. and trans. David Magarshack (Evanston, IL: Northwestern University Press, 1997), 58–59.

15. Erik Egeberg, "How Should We Then Read *The Idiot*?," in *Celebrating Creativity: Essays in Honor of Jostein Børtnes*, ed. Kurt Andreas Grimstad and Ingunn Lunde (Bergen, Norway: University of Bergen, Department of Russian Studies, 1997), 163.

16. All citations to *The Idiot* will be given parenthetically within the text by part, chapter, and page number from the Alan Myers translation (Oxford: Oxford University Press, 1992), with modifications by me where necessary.

17. Myshkin repeats this same speech at the end of the novel at his and Aglaya's engagement party: "I'm always afraid my comic/ridiculous appearance will detract from the thought and the *main point*. My gestures are all wrong. I always use them in the opposite way to what I am saying, and that raises a laugh and takes away from the idea. The sense of proportion just isn't there either, that's the main thing; that really is the main thing" (4:7:583).

18. In an argument at the Ptitsyn household, Ippolit acknowledges the Prince is "a truly good man … although absurd/comical as well" (4:2:505). Princess Belokonskaia's pronouncement later in part 4 is especially conspicuous, as it reflects the judgment of Russian high society (4:7:581). A few pages later, Myshkin uses the epithet to describe himself (4:7:584).

19. Rogozhin calls Myshkin a holy fool (1:1:14); the inhabitants of the lost paradise call the Ridiculous Man the same thing in the final pages of the story (see Dostoevskii, *PSS* 25:117); for an English translation, see "The Dream of a Ridiculous Man," in *Notes from Underground, The Double and Other Stories*, translated by Constance Garnett, introduction and notes by Deborah Martinsen (New York: Barnes and Noble, 2003), 407–28 (here, 426).

20. The Ridiculous Man speaks of his dream as being induced "not by reason but by desire, not by the head but by the heart" (Dostoevskii, *PSS* 25:108; Dostoevsky, "The Dream," 413). Elsewhere he notes that the singing of the people in his dream was "beyond the grasp of my mind, yet my heart unconsciously absorbed it more and more" (*PSS* 25:114, "The Dream," 421).

21. "Я потерял слов" (Dostoevskii, *PSS* 25:118; Dostoevsky, "The Dream," 427).

22. Here, he looks more like the first incarnation of Myshkin in Dostoevsky's notebooks: "*The Idiot*'s passions are violent, he has a burning need of love, a boundless pride, and out of pride he means to dominate himself, conquer himself. He takes delight in humiliation. Those who do not know him make fun of him; those who do know him begin to fear him." Dostoevsky, *The Notebooks for* The Idiot, 31. Russian text in *PSS* 9:141.

23. To cite two differing opinions: Edward Wasiolek argues that "The Dream of a Ridiculous Man" depicts a corruption of the truth "to its highest point, the blasphemy of Christ." See his *Dostoevsky: The Major Fiction* (Cambridge, MA: MIT Press, 1964), 147. Robin Feuer Miller, by contrast, reads the story as a straight conversion narrative, likening it to Dickens's *A Christmas Carol*. See her chapter "Unsealing the Generic Envelope and Deciphering 'The Dream of a Ridiculous Man,'" in her *Dostoevsky's Unfinished Journey* (New Haven, CT: Yale University Press, 2007), 105–27.

24. My thanks to Olga Meerson for this observation.

25. Ashimbaeva's short analysis "Comedy between the Poles of Humour and Tragedy" discusses Myshkin as a comic character, but does not link his comicality to a Christian worldview.

26. The definitive treatment is Harriet Murav, *Holy Foolishness: Dostoevsky's Novels and the Poetics of Cultural Critique* (Stanford, CA: Stanford University Press, 1992), 71–98. See also Robin Feuer Miller, *Dostoevsky and* The Idiot: *Author, Narrator, and Reader* (Cambridge, MA: Harvard University Press, 1981), 65–67; Jostein Børtnes, "The Function of Hagiography in Dostoevskii's Novels," *Scando-Slavica* 24 (1978): 27–33; Frank, *Miraculous Years*, 288–89.

27. Frank, *Miraculous Years*, 340.

28. Mikhail Bakhtin, *Problems of Dostoevsky's Poetics,* ed. and trans. Caryl Emerson (Minneapolis, MN: University of Minnesota Press, 1984), his emphasis.

29. Bakhtin writes: "Wherever Prince Myshkin appears, hierarchical barriers between people suddenly become penetrable, an inner contact is formed between them, a carnival frankness is born. His personality possesses the peculiar capacity to relativize everything that disunifies people and imparts a *false seriousness* to life." Ibid., 174.

30. Ibid., 175.

31. Part 1, chapter 3 (28), chapter 6 (79), chapter 7 (83, 92, 93), chapter 8 (108), chapter 9 (111), chapter 11 (127), chapter 13 (145), chapter 16 (177, 179).

32. Part 1, chapter 3 (26, 28, 29, 37), chapter 6 (79), chapter 12 (141), chapter 15 (174).

33. Northrop Frye, Sheridan Baker, and George Perkins, *The Harper Handbook to Literature* (New York: Harper & Rowe, 1985), 110.

34. Ibid., 111.

35. Richard Pearce, *Stages of the Clown: Perspectives on Modern Fiction from Dostoyevsky to Beckett* (Carbondale: Southern Illinois University Press, 1970), 18.

36. Ibid., 18–19.

37. Dostoevskii, *PSS* 28:251. The letter is dated January 1/13, 1868. English translation from Knapp, *Dostoevsky's* The Idiot, 242–43.

38. Dostoevskii, *PSS* 9:239. English translation from *The Notebooks for* The Idiot, 191. Dostoevsky's emphasis.

39. See 1:4:53; 1:7:87; and 2:12:335–36. Aglaya, in an obvious allusion to Christ, tells Myshkin at one point: "There are some not worthy of bending down and picking up the handkerchief you've just dropped" (3:2:360). Lebedev refers to him as "Providence" at one point (3:9:466).

40. A brief summary of the major comic highlights would include the Prince's crashing of Nastasia Filippovna's name-day party and marriage proposal in part 1; the scandal scene with Burdovskii's crew in part 2 involving the hilarious public reading of the satirical feuilleton on Myshkin; Lebedev's ridiculous discourse on cannibals and the raucous reception of Ippolit Terent'ev's "Necessary Explanation" (itself a self-aggrandizing and self-pitying document that verges on the absurd) at the Prince's birthday party in part 3; and Myshkin's breaking of an expensive vase at his own engagement party at the end of the novel.

41. See part 2, chapters 1 and 6.

42. These are Eric J. Ziolkowski's characterizations, which he asserts are shared by "Dostoevsky's three most religiously significant heroes, Myshkin, Alyosha and Father

Zosima" and link them to Don Quixote. See his *The Sanctification of Don Quixote: From Hidalgo to Priest* (University Park: Pennsylvania State University Press, 1991), 120. See also the discussion in "Primechaniia" in *PSS* 9:400–402 for more on the influence of *Don Quixote* on Dostoevsky while he was writing *The Idiot*. Miguel de Unamuno's 1905 work, *Our Lord Don Quixote: The Life of Don Quixote and Sancho with Related Essays*, trans. Anthony Kerrigan (Princeton, NJ: Princeton University Press, 1976), is the most influential treatment of Quixote as a Christ figure. In his analysis, Michael Holquist considers Myshkin to be "a black parody" of both Christ and Don Quixote. See his *Dostoevsky and the Novel* (Princeton, NJ: Princeton University Press, 1977), 108.

43. Ziolkowski argues that in Myshkin "Christ and Don Quixote are combined." *Sanctification of Don Quixote*, 126.

44. Nathan A. Scott, Jr., "The Bias of Comedy and the Narrow Escape into Faith," in *Holy Laughter: Essays on Religion in the Comic Perspective*, ed. M. Conrad Hyers (New York: Seabury Press, 1969), 52. Scott here is referring to Aldous Huxley's famous essay, "Tragedy and the Whole Truth," in which Huxley calls Homer a poet of the "Whole Truth" because he shows not just tragedy and tears in the *Odyssey*, but supper and sleep as well. When Odysseus and his men mourn their comrades who have been eaten by the monster Scylla, they nevertheless "expertly" prepare dinner and sleep afterwards. "In other words," Huxley argues, "Homer refused to threat the theme tragically. He preferred to tell the Whole Truth" (quoted by Scott, 52). Scott associates the "Whole Truth" with the "art of comedy" (52).

45. I have in mind Myshkin's story of Marie in part 1, chapter 6, as well the four anecdotes of Christian faith he tells to Rogozhin in part 2, chapter 4.

46. These epithets (and their emphasis) are Bakhtin's. "Myshkin is in carnival *paradise*," he argues, "Nastasya Filippovna in carnival *hell*; but this hell and paradise in the novel intersect, intertwine in various ways, and are reflected in each other according to the laws of a profound carnival ambivalence." See *Problems of Dostoevsky's Poetics*, 173–74.

47. Conrad Hyers, *The Comic Vision and the Christian Faith: A Celebration of Life and Laughter* (New York: Pilgrim Press, 1981), 155.

48. Dominic Crossan, *Raid on the Articulate: Comic Eschatology in Jesus and Borges* (New York: Harper and Row, 1976), 22.

49. Scott, "Bias of Comedy," 72.

50. Ibid., 65–66.

51. Kunil'skii, *Smekh v mire Dostoevskogo*, 84.

52. Scott, "Bias of Comedy," 50.

53. Elena Mestergazi provides an opposite interpretation of Myshkin's materialism, viewing it as a sign of his unbelief. See her "Vera i kniaz' Myshkin: Opyt 'naivnogo' chteniia romana *Idiot*," in *Roman F. M. Dostoevskogo* Idiot: *Sovremennoe sostoianie izucheniia*, ed. Tat'iana Kasatkina (Moscow: Nasledie, 2001), 291–318, especially 306–10.

54. Hyers, *The Comic Vision*, 166.

55. When Myshkin first beholds Holbein's dead Christ, he gasps: "That picture! That picture! A man could lose his faith by looking at that picture!" "It's fading as it is," Rogozhin agrees (2:4:229).

56. An excellent treatment of this topic is Leslie A. Johnson, "The Face of the Other in *Idiot*," *Slavic Review* 50, no. 4 (Winter 1991): 867–78.

57. See, for instance, David M. Bethea, *The Shape of Apocalypse in Modern Russian Fiction* (Princeton, NJ: Princeton University Press, 1989), 83, and Liza Knapp, "Introduction to *The Idiot* Part 2: The Novel," in *Dostoevsky's* The Idiot, 32.

58. See, for example, Elizabeth Dalton, *Unconscious Structure in* The Idiot: *A Study in Literature and Psychoanalysis* (Princeton, NJ: Princeton University Press, 1979), 172; Nina Pelikan Straus, "Flights from *The Idiot's* Womanhood," in Knapp, *Dostoevsky's* The Idiot, 112–13; and Michael C. Finke, *Metapoesis: The Russian Tradition from Pushkin to Chekhov* (Durham, NC: Duke University Press, 1995), 107.

59. Zinaida Malenko and James J. Gebhard, "The Artistic Use of Portraits in Dostoevskij's *Idiot*," *Slavic and East European Journal* 5, no. 3 (Autumn 1961): 249. Twice in part 1 Myshkin comments on the suffering he sees in Nastasia Filippovna's photograph. He remarks: "The face is cheerful, but she's suffered dreadfully, hasn't she?" (1:3:37). A few chapters later he repeats the sentiment: "In that face … there's a great deal of suffering" (1:7:85).

60. As early as chapter 3, part 2, Nastasia Filippovna declares her belief that Rogozhin will murder her, yet she repeatedly flies to him as if hastening that outcome. See also chapter 10, part 4.

61. At the end of part 1 (1:16:186), the moneylender Ptitsyn correctly likens Nastasia Filippovna's scandalous behavior to seppuku, or Japanese ritualistic suicide. Ptitsyn, however, speaks of seppuku only as a passive-aggressive act against one's enemies, rather than a ritual of atonement for shame, which is the common understanding of seppuku. Nastasia Filippovna's murder/suicide can be understood as both.

62. Dostoevskii, *PSS* 20:172. English translation from Knapp, *Dostoevsky's* The Idiot, 219. A. B. Galkin makes the same connection between Myshkin's lapse into idiocy and Dostoevsky's diary entry on the death of his first wife ("Obraz Khrista i kontseptsiia cheloveka v romane F. M. Dostoevskogo *Idiot*," in *Roman F. M. Dostoevskogo* Idiot: *Sovremennoe sostoianie izucheniia*, ed. Tat'iana Kasatkina [Moscow: Nasledie, 2001], 322). Steven Cassedy also discusses Dostoevsky's diary entry, but he links it not to Myshkin's lapse into idiocy at novel's end, but rather to the "long passage about epileptic auras" in chapter 5 of part 2. See his *Dostoevsky's Religion* (Stanford, CA: Stanford Unversity Press, 2005), 124–38 (here, 126).

63. Dostoevskii, *PSS* 9:270. English translation: Dostoevsky, *The Notebooks for* The Idiot, 230.

64. In his classic study, James Rice argues that "*The Idiot* is a book about epilepsy, and not just 'among other things' but above all." He explains Myshkin's fate (and Dostoevsky's life and art) in medical terms, as the artistic working out on Dostoevsky's part of the *morbus sacer* ("sacred disease") of epilepsy. See his *Dostoevsky and the Healing Art: An Essay in Literary and Medical History* (Ann Arbor, MI: Ardis, 1985), 247 (also 82–85, 90, 163, 245–46, 288–90).

65. Cassedy, *Dostoevsky's Religion*, 138.

66. Dalton, *Unconscious Structure*, 139.

67. "Idiocy is the condition of the great divestment; for in idiocy instinct is set to operating with the least possible impairment by reason. [. . .] Idiocy, then, is the very condition of dramatic necessity for the novelist who would, like Dostoevsky, attempt to dramatize instinctive goodness and pity as the essence of Christianity." R. P. Blackmur, "A Rage of Goodness: *The Idiot* of Dostoevsky," in *The Critical Performance: An Anthology of American and British Literary Criticism of Our Century*, ed. Stanley Edgar Hyman (New York: Random House, 1956), 239.

68. She goes on to say: "You need brains too of course … perhaps that is what matters, after all. Stop smiling Aglaya, I'm not contradicting myself. [. . .] I'm the fool with the

heart and no brain, you're the other way round; we're both miserable and we both suffer" (1:7:86–87). Thus Aglaya's incompatibility with Myshkin is foreordained: she's all brain and no heart.

69. On his way to meet Aglaya on the green park bench, Myshkin is deliriously happy. He even takes her note from his pocket and kisses it. But, as the narrator informs us, "If anyone had told him at that moment that he had fallen in love, passionately in love, he would have rejected such a notion in astonishment, perhaps even indignation. And if anyone had added that Aglaya's note was a love-letter, appointing a tryst, he would have burned with shame for the man and perhaps challenged him to a duel. All this was perfectly sincere and he never had the least doubt of it or permitted the slightest 'ambivalent' thought of the possibility of this girl loving him, or even of him loving this girl" (3:3:381). For an interesting treatment of love as "taboo" in *The Idiot*, see Olga Meerson, *Dostoevsky's Taboos* (Dresden: Dresden University Press, 1998), 93–101.

70. At their tryst on the green park bench, Aglaya tells Myshkin, "Your mind is superior to all of theirs, it's the sort of mind they've never even dreamed of" (3:8:452). She is disappointed a page later to hear him admit that he is not a learned man.

71. Dostoevsky, "The Dream," 427.

72. "Weak and foolish—such is Christ in His kenosis to the eyes of a Nietzsche just as he was to the eyes of the ancient pagan world. The semipagan Christian societies, such as in Byzantium or the western Dark Ages, turned away with fear and discomfort from the face of the humiliated God." George P. Fedotov, *The Russian Religious Mind: Kievan Christianity, the Tenth to the Thirteenth Centuries* (New York: Harper, 1960), 130.

73. Shortly after sending off the first chapters of *The Idiot*, Dostoevsky wrote to Apollon Maikov, discussing the novel and contrasting the "Russian idea" with Roman Catholicism in a way that distinctly anticipates Myshkin's speech. See *PSS* 28:2:243–44; English translation in *Selected Letters of Fyodor Dostoevsky*, trans. Andrew MacAndrew, ed. Joseph Frank and David I. Goldstein (New Brunswick, NJ: Rutgers University Press), 265. See Frank, *Miraculous Years*, 252–54, for a discussion of this letter, Dostoevsky's Russian Messianism, and its link to this scene at the Yepanchins'.

74. This is Elizabeth Dalton's characterization of the speech. See her *Unconscious Structure*, 163.

75. In this same speech, Myshkin evokes Christ again when he urges all present to "become servants in order to be masters" (4:7:585).

76. Sergius Bulgakov writes that the Russian Christ is "the image of Christ, meek and lowly, Lamb of God, Who has taken on Himself the sins of the world, and Who has humbled Himself to take a human form; He Who came into this world to serve all men and not to be served; He Who submitted without a murmur to outrage and dishonor, and Who answered these with love." See his *The Orthodox Church*, trans. Lydia Kesich (1935; repr., Crestwood, NY: St. Vladimir's Seminary Press, 1988), 150.

77. Myshkin's speech is obviously the "inspired discourse" Dostoevsky mentions in his note dated September 8, 1868: "The inspired discourse of the Prince (*Don Quixote* and the acorn)" (*Notebooks for* The Idiot, 233; *PSS* 9:277). The reference associates Myshkin's speech with Quixote's address to the goatherds about his dream of a Golden Age (see Ziolkowski, *Sanctification of Don Quixote*, 114). According to the note, Myshkin was to speak of "each blade of grass, each step, Christ," as he does in the novel just before his final epileptic fit: "Do you know, I can't understand how one can pass a tree and not be happy at seeing it! Talk to a man and not be happy at loving him! Oh, it's just that I can't find the

words ... and so many beautiful things at every step that even the most desperate man finds beautiful! Look at a child, look at God's dawn, look at the grass growing, look into the eyes that look at you and love you" (4:7:585).

78. Pearce, *Stages of the Clown*, 11.

79. Dostoevsky writes in his notebooks for the novel, "wherever he even made an appearance—everywhere he left a permanent trace." See his *Notebooks for* The Idiot, 193. Russian original in *PSS* 9:242.

80. Peace, *Dostoevsky*, 100.

81. Earlier, he ponders what a "dear, sweet face Lebedev's elder daughter has" with its "innocent, childlike expression" and even chides himself "that he'd almost forgotten that face and only now brought it to mind" (2:5:240), thus linking Vera to the novel's interest in the human face.

82. The first is Marie, the consumptive girl he befriends in Switzerland. For more on Vera's role in the novel, see Peace, *Dostoevsky*, 97–100, and Mestergazi, "Vera i kniaz' Myshkin," 314–16. Mestergazi calls Vera "both the symbol and the personification of Christian faith in the novel" (315).

83. In *Dostoevsky and the Dynamics of Religious Experience* (London: Anthem, 2005), Malcom Jones speaks of "delicate shoots of new life" that are "beginning to show through in the closing pages" of *The Idiot*, adding "Kolia, Radomsky and Vera Lebedeva seem to sense this" (47). Tat'iana Kasatkina's "Posle znakomstva s podlinnikom: Kartina Gansa Gol'beina Mladshego 'Khristos v mogile' v structure romana F. M. Dostoevskogo *Idiot*," *Novyi mir* 2 (2006): 154–68, argues that the final chapter of the novel must be read as a verbal icon of the *Polozhenie vo grob* or "Entombment of Christ," and thus is pregnant with the "promise of resurrection" (168).

84. See Knapp, "Myshkin," 203–9, for an extended discussion of the theme of the accidental family in the novel.

85. Murray Kreiger, "Dostoevsky's *Idiot*: The Curse of Saintliness," in *Dostoevsky: A Collection of Critical Essays*, ed. René Wellek (Englewood Cliffs, NJ: Prentice-Hall, 1962), 51–52. "For Myshkin has not spoken the last word, although he has spoken the most extreme word. Whatever is spoken beyond this is not spoken out of the tragic vision."

86. Christopher Fry, "Comedy," in *Comedy: Meaning and Form*, ed. Robert W. Corrigan (San Francisco: Chandler, 1965), 15.

87. Gary Rosenshield argues that Myshkin's fate presents "a test of faith," but "not so much of the characters as of the reader—and even the author himself." See his "Chaos, Apocalypse, the Laws of Nature: Autonomy and 'Unity' in Dostoevskii's *Idiot*," *Slavic Review* 50, no. 4 (Winter 1991), 879–89 (here, 888).

88. Marina Kostalevsky, *Dostoevsky and Soloviev: The Art of Integral Vision* (New Haven, CT: Yale University Press, 1997), 97–98.

CHAPTER 4

1. Lev Nikolaevich Tolstoi, *Polnoe sobranie sochinenii* (herafter *PSS*), ed. V. G. Chertkov et al., 90 vols. (Moscow: Khudozhestvennaia literatura, 1928–1964), 60:293.

2. Leo Tolstoy, *On Life and Essays on Religion*, trans. Aylmer Maude (Oxford: Oxford University Press, 1934), 225.

3. Leo Tolstoy, *A Confession, The Gospel in Brief, and What I Believe*, trans. Aylmer Maude (London: Oxford University Press, 1971), 462; Tolstoi, *PSS* 23:411.

4. "Love all God's creation, the whole and every grain of sand in it. Love every leaf, every ray of God's light. Love the animals, love the plants, love everything. If you love everything, you will perceive the divine mystery in things. Once you perceive it, you will begin to comprehend it better every day. And you will come at last to love the whole world with an all-embracing love. Love the animals: God has given them the rudiments of thought and joy untroubled. Do not trouble it, don't harass them, don't deprive them of their happiness, don't work against God's intent. Man, do not pride yourself on superiority to the animals; they are without sin, and you, with your greatness, defile the earth by your appearance on it, and leave the traces of your foulness after you—alas, it is true of almost every one of us!" Fyodor Dostoevsky, *The Brothers Karamazov*, translated by Constance Garnett, revised by Ralph E. Matlaw (New York, W.W. Norton: 1976), 298.

5. Tolstoi, *PSS* 53:172.

6. Tolstoi, *PSS* 45:50–51, cited in Richard Gustafson, *Leo Tolstoy: Resident and Stranger* (Princeton, NJ: Princeton University Press, 1986), 185.

7. See, respectively, book 4, chapter 1, 164, and book 6, chapter 3, 320–21, of *Brothers Karamazov*, here in the Richard Pevear and Larissa Volokhonsky translation (San Francisco: North Point Press, 1990).

8. Leo Tolstoy, *Resurrection*, trans. Anthony Briggs (London: Penguin, 2009), 507; Tolstoi, *PSS* 32:442.

9. Tolstoy, *A Confession, The Gospel in Brief, and What I Believe*, 124.

10. Tolstoi, *On Life and Essays on Religion*, 223.

11. Tolstoi, *PSS* 24:980. Ivakin's memoirs were unpublished and are cited in the commentary to Tolstoy's *Kratkoe izlozhenie evangeliia*, *PSS* 24:801–938. See "Soedinenie i perevod chetyrekh evangelii: istoriia pisaniia," *PSS* 24:973–984.

12. Leo Tolstoy, *Tolstoy's Diaries, vol. 1, 1847–1894*, ed. and trans. R. F. Christian (New York: Scribner, 1985), 101.

13. Gary Saul Morson, *Anna Karenina in Our Time: Seeing More Wisely* (New Haven, CT: Yale University Press, 2007), 176.

14. Ibid., 188.

15. Tolstoy, *A Confession, The Gospel in Brief, and What I Believe*, 478–79.

16. This and all references to *War and Peace* will be given parenthetically in the text citing the volume, part, chapter, and page, with translations taken from the Richard Pevear and Larissa Volokhonsky version (New York: Knopf, 2007), with occasional modifications by me.

17. Edward Wasiolek, *Tolstoy's Major Fiction* (Chicago: University of Chicago Press, 1978), 82.

18. Inessa Medzhibovskaya, *Tolstoy and the Religious Culture of His Time: A Biography of a Long Conversion, 1845–1887* (Lanham, MD: Lexington Books, 2008), 135.

19. Wasiolek, *Tolstoy's Major Fiction*, 93.

20. Tolstoy himself would later profess such a philosophy of love. In his diary entry for June 12, 1898, he writes: "The time is now, this minute; the person is the one you are now dealing with; and the act is to save your own soul, i.e., to perform an act of love." See Leo Tolstoy, *Tolstoy's Diaries, vol. 2, 1895–1910*, ed. and trans. R. F. Christian (New York: Scribner, 1985), 458.

21. Nicolas Berdyaev, *The Divine and the Human*, trans. R. M. French (San Rafael, CA: Semantron Press, 2009), 116.

22. This and all references to *Anna Karenina* will be given parenthetically in the text citing the part, chapter, and page, with translations taken from the Richard Pevear and Larissa Volokhonsky version (New York: Viking, 2001).

23. Vladimir E. Alexandrov, *Limits to Interpretation: The Meanings of Anna Karenina* (Madison: University of Wisconsin Press, 2004), 128.

24. Morson, *Anna Karenina*, 186.

25. Ibid., 190.

26. Ibid., 189–90.

27. In part 5, chapter 25, Karenin already regrets having forgiven Anna: "The memory of the letter he had written her also tormented him, and in particular his forgiveness, needed by no one, and his taking care of another man's child, burned his heart with shame and remorse" (5:25:520).

28. For more on this argument, see John Givens, "The Fiction of Fact and the Fact of Fiction: Hayden White and *War and Peace*," *Tolstoy Studies Journal* 21 (2009): 22–26.

29. Alexandrov, *Limits to Interpretation*, 192.

30. Levin's mild inebriation is not to be confused with a state of intoxication, which, in his 1896 work "Christian Doctrine" ("Khristianskoe uchenie"), Tolstoy condemns as one of the six cardinal sins that subvert one's faculty of reasoning and pervert one's natural and good proclivities. See Tolstoi, *PSS* 39:116–91, especially 140–41.

31. Here, I disagree with Nikolai Strakhov, who reproached Tolstoy for his pitiless attitude toward Anna's death: "But you have deprived me of that tender emotion which I experienced three years ago in your study and which I was waiting for now. You are pitiless; you did not forgive Anna even at the moment of her death; her bitterness and spite increase to the last instant, and you have cut out, it seems to me, certain passages that expressed a softening of the soul and pity for herself. Thus, I did not burst into tears, but sank into painful thought. Yes, it is truer than what I had imagined. It is very true, and therefore more terrible!" Quoted in Boris Eikhenbaum, *Tolstoy in the Seventies*, trans. Albert Kaspin (Ann Arbor, MI: Ardis, 1982), 125. Having forgiven Anna alongside Levin, we cannot but view her suicide in a compassionate light.

32. Amy Mandelker argues that in his meeting with Anna, Levin "plays the role of Christ asked to judge the fallen woman" from John 8:3–11. See her *Framing Anna Karenina: Tolstoy, the Woman Question, and the Victorian Novel* (Columbus: Ohio State University Press, 1993), 115. Just as Christ pities and forgives the fallen woman, he pities and forgives Anna.

33. See Jefferson J. A. Gatrall, *The Real and the Sacred: Picturing Jesus in Nineteenth-Century Fiction* (Ann Arbor: University of Michigan Press, 2014), 226–34, for a detailed treatment of Mikhailov's painting in the novel.

34. Gustafson, *Leo Tolstoy*, 143.

35. Dostoevsky, *Brothers Karamazov*, trans. Pevear and Volokhonsky, book 5, chapter 3, 236.

36. Vladimir Lossky, *The Mystical Theology of the Eastern Church* (Crestwood, NY: St. Vladimir's Seminary Press, 1998), 27.

37. Tolstoi, *PSS* 56:55.

Chapter 5

1. Leo Tolstoy, *A Confession, The Gospel in Brief, and What I Believe*, trans. Aylmer Maude (London: Oxford University Press, 1971), 78, 80.

2. Leo Tolstoy, *Tolstoy's Diaries, vol. 2, 1895–1910*, ed. and trans. R. F. Christian (New York: Scribner, 1985), 156. Tolstoy later modified his views on this question: "Prayer is addressed to the personal God. Not because he is personal (indeed, I know for certain that

he is not personal, because personality is limitation, while God is unlimited), but because I am a personal being." Leo Tolstoy, *My Religion; On Life; Thoughts on God; On the Meaning of Life,* trans. Leo Wiener (Boston, 1904), 416.

3. Richard Gustafson writes: "Tolstoy's doctrine of god is panentheistic (all-in-God). His God is in everything and everything is in God, but God is not everything and everything is not God." See his *Leo Tolstoy: Resident and Stranger* (Princeton, NJ: Princeton University Press, 1986), 101.

4. *Tolstoy's Diaries,* 2:70.

5. Leo Tolstoy, "Thoughts on God," in *My Religion,* 409.

6. Tolstoy, *A Confession, The Gospel in Brief, and What I Believe,* 6.

7. Gustafson, *Leo Tolstoy,* 434.

8. Tolstoi, *PSS* 45:34–35, cited in David Matual, *Tolstoy's Translation of the Gospels: A Critical Study* (Lewiston, NY: Edwin Mellen Press, 1992), 167.

9. Tolstoy, *A Confession, The Gospel in Brief, and What I Believe,* 123.

10. Ibid., 129, 128.

11. See Pål Kolstø, "Leo Tolstoy: A Church Critic Influenced by Orthodox Thought," in *Church, Nation and State in Russia and Ukraine,* ed. Geoffrey Hosking (London: Macmillan, 1991), 148–66.

12. Gustafson writes: "[D]eification entails a total transfiguration of self, a turning away from all personal passion, desire, perception, and reasoning which returns you to your life 'in God.' Tolstoy's conception of the career of life follows the pattern of this doctrine of deification. It assumes an 'eternally growing soul' which exists in a process of increasing participation in true life and ends up becoming one with the All." *Leo Tolstoy,* 104–5.

13. Tolstoy, *A Confession, The Gospel in Brief, and What I Believe,* 123.

14. Ibid., 131–32.

15. Lev Tolstoi to N. N. Strakhov, April 17–18, 1878, in Tolstoi, *PSS* 62:413.

16. Ani Kokobobo, "Authoring Jesus: Novelistic Echoes in Tolstoy's Harmonization and Translation of the Four Gospels," *Tolstoy Studies Journal* 20 (2008): 10.

17. Matual, *Tolstoy's Translation,* 14.

18. Tolstoi, *PSS* 24:981.

19. Matual, *Tolstoy's Translation,* 54.

20. Cited in N. N. Gusev, "'Soedinenie i perevod chetyrekh evangelii: Istoriia pisaniia," in Tolstoi, *PSS* 24:980.

21. *Tolstoy's Letters, vol. 2, 1880–1910,* ed. and trans. R. F. Christian (London: Athlone Press, 1978), 421; *PSS* 24:982.

22. *Tolstoy's Diaries,* 1:239.

23. Tolstoy, *A Confession, The Gospel in Brief, and What I Believe,* 272; Tolstoi, *PSS* 24:848.

24. Tolstoy, *A Confession, The Gospel in Brief, and What I Believe,* 273; Tolstoi, *PSS* 24:849.

25. Tolstoy, *A Confession, The Gospel in Brief, and What I Believe,* 207; Tolstoi, *PSS* 24:881.

26. Tolstoy, *A Confession, The Gospel in Brief, and What I Believe,* 135–36, translation modified by me to reflect the original more closely; Tolstoi, *PSS* 24:817.

27. See *A Confession, The Gospel in Brief, and What I Believe,* 370–406, for Tolstoy's explanation of these "five commandments." By the time he wrote *What I Believe,* Tolstoy's understanding of Jesus's commandment to love your enemies had changed, as it smacked

too much of "an unattainable moral ideal" to him (394). By enemies here, Tolstoy explains, Jesus had in mind foreigners, those who are not our neighbors, since the commandment explicitly compares those who are our neigbors and those who are our enemies: "You have heard that it was said, Thou shalt love thy neighbor and hate thine enemy" (see 393–97). This understanding, however, ignores Jesus's reference in Matthew to love "those who persecute you" and those who are "bad" and "unjust" (Matthew 5:44–45). In Luke, Jesus also says "do good to those who hate you, bless those who curse you, pray for those who mistreat you" (Luke 6:27–28), also indicating that loving enemies meant loving those who hate you—Tolstoy's original understanding from his treatment of this theme in *War and Peace* and *Anna Karenina*. By 1907, Tolstoy had returned to his original conception: "Yes, loving one's enemies, loving those who hate you is not an exaggeration, like it seemed at first. It is the main meaning of love" (*PSS* 56:55).

28. Tolstoy, *A Confession, The Gospel in Brief, and What I Believe*, 401, 404; Tolstoi, *PSS* 23:368, 370.

29. Ernest Renan, *The Life of Jesus* (Buffalo, NY: Prometheus Books, 1991), 165.

30. Leo Tolstoy, "Three Letters on Reason, Faith and Prayer," in *The Complete Works of Count Tolstoy: Miscellaneous Letters and Essays*, trans. Leo Weiner (Boston: D. Estes and Company, 1905), 464.

31. Tolstoy, *A Confession, The Gospel in Brief, and What I Believe*, 135–36.

32. On the genesis of *Resurrection*, see Viktor Shklovskii, *Lev Tolstoi* (Moscow: Molodaia gvardiia, 1963), 690–95; Hugh McLean, "Resurrection," in *The Cambridge Companion to Tolstoy*, ed. Donna Tussing Orwin (Cambridge: Cambridge University Press, 2002), 96–99; and Henri Troyat, *Tolstoy*, trans. Nancy Amphoux (New York: Dell, 1967), 654–56.

33. Anton Chekhov to Mikhail Menshikov, 28 January 1900, in *Anton Chekhov's Life and Thought: Selected Letters and Commentary*, trans. Michael Henry Heim with Simon Karlinsky, ed. Simon Karlinsky (Berkeley: University of California Press, 1973), 374.

34. Gustafson, *Leo Tolstoy*, 48.

35. English translations are from Leo Tolstoy, *Resurrection*, trans. Anthony Briggs (London: Penguin, 2009), and will be given parenthetically in the text listing part, chapter, and page number, respectively.

36. John Bayley, *Tolstoy and the Novel* (New York: Viking, 1968), 258.

37. Viktor Shklovsky, "Art as Device," in his *Theory of Prose*, trans. Benjamin Sher (Elmwood Park, IL: Dalkey Archive Press, 1990). Shklovsky writes: "The purpose of art, then, is to lead us to a knowledge of a thing through the organ of sight instead of recognition. By 'enstranging' objects and complicating form, the device of art makes perception long and 'laborious'" (6).

38. Donna Tussing Orwin, Introduction to *Resurrection*, by Leo Tolstoy, trans. Louise Maude (New York: Barnes and Noble, 2006), xiii.

39. See chapter 19 of part 3.

40. Tolstoy, *The Gospel in Brief: The Life of Jesus*, trans. Dustin Condren (New York: Harper Perennial, 2011), xxiii–xxiv; Tolstoi, *PSS* 24:808. Condren's translation is cited here, as Maude's version of this passage is incomplete and leaves out Tolstoy's direct references to St. Paul as well as several sentences of Tolstoy's original text.

41. The Hegelian Ferdinand Christian Baur's 1845 book, *Paul: His Life and Works*, is the first serious scholarly work to advance this theory. He was followed by many others, most notably Friedrich Nietzsche in his 1895 work *The Antichrist*, in which Paul is accused of "exceeding and summing up the subterranean cults of all varieties," including

"that of Osiris, that of the Great Mother, that of Mithras." See his *The Antichrist*, trans. H. L. Mencken (New York: A. A. Knopf, 1920), 171. In his 1907 book *Paulus*, the Lutheran theologian Georg Friedrich Eduard William Wrede asserts that there was "an enormous gulf" between Jesus and "the Pauline Son of God" (*Paul*, trans. Edward Lummis [London: Green, 1907], 147). More recent works on Paul as "mythologizer" of Jesus include Hyam Maccoby's *The Mythmaker: Paul and the Invention of Christianity* (New York: Harper and Row, 1986), and A. N. Wilson's *Paul: The Mind of the Apostle* (New York: W. W. Norton, 1998).

42. Tolstoi, *PSS* 50:54.

43. Ibid., 24:316–17.

44. Ibid., 24:611.

45. Ibid., 24:25, 817.

46. Shklovskii, *Lev Tolstoi*, 703.

47. Anton Chekhov to Mikhail Menshikov, 28 January 1900, in *Anton Chekhov's Life and Thought*, 374. Chekhov writes: "The novel has no ending; what it does have can't be called an ending. To write so much and then suddenly make a Gospel text responsible for it all smacks a bit too much of the seminary. [...] Why a Gospel text and not a text from the Koran? First he has to force his readers to believe in the Gospel, to believe that it alone is the truth, and only then can he resolve everything by the text."

48. Richard Gustafson, Introduction to *Resurrection*, by Leo Tolstoy, trans. Louise Maude (Oxford: Oxford University Press, 2009), xiv.

49. *Tolstoy's Diaries*, 1:241.

50. *Tolstoy's Diaries*, 2:460.

51. Ibid., 658.

52. *Tolstoy's Letters*, 2:640.

53. Ibid., 476.

54. Ibid., 512.

55. See Jesse Stavis, "Double Thoughts on the Single Tax: Tolstoy, Henry George, and the Meaning(s) of Progress," *Tolstoy Studies Journal* 28 (2016): 75–93.

Chapter 6

1. Aleksandr Blok, "Bezvremen'e," in *Sobranie sochinenii v vos'mi tomakh* (Moscow: Khudozhestvennaia literatura, 1962), 5:68.

2. M. Menshikov, "On Literature and Writers," in *The Noise of Change: Russian Literature and the Critics, 1891–1917*, ed. and trans. Stanley Rabinowitz (Ann Arbor, MI: Ardis, 1989), 30. Originally: M. Menshikov, "O literature i pisateliakh," *Knizhki nedeli* 11 (1891): 206–23.

3. Menshikov, "On Literature and Writers," 33.

4. Dmitrii Sergeevich Merezhkovskii, "O prichinakh upadka i o novykh techeniiakh sovremennoi russkoi literatury," in *Polnoe sobranie sochinenii* (Moscow: Tip. I. D. Sytina, 1914), 18:536. Further citations will be given parenthetically.

5. See his 1899 article "O isskustve" (*sic*—"About Art").

6. Michael Basker, "The Silver Age," in *The Routledge Companion to Russian Literature*, ed. Neil Cornwell (London: Routledge, 2001), 138.

7. Bryusov wrote in 1902: "The reign of positive science is passing. [...] We feel crowded, we are stifling, we can bear it no longer. We are oppressed by society's conventions; we are suffering from the conditional forms of morality, from the very conditions of

knowledge, from all that is superimposed upon us." Cited in D. S. von Mohrenschildt, "The Russian Symbolist Movement," *PMLA* 53, no. 4 (December 1938): 1193.

8. See Bernice Glatzer Rosenthal's excellent treatment of these writers on this topic: "Eschatology and the Appeal of Revolution: Merezhkovsky, Bely, Blok," *California Slavic Studies* 11 (1980): 105–39.

9. Ibid., 114.

10. Marc Slonim, *From Chekhov to the Revolution: Russian Literature 1900–1917* (New York: Oxford University Press, 1962), 193.

11. See Jay Bergman, "The Image of Jesus in the Russian Revolutionary Movement: The Case of Russian Marxism," *International Review of Social History* 35 (1990): 220–48, for an excellent treatment of this topic.

12. Quoted in *Delo pervogo marta 1881* (St. Petersburg: Izdanie I. Balashova, 1906), 6–7. Attached to the letter that the Executive Committee of the revolutionary movement Narodnaia volia (People's Will) sent to Alexander III was a statement that "[t]he gallows are as powerless to save the old order [in Russia] as was the death of the Savior on the cross to save the corrupt, ancient world from the triumph of reforming Christianity." Reprinted in Vera Figner, *Memoirs of a Revolutionist*, trans. Alexander Kaun (New York: Greenwood Press, 1968), 312. These two citations come from Bergman, "The Image of Jesus," 224.

13. Nikolai Valentinov [N. V. Vol'skii], *The Early Years of Lenin*, trans. Rolf H. W. Theen (Ann Arbor: University of Michigan Press, 1969), 104–5. Cited in Nina Tumarkin, *Lenin Lives: The Lenin Cult in Soviet Russia*, enlarged ed. (Cambridge, MA: Harvard University Press, 1997), 17.

14. Cited in Konstantin Mochulsky, *Alexander Blok*, trans. Doris V. Johnson (Detroit, MI: Wayne State University Press, 1983), 402.

15. Ibid., 390.

16. Leon Trotsky, *Literature and Revolution*, trans. Rose Strunsky (Ann Arbor: University of Michigan Press, 1960), 121. Further citations will be given parenthetically in the text.

17. Vladimir Il'ich Lenin to Gorky, November 13 or 14, 1913, in *Polnoe sobranie sochineniia*, by Vladimir Il'ich Lenin, 5th ed. (Moscow: Politicheskaia literatura, 1970), 48:228.

18. See Bergman, "The Image of Jesus," 230–36.

19. In 1927, he declared the story of Jesus to be "the purest myth" in a public debate with the prelate and Christian Socialist Alexander Vvedenskii. See Bergman's discussion in "The Image of Jesus," 231–36. The quotes from Lunacharskii, cited by Bergman on p. 235, are originally from A. V. Lunacharskii, "T'ma," reprinted in *Literaturnyi raspad* (St. Petersburg: Izd. T-va Izdatel'skoe biuro, 1909), 1:155, and "Lichnost' Khrista," in *A. V. Lunacharskii ob ateizme i religii* (Moscow: Mysl', 1972), 233.

20. See Bergman, "The Image of Jesus," 238–42, for a nice summation of the God-building impulse in the early Bolshevik state.

21. Mark D. Steinberg, *Proletarian Imagination: Self, Modernity, and the Sacred in Russia, 1910–1925* (Ithaca, NY: Cornell University Press, 2002), 250.

22. See Steinberg, *Proletarian Imagination*, 254, 262–67, and Richard Stites, *Revolutionary Dreams: Utopian Vision and Experimental Life in the Russian Revolution* (Oxford: Oxford University Press, 1989), 109–23.

23. V. V. Maiakovskii, "Vladimir Il'ich," *Sochineniia v trekh tomakh* (Moscow: Khudozhestvennaia literatura, 1965), 1:172–74. Cited in Tumarkin, *Lenin Lives*, 100.

24. See Victoria Bonnell, *Iconography of Power: Soviet Political Posters under Lenin and Stalin* (Berkeley: University of California Press, 1997).

25. Tumarkin, *Lenin Lives*, 82–90.

26. Maksim Gor'kii, "Vladimir Il'ich Lenin," *Kommunisticheskii Internatsional*, no. 12 (1920) no page, column 1933. English translation from the Maxim Gorky online archive: https://www.marxists.org/archive/gorky-maxim/1920/07/lenin.htm (accessed 21 October 2017). See also Olga Velikanova, *Making of an Idol: On Uses of Lenin* (Göttingen: Muster-Schmidt, 1996), 36.

27. Iu. Steklov, "Mogila Lenina," *Izvestiia*, January 27, 1924, 1. Cited in Bergman, "The Image of Jesus," 244.

28. Vladimir Vladimirovich Maiakovskii, "Komsomol'skaia," *Molodaia gvardiia*, nos. 2–3 (1924): 10–14.

29. Stites, *Revolutionary Dreams*, 103. See also Ol'ga Velikanova, *Obraz Lenina v massovom vospriatii sovetskikh liudei po arkhivnym materialam* (Lewiston, NY: Edwin Mellen Press, 2001), especially "Religioznyi simvol: Obraz, leksika," 163–90.

30. Bergman, "The Image of Jesus," 244.

31. Tumarkin, *Lenin Lives*, 180–81.

32. Philip T. Grier, "The Russian Idea and the West," in *Russia and Western Civilization: Cultural and Historical Encounters*, ed. Russell Bova (Armonk, NY: M. E. Sharpe, 2003), 70.

33. M. Ol'minskii, "Kriticheskie stat'i i zametki," *Proletarskaia revoliutstiia*, no. 1 (1931): 149–50. Cited in Tumarkin, *Lenin Lives*, 181.

34. George M. Young, *The Russian Cosmists: The Esoteric Futurism of Nikolai Fedorov and His Followers* (Oxford: Oxford University Press, 2012), 180.

35. Catherine Merridale, *Night of Stone: Death and Memory in Twentieth-Century Russia* (New York: Viking, 2000), 153.

36. Steinberg, *Proletarian Imagination*, 264. See chapter 7 of his study, "Sacred Vision in the Revolution," 247–81, for a detailed discussion.

37. All quotations will be taken from Mirra Ginsburg's translation of the novel (New York: Harper, 1972), and cited parenthetically in the text.

38. Richard A. Gregg, "Two Adams and Eve in the Crystal Palace: Dostoevsky, the Bible and *We*," in *Zamyatin's We: A Collection of Critical Essays*, ed. Gary Kern (Ann Arbor, MI: Ardis, 1988), 61–69 (here, 66). Originally published in *Slavic Review* 4 (1965): 680–87.

39. Yuri Olesha, *Envy*, trans. Marian Schwartz (New York: New York Review, 2004). All citations will be given parenthetically within the text, with slight adjustments in the translation by me.

40. Isaac Babel, *Collected Stories*, trans. David McDuff (London: Penguin, 1994), 109. Further citations to this edition will be made parenthetically.

41. Isaac Babel, "The Sin of Jesus," trans. Mirra Ginsburg, in *The Collected Stories*, ed. and trans. Walter Morrison (New York: Criterion, 1955), 247. The story was first published in 1922. Further citations to this edition will be made parenthetically.

42. Ilya Ilf and Evgeny Petrov, *The Golden Calf*, trans. Konstantin Gurevich and Helen Anderson (Rochester, NY: Open Letter, 2009), 160. Further citations to this edition will be given parenthetically within the text.

43. The definitive study of Soviet socialist realism on which these comments are based is Katerina Clark, *The Soviet Novel: History as Ritual* (Chicago: University of Chicago Press, 1985).

44. Cited in Natal'ia Ivanova, "Cryptic Precision: The Poet and the Master," trans. Liv Bliss, *Russian Studies in Literature* 39, no. 1 (Winter 2002–2003): 70. The Russian original is "Tochnost' tain: Poet i Master," *Znamia* 11 (2001): 189–99.

45. See chapter 5 of part 2 of the novel.

46. Pyotr Pavlenko, *Happiness*, trans. J. Fineberg (Moscow: Foreign Languages Publishing House, 1950), 346. Emphasis added. Further references will be provided parenthetically within the text.

47. Mikhail Bulgakov, Letter to the Soviet Government, in *Manuscripts Don't Burn: Mikhail Bulgakov; A Life in Letters and Diaries*, ed. J. A. E. Curtis (Woodstock, NY: Overlook Press, 1992), 103–10.

48. This is Christopher Barnes's account from his biography of Pasternak, *Boris Pasternak: A Literary Biography, vol. 2, 1928–1960* (Cambridge: Cambridge University Press, 1998), 92.

49. Curtis, *Manuscripts Don't Burn*, 112.

50. Natal'ia Ivanova, "The 'Companion of Groves' and the Leader: A Certain Assonance," trans. Liv Bliss, *Russian Studies in Literature* 39, no. 1 (Winter 2002–2003): 37. Originally "'Sobesednik roshch' i vozhd': K voprosu ob odnoi rifme," *Znamia* 10 (2001): 186–200.

51. Ibid, 65. The poems are "Mne po dushe stroptivyi norov" (the full, thirteen-stanza version, not the shorter version published in later collections that exclude references to Stalin) and "Ia ponial, vse zhivo," in which both Lenin and Stalin are mentioned by name.

52. Mikhail Bulgakov, *The Master and Margarita*, trans. Diana Burgin and Katherine Tiernan O'Connor (New York: Vintage International, 1995), 21, 22.

53. Barnes, *Boris Pasternak*, 2:90.

54. Boris Pasternak, *Doctor Zhivago*, trans. Max Hayward and Manya Harari (1958; repr., New York: Knopf, 1991), 10. Further citations to this edition will be given parenthetically within the text.

55. Boris Pasternak to Olga Freidenberg, October 13, 1946, trans. Charlotte Hoss and Edith W. Clowes, in *Doctor Zhivago: A Critical Companion*, ed. Edith W. Clowes (Evanston, IL: Northwestern University Press, 1995), 128.

CHAPTER 7

1. Boris Sokolov, *Rasshifrovannyi Bulgkaov: Tainy* Mastera i Margarita (Moscow: Eksmo, 2006), 519.

2. The earliest version of the first chapter of the Pilate novel is titled "The Gospel according to Woland." See *Kopyta inzhenera* in *Moi bednyi, bednyi Master: Polnoe sobranie redaktsii i variantov romana Master i Margarita*, ed. Viktor Losev (Moscow: Vagrius, 2006), 41.

3. The Master tells Woland that the subject of his novel is Pontius Pilate (not Jesus Christ). See chapter 24 of the novel.

4. Gleb Struve, *Russian Literature under Lenin and Stalin: 1917–1953* (Norman: University of Oklahoma Press, 1971), 30.

5. Demian Bednyi, "Novyi zavet bez iz"iana evangelista Demiana," in Bednyi, *Sobranie sochinenii*, ed. S. A. Vasil'ev et al. (Moscow: Khudozhestvennaia literatura, 1965), 5:380.

6. Mikhail Bulgakov and Elena Bulgakov, *Dnevnik Mastera i Margarity*, ed. V. I. Losev (Moscow: Vagrius, 2001), 55.

7. David M. Bethea, *The Shape of Apocalypse in Modern Russian Fiction* (Princeton, NJ: Princeton University Press, 1989), 201n29.

8. Sokolov, *Entsiklopediia Bulgakova* (Moscow: Lokid, Mif, 1996), 511.

9. "My illness is complicated and protracted. I feel completely broken. It may interfere with my work, that's why I fear it, that's why I put my faith in God." Diary entry for October 26, 1923. Bulgakov and Bulgakov, *Dnevnik Mastera i Margarity*, 34. See also 32, 35.

10. Marietta Chudakova, "Arkhiv M. A. Bulgakova: Materialy dlia tvorcheskoi biografii pisatelia," *Zapiski otdela rukopisei gosudarstvennoi biblioteki imeni V. I. Lenina*, vypusk 37 (Moscow: Kniga, 1976), 97.

11. Ellendea Proffer, *Bulgakov: Life and Work* (Ann Arbor, MI: Ardis, 1984), 3, 178, 525. See M. A. Bulgakov, "Zametki avtobiograficheskogo kharaktera," Otdel rukopisei Gosudarstvennoi biblioteki imeni V. I. Lenina, fond 281, karton 1269, ed. khr. 6. The note was written down by Bulgakov's friend, P. S. Popov.

12. Bethea, *The Shape of Apocalypse*, 201.

13. Mikhail Bulgakov, *The Master and Margarita*, trans. Diana Burgin and Katherine Tiernan O'Connor (New York: Vintage International, 1995), 12. Further translations from the novel will be cited parenthetically within the text using this edition.

14. With the exception of the mention of Thomas Aquinas, these references are all from the annotations to the novel by Richard Pevear and Larissa Volokhonsky in their translation of Mikhail Bulgakov, *The Master and Margarita* (New York: Penguin, 1997), 397–99.

15. A. Vilus, the author of the afterword to the journal *Moskva*'s publication of the censored version of the novel, was also mystified by it, and confessed to being woefully unprepared to understand the novel's treatment of theology, demonology, the occult, and biblical history. His reaction is characteristic of many of the novel's readers at that time. See Lesley Milne, *Mikhail Bulgakov: A Critical Biography* (Cambridge: Cambridge University Press, 1990), 228.

16. Proffer, *Bulgakov*, 6.

17. Chudakova, "Arkhiv M. A. Bulgakova," 136.

18. In fact, as Boris Sokolov argues, Berlioz is but superficially educated. Sokolov asserts that all of Berlioz's information about mythology, philosophy, and religion is taken straight from the pages of the *Brockhaus and Efron Encyclopedic Dictionary*, one of the sources Bulgakov himself consulted in writing his novel (*Rasshifrovannyi Bulgakov*, 541–546).

19. This detail can be found in Bulgakov's 1929 manuscript version of the novel, *Kopyta inzhenera*. See *Moi bednyi, bednyi Master*, 54. *Bogoborets* is also a possible translation of the Hebrew word "Israel" (ישראל)—i.e., the name given to the founder of Israel's monotheism by God himself, as a reward for fighting God. Ironically, scripture itself calls the pillar of faith a God-Fighter/God-Resister, a point relevant to characters discussed in this study who resist God but bear a Christological message, such as Ivan Karamazov, Stavrogin, Shatov, Kirillov, Nekhliudov, and the converted Ivan Bezdomny in *The Master and Margarita* itself. I am grateful to an anonymous reader for this observation.

20. The title of chapter 3, "The Seventh Proof," announces this in no uncertain terms.

21. This conversion process actually begins two chapters earlier in chapter 11, "Ivan Is Split in Two." There the "old Ivan" converses with the "new Ivan" moments before the Master steals into his room.

22. In one of the earliest Soviet reactions to the novel, V. Lakshin asserts that Yeshua is "not an omnipotent god" but a mortal man who perished for his convictions, and is thus no different from Joan of Arc or the Decembrists. See V. Lakshin, "M. Bulgakov's novel *The Master and Margarita*," in *The Master and Margarita: A Critical Companion*, ed. Laura D. Weeks (Evanston, IL: Northwestern University Press, 1996), 80–81. This interpretation has found many adherents. In her definitive biography, Proffer describes Yeshua as "an ordinary man who suffers for his beliefs" and who is not "in any way meant to be seen as a god" (Proffer, *Bulgakov*, 548, 641n32). Henry Elbaum likens him to Socrates—another philosopher executed for his ideals whose humility, simplicity of heart, and benevolence are qualities Yeshua shares. See Genrikh El'baum, *Analiz iudeiskikh glav Mastera i Margarity M. Bulgakova* (Ann Arbor, MI: Ardis, 1981), 52. In Lesley Milne's reading, Yeshua is "the archetypal victim-other who has power to forgive" (*Mikhail Bulgakov*, 246). Laura Weeks recognizes in him the "wandering philosopher" of the Jesus Seminar who preaches "free healing," "free eating," "religious and economic egalitarianism," and "unmediated physical and spiritual contact with one another." See Laura D. Weeks, "'What I Have Written, I Have Written,'" in *The Master and Margarita*, 50; she quotes from John Dominic Crossan, *The Historical Jesus: The Life of a Mediterranean Peasant* (San Francisco: Harper, 1991), 421–22. Russian Orthodox deacon Andrei Kuraev agrees that Bulgakov's Yeshua is no Christ, but for a different reason. In his view, the Pilate chapters are "blasphemous and atheist" and Yeshua himself is but "a caricature of the atheist (Tolstoyan) Christ." See Andrei Kuraev, *Master i Margarita: Za Khrista ili protiv?* (Moscow: Izdatel'skii sovet Russkoi Pravoslavnoi Tserkvi, 2006), 34, 38. Several other scholars link Yeshua with Gnosticism, claiming that he and the novel as a whole are imparters of "secret knowledge." In his monograph-length study, George Krugovoy attempts to show how this "'knowledge,' *gnosis*" is "laboriously encoded in the complex structural texture of the novel." See George Krugovoy, *The Gnostic Novel of Mikhail Bulgakov: Sources and Exegesis* (Lanham, MD: University Press of America, 1991), 292. See also Andrew Barratt, *Between Two Worlds: A Critical Introduction to* The Master and Margarita (Oxford: Clarendon Press, 1987), 171–72, 320–23; and Edythe C. Haber, "The Mythic Bulgakov: *The Master and Margarita* and Arthur Drews's *The Christ Myth*," *Slavic and East European Journal* 43, no. 2 (1999): 347–60. Edythe Haber argues that as a Gnostic Christ, Yeshua is more spirit than body, someone who "never appears in the novel in actuality, but only through the mediation of the 'messenger' Woland, the dreams of Ivan Bezdomny, the artistic intuition of the Master" ("Mythic Bulgakov," 356). Still other scholars assert that, his differences from the Gospel Christ notwithstanding, Yeshua is nevertheless ultimately "the biblical Khristos," largely on the basis of his supernatural appearance at novel's end. See Margot K. Frank, "The Mystery of the Master's Final Destination," *Canadian-American Slavic Studies* 15, nos. 2–3 (Summer–Fall 1981): 292. See also Gary Rosenshield, "*The Master and Margarita* and the Poetics of Aporia: A Polemical Article," *Slavic Review* 56, no. 2 (Summer 1997): 199n30; and Edward E. Ericson, *The Apocalyptic Vision of Mikhail Bulgakov's* The Master and Margarita (Lewiston, NY: Edwin Mellen Press, 1991). Margot Frank goes so far as to claim that the Master's "primary transgression," for which he is denied "the light" but not "peace," is the omission in his novel of Yeshua's divine identity ("Mystery," 292).

23. See J. A. E. Curtis, *Bulgakov's Last Decade: The Writer as Hero* (Cambridge: Cambridge University Press, 1987), 132, for a nice summary of inconsistencies and discrepancies arising from the novel's "unfinished" status.

24. Viktor Losev, "Kommentarii," in Bulgakov and Bulgakov, *Dnevnik Mastera i Margarity*, 552.

25. Chudakova, "Arkhiv M. A. Bulgakova," 140–41.

26. Frank, "Mystery," 294. Anthony Colin Wright states that "*The Master and Margarita* is not a tidy work, nor does it present a logically structured argument." He also cites the novel's "bewildering mass of detail" as a potential impediment to readers' comprehension. *Mikhail Bulgakov: Life and Interpretations* (Toronto: University of Toronto Press, 1978), 261.

27. Ellendea Proffer writes: "Many great cathedrals remain unfinished, as do many famous works, from *Dead Souls* to *Remembrance of Things Passed*. Fate decreed that this novel be left as it is, something Bulgakov would have understood." Proffer, *Bulgakov*, 530. See also Aleksei Varlamov, *Mikhail Bulgakov* (Moscow: Molodaia gvardiia, 2008), 734.

28. Proffer, *Bulgakov*, 559.

29. J. A. E. Curtis notes that Bulgakov's "conception of the Master's inspiration aligns Bulgakov's approach with a neo-Platonic Romantic tradition, where ultimate truth is held to exist on a higher plane occasionally accessible only to the artist through the power of his genius." *Bulgakov's Last Decade*, 147.

30. Barratt, *Between Two Worlds*, 100.

31. Ellendea Proffer, "Bulgakov's *The Master and Margarita*: Genre and Motif," in Weeks, *The Master and Margarita*, 100.

32. Rosenshield, "*The Master and Margarita*," 190.

33. Ibid., 210.

34. Neither the substantial annotations by Ellendea Proffer for the translation by Diana Burgin and Katherine Tiernan O'Connor nor those by Richard Pevear and Larissa Volokhonsky for their translation identify Thomas Aquinas as the author of the five proofs of God that Woland references in his discussion with Berlioz nor do they summarize what those five proofs are. Mention of Aquinas is also curiously absent from critical discussions about the novel, in Russia as well as the West. One exception is Ericson, who mentions Aquinas's Five Ways in his study *The Apocalyptic Vision*, 19.

35. Thomas Aquinas, *Summa Theologica*, part 1, question 2, article 3.

36. Ibid.

37. Barratt notes how "the three sections of the Jerusalem story display a straight-forward linear sequentiality which alone creates a powerful impression of unity" between the four chapters. At the same time, Barratt adds that "shifts of focus" between the different Jerusalem chapters are so great that "it is necessary to talk in terms of three largely separate stories, which deal, respectively, with Pilate's act of cowardice (chapter 2); Matthew's agonized impotence (chapter 16); and Aphranius's ambiguous performance of his duty (chapters 25 and 26)." *Between Two Worlds*, 197, 198.

38. Curtis, *Bulgakov's Last Decade*, 151. Proffer cites Marietta Chudakova, Aleksandr Zerkalov, and Genrikh El'baum, among others, for evidence suggesting that Bulgakov consulted the ancient historians Josephus and Tacitus and the nineteenth-century biblical scholars Ernest Renan, Frederic William Farrar, and Friedrich Strauss for information concerning Jesus, first-century Judea, and questions of Christology (*Bulgakov*, 640n30). Edythe Haber also makes a case for Arthur Drews's *The Christ Myth* ("Mythic Bulgakov").

39. These are summarized from Proffer's annotations of the Burgin-O'Connor translation, 340–41. Proffer suggests that "it is noteworthy that the only main character to be given a Hebrew version of his name is Yeshua Ha-Notsri" (340). See also El'baum's discussion, *Analiz iudeiskikh glav*, 45–46, 104, and 116.

40. According to El'baum, "As if desiring to disassociate himself from the traditional Christian interpretation of the death of Jesus, Bulgakov carefully avoids words rich in symbolism like 'cross' and 'crucifixion.'" *Analiz iudeiskikh glav*, 45–46.

41. Leonid Rzhevsky, "Pilate's Sin: Cryptography in Bulgakov's Novel, *The Master and Margarita*," *Canadian Slavonic Papers* 13, no. 1 (Spring 1971), 14. See also Weeks, "'What I Have Written,'" 42.

42. See, respectively, Weeks, "'What I Have Written,'" 42, and Proffer, *Bulgakov*, 540.

43. *Kopyto inzhenera*, in Bulgakov, *Moi bednyi, bednyi Master*, 43, 51. Yeshua also utters "It is finished" in the 1934–1936 manuscript variant, *Fantasticheskii roman*. See *Moi bednyi, bednyi Master*, 237.

44. Marietta Chudakova, "*The Master and Margarita*: The Development of a Novel," trans. Phyllis Powell, *Russian Literature Triquarterly* 15 (1978): 179. Bulgakov's first notebooks date to early 1929 and were ripped in half in March 1930, when, according to Proffer, "he became convinced of the hopelessness of a literary career in Russia" (*Bulgakov*, 527). He burned one half and preserved the other as a record of its existence. Chudakova's reconstructed text was not included in the complete collection of editions and variants of the novel published as *Moi bednyi, bednyi Master* in 2006.

45. *Kopyto inzhenera*, in Bulgakov, *Moi bednyi, bednyi Master*, 54.

46. See *Master i Margarita: Polnaia rukopisnaia redaktsiia* in Bulgakov, *Moi bednyi, bednyi Master*, 367–644.

47. *Kopyto inzhenera: Chernoviki romana, tetrad' 2, 1928–29*, in Bulgakov, *Moi bednyi, bednyi Master*, 41.

48. Ericson, *The Apocalyptic Vision*, 71.

49. Ericson lists them thusly: "Judas betrays Jesus, for which the price is thirty pieces of silver. Pilate sentences Jesus. Pilate asks his famous 'What is truth?' question. The Jewish religious leaders, Caiaphas in particular, insist that Jesus be put to death, even at the cost of the freeing of Barabbas. Jesus is crucified, and the crucifixion occurs on Mount Golgotha and on Friday. The event is accompanied by a major storm." *The Apocalyptic Vision*, 72. See 72–73 for a list of further parallels to the Gospels and prophetic passages of the Old Testament that have been imaginatively reworked in the Jerusalem chapters.

50. Barratt, "*The Master and Margarita* in Recent Criticism: An Overview," in Weeks, *The Master and Margarita*, 88.

51. Ericson, *The Apocalypstic Vision*, 20–21.

52. Weeks, "'What I Have Written,'" 34. See also See Proffer, *Bulgakov*, 559; Krugovoy, *Gnostic Novel*, 173. Ericson, *The Apocalyptic Vision*, 121–24.

53. See Ericson, *The Apocalyptic Vision*, 124–25.

54. Barratt, *Between Two Worlds*, 251.

55. See, for instance, Sona Hoisington, "Fairy-Tale Elements in Bulgakov's *The Master and Margarita*," *Slavic and East European Journal* 25, no. 2 (1981): 44–55. Rosenshield likens the love story to the märchen of German Romantic literature. See his "*The Master and Margarita*," 191n11.

56. See, in particular, Ericson, *The Apocalyptic Vision*, 99–105 and 115–37, and Weeks, "'What I Have Written,'" 33–43.

57. See chapter 4 of book 5 of *The Brothers Karamazov*.

58. Woland assures Margarita in chapter 32: "Everything will be made right, that is what the world is built on" (323).

59. In this way, Bulgakov's novel mirrors the Master's: it is a text that, as Woland puts it, has "more surprises" in store than the author himself may be aware of (250).

CHAPTER 8

1. Boris Pasternak, *Doctor Zhivago*, trans. Max Hayward and Manya Harari (1958; repr., New York: Knopf, 1991), 414. Further citations to this edition will be given parenthetically within the text listing part, subsection, and page number: (13:17:414).

2. Guy de Mallac, *Boris Pasternak: His Life and Art* (Norman: University of Oklahoma Press, 1981), 331.

3. Lazar Fleishman, "Boris Pasternak i Khristianstvo," *Christianity and the Eastern Slavs, vol. 3, Russian Literature in Modern Times*, ed. Boris Gasparov, Robert P. Hughes, Irina Paperno, and Olga Raevsky-Hughes (Berkeley: University of California Press, 1995), 292.

4. This first version of "Hamlet" is reproduced in Boris Pasternak, *Polnoe sobranie sochinenii s prilozheniiami v odinnadtsati tomakh* (Moscow: Slovo, 2003–2005), 4:639.

5. Fleishman, "Boris Pasternak i Khristianstvo," 292.

6. Ibid., 298.

7. Christopher Barnes, *Boris Pasternak: A Literary Biography, vol. 1, 1890–1928* (Cambridge: Cambridge University Press, 1989), 27.

8. Cited in Mallac, *Boris Pasternak*, 9. The original letter is dated May 2, 1959, and is reproduced in Jacqueline de Proyart, *Boris Pasternak* (Paris: Gallimard, 1964), 41. This letter is also published in *Novyi zhurnal* 80 (1975): 77.

9. Statement by Pasternak to Mme. Z. I. Konchalovskii, 1929–1930. Cited in Mallac, *Boris Pasternak*, 331.

10. Cited in Boris Pasternak, *The Poems of Doctor Zhivago*, translated with commentary by Donald Davie (New York: Barnes and Noble, 1965), 126–27.

11. Per-Arne Bodin, *Nine Poems from Doktor Živago: A Study of Christian Motifs in Boris Pasternak's Poetry* (Stockholm: Almqvist & Wiksell, 1976), 4–5.

12. Ibid., 5–7.

13. Ibid., 8.

14. Gerd Ruge, "A Visit to Pasternak," *Encounter* 10, no. 3 (March 1958), 24.

15. James Billington, *The Icon and the Axe: An Interpretive History of Russian Culture* (New York: Knopf, 1966), 559.

16. Vadim Borisov and Evgenii Pasternak, "Materialy k tvorcheskoi istorii romana B. Pasternaka Doktor Zhivago," *Novyi mir* 6 (1988): 228.

17. Cited in Evgenii Pasternak, "Khronika proshedshikh let," *Znamia* 12 (2008): 135.

18. I have altered the translation to more literally match the original.

19. See Timothy Ware [Bishop Kallistos of Diokleia], *The Orthodox Church* (London: Penguin, 1993), 234.

20. The poems are: "Hamlet," "Holy Week," "August," "Star of the Nativity," "Miracle," "Evil Days," "Magdalene I," "Magdalene II," and "Garden of Gethsemane."

21. Fleishman, "Boris Pasternak i Khristianstvo," 296, 298.

22. "The belief that man—when fully aware of his true powers—is capable of totally transforming the world in which he lives." See Billington, *The Icon and the Axe*, 478.

23. Walter Vickery, "Symbolism Aside: *Doktor Živago*," *Slavic and East European Journal* 3, no. 4 (Winter 1959), 344. See also Edmund Wilson, "Legend and Symbol in *Doctor Zhivago*," in *The Bit between My Teeth: A Literary Chronicle of 1950–1965* (New York: Farrar, Straus & Giroux, 1965), 468. Originally published in *Encounter 12, no. 6* (June 1959): 5–15.

24. Max Hayward, "Pasternak's *Doctor Zhivago*," *Encounter* 11, no. 5 (May 1958), 43; cited in Mallac, *Boris Pasternak*, 327.

25. Josephine Pasternak, "Patior," *The London Magazine* 4, no. 6 (September 1964): 44.

26. Mallac, *Boris Pasternak*, 337.

27. Pasternak, "Translating Shakespeare," trans. Manya Harari, in *I Remember: Sketch for an Autobiography*, by Boris Pasternak, trans. David Magarshack (Cambridge, MA: Harvard University Press), 130.

28. Per-Arne Bodin, "Boris Pasternak and the Christian Tradition," *Forum for Modern Language Studies* 26, no. 4 (1990): 396.

29. The interview with Pasternak appeared in *Nation* on September 12, 1959, and is cited by Edmund Wilson in "Legend and Symbol," 471.

30. Wilson, "Legend and Symbol," 468, 447.

31. Mary F. Rowland and Paul Rowland, *Pasternak's Doctor Zhivago* (Carbondale: Southern Illinois University Press, 1967), 171, 175.

32. Mallac, *Boris Pasternak*, 334.

33. John Bayley, "Tolstoy's Legacy: *Dr. Zhivago*," in *Tolstoy and the Novel* (New York: Viking, 1968), 300–301.

34. "Provokatsionnaia vylazka mezhdunarodnoi reaktsii," *Literaturnaia gazeta* 128 (October 25, 1958). English translation from Robert Conquest, *The Pasternak Affair: Courage of Genius* (New York: J. B. Lippincott, 1962), 139–63 (here, 159).

35. Dmitrii Bykov, "*Doctor Zhivago*," trans. Liv Bliss, *Russian Studies in Literature* 48, no. 2 (Spring 2012): 4–19 (here, 15). Originally in Bykov, *Boris Pasternak* (Moscow: Molodaia gvardiia, 2010), 731.

36. Ibid., 16.

37. Luke Timothy Johnson, *The Writings of the New Testament: An Interpretation*, rev. ed. (Minneapolis, MN: Fortress Press, 1999), 145.

38. Billington, *The Icon and the Axe*, 562.

39. Davie, commentary, in Pasternak, *The Poems of Doctor Zhivago*, 128–29.

40. Vladimir Solovyov, *The Meaning of Love*, trans. Jane Marshall, ed. and rev. Thomas R. Beyer (West Stockbridge, MA: Lindisfarne Press, 1985), 60–61. Further citations to this edition will be given parenthetically in the text.

41. See Jerome Spencer, "'Soaked in *The Meaning of Love* and *The Kreutzer Sonata*': The Nature of Love in *Doctor Zhivago*," in *Doctor Zhivago: A Critical Companion*, ed. Edith W. Clowes (Evanston, IL: Northwestern University Press, 1995), 76–88, for such an analysis.

42. Vickery, "Symbolism Aside," 346.

43. Bykov, "*Doctor Zhivago*," 17.

44. Both the Catholic and the Orthodox Church now teach that Mary Magdalene was not the sinful woman from Luke's Gospel. A homily by Pope Gregory the Great in 591 first suggested that Mary Magdalene was the sinful woman, drawing a parallel between the seven demons cast from Mary Magdalene and the vices of sexual incontinence, and since then, the confusion has persisted in the popular imagination.

45. Pasternak, "Translating Shakespeare," 133. He writes: "Compared to other feelings, love is an elemental cosmic force wearing a disguise of meekness. In itself it is as simple and unconditional as consciousness and as death, as oxygen or uranium. It is not a state of mind, it is the foundation of the universe. Being thus basic and primordial, it is the equal of artistic creation."

46. In a letter Tonya writes to Yuri from Paris, she declares: "The whole trouble is that I love you and that you don't love me. [...] If only you knew how much I love you! I love all that is unusual in you, the good with the bad, and all the ordinary traits of your character, whose extraordinary combination is so dear to me, your face ennobled by your thoughts, which otherwise might not seem handsome, your great gifts and intelligence which, as it were, have taken the place of the will that is lacking" (13:18:418).

47. Leo Tolstoy, *War and Peace*, trans. Richard Pevear and Larissa Volokhonsky (New York: Knopf, 2007), 3:3:32:921.

48. Nicolas Berdyaev, *The Divine and the Human*, trans. R. M. French (San Rafael, CA: Semantron, 2008), 116 (translation slightly modified).

CONCLUSION

1. Gregory L. Freeze, "From Stalinism to Stagnation: 1953–1985," in *Russia: A History*, ed. Gregory L. Freeze (Oxford: Oxford University Press, 2002), 364.

2. Nicholas Zernov, *The Russians and Their Church*, 3rd ed. (Crestwood, NY: St. Vladimir's Seminary Press, 1994), 166.

3. Quoted by M. O. Chudakova, "Zhizneopisanie Mikhaila Bulgakova," *Moskva* 6 (1987): 13. Cited in Lesley Milne, *Mikhail Bulgakov: A Critical Biography* (Cambridge: Cambridge University Press, 1990), 228.

4. Margaret Ziolkowski, *Hagiography and Modern Russian Literature* (Princeton, NJ: Princeton University Press, 1988), 126.

5. In her "parameters of Village Prose," Kathleen Parthé lists "the village," "nature," "home," "native realms, kindred places," "time," and "a native language," but not "faith," "religious belief," or even "spirituality." See chapter 1 of her study *Russian Village Prose: The Radiant Past* (Princeton, NJ: Princeton University Press, 1992), 3–12.

6. Alexander Solzhenitsyn, "Matryona's Home," trans. H. T. Willetts, in *The Portable Twentieth-Century Russian Reader*, ed. Clarence Brown (New York: Viking, 1985), 422–64 (here, 464).

7. Ziolkowski, *Hagiography*, 189.

8. Valentin Rasputin, *Farewell to Matyora*, trans. Antonina W. Bouis (Evanston, IL: Northwestern University Press, 1991), 70.

9. Vasilii Shukshin, *Stories from a Siberian Village*, trans. Laura Michael and John Givens (DeKalb: Northern Illinois University Press, 1996), 11.

10. Ibid., 16, 18. See John Givens, *Prodigal Son: Vasilii Shukshin in Soviet Russian Culture* (Evanston, IL: Northwestern University Press, 2000), 61–63.

11. Alexander Solzhenitsyn, *Invisible Allies*, trans. Alexis Klimoff and Michael Nicholson (Washington, DC: Counterpoint, 1995), 111.

12. Robert Mann, "St. George in Russian Folklore and Vasilii Shukshin's *Kalina krasnaia*," in *Kalina krasnaia*, by Vasilii Shukshin (St. Petersburg: Terra Fantastika Kompanii "Korpus," 1994), 19.

13. Donald Fiene, "Vasily Shukshin's *Kalina krasnaia*," in *Snowball Berry Red and Other Stories*, by Vasily Shukshin, ed. Donald Fiene (Ann Arbor, MI: Ardis, 1979), 207, 208.

14. The verse runs: "He was despised and rejected by mankind, a man of suffering, and familiar with pain. Like one from whom people hide their faces he was despised, and we held him in low esteem." Fiene, "Vasily Shukshin's *Kalina krasnaia*," 208.

15. Ibid., 206–11.

16. Margaret Ziolkowski, "Pilate and Pilatism in Recent Russian Literature," in *New Directions in Soviet Literature: Selected Papers from the Fourth World Congress for Soviet and East European Studies, Harrogate, 1990*, ed. Sheelagh Duffin Graham (New York: St. Martin's Press, 1992), 164–81 (here, 178).

17. Ibid., 164–65.

18. Yury Dombrovsky, *The Faculty of Useless Knowledge*, trans. Alan Myers (London: Harvill, 1996), 313. Further references will be given parenthetically within the text.

19. The interrogator continues: "You hear everybody talking about 'Trial by jury, trial by jury.' But who jailed Katyusha Maslova [from Tolstoy's *Resurrection*]? A jury. Who sent Dmitri Karamazov to forced labour? A jury" (266).

20. See Peter Doyle, *Iurii Dombrovskii: Freedom under Totalitarianism* (Amsterdam: Harwood Academic, 2000), 152.

21. See Robert Porter, *Four Contemporary Russian Writers* (Oxford: Berg, 1989), 82–83; Joseph P. Mozur, Jr., *Parables from the Past: The Prose Fiction of Chingiz Aitmatov* (Pittsburgh, PA: University of Pittsburgh Press, 1995), 140–43; and Nina Kolesnikoff, "Biblical Motifs in Chingiz Aitmatov's *The Place of the Skull*," *Canadian Slavonic Papers* 40, nos. 1–2 (March–June 1998), 17–18.

22. Porter, *Four Contemporary Russian Writers*, 80.

23. Chingiz Aitmatov, *The Place of the Skull*, trans. Natasha Ward (New York: Grove Press, 1989), 126. All further citations will be given parenthetically within the text.

24. See Porter, *Four Contemporary Russian Writers*, 82.

25. In his harmonized Gospel, Tolstoy's Jesus does not speak of resurrection but rather of an awakening to life: "My teaching is an awakening of life. Whoever believes in my teaching, although he may die in the flesh, will remain living and everyone who lives and believes in me will not die." From chapter 7 of the harmonized Gospels, here in Dustin Condren's translation, *The Gospel in Brief: The Life of Jesus* (New York: Harper Perennial, 2011), 92.

26. David Friedrich Strauss, *Life of Jesus Critically Examined*, trans. George Eliot (New York: Gloger Family Books, 1993), 780.

27. Ibid., 152.

28. Venedikt Erofeev, *Moscow to the End of the Line*, trans. H. William Tjalsma (Evanston, IL: Northwestern University Press, 1994), 164. Further references will be given parenthetically within the text.

29. Roland Barthes, *Image, Music, Text*, trans. Stephen Heath (New York: Hill and Wang, 1978), 146, 148.

30. See the edition annotated and edited by Eduard Vlasov: Venedikt Erofeev, *Moskva-Petushki* (Moscow: Vagrius, 2000).

31. Mark Lipovetsky, *Russian Postmodernist Fiction: Dialogue with Chaos*, ed. Eliot Borenstein (Armonk, NY: M. E. Sharpe, 1999), 68.

32. Victor Terras, "A Christian Revolution in Russian Literary Criticism," *Slavic and East European Journal* 46, no. 4 (Winter 2002): 769–76 (here, 769).

33. V. N. Zakharov, ed., *Evangel'skii tekst v russkoi literature XVIII–XX vekov: Tsitata, reministsentsiia, motiv, siuzhet, zhanr* (Petrozavodsk: Izdatel'svo Petrozavodskogo universiteta, 1999–2013), vol. 1, 1994; vol. 2, 1998; vol. 3, 2001; vol. 4, 2005; vol. 5, 2008; vol. 6, 2011; vol. 7, 2012; vol. 8, 2013; vol. 9, 2014.

34. V. N. Zakharov, "Russkaia literatura i khristianstvo," in Zakharov, *Evangel'skii tekst*, 5.

35. Terras, "A Christian Revolution," 770.

36. Vol. 1, 1994; vol. 2, 1996; vol. 3, 1999; vol. 4, 2002; vol. 5, 2006; vol. 6, 2010; vol. 7, 2012.

37. For a 2014 survey of the appearance and growth of Christian literature in post-Soviet Russia, see Svetlana Boiko, "Dlia bessmertnykh: Instruktsii; Pravoslavnaia kniga segodnia," *Voprosy literatury* 5 (2014): 61–88. Translated as "Instruction for Immortals: Orthodox Literature Today," trans. Liv Bliss, *Russian Studies in Literature* 51, no. 4 (2015): 7–33.

38. Natal'ia Ivanova, "Vysokoe chtivo: Strategiia literaturnogo vyzhivaniia," *Znamia* 10 (2013): 181–88 (here, 183).

39. Vladimir Bondarenko et al., "A Consciousness of the Boundaries or on the Outside Looking In? The Virtual Roundtable: A Literary Roundup for 2012," trans. Liv Bliss, *Russian Studies in Literature* 50, no. 1 (Winter 2013–2014): 27.

40. Ibid., 27–28.

41. Ibid., 28–29.

42. See Milne, *Mikhail Bulgakov*, 230–32.

BIBLIOGRAPHY

PRIMARY SOURCES

Aitmatov, Chingiz. *The Place of the Skull*. Translated by Natasha Ward. New York: Grove Press, 1989.

Babel, Isaac. *The Collected Stories*. Edited and translated by Walter Morison. New York: Criterion, 1955.

———. *Collected Stories*. Translated by David McDuff. London: Penguin, 1994.

Bednyi, Demian. *Sobranie sochinenii*. 8 vols. Edited by S. A. Vasil'ev et al. Moscow: Khudozhestvennaia literatura, 1963–1965.

Blok, Aleksandr. *Sobranie sochinenii v vos'mi tomakh*. Moscow: Khudozhestvennaia literatura, 1962.

Bulgakov, Mikhail. *The Master and Margarita*. Translated by Diana Burgin and Katherine Tiernan O'Connor. New York: Vintage International, 1995.

———. *The Master and Margarita*. Translated by Richard Pevear and Larissa Volokhonsky. New York: Penguin, 1997.

———. *Moi bednyi, bednyi Master: Polnoe sobranie redaktsii i variantov romana Master i Margarita*. Edited by Viktor Losev. Moscow: Vagrius, 2006.

———. *White Guard*. Translated by Marian Schwartz. New Haven, CT: Yale University Press, 2008.

Bulgakov, Mikhail, and Elena Bulgakov. *Dnevnik Mastera i Margarity*. Edited by Viktor Losev. Moscow: Vagrius, 2001.

Chekhov, Anton. *Anton Chekhov's Life and Thought: Selected Letters and Commentary*. Translated by Michael Henry Heim with Simon Karlinsky. Edited by Simon Karlinsky. Berkeley: University of California Press, 1973.

———. "Peasants." In *Selected Stories*. Translated by Anne Dunnigan. New York: New American Library, 1960.

Chernyshevsky, Nikolai. *What Is to Be Done?* Translated by Michael R. Katz. Ithaca, NY: Cornell University Press, 1989.

Dombrovsky, Yury. *The Faculty of Useless Knowledge*. Translated by Alan Myers. London: Harvill, 1996.

Dostoevskii, Fedor Mikhailovich. *Polnoe sobranie sochinenii*. 30 vols. Leningrad: Nauka, 1972–1990.

Dostoevsky, Fyodor. *The Brothers Karamazov*. Translated by Constance Garnett. Revised by Ralph E. Matlaw. New York, W.W. Norton: 1976.

———. *The Brothers Karamazov*. Translated by Richard Pevear and Larissa Volokhonsky. San Francisco: North Point Press, 1990.

———. *Complete Letters*. 5 vols. Edited and translated by David A. Lowe. Ann Arbor, MI: Ardis, 1988–1991.

———. *Crime and Punishment*. Translated by Richard Pevear and Larissa Volokhonsky. New York: Knopf, 1992.

———. *Demons*. Translated by Richard Pevear and Larissa Volokhonsky. New York: Vintage, 1994.

———. *Dostoevsky's Occasional Writings*. Edited and translated by David Magarshack. Evanston, IL: Northwestern University Press, 1997.

———. "The Dream of a Ridiculous Man." In *Notes from Underground, The Double and Other Stories*, translated by Constance Garnett, introduction and notes by Deborah Martinsen, 407–28. New York: Barnes and Noble, 2003.

———. *The Idiot*. Translated by Alan Myers. Oxford: Oxford University Press, 1992.

———. *The Notebooks for* The Idiot. Translated by Katharine Strelsky. Edited by Edward Wasiolek. Chicago: University of Chicago Press, 1967.

———. *The Notebooks for* The Possessed. Translated by Victor Terras. Edited by Edward Wasiolek. Chicago: University of Chicago Press, 1968.

———. *Notes from Underground*. Translated by Michael R. Katz. New York: Norton, 1989.

———. *Notes from Underground*. Translated by Mirra Ginsburg. New York: Bantam, 1974.

———. *Selected Letters of Fyodor Dostoyevsky*. Translated by Andrew MacAndrew. Edited by Joseph Frank and David I. Goldstein. New Brunswick, NJ: Rutgers University Press, 1987.

———. *A Writer's Diary*. Vol. 1, *1873–1876*. Translated by Kenneth Lantz. Evanston, IL: Northwestern University Press, 1993.

Erofeev, Venedikt. *Moscow to the End of the Line*. Translated by H. William Tjalsma. Evanston, IL: Northwestern University Press, 1994.

———. *Moskva-Petushki*. Edited and annotated by Eduard Vlasov. Moscow: Vagrius, 2000.

Gogol, Nikolai. *Dead Souls*. Translated by Bernard Guilbert Guerney, revised and edited by Susanne Fusso. New Haven, CT: Yale University Press, 1996.

Goncharov, Ivan. *Oblomov*. Translated by Marian Schwartz. New Haven, CT: Yale University Press, 2008.

Ilf, Ilya, and Evgeny Petrov. *The Golden Calf*. Translated by Konstantin Gurevich and Helen Anderson. Rochester, NY: Open Letter, 2009.

Lenin, Vladimir Il'ich. *Polnoe sobranie sochinenii*. 5th ed. Moscow: Politicheskaia literatura, 1967–1970.

Lermontov, Mikhail. *A Hero of Our Time*. Translated by Vladimir Nabokov in collaboration with Dmitri Nabokov. Garden City, NY: Doubleday, 1958.

Leskov, Nikolai. *The Cathedral Clergy*. Translated by Margaret Winchell. Bloomington, IN: Slavica, 2010.

Maiakovskii, Vladimir Vladimirovich. "Komsomol'skaia." *Molodaia gvardiia*, nos. 2–3 (1924): 10–14.

Merezhkovskii, Dmitrii Sergeevich. *Polnoe sobranie sochinenii*. Moscow: Tip. I. D. Sytina, 1914.

Olesha, Yuri. *Envy*. Translated by Marian Schwartz. New York: New York Review, 2004.

Pasternak, Boris. *Doctor Zhivago*. Translated by Max Hayward and Manya Harari. 1958. Reprint, New York: Knopf, 1991.

———. *I Remember: Sketch for an Autobiography*. Translated by David Magarshack. Cambridge, MA: Harvard University Press, 1983.

——. *The Poems of Doctor Zhivago*. Translated with commentary by Donald Davie. New York: Barnes and Noble, 1965.

——. *Polnoe sobranie sochinenii s prilozheniiami v odinnadtsati tomakh*. Moscow: Slovo, 2003–2005.

Pavlenko, Pyotr. *Happiness*. Translated by J. Fineberg. Moscow: Foreign Languages Publishing House, 1950.

Pushkin, Aleksandr Sergeevich. *Polnoe sobranie sochinenii v desiati tomakh*. Leningrad: Nauka, 1977–1979.

Rasputin, Valentin. *Farewell to Matyora*. Translated by Antonina W. Bouis. Evanston, IL: Northwestern University Press, 1991.

Shukshin, Vasilii. *Snowball Berry Red and Other Stories*. Edited by Donald Fiene. Ann Arbor, MI: Ardis, 1979.

——. *Stories from a Siberian Village*. Translated by Laura Michael and John Givens. DeKalb: Northern Illinois University Press, 1996.

Solovyov, Vladimir. *Lectures on Divine Humanity*. Translated by Peter Zouboff. Edited and revised by Boris Jakim. Hudson, NY: Lindisfarne Press, 1995.

——. *The Meaning of Love*. Translated by Jane Marshall. Edited and revised by Thomas R. Beyer. West Stockbridge, MA: Lindisfarne Press, 1985.

——. *A Solovyov Anthology*. Edited by S. L. Frank. Translated by Natalie Duddington. London: SCM Press, 1950.

Solzhenitsyn, Aleksandr. *Invisible Allies*. Translated by Alexis Klimoff and Michael Nicholson. Washington, DC: Counterpoint, 1995.

——. "Matryona's Home." Translated by H. T. Willetts. In *The Portable Twentieth-Century Russian Reader*, edited by Clarence Brown, 422–64. New York: Viking, 1985.

Tolstoi, Lev Nikolaevich. *Polnoe sobranie sochinenii*. 90 vols. Edited by V. G. Chertkov et al. Moscow: Khudozhestvennaia literatura, 1928–1964.

Tolstoy, Leo. *Anna Karenina*. Translated by Richard Pevear and Larissa Volokhonsky. New York: Viking, 2001.

——. *The Awakening (The Resurrection)*. Translated by William E. Smith. New York: Dodd, Mead and Company, 1900.

——. *Complete Works of Count Tolstoy*. 28 vols. Translated and edited by Leo Weiner. Boston: Estes and Company, 1904–1912.

——. *A Confession, The Gospel in Brief, and What I Believe*. Translated by Aylmer Maude. London: Oxford University Press, 1971.

——. *The Gospel in Brief: The Life of Jesus*. Translated by Dustin Condren. New York: Harper Perennial, 2011.

——. *The Gospel in Brief*. Translated by Isabel Hapgood. Lincoln: University of Nebraska Press, 1997.

——. *Miscellaneous Letters and Essays*. Edited and translated by Leo Wiener. Boston: Dana Estes & Co., 1905.

——. *My Religion; On Life; Thoughts on God; On The Meaning of Life*. Translated by Leo Wiener. Boston: Dana Estes & Co., 1904.

——. *On Life and Essays on Religion*. Translated by Aylmer Maude. Oxford: Oxford University Press, 1934.

——. *Resurrection*. Translated by Anthony Briggs. London: Penguin, 2009.

——. *Tolstoy's Diaries*. Vol. 1, *1847–1894*. Edited and translated by R. F. Christian. New York: Scribner, 1985.

————. *Tolstoy's Diaries*. Vol. 2, *1895–1910*. Edited and translated by R. F. Christian. New York: Scribner, 1985.

————. *Tolstoy's Letters*. Vol. 2, *1880–1910*. Edited and translated by R. F. Christian. London: Athlone Press, 1978.

————. *War and Peace*. Translated by Richard Pevear and Larissa Volokhonsky. New York: Knopf, 2007.

Turgenev, Ivan. *Polnoe sobranie sochinenii i pisem v dvadtsati vos'mi tomakh*. Moscow: Nauka, 1964–1969.

Zamyatin, Yevgeny. *Soviet Heretic*. Edited and translated by Mirra Ginsburg. Chicago: University of Chicago Press, 1970.

————. *We*. Translated by Mirra Ginsburg. New York: Harper, 1972.

Secondary Sources

Alexandrov, Vladimir E. *Limits to Interpretation: The Meanings of* Anna Karenina. Madison: University of Wisconsin Press, 2004.

Apollonio, Carol. *Dostoevsky's Secrets: Reading against the Grain*. Evanston, IL: Northwestern University Press, 2009.

Ashimbaeva, Natalia. "Comedy between the Poles of Humour and Tragedy, Beauty and Ugliness: Prince Myshkin as a Comic Character." Translated by Sarah Young. In *Reflective Laughter: Aspects of Humour in Russian Culture*, edited by Lesley Milne, 49–56. Anthem Russian and Slavonic Studies. London: Anthem, 2004.

Bailey, Heather. *Orthodoxy, Modernity, and Authenticity: The Reception of Ernest Renan's* Life of Jesus *in Russia*. Newcastle: Cambridge Scholars Publishing, 2008.

Bakhtin, Mikhail. *Problems of Dostoevsky's Poetics*. Edited and translated by Caryl Emerson. Theory and History of Literature 8. Minneapolis: University of Minnesota Press, 1984.

Barnes, Christopher. *Boris Pasternak: A Literary Biography*. Vol. 1, *1890–1928*. Cambridge: Cambridge University Press, 1989.

————. *Boris Pasternak: A Literary Biography*. Vol. 2, *1928–1960*. Cambridge: Cambridge University Press, 1998.

Barratt, Andrew. *Between Two Worlds: A Critical Introduction to* The Master and Margarita. Oxford: Clarendon Press, 1987.

————. "*The Master and Margarita* in Recent Criticism: An Overview." In Weeks, *The Master and Margarita*, 84–97.

Barthes, Roland. *Image, Music, Text*. Translated by Stephen Heath. New York: Hill and Wang, 1978.

Basker, Michael. "The Silver Age." In *The Routledge Companion to Russian Literature*, edited by Neil Cornwell, 136–49. London: Routledge, 2001.

Bayley, John. Introduction to *Doctor Zhivago*, by Boris Pasternak, translated by Max Hayward and Manya Harari, xi–xxiii. New York: Knopf, 1991.

————. *Tolstoy and the Novel*. New York: Viking, 1968.

Belinsky, Vissarion. "Letter to N. V. Gogol." In *Belinsky, Chernyshevsky, and Dobrolyubov: Selected Criticism*, edited by Ralph E. Matlaw, 83–92. Bloomington: Indiana University Press, 1977.

Belknap, Robert L. *The Structure of* The Brothers Karamazov. The Hague: Mouton, 1967.

Bercken, Wil van den. *Christian Fiction and Religious Realism in the Novels of Dostoevsky.* London: Anthem, 2011.

Berdyaev, Nicolas. *The Divine and the Human.* Translated by R. M. French. San Rafael, CA: Semantron Press, 2009.

Berdyaev, Nikolai. *The Russian Idea.* Translated by R. M. French. Hudson, NY: Lindisfarne Press, 1992.

Bergman, Jay. "The Image of Jesus in the Russian Revolutionary Movement: The Case of Russian Marxism." *International Review of Social History* 35 (1990): 220–48.

Berlin, Isaiah. *Russian Thinkers.* New York: Penguin, 1984.

Bethea, David M. *The Shape of Apocalypse in Modern Russian Fiction.* Princeton, NJ: Princeton University Press, 1989.

Billington, James. *The Icon and the Axe: An Interpretive History of Russian Culture.* New York: Knopf, 1966.

Bitsilli, P. M. *Izbrannye trudy po filologii.* Moscow: Nasledie, 1996.

Blackmur, R. P. "A Rage of Goodness: *The Idiot* of Dostoevsky." In *The Critical Performance: An Anthology of American and British Literary Criticism of Our Century,* edited by Stanley Edgar Hyman, 235–57. New York: Random House, 1956.

Bodin, Per-Arne. "Boris Pasternak and the Christian Tradition." *Forum for Modern Language Studies* 26, no 4 (1990): 382–401.

———. *Nine Poems from Doktor Živago: A Study of Christian Motifs in Boris Pasternak's Poetry.* Stockholm: Almqvist & Wiksell, 1976.

Boiko, Svetlana. "Dlia bessmertnykh: Instruktsii; Pravoslavnaia kniga segodnia." *Voprosy literatury* 5 (2014): 61–88.

Bondarenko, Vladimir, et al. "A Consciousness of the Boundaries or on the Outside Looking In? The Virtual Roundtable: A Literary Roundup for 2012." Translated by Liv Bliss. *Russian Studies in Literature* 50, no. 1 (Winter 2013–2014): 8–56.

Bonnell, Victoria. *Iconography of Power: Soviet Political Posters under Lenin and Stalin.* Berkeley: University of California Press, 1997.

Borisov, Vadim, and Evgenii Pasternak. "Materialy k tvorcheskoi istorii romana B. Pasternaka Doktor Zhivago." *Novyi mir* 6 (1988): 205–48.

Børtnes, Jostein. "Dostoevskij's *Idiot* or the Poetics of Emptiness." *Scando-Slavica* 40, no. 1 (1994): 5–14.

———. "The Function of Hagiography in Dostoevskii's Novels." *Scando-Slavica* 24 (1978): 27–33.

Bulgakov, Sergius. *The Orthodox Church.* Translated by Lydia Kesich. 1935. Reprint, Crestwood, NY: St. Vladimir's Seminary Press, 1988.

Busch, R. L. *Humor in the Major Novels of F. M. Dostoevsky.* Columbus, OH: Slavica, 1987.

Bykov, Dmitrii. *Boris Pasternak.* Moscow: Molodaia gvardiia, 2010.

———. "Doctor Zhivago." Translated by Liv Bliss. *Russian Studies in Literature* 48, no. 2 (Spring 2012): 4–19.

Cassedy, Steven. *Dostoevsky's Religion.* Stanford, CA: Stanford University Press, 2005.

Chudakova, Marietta. "Arkhiv M. A. Bulgakova: Materialy dlia tvorcheskoi biografii pisatelia." *Zapiski otdela rukopisei gosudarstvennoi biblioteki imeni V. I. Lenina.* Vypusk 37. Moscow: Kniga, 1976.

———. "*The Master and Margarita*: The Development of a Novel." Translated by Phyllis Powell. *Russian Literature Triquarterly* 15 (1978): 177–209.

———. *Zhizneopisanie Mikhail Bulgakova*. Moscow: Kniga, 1988.

Clark, Katerina. *The Soviet Novel: History as Ritual*. Chicago: University of Chicago Press, 1985.

Clowes, Edith W., ed. *Doctor Zhivago: A Critical Companion*. Evanston, IL: Northwestern University Press, 1995.

Conquest, Robert. *The Pasternak Affair: Courage of Genius*. New York: J. B. Lippincott, 1962.

Crone, Anna Lisa. *Eros and Creativity in Russian Religious Renewal: The Philosophers and the Freudians*. Leiden: Brill, 2010.

Crossan, John Dominic. *The Historical Jesus: The Life of a Mediterranean Jewish Peasant*. San Francisco: Harper, 1991.

———. *Raid on the Articulate: Comic Eschatology in Jesus and Borges*. New York: Harper and Row, 1976.

Curtis, J. A. E. *Bulgakov's Last Decade: The Writer as Hero*. Cambridge: Cambridge University Press, 1987.

———. *Manuscripts Don't Burn: Mikhail Bulgakov; A Life in Letters and Diaries*. Woodstock, NY: Overlook Press, 1992.

Dalton, Elizabeth. Introduction to *The Possessed*, by Fyodor Dostoevsky, translated by Constance Garnett, xiii–xxxxv. New York: Barnes and Noble, 2005.

———. *Unconscious Structure in* The Idiot: *A Study in Literature and Psychoanalysis*. Princeton, NJ: Princeton University Press, 1979.

DeSherbinin, Julie. "Chekhov and Christianity: The Critical Evolution." *Chekhov Then and Now: The Reception of Chekhov in World Culture*. Edited by J. Douglas Clayton. New York: Lang, 1997. 285–99.

Doyle, Peter. *Iurii Dombrovskii: Freedom under Totalitarianism*. Amsterdam: Harwood Academic, 2000.

Dyck, J. W. "Boris Pasternak: The Caprice of Beauty." *Canadian Slavonic Papers* 16, no. 4 (Winter 1974): 612–26.

———. "Doktor Živago: A Quest for Self-Realization." *Slavic and East European Journal* 6, no. 2 (Summer 1962): 117–24.

Edie, James M., James P. Scanlan, and Mary-Barbara Zeldin, with the collaboration of George L. Kline. *Russian Philosophy*. Vol. 1, *The Beginnings of Russian Philosophy: The Slavophiles, the Westernizers*. Knoxville: University of Tennessee Press, 1976.

———. *Russian Philosophy*. Volume 2, *The Nihilists, the Populists, Critics of Religion and Culture*. Knoxville: University of Tennessee Press, 1976.

Egeberg, Erik. "How Should We Then Read *The Idiot*?" In *Celebrating Creativity: Essays in Honor of Jostein Børtnes*, edited by Kurt Andreas Grimstad and Ingunn Lunde, 163–69. Bergen, Norway: University of Bergen, Department of Russian Studies, 1997.

Eikhenbaum, Boris. *Tolstoy in the Seventies*. Translated by Albert Kaspin. Ann Arbor, MI: Ardis, 1982.

Elbaum, Henry. "The Evolution of *The Master and Margarita*: Text, Context, Intertext." *Canadian Slavonic Papers* 37, nos. 1–2 (March–June 1995): 59–87.

El'baum, Genrikh. *Analiz iudeiskikh glav Mastera i Margarity M. Bulgakova*. Ann Arbor, MI: Ardis, 1981.

Ericson, Edward E. *The Apocalyptic Vision of Mikhail Bulgakov's* The Master and Margarita. Lewiston, NY: Edwin Mellen, 1991.

Erlich, Victor. *Gogol*. New Haven, CT: Yale University Press, 1969.

———. *Modernism and Revolution: Russian Literature in Transition*. Cambridge, MA: Harvard University Press, 1994.

Ermilov, Vladimir. *Tolstoi—romanist*. Moscow: Khudozhestvennaia literatura, 1965.

Esaulov, I. A. *Paskhal'nost' russkoi slovesnosti*. Moscow: Krug, 2004.

Etkind, Aleksandr. "Kto pisal *Doktora Zhivago?*" *Novoe literaturnoe obozrenie* 3 (1999): 70–82.

Evdokimova, Svetlana, and Vladimir Golstein. "Pushkiniana as an Encyclopedia of Contemporary Literary Criticism." In *The Pushkin Handbook*, edited by David M. Bethea, 609–38. Madison: University of Wisconsin Press, 2005.

Fedotov, George P. *The Russian Religious Mind: Kievan Christianity, the Tenth to the Thirteenth Centuries*. New York: Harper, 1960.

Fiene, Donald. "Vasily Shukshin's *Kalina krasnaia*." In *Snowball Berry Red and Other Stories*, by Vasily Shukshin, edited by Donald Fiene, 200–212. Ann Arbor, MI: Ardis, 1979.

Figner, Vera. *Memoirs of a Revolutionist*. Translated by Alexander Kaun. New York: Greenwood Press, 1968.

Finke, Michael C. *Metapoesis: The Russian Tradition from Pushkin to Chekhov*. Durham, NC: Duke University Press, 1995.

Flath, Carol A. "Fear of Faith: The Hidden Religious Message of *Notes from Underground*." *Slavic and East European Journal* 37, no. 4 (1993): 510–29.

Fleishman, Lazar. "Boris Pasternak i Khristianstvo." In *Christianity and the Eastern Slavs*. Vol. 3, *Russian Literature in Modern Times*, edited by Boris Gasparov, Robert P. Hughes, Irina Paperno, and Olga Raevsky-Hughes, 288–301. Berkeley: University of California Press, 1995.

Florensky, Pavel. *Iconostasis*. Translated by Donald Sheehan and Olga Andrejev. Crestwood, NY: St. Vladimir's Seminary Press, 2000.

Fokin, Pavel. *Bulgakov bez gliantsa*. St. Petersburg: Amfora, 2010.

Frank, Joseph. *Dostoevsky: The Miraculous Years, 1865–1871*. Princeton, NJ: Princeton University Press, 1995.

———. *Dostoevsky: The Seeds of Revolt, 1821–1849*. Princeton, NJ: Princeton University Press, 1976.

———. *Dostoevsky: The Stir of Liberation, 1860–1865*. Princeton, NJ: Princeton University Press, 1986.

———. *Dostoevsky: The Years of Ordeal, 1850–1859*. Princeton, NJ: Princeton University Press, 1983.

———. *The Mantle of the Prophet, 1871–1881*. Princeton, NJ: Princeton University Press, 2002.

Frank, Margot K. "The Mystery of the Master's Final Destination." *Canadian-American Slavic Studies* 15, nos. 2–3 (Summer–Fall 1981): 287–94.

Frede, Victoria S. "Materialism and the Radical Intelligentsia: The 1860s." In *A History of Russian Philosophy, 1830–1930: Faith, Reason, and the Defense of Human Dignity*, edited by Gary M. Hamburg and Randall A. Poole, 69–89. Cambridge: Cambridge University Press, 2010.

Freeze, Gregory L. "From Stalinism to Stagnation: 1953–1985." In *Russia: A History*, edited by Gregory L. Freeze, 347–82. Oxford: Oxford University Press, 2002.

Fry, Christopher. "Comedy." In *Comedy: Meaning and Form*, edited by Robert W. Corrigan, 15–17. San Francisco: Chandler, 1965.

Frye, Northrop, Sheridan Baker, and George Perkins. *The Harper Handbook to Literature*. New York: Harper & Rowe, 1985.

Galkin, A. B. "Obraz Khrista i kontseptsiia cheloveka v romane F. M. Dostoevskogo *Idiot*." In *Roman F. M. Dostoevskogo* Idiot: *Sovremennoe sostoianie izucheniia*, edited by Tat'iana Kasatkina, 319–36. Moscow: Nasledie, 2001.

Gatrall, Jefferson J. A. *The Real and the Sacred: Picturing Jesus in Nineteenth-Century Fiction*. Ann Arbor: University of Michigan Press, 2014.

Givens, John. "The Fiction of Fact and the Fact of Fiction: Hayden White and *War and Peace*." *Tolstoy Studies Journal* 21 (2009): 16–33.

———. "A Narrow Escape into Faith? Dostoevsky's Idiot and the Christology of Comedy." *Russian Review* 70, no. 1 (January 2011): 95–117.

———. *Prodigal Son: Vasilii Shukshin in Soviet Russian Culture*. Evanston, IL: Northwestern University Press, 2000.

Greenwood, E. B. "Tolstoy and Religion." In *New Essays on Tolstoy*, edited by Malcolm Jones, 149–74. Cambridge: Cambridge University Press, 1978.

Gregg, Richard A. "Two Adams and Eve in the Crystal Palace: Dostoevsky, the Bible and *We*." In *Zamyatin's* We: *A Collection of Critical Essays*, edited by Gary Kern, 61–69. Ann Arbor, MI: Ardis, 1988.

Grier, Philip T. "The Russian Idea and the West." In *Russia and Western Civilization: Cultural and Historical Encounters*, edited by Russell Bova, 23–77. Armonk, NY: M. E. Sharpe, 2003.

Grigorieff, Dmitry Felix. "Pasternak and Dostoevskij." *Slavic and East European Journal* 3, no. 4 (1959): 335–42.

Guardini, Romano. "Dostoyevsky's *Idiot*, A Symbol of Christ." Translated by Francis X. Quinn. *Cross Currents* 6, no. 4 (Fall 1956): 359–82.

Gusev, N. N. "'Soedinenie i perevod chetyrekh evangelii: Istoriia pisaniia." In Tolstoi, *Polnoe sobranie sochinenii*, 24:973–84.

Gustafson, Richard. Introduction to *Resurrection*, by Leo Tolstoy. Translated by Louise Maude. Oxford: Oxford Unversity Press, 2009.

———. *Leo Tolstoy: Resident and Stranger*. Princeton, NJ: Princeton University Press, 1986.

Haber, Edythe C. "The Lamp with the Green Shade: Mikhail Bulgakov and His Father." *Russian Review* 44, no. 4 (1985): 333–50.

———. "The Mythic Bulgakov: *The Master and Margarita* and Arthur Drews's *The Christ Myth*." *Slavic and East European Journal* 43, no. 2 (1999): 347–60.

Hahn, Beverly. *Chekhov: A Study of the Major Stories and Plays*. Cambridge: Cambridge University Press, 1977.

Hamburg, Gary M., and Randall A. Poole, eds. *A History of Russian Philosophy, 1830–1930: Faith, Reason, and the Defense of Human Dignity*. Cambridge: Cambridge University Press, 2010.

Hayward, Max. "Pasternak's *Doctor Zhivago*." *Encounter* 56 (May 1958): 38–48.

Herzen, Alexander. *Childhood, Youth and Exile*. Translated by J. D. Duff. Oxford: Oxford University Press, 1980.

———. *My Past and Thoughts*. Translated by Constance Garnett, revised by Humphrey Higgens. 4 vols. New York: Knopf, 1968.

Hingley, Ronald. *The Undiscovered Dostoevsky*. Westport, CT: Greenwood Press, 1977.

Hoisington, Sona. "Fairy-Tale Elements in Bulgakov's *The Master and Margarita*." *Slavic and East European Journal* 25, no. 2 (1981): 44–55.

Holquist, Michael. *Dostoevsky and the Novel*. Princeton, NJ: Princeton University Press, 1977.

Holtrop, Pieter N., and C. H. Slechte. "Foreign Churches along the Nevski Prospekt: An Introduction." In *Foreign Churches in St. Petersburg and Their Archives: 1703–1917*, edited by Pieter N. Holtrop and C. H. Slechte, 1–14. Leiden: Brill, 2007.

Hyers, Conrad. *The Comic Vision and the Christian Faith: A Celebration of Life and Laughter*. New York: Pilgrim Press, 1981.

Ivanov, V. V. *Sakral'nyi Dostoevskii*. Petrozavodsk: Izdatel'stvo PetrGU, 2008.

Ivanova, Natal'ia. "The 'Companion of Groves' and the Leader: A Certain Assonance." Translated by Liv Bliss. *Russian Studies in Literature* 39, no. 1 (Winter 2002–2003): 33–59.

———. "Cryptic Precision: The Poet and the Master." Translated by Liv Bliss. *Russian Studies in Literature* 39, no. 1 (Winter 2002–2003): 60–79.

———. "Smert' i voskresenie Doktora Zhivago." *Iunost'* 5 (1988): 78–82.

———. "Vysokoe chtivo: Strategiia literaturnogo vyzhivaniia." *Znamia* 10 (2013): 181–88.

Johnson, Leslie A. "The Face of the Other in *Idiot*." *Slavic Review* 50, no. 4 (Winter 1991): 867–78.

Johnson, Luke Timothy. *The Writings of the New Testament: An Interpretation*. Rev. ed. Minneapolis, MN: Fortress Press, 1999.

Jones, Malcolm. *Dostoevsky and the Dynamics of Religious Experience*. London: Anthem, 2005.

Kasack, Wolfgang. *Christus in der russischen Literatur: Ein Gang durch die Literaturgeschichte von ihren Anfängen biz zum Ende des 20. Jahrhunderts*. Munich: Otto Sagner, 1999.

Kasatkina, Tat'iana. "Posle znakomstva s podlinnikom: Kartina Gansa Gol'beina Mladshego 'Khristos v mogile' v structure romana F. M. Dostoevskogo *Idiot*." *Novyi mir* 2 (2006): 154–68.

Katkov, M. N. "Starye bogi i novye bogi." *Russkii vestnik* 31 (1861): 891–904.

Kerr, Walter. *Tragedy and Comedy*. New York: Simon and Schuster, 1967.

Kirillova, Irina. *Obraz Khrista v tvorchestve Dostoevskogo: Razmyshleniia*. Moscow: Tsentr knigi Vseros. gos. biblioteki innostrannoi literatury, 2010.

Knapp, Liza, ed. *Dostoevsky's The Idiot: A Critical Companion*. Evanston, IL: Northwestern University Press, 1998.

———. "Introduction to *The Idiot* Part 2: The Novel." In Knapp, *Dostoevsky's The Idiot*, 27–50.

———. "Myshkin through a Murky Glass, Guessingly." In Knapp, *Dostoevsky's The Idiot*, 191–215.

Kokobobo, Ani. "Authoring Jesus: Novelistic Echoes in Tolstoy's Harmonization and Translation of the Four Gospels." *Tolstoy Studies Journal* 20 (2008): 1–13.

Kolesnikoff, Nina. "Biblical Motifs in Chingiz Aitmatov's *The Place of the Skull*." *Canadian Slavonic Papers* 40, nos. 1–2 (March–June 1998): 17–26.

Kolstø, Pål. "Leo Tolstoy: A Church Critic Influenced by Orthodox Thought." In *Church, Nation and State in Russia and Ukraine*, edited by Geoffrey Hosking, 148–66. London: Macmillan, 1991.

Kostalevsky, Marina. *Dostoevsky and Soloviev: The Art of Integral Vision*. New Haven, CT: Yale University Press, 1997.

Kreiger, Murray. "Dostoevsky's *Idiot*: The Curse of Saintliness." In *Dostoevsky: A Collection of Critical Essays*, edited by René Wellek, 39–52. Englewood Cliffs, NJ: Prentice-Hall, 1962.

Krugovoy, George. *The Gnostic Novel of Mikhail Bulgakov: Sources and Exegesis*. Lanham, MD: University Press of America, 1991.

Kunil'skii, A. E. *Smekh v mire Dostoevskogo*. Petrozavodsk: Izdatel'stvo Petrozavodskogo universiteta, 1994.

Kuraev, Andrei. *Master i Margarita: Za Khrista ili protiv?* Moscow: Izdatel'skii sovet Russkoi Pravoslavnoi Tserkvi, 2006.

Lakshin, V. "M. Bulgakov's Novel *The Master and Margarita.*" In Weeks, *The Master and Margarita*, 73–83.

———. "Roman M. Bulgakova *Master i Margarita.*" *Novyi mir* 6 (1968): 284–311.

Lange, Nicholas de. *Judaism*. Oxford: Oxford University Press, 1986.

Lantz, Kenneth. *The Dostoevsky Encyclopedia*. Westport, CT: Greenwood, 2004.

Lapshin, I. I. "Komicheskoe v proizvedeniiakh Dostoevskogo." In *O Dostoevksom: Sbornik statei*, edited by A. L. Bem, 2:31–50. Prague, 1933.

Lawrence, D. H. "Preface to Dostoevsky's *The Grand Inquisitor.*" In *Dostoevsky: A Collection of Critical Essays*, edited by René Wellek. Englewood Cliffs, NJ: Prentice-Hall, 1962. 90–97.

———. *Selected Literary Criticism*. Edited by Anthony Beal. London: Heinemann, 1955.

Lesser, Simon O. "Saint and Sinner—Dostoevsky's *Idiot.*" *Modern Fiction Studies* 4, no. 3 (Autumn 1958): 211–24.

Levitskii, Sergei. "Svoboda i bessmertie: O romane Pasternaka *Doktor Zhivago.*" *Mosty* 2 (1959): 224–36.

Likhachev, Dmitry. "Religion: Russian Orthodoxy." Translated by Nicholas Rzhevsky and Rama Sohonee. In *The Cambridge Companion to Modern Russian Culture*, edited by Nicholas Rzhevsky, 38–56. Cambridge: Cambridge University Press, 1998.

Lipovetsky, Mark. *Russian Postmodernist Fiction: Dialogue with Chaos*. Edited by Eliot Borenstein. Armonk, NY: M. E. Sharpe, 1999.

Lord, Robert. "An Epileptic Mode of Being." In *Dostoevsky: Essays and Perspectives*, 81–101. Berkeley: University of California Press, 1970.

Lossky, Vladimir. *The Mystical Theology of the Eastern Church*. Crestwood, NY: St. Vladimir's Seminary Press, 1998.

———. *Orthodox Theology: An Introduction*. Translated by Ian and Ihita Kesarcodi-Watson. Crestwood, NY: St. Vladimir's Seminary Press, 2001.

Love, Jeff. *The Overcoming of History in* War and Peace. Amsterdam: Rodopi, 2004.

Maccoby, Hyam. *The Mythmaker: Paul and the Invention of Christianity*. New York: Harper and Row, 1986.

Magomedova, Dina. "Lyrical and Narrative 'Plot' in *Doctor Zhivago.*" In Clowes, *Doctor Zhivago*, 115–24.

Malenko, Zinaida, and James J. Gebhard. "The Artistic Use of Portraits in Dostoevskij's *Idiot.*" *Slavic and East European Journal* 5, no. 3 (Autumn 1961): 243–54.

Mallac, Guy de. *Boris Pasternak: His Life and Art*. Norman: University of Oklahoma Press, 1981.

Mandelker, Amy. *Framing Anna Karenina: Tolstoy, the Woman Question, and the Victorian Novel*. Columbus: Ohio State University Press, 1993.

Mann, Robert. "St. George in Russian Folklore and Vasilii Shukshin's *Kalina krasnaia.*" In *Kalina krasnaia*, by Vasilii Shukshin, edited by Robert Mann, 5–19. St. Petersburg: Terra Fantastika Kompanii "Korpus," 1994.

Mathewson, Rufus W., Jr. *The Positive Hero in Russian Literature*. 2nd ed. Stanford, CA: Stanford University Press, 1975.

Matual, David. *Tolstoy's Translation of the Gospels: A Critical Study*. Lewiston, NY: Edwin Mellen Press, 1992.

McFadden, William C. "Kenosis." In *The Modern Catholic Encyclopedia*, edited by Michael Glazier and Monika Hellweg, 458. Rev. ed. Collegeville, MN: Liturgical Press, 2004.

McLean, Hugh. *Nikolai Leskov: The Man and His Art*. Cambridge, MA,: Harvard University Press, 1977.

———. "Resurrection." In *The Cambridge Companion to Tolstoy*, edited by Donna Tussing Orwin, 96–110. Cambridge: Cambridge University Press, 2002.

———. "Tolstoy and Jesus." In *In Quest of Tolstoy*, 117–42. Boston: Academic Studies Press, 2008.

Medzhibovskaya, Inessa. *Tolstoy and the Religious Culture of His Time: A Biography of a Long Conversion, 1845–1887*. Lanham, MD: Lexington Books, 2008.

Meerson, Olga. *Dostoevsky's Taboos*. Dresden: Dresden University Press, 1998.

———. "Ivolgin and Holbein: Non-Christ Risen vs. Christ Non-Risen." *Slavic and East European Journal* 39, no. 2 (1995): 200–213.

———. "Old Testament Lamentation in the Underground Man's Monologue: A Refutation of the Existentialist Reading of *Notes from the Underground*." *Slavic and East European Journal* 36, no. 3 (1992): 317–22.

———. *Personalizm kak poetika: Literaturnyi mir glazami ego obitalei*. St. Petersburg: Pushkinskii dom, 2009.

Meerson, Michael Aksionov. *The Trinity of Love in Modern Russian Theology*. Quincy, IL: Franciscan Press, 1998.

Menshikov, M. "On Literature and Writers." In *The Noise of Change: Russian Literature and the Critics, 1891–1917*, edited and translated by Stanley Rabinowitz, 29–35. Ann Arbor, MI: Ardis, 1989.

Merridale, Catherine. *Night of Stone: Death and Memory in Twentieth-Century Russia*. New York: Viking, 2000.

Mestergazi, Elena. "Vera i kniaz' Myshkin: Opyt 'naivnogo' chteniia romana *Idiot*." In *Roman F. M. Dostoevskogo* Idiot: *Sovremennoe sostoianie izucheniia*, edited by Tat'iana Kasatkina, 291–318. Moscow: Nasledie, 2001.

Michelson, Patrick Lally. "Slavophile Religious Thought and the Dilemma of Russian Modernity, 1830–1860." *Modern Intellectual History* 7, no. 2 (2010): 239–67.

Miller, Robin Feuer. *The Brothers Karamazov: Worlds of the Novel*. New York: Twayne Publishers, 1992.

———. *Dostoevsky and* The Idiot: *Author, Narrator, and Reader*. Cambridge, MA: Harvard University Press, 1981.

———. *Dostoevsky's Unfinished Journey*. New Haven, CT: Yale University Press, 2007.

Milne, Lesley. *Mikhail Bulgakov: A Critical Biography*. Cambridge: Cambridge University Press, 1990.

Mirsky, D. S. *A History of Russian Literature From Its Beginnings to 1900*. New York: Vintage, 1958.

———. *Pushkin*. New York: Dutton, 1963.

Mochulsky, Konstantin. *Alexander Blok*. Translated by Doris V. Johnson. Detroit, MI: Wayne State University Press, 1983.

———. *Dostoevsky: His Life and Work*. Translated by Michael A. Minihan. Princeton, NJ: Princeton University Press, 1967.

Mohrenschildt, D. S. von. "The Russian Symbolist Movement." *PMLA* 53, no. 4 (December 1938): 1193–1209.

Molchanova, Lidiia. *Obraz Khrista v russkoi literature*. 2 vols. St. Petersburg: Novoe i staroe, 2013.

Moreau, Jean Luc. "The Passion according to Zhivago." Translated by Constance Wagner. *Books Abroad* 44, no. 2 (Spring 1970): 237–42.

Morson, Gary Saul. *Anna Karenina in Our Time: Seeing More Wisely*. New Haven, CT: Yale University Press, 2007.

———. *Hidden in Plain View: Narrative and Creative Potentials in* War and Peace. Stanford, CA: Stanford University Press, 1987.

Mozur, Joseph P., Jr. *Parables from the Past: The Prose Fiction of Chingiz Aitmatov*. Pittsburgh, PA: University of Pittsburgh Press, 1995.

Muchnic, Helen. "Boris Pasternak and the Poems of Yurii Zhivago." In *From Gorky to Pasternak: Six Writers in Soviet Russia*, 341–404. New York: Random House, 1961.

Murav, Harriet. *Holy Foolishness: Dostoevsky's Novels and the Poetics of Cultural Critique*. Stanford, CA: Stanford University Press, 1992.

Nabokov, Vladimir. *Lectures on Russian Literature*. New York: Harcourt Brace Jovanovich, 1981.

Nietzsche, Friedrich. *The Antichrist*. Translated by H. L. Mencken. New York: A. A. Knopf, 1920.

Obolensky, Dmitri. "The Poems of *Doctor Zhivago*." In *Pasternak: A Collection of Critical Essays*, edited by Victor Erlich, 151–65. Englewood Cliffs, NJ: Prentice-Hall, 1978.

Oravesz, Johannes Miroslav. *God As Love:The Concept and Spiritual Aspects of Agape in Modern Russian Religious Thought*. Grand Rapids, Michigan: Eerdmans, 2014.

Orwin, Donna Tussing. Introduction to *Resurrection*, by Leo Tolstoy. Translated by Louise Maude. New York: Barnes and Noble, 2006.

———. *Tolstoy's Art and Thought, 1847–1880*. Princeton, NJ: Princeton University Press, 1993.

Ouspensky, Leonid, and Vladimir Lossky. *The Meaning of Icons*. Edited by Titus Burckhardt. Translated by G. E. H. Palmer and E. Kadloubovsky. Crestwood, NY: St. Vladimir's Seminary Press, 1994.

Paperno, I. A., and B. M. Gasparov. "'Vstan' i idi.'" *Slavica Hierosolymitana* 5–6 (1981): 387–400.

Paperno, Irina. *Chernyshevsky and the Age of Realism: A Study in the Semiotics of Behavior*. Stanford, CA: Stanford University Press, 1988.

Parthé, Kathleen. *Russian Village Prose: The Radiant Past*. Princeton, NJ: Princeton University Press, 1992.

Pasternak, Evgenii. *Boris Pasternak: Materialy dlia biografii*. Moscow: Sovetskii pisatel', 1989.

———. "Khronika proshedshikh let." *Znamia* 12 (2008): 135–65.

Pasternak, Josephine. "Patior." *The London Magazine* 4, no. 6 (September 1964): 42–57.

Pattison, George, and Diane Oenning Thompson, eds. *Dostoevsky and the Christian Tradition*. Cambridge: Cambridge University Press, 2001.

Peace, Richard. *Dostoevsky: An Examination of the Major Novels*. Cambridge: Cambridge University Press, 1971.

———. "Dostoevsky and the 'Golden Age.'" *Dostoevsky Studies* 3 (1982): 62–79.

Pearce, Richard. *Stages of the Clown: Perspectives on Modern Fiction from Dostoyevsky to Beckett*. Carbondale: Southern Illinois University Press, 1970.

Pelikan, Jaroslav. *Jesus through the Centuries: His Place in the History of Culture*. New Haven, CT: Yale University Press, 1985.

Pevear, Richard. Foreword to *Demons*, by Fyodor Dostoevsky, 7–23. New York: Vintage, 1995.

Porter, Robert. *Four Contemporary Russian Writers*. Oxford: Berg, 1989.

Proffer, Ellendea. *Bulgakov: Life and Work*. Ann Arbor, MI: Ardis, 1984.

——. "Bulgakov's *The Master and Margarita*: Genre and Motif." In Weeks, *The Master and Margarita*, 98–112.

——. Commentary to *The Master and Margarita*, by Mikhail Bulgakov, translated by Diana Burgin and Katherine Tiernan O'Connor, 337–60. New York: Vintage International, 1995.

Proyart, Jacqueline de. *Boris Pasternak*. Paris: Gallimard, 1964.

Pseudo-Dionysius. "The Mystical Theology." In his *The Complete Works*. Translated by Colm Luibheid. New York: Paulist Press, 1987.

Raskolnikov, Felix. "Pushkin and Religion." Translated by Liv Bliss. *Russian Studies in Literature* 42, no. 1 (Winter 2005–2006): 7–35.

Renan, Ernest. *The Life of Jesus*. Buffalo, NY: Prometheus Books, 1991.

Rice, James L. *Dostoevsky and the Healing Art: An Essay in Literary and Medical History*. Ann Arbor, MI: Ardis, 1985.

——. "Dostoevsky's Endgame: The Projected Sequel to *The Brothers Karamazov*." *Russian History/Histoire Russe* 33, no. 1 (Spring 2006): 45–62.

——. *Who Was Dostoevsky? Essays New and Revised*. Oakland, CA: Berkeley Slavic Specialties, 2011.

Rogers, Thomas F. "The Implications of Christ's Passion in *Doktor Živago*." *Slavic and East European Journal* 18, no. 4 (1974): 384–91.

Rosenshield, Gary. Afterword to *The Idiot*, by Fyodor Dostoyevsky, translated by Henry and Olga Carlisle, 645–55. New York: Signet, 2002.

——. "Chaos, Apocalypse, the Laws of Nature: Autonomy and 'Unity' in Dostoevskii's *Idiot*." *Slavic Review* 50, no. 4 (Winter 1991): 879–89.

——. "*The Master and Margarita* and the Poetics of Aporia: A Polemical Article." *Slavic Review* 56, no. 2 (Summer 1997): 187–211.

Rosenthal, Bernice Glatzer. "Eschatology and the Appeal of Revolution: Merezhkovsky, Bely, Blok." *California Slavic Studies* 11 (1980): 105–39.

——. Introduction to *A Revolution of the Spirit: Crisis of Value in Russia, 1900–1924*, edited by Bernice Glatzer Rosenthal and Martha Bohachevky-Chomiak, 1–40. New York: Fordham University Press, 1990.

Rowland, Mary F., and Paul Rowland. *Pasternak's Doctor Zhivago*. Carbondale: Southern Illinois University Press, 1967.

Ruge, Gerd. "A Visit to Pasternak." *Encounter* 10, no. 3 (March 1958): 22–25.

Rzhevsky, Leonid. "Pilate's Sin: Cryptography in Bulgakov's Novel, *The Master and Margarita*." *Canadian Slavonic Papers* 13, no. 1 (Spring 1971): 1–19.

Schapiro, Leonard. *Turgenev: His Life and Times*. Cambridge, MA: Harvard University Press, 1982.

Schweitzer, Albert. *The Quest of the Historical Jesus: A Critical Study of Its Progress from Reimarus to Wrede*. Translated by W. Montgomery. London: SCM Press, 1981.

Scott, Nathan A., Jr. "The Bias of Comedy and the Narrow Escape into Faith." In *Holy Laughter: Essays on Religion in the Comic Perspective*, edited by M. Conrad Hyers, 45–74. New York: Seabury Press, 1969.

Serdiuchenko, V. "The Futurology of Dostoevsky and Chernyshevsky." Translated by Liv Bliss. *Russian Studies in Literature* 38, no. 4 (Fall 2002): 58–76.

Shestov, Lev. "The Gift of Prophecy." In *Chekhov and Other Essays*, 63–85. 1916. Reprint, Ann Arbor: University of Michigan Press, 1966.

Shklovskii, Viktor. *Lev Tolstoi*. Moscow: Molodaia gvardiia, 1963.

Shklovsky, Viktor. *Theory of Prose*. Translated by Benjamin Sher. Elmwood Park, IL: Dalkey Archive Press, 1990.

Simmons, Ernest J. *Chekhov: A Biography*. Chicago: University of Chicago Press, 1962.

Slattery, Dennis Patrick. "Idols and Icons: Comic Transformation in Dostoevsky's *The Possessed*." *Dostoevsky Studies* 6 (1985): 35–50.

Slonim, Marc. *From Chekhov to the Revolution: Russian Literature 1900–1917*. New York: Oxford University Press, 1962.

Sokolov, Boris. *Entsiklopediia Bulgakova*. Moscow: Lokid, Mif, 1996.

——. *Rasshifrovannyi Bulgakov: Tainy* Mastera i Margarita. Moscow: Eksmo, 2006.

——. *Rasshifrovannyi Pasternak: Kto vy, Doktor Zhivago?* Moscow: Eksmo, 2006.

Sorkina, D. L. "Ob odnom iz istochnikov obraza L'va Nikolaevicha Myshkina." *Uchenye zapiski Tomskogo gosudarstvennogo universiteta: Voprosy khudozhestvennogo metoda i stilia*. 48 (1964): 145–51.

Spencer, Jerome. "'Soaked in *The Meaning of Love* and *The Kreutzer Sonata*': The Nature of Love in *Doctor Zhivago*." In Clowes, *Doctor Zhivago*, 76–88.

Spivak, M. L. "Mesto i funktsiia smekha v tvorchestve F. M. Dostoevskogo." *Vestnik Moskovskogo universiteta, Seriia 9: Filologiia* 5 (1986): 70–76.

Stavis, Jesse. "Double Thoughts on the Single Tax: Tolstoy, Henry George, and the Meaning(s) of Progress." *Tolstoy Studies Journal* 28 (2016): 75–93.

Steinberg, Mark D. *Proletarian Imagination: Self, Modernity, and the Sacred in Russia, 1910–1925*. Ithaca, NY: Cornell University Press, 2002.

Stepanian, Karen. "'It Will Be, but Not Until the End Has Been Achieved' (David Friedrich Strauss's *Das Leben Jesu*, Joseph Ernest Renan's *La Vie de Jésus*, and Dostoevsky's *Idiot*)." Translated by Liv Bliss. *Russian Studies in Literature* 42, no. 1 (Winter 2005–2006): 36–54.

Stites, Richard. *Revolutionary Dreams: Utopian Vision and Experimental Life in the Russian Revolution*. Oxford: Oxford University Press, 1989.

Straus, Nina Pelikan. "Flights from *The Idiot's* Womanhood." In Knapp, *Dostoevsky's* The Idiot, 105–29.

Strauss, David Friedrich. *Life of Jesus Critically Examined*. Translated by George Eliot. New York: Gloger Family Books, 1993.

Struve, Gleb. *Russian Literature under Lenin and Stalin: 1917–1953*. Norman: University of Oklahoma Press, 1971.

Suzi, V. N. *Podrazhanie Khristu v romannoi poetike F. M. Dostoevskogo*. Petrozavodsk: PetrGU, 2008.

Taylor, Charles. *A Secular Age*. Cambridge, MA: Belknap Press of Harvard University Press, 2007.

Terras, Victor. "A Christian Revolution in Russian Literary Criticism." *Slavic and East European Journal* 46, no. 4 (Winter 2002): 769–76.

——. *The Idiot: An Interpretation*. Boston: Twayne Publishers, 1990.

——. *Reading Dostoevsky*. Madison: University of Wisconsin Press, 1998.

Tiupa, Valerii. "*Doktor Zhivago*: Kompozitsiia i arkhitektonika." *Voprosy literatury* 1 (2011): 380–410.

Trotsky, Leon. *Literature and Revolution*. Translated by Rose Strunsky. Ann Arbor: University of Michigan Press, 1960.

Troyat, Henri. *Chekhov*. Translated by Michael Henry Heim. New York: Fawcett Columbine, 1986.

———. *Pushkin*. Translated by Nancy Amphoux. Garden City, NY: Doubleday, 1970.

———. *Tolstoy*. Translated by Nancy Amphoux. New York: Dell, 1967.

Tumarkin, Nina. *Lenin Lives: The Lenin Cult in Soviet Russia*. Enlarged ed. Cambridge, MA: Harvard University Press, 1997.

Turner, C. J. G. "Dostoevsky's *Idiot*: Treasure in Earthen Vessels." *Dostoevsky Studies* 6 (1985): 173–80.

Unamuno, Miguel de. *Our Lord Don Quixote: The Life of Don Quixote and Sancho with Related Essays*. Translated by Anthony Kerrigan. Princeton, NJ: Princeton University Press, 1976.

Valentinov, Nikolai [N. V. Vol'skii]. *The Early Years of Lenin*. Translated by Rolf H. W. Theen. Ann Arbor: University of Michigan Press, 1969.

Valliere, Paul. *Modern Russian Theology: Bukharev, Soloviev, Bulgakov*. Grand Rapids, MI: William B. Eerdmans, 2000.

Varlamov, Aleksei. *Mikhail Bulgakov*. Moscow: Molodaia gvardiia, 2008.

Velikanova, Olga. *Making of an Idol: On Uses of Lenin*. Göttingen: Muster-Schmidt, 1996.

———. *Obraz Lenina v massovom vospriatii sovetskikh liudei po arkhivnym materialam*. Lewiston, NY: Edwin Mellen Press, 2001.

Vickery, Walter. "Symbolism Aside: *Doktor Živago*." *Slavic and East European Journal* 3, no. 4 (Winter 1959): 343–48.

Volgin, Igor. "Alyosha's Destiny." In *The New Russian Dostoevsky*, edited and translated by Carol A. Flath, 271–86. Bloomington, IN: Slavica, 2010.

Ware, Timothy [Bishop Kallistos of Diokleia]. *The Orthodox Church*. London: Penguin, 1993.

Wasiolek, Edward. *Dostoevsky: The Major Fiction*. Cambridge: MIT Press, 1964.

———. *Tolstoy's Major Fiction*. Chicago: University of Chicago Press, 1978.

Weeks, Laura D., ed. *The Master and Margarita: A Critical Companion*. Evanston, IL: Northwestern University Press, 1996.

———. "'What I Have Written, I Have Written.'" In Weeks, *The Master and Margarita*, 3–67.

Williams, Rowan. *Dostoevsky: Language, Faith and Fiction*. Waco, TX: Baylor University Press, 2008.

Wilson, A. N. *Paul: The Mind of the Apostle*. New York: W. W. Norton, 1998.

———. *Tolstoy*. New York: W. W. Norton, 1988.

Wilson, Edmund. "Doctor Life and His Guardian Angel." In *The Bit between My Teeth: A Literary Chronicle of 1950–1965*, 420–46. New York: Farrar, Straus & Giroux, 1965.

———. "Legend and Symbol in Doctor Zhivago." In *The Bit between My Teeth: A Literary Chronicle of 1950–1965*, 446–72. New York: Farrar, Straus & Giroux, 1965.

Wrede, Georg Friedrich Eduard William. *Paul*. Translated by Edward Lummis. London: Green, 1907.

Wright, Anthony Colin. *Mikhail Bulgakov: Life and Interpretations*. Toronto: University of Toronto Press, 1978.

Yarmolinsky, Avrahm. *Turgenev: The Man, His Art and His Age*. New York: Collier, 1961.

Young, George M. *The Russian Cosmists: The Esoteric Futurism of Nikolai Fedorov and His Followers*. Oxford: Oxford University Press, 2012.

Young, Sarah. *Dostoevsky's* The Idiot *and the Ethical Foundations of Narrative: Reading, Narrating, Scripting*. London: Anthem, 2004.

Zakharov, V. N., ed. *Evangel'skii tekst v russkoi literature XVIII–XX vekov: Tsitata, reminist-sentsiia, motiv, siuzhet, zhanr*. 8 volumes. Petrozavodsk: Izdatel'stvo Petrozavodsk-ogo universiteta, 1994–2013.

———. "Russkaia literatura i khristianstvo." In Zakharov, *Evangel'skii tekst*, 5–11.

———. "Simvolika khristianskogo kalendaria v proizvedeniiakh Dostoevskogo," *Novye aspekty v izuchenii Dostoevskogo: Sbornik nauchnykh trudov*, edited by V. N. Zakharov, 37–49. Petrozavodsk: Izdatel'stvo Petrozavodskogo universiteta, 1994.

Zerkalov, Aleksandr. *Evangelie Mikhaila Bulgakova*. Moscow: Tekst, 2003.

Zernov, Nicholas. *The Russians and Their Church*. 3rd ed. Crestwood, NY: St. Vladimir's Seminary Press, 1994.

Zhozhikashvili, V. N. "Notes on Contemporary Dostoevsky Studies." Translated by Laura Givens. *Russian Studies in Literature* 34, no. 4 (Fall 1998): 56–91.

Ziolkowski, Eric J. *The Sanctification of Don Quixote: From Hidalgo to Priest*. University Park: Pennsylvania State University Press, 1991.

Ziolkowski, Margaret. *Hagiography and Modern Russian Literature*. Princeton, NJ: Princeton University Press, 1988.

———. "Pilate and Pilatism in Recent Russian Literature." In *New Directions in Soviet Literature: Selected Papers from the Fourth World Congress for Soviet and East European Studies, Harrogate, 1990*, edited by Sheelagh Duffin Graham, 164–81. New York: St. Martin's Press, 1992.

Ziolkowski, Theodore. *Fictional Transfigurations of Jesus*. Princeton, NJ: Princeton University Press, 1972.

Zlochevskaia, Alla. "Stikhiia smekha v romane *Idiot*." *Dostoevskii i mirovaia kul'tura* 1 (1993): 25–47.

Index